AN ACCOUNT

OF

TIMBUCTOO AND HOUSA,

TERRITORIES IN THE INTERIOR OF
Africa,

By; EL HAGE ABD SALAM SHABEENY;

WITH

NOTES, CRITICAL AND EXPLANATORY.

TO WHICH IS ADDED,

LETTERS DESCRIPTIVE OF

TRAVELS THROUGH WEST AND SOUTH BARBARY,

AND ACROSS THE MOUNTAIN'S OF ATLAS;

ALSO,

FRAGMENTS, NOTES, AND ANECDOTES;

SPECIMENS OF THE ARABIC EPISTOLARY STYLE,
&c. &c.

"L'Univers est une espèce de livre, dont on n'a lu que la première page, quand on n'a vu que son pays." LE COSMOPOLITE.

By JAMES GREY JACKSON,

RESIDENT UPWARDS OF SIXTEEN YEARS IN SOUTH AND WEST BARBARY, IN A DIPLOMATIC AND IN A COMMERCIAL CAPACITY.

ZuuBooks specialize in offering rare printed and ebooks for affordable prices. For more information on our products and services for authors please contact us at
ilifeebooks@gmail.com

This has been a ZuuBooks.com Publication. For New and Classic titles in Audiobooks, ebooks, and Paperback please visit us at www.zuuBooks.com

Authors who are interested in publishing and distributing their works can contact us at
ilifeebooks@gmail.com

AN ACCOUNT

OF

TIMBUCTOO AND HOUSA,

TERRITORIES IN THE INTERIOR OF Africa,
By; EL HAGE ABD SALAM SHABEENY;

WITH

NOTES, CRITICAL AND EXPLANATORY.

LONDON:
PRINTED FOR LONGMAN, HURST, REES, ORME, AND BROWN,
PATERNOSTER-ROW.
1820.

Printed by A. and R. Spottiswoode,
Printers Street, London.

TO HIS MOST EXCELLENT MAJESTY

GEORGE THE FOURTH,

&c. &c. &c.

THIS WORK
IS
WITH PERMISSION,
RESPECTFULLY INSCRIBED,
BY
HIS MAJESTY'S
MOST DUTIFUL SUBJECT
AND SERVANT,

JAMES GREY JACKSON.

INTRODUCTION.

The person who communicated the following intelligence respecting Timbuctoo and Housa, is a Muselman, and a native of Tetuan, whose father and mother are personally known to Mr. Lucas, the British Consul. His name is Asseed El Hage Abd Salam Shabeeny. His account of himself is, that at the age of fourteen years he accompanied his father to Timbuctoo, from which town, after a residence of three years, he proceeded to Housa; and after residing at the latter two years, he returned to Timbuctoo, where he continued seven years, and then came back to Tetuan.

Being now in the twenty-seventh year of his age, he proceeded from Tetuan as a pilgrim and merchant, with the caravan for Egypt to Mecca and Medina, and on his return, established himself as a merchant at Tetuan, his native place, from whence he embarked on board a vessel bound for Hamburgh, in order to purchase linens and other merchandize that were requisite for his commerce.

On his return from Hamburgh in an English vessel, he was captured, and carried prisoner to Ostend, by a ship manned by Englishmen, but under Russian colours, the captain of which pretended that his Imperial mistress was at war with all Muselmen. There he was released by the good offices of the British consul, Sir John Peters [a], and embarked once more in the same vessel, which, by the same mediation, was also released; but as the captain either was or pretended to be afraid of a second capture, El Hage Abd Salam was sent ashore at Dover, and is now [b], by the orders of government, to take his passage on board a king's ship that will sail in a few days.

In the following communications, Mr. Beaufoy proposed the questions, and Mr. Lucas was the interpreter.

Shabeeny was two years on his journey from Tetuan to Mekka, before he returned to Fas. He made some profit on his merchandise, which consisted of haiks [c], red caps, and slippers, cochineal and saffron; the returns were, fine Indian muslins [d] for turbans, raw silk, musk, and *gebalia* [e], a fine perfume that resembles black paste.

He made a great profit by his traffic at Timbuctoo and Housa; but, *he says*, money gained among the Negroes [f] has not the blessing of God on it, but vanishes away without benefit to the owner; but, acquired in a journey to Mecca, proves fortunate, and becomes a permanent acquisition.

On his return with his father from Mecca, they settled at Tetuan, and often carried cattle, poultry, &c. to Gibraltar; his father passed the last fifteen years of his life at Gibraltar, and died there about the year 1793. He was born at Mequinas; his family is descended from the tribe of Shabban [g], which possesses the country between Santa Cruz and Wedinoon. They were entitled to the office of pitching the Emperor's tent, and attending his person. They can raise 40,000 men, and they were the first who accompanied Muley Hamed Dehebby [h] in his march to Timbuctoo.

Footnote a: (return) Confirmed by Sir John Peters.

Footnote b: (return) In the year 1795.

Footnote c: (return) The haiks are light cotton, woollen, or silk garments, about five feet wide and four yards long, manufactured at Fas, as are also the red caps which are generally made of the finest Tedla wool, which is equal to the Spanish, and is the produce of the province of that name, (for the situation of which see the map of the empire of Marocco, facing page 55.) The slippers are also manufactured from leather made from goat-skins, at Fas and at Mequinas. The cochineal is imported from Spain, although the opuntia, or the tree that nourishes the cochineal-fly, abounds in many of the provinces of West Barbary, particularly in the province of Suse. The saffron abounds in the Atlas mountains in Lower Suse, and is used in most articles of food by the Muhamedans.

Footnote d: (return) Muls.

Footnote e: (return) *Gebalia* resembles frankincense, or Gum Benjamin, and is used for fumigations by the Africans.

Footnote f: (return) Being idolaters.

Footnote g: (return) Shâban is (probably) a tribe of the Howara Arabs, who possess the beautiful plains and fine country situated between the city of Terodant and the port of Santa Cruz. There is an emigration of the Mograffra Arabs, who are in possession of the country between Terodant and the port of Messa. The encampments of an emigration of the Woled Abusebah (vulgarly called, in the maps, *Labdessebas*) Arabs of Sahara, occupy a considerable district between Tomie, on the coast, and Terodant. The coast from Messa to Wedinoon is occupied by a trading race of Arabs and Shelluhs, who have inter-married, called *Ait Bamaran*. These people are very anxious to have a port opened in their country, and some sheiks among them have assured me, that there is a peninsula on their coast conveniently situated for a port. *This circumstance is well deserving the attention of the maritime and commercial nations of the world.*

Footnote h: (return) The youngest son of the Emperor Muley Ismael conducted the expedition here alluded to, about the year of Christ 1727. For an account of which see the Appendix, page 523.

He considers himself now as settled at Tetuan, where he has a wife and children. He left it about twelve months ago, with three friends, to go to Hamburg (as before mentioned.) They were confined forty-seven days at Ostend, were taken the second day of their voyage; the English captain put them ashore at Dover against their inclination, and proceeded to Gibraltar with their goods: this was in December, 1789.

THE CONTINENT.

The continent of Africa, the discovery of which has baffled the enterprise of Europe, (unlike every other part of the habitable world,) still remains, as it were, a sealed book, at least, if the book has been opened, we have scarcely got beyond the title-page.

Great merit is due to the enterprise of travellers. The good intention of the African Association, in promoting scientific researches in this continent, cannot (by the liberal) be doubted. But something more than this is necessary to embark *successfully* in this gigantic undertaking. I never thought that the system of solitary travellers would produce any beneficial result. The plan of the expedition of Major Peddie and Captain Tuckie was still more objectionable than the solitary plan, and I have reason to think, that no man possessing any personal knowledge of Africa, ever entertained hopes of the success of those expeditions. Twenty years ago I declared it as MY decided opinion, that the only way to obtain a knowledge of this interesting continent, is through the medium of commercial intercourse. The more our experience of the successive failure of our African expeditions advances, the more strongly am I confirmed in this opinion. If we are to succeed in this great enterprise, we must step out of the beaten path--the road of error, that leads to disappointment--the road that has been so fatal to all our ill-concerted enterprises; we must shake off the rust of precedent, and strike into a new path altogether.

Do we not lack that *spirit of union* so expedient and necessary to all great enterprises? Is not the public good sacrificed to self-aggrandisement and individual interest.--Let the African Institution unite its funds to those of the African Association, and co-operate with the efforts of that society! Let the African Company also throw in their share of intelligence. The separated and sometimes discordant interests of all these societies, if united, might effect much. The *united* efforts of such societies would do more in a year towards the civilization of Africa, and the abolition of slavery, than they will do in ten, unconnected as they now are. *Concordia parva res crescunt.*--When each looks to particular interests, we cannot expect the result to be the general good.

It is probable that the magnificent enterprises of the Portuguese and Spaniards, would, ere this, have colonised and converted to Christianity, all the eligible spots of idolatrous Africa, if their attention to this grand object had not been diverted by the discovery of America, and their establishments in Brazil, Mexico, &c.

I was established upwards of sixteen years in West and South Barbary; territories that maintain an uninterrupted intercourse with all those countries that Major Houghton, Hornemann, Park, Rontgen, Burckhardt, Ritchie, and others have attempted to explore. I was diplomatic agent to several maritime nations of Europe, which familiarised me with all ranks of society in those countries. I had a perfect knowledge of the commercial and travelling language of Africa, (the Arabic.) I corresponded *myself* with the Emperors, Princes, and Bashaws in this language; my commercial connections were *very* extensive, amongst all the most respectable merchants who traded with Timbuctoo and other countries of Sudan. My residence at Agadeer, or Santa Cruz, in Suse, afforded me eligible opportunities of procuring information respecting the trade with Sudan, and the interior of Africa. A long residence in the country, and extensive connections, enabled me to discriminate, and to ascertain who were competent and who were not competent to give me the information I required. I had opportunities at my leisure of investigating the motives that any might have to deceive me; I had time and leisure also to investigate their moral character, and to ascertain the principles that regulated their respective conduct. Possessed of all these sources of information, how could I fail of procuring correct and authentic intelligence of the interior of Africa; yet my account of the two Niles has been doubted by our fire-side critics, and the desultory intelligence of other travellers, who certainly did not possess those opportunities of procuring information that I did, has been substituted: but, notwithstanding this unaccountable scepticism, my uncredited account of the connection of the two Niles of Africa, continues daily to receive additional confirmation from all the African travellers themselves. And thus, Time , (to use the words of a [j]learned and most intelligent writer), "which is more obscure in its course than the Nile, and in its termination than the Niger," is disclosing all these things: so that I now begin to think that the before-mentioned critics will not be able much longer to maintain their theoretical hypothesis. [k]

Footnote j: (return) Vide the Rev. C. C. Colton's Lacon, sect. 587. p. 260, 261.

Footnote k: (return) See various letters on Africa, in this work, p. 443.

The talents, the extraordinary prudence and forbearance, the knowledge of the Arabic language, and other essential qualifications in an African traveller, which the ever-to-be-lamented Burckhardt so eminently possessed, gave me the greatest hopes of his success in his arduous enterprise, until I discovered, when reading his Travels, that he was *poor and despised, though a Muselman.*

There is too much reason to apprehend that he was suspected, if not discovered by the Muselmen, or he would not have been *secluded from their meals* and society: the Muselmen never (*sherik taam*) eat or divide food with those they suspect of deception, nor do they ever *refuse to partake of food with a Muselman,* unless they do suspect him of treachery or deception; this principle prevails so universally among them, that artful and designing people have practised as many deceptions on the Bedouin under the cloak of hospitality, as are practised in Christian countries under the cloak of religion! I cannot but suspect, therefore, from the circumstance before recited, that the Muselmism of Burckhardt was seriously suspected, and that his companions only waited a convenient opportunity in the Sahara for executing their revenge on him for the deception.

The very favourable reception that my account of Marocco met with from the British public; the many things therein stated, which are daily gaining confirmation, although they were doubted at the period of their publication, have contributed in no small degree, to the production of the following sheets, in which I can conscientiously declare, that truth has been my guide; I have never sacrificed it to ambition, vanity, avarice, or any other passion.

The learned, I am flattered to see, are now beginning to adopt my orthography of African names; they have lately adopted *Timbuctoo* for the old and barbarous orthography of *Timbuctoo*; they have, however, been upwards of ten years about it. In ten years more, I anticipate that *Fez* will be changed into *Fas*, and *Morocco* into *Marocco*, for this plain and uncontrovertible reason,-- because they are so spelled in the original language of the countries, of which they are the chief cities. Since the publication of my account of Marocco, I have seen Arabic words spelled various ways by the same author (I have committed the same error myself); but in the following work I have adopted a plan to correct this prevailing error in Oriental orthography, which, I think, ought to be followed by every Oriental scholar, as the only correct way of transcribing them in English; viz. by writing them exactly according to the original Arabic orthography, substituting *gr* (not *gh*, as Richardson directs) for the Arabic guttural [غ Arabic] grain, and *kh* for the guttural *k* or [خ Arabic]--

Note. We should be careful not to copy the orthography of Oriental or African names from the French, which has too often been done, although their pronunciation of European letters is very dissimilar from our own.

CONTENTS.

Science, and the Arts, edited at the Royal Institution of Great Britain, No. 15, published October, 1819
186

*Journey from Tangier to Rabat, through the Plains of Seboo, in Company with Doctor Bell and the Prince Muley Teib and an Army of Cavalry*191

Officiated as Interpreter between the Prince and Dr. Bell.--Description of Food sent to us by the Prince.--The Plains of M'sharrah Rummellah, an incomparably fine and productive Country.--The Cavalry of the Amorites;--their unique Observations on Dr. Bell: their mean opinion of his Art, because he could not cure Death.--Passage of the River Seboo on Rafts of inflated Skins.-- Spacious tent of Goat's Hair erected for the Sheik, and appropriated to the Use of the Prince.-- Description of the magnificent Plains of M'sharrah Rummellah and Seboo.--Arabian Royalty.-- Prodigious Quantity of Corn grown in these Plains.--Matamores, what they are.--Mode of Reaping.--

The Prince presents the Doctor with a Horse, and approves of his Medicines.--The Prince and the Doctor depart south-eastwardly, and the Author pursues his Journey to Rabat and Mogodor191

*Of the excavated Residences of the Inhabitants of Atlas: the Acephali, Hel Shoual, and Hel el Kitteb*198

The Discovery of Africa not to be effected by the present System of solitary Travellers; but by a grand Plan, with a numerous Company; beginning with Commerce, as the natural Prelude to Discovery, the Fore-runner of Civilization, and a preliminary Step, indispensable to the Conversion of the native Negroes to Christianity.

*Cautions to be used in Travelling*202

Danger of Travelling after Sun-set.--The Emperor holds himself accountable for Thefts committed on Travellers, whilst travelling between the rising and the setting Sun.--Emigration of Arabs.--Patriarchal Style of Living among the Arabs; Food, Clothing, domestic Looms, and Manufactures.--Riches of the Arabs calculated by the Number of Camels they possess.--Arabian Women are good Figures, and have personal Beauty; delicate in their Food; poetical Geniuses; Dancing and Amusements; Musical Instruments; their Manners are courteous.

*Abundance of Corn produced in West Barbary*208

Costly Presents made by Spain to the Emperor.--Bashaw of Duquella's Weekly Present of a Bar of Gold.--Mitferes or Subterranneous Depositaries for Corn.

*Domestic Serpents of Marocco*213

*Manufactures of Fas*214

Superior Manufactory of Gold Thread.--Imitation of precious Stones.--Manufactory of Gun-barrels in Suse.--Silver-mine.

Their incredible Destruction.--Used as Food.--Remarkable Instance of their destroying every Green Herb on one Side of a River, and not on the other.

Of the Propagation of Christianity in Africa.--Causes that prevent it.--The Mode of promoting it is through a friendly and commercial Intercourse with the Natives.--Exhortation to Great Britain to attend to the Intercourse with Africa.--Danger of the French colonizing Senegal, and supplanting us, and thereby depreciating the Value of our West-India Islands.

Application of the Superflux of Property or Capital.

On the Commercial Intercourse with Africa, through the Sahara and Ashantee.

Appendix to the foregoing Prospectus, being an Epitome of the Trade carried on by Great Britain and the European States in the Mediterranean, indirectly with Timbuctoo, the Commercial Depot of North Africa, and with other States of Sudan254

Letter from Vasco de Gama, in Elucidation of this Plan258

Letter on the Commercial Intercourse with Africa, in further Elucidation of this Plan264

Impediments to our Intercourse with Africa266

DIRECTIONS TO THE BINDER.

Larger format

[Page 1]

AN

ACCOUNT OF A JOURNEY

FROM

FAS TO TIMBUCTOO,

PERFORMED IN OR ABOUT THE YEAR 1787, A.C.

BY

EL HAGE ABD SALAM SHABEENY.

The Moors always prefer the spring and summer for travelling, because they suffer very much from the severe cold of the mornings in winter. They generally leave Fas in the beginning of April to proceed to Timbuctoo, and they leave Timbuctoo to return to Fas in the month of January.

The Mecca caravan takes its departure from Fas the beginning of March.

In travelling, the Moors hire their camels from stage to stage. Shabeeny's first stage was from Fas [1] to Tafilelt, which is generally performed in about twenty days.

Footnote 1: (return) This is a journey of crooked and rugged roads across the Atlas mountains, where they often sojourn in spots which invite the traveller, so that it takes a longer time to perform it than the distance would indicate.

[2]

The hire of every camel was from ten to twelve ducats, at five shillings sterling per ducat; as this route is through a very mountainous country, and the travelling is very bad, the charges were proportionally high; the weight which every camel carried was between four and five quintals, the camels in this country being strong and very large. [2]

Tafilelt is the place of general meeting of all the merchants who go to Timbuctoo. [3]

The territory of Tafilelt contains no towns, but abounds in fortresses with mud-walls [4], which the natives call El Kassar, and which contain from three to four hundred families; in these fortresses there is a public market (in Arabic, *soke*) every week, where the inhabitants purchase provisions, &c.

The natives of Tafilelt are descendants of the shereefs [5] or princes of Marocco, and are therefore of the Imperial family.

Footnote 2: (return) This charge of carriage by the camels from Fas to Tafilelt, is equal to 55s., sterling per camel; to 1-1/2d. per mile for each camel, and to one farthing and one third per quintal of merchandise per mile.

Footnote 3: (return) That is for all who go from the Emperor of Marocco's dominions, north of the river Morbeya, which is called El Garb, or the North Western Division.

Footnote 4: (return) These mud walls are made in cases, and the mode of erecting them is called *tabia*. See Jackson's Account of the Empire of Marocco, &c. &c. 2d or 3d edition, page 298.

Footnote 5: (return) Hence it is called *Bled Shereef*, i.e. the Country of Princes.

[3]

Shabeeny's next stage was to Draha [6], which he reached in six days. The expense per camel was about six ducats, or thirty shillings sterling. The district of Draha abounds in the small hard date [7], which is very fine; from four to six drahems [8] (equal to two to three shillings sterling) is the price of a camel load of these dates.

The province of Draha is larger than that of Tafilelt, its circumference being about four or five days' journey. The natives [9] of Draha are very dark, approaching to black, in their complexion: this province abounds in fortresses, like those of Tafilelt.

Footnote 6: (return) A province at the foot of the mountains of Atlas, south of Marocco, for which see the Map of West Barbary, in Jackson's Account of the Empire of Marocco, &c. &c. p. 1.

Footnote 7: (return) This date is called by the natives *bouskree:* it contains a larger quantity of saccharine juice than any other date. This province also produces a date called *bûtube*, which is the best that grows, and is called *sultan de timmar*, i.e. the king of dates. It is not used as an article of commerce, but is sent as presents to the great, and costs nearly double the price of those of any other quality: the quality mostly used for foreign commerce, is the Tafilelt date, called *timmar adamoh*, which is sold by the grocers in London. This species is, however, considered very unwholesome food, and accordingly is never eaten by the Filellies, or inhabitants of Tafilelt, but is food for the camels. The district of Tafilelt abounds in dates of all kinds: there are not less than thirty different kinds; and the plantations of dates belonging to the princes of Tafilelt are very extensive, insomuch that the annual produce of one plantation is often sold for a thousand dollars, or 220£ sterling. Half a dollar, or five drahems per camel load of three quintals.

Footnote 8: (return) A drahem is a silver coin, ten of which are equal to a Mexico dollar.

Footnote 9: (return) Their colour is darker than new copper, but not black, It may be compared to the colour of *old* mahogany, with a black hue. The natives of Draha are proverbially stupid.

[4]

The caravans have not, as in the journey to Mecca, their sheiks [10] or commanders. From Fas to Tafilelt they had no chief, but as there are generally a few old, rich, and respectable men in the caravan, its direction and government are committed to their care.

Footnote 10: (return) The *sheik akkabar*, or chief of the accumulated caravan, is generally a *shereef* or prince.

From Tafilelt, which, as before observed, is the country of the shereefs, they are guided by such of the trading shereefs as accompany the caravan, and who have always great respect paid them, till they arrive at Timbuctoo. The caravan increases as it proceeds in its journey: at Fas it consisted of about thirty or forty; at Draha, of from 300 to 400 camels. From Draha, at the distance of three days' travelling, they found water by digging, and on the next morning they entered the *Sahara*, which, for the first twenty days is a plain sandy desert resembling the sea. In this desert, when they pitch their tents at night, they are obliged frequently to shake the sand from their tops, as they would otherwise be overwhelmed before the morning.

Some part of this desert is hard, and the camels do not sink deep into it; in others the sand is very loose, which fatigues the camels exceedingly. In travelling, the caravan is directed by the stars at night, and by the sun in [5] the day, and occasionally by the smell of the earth, which they take up in their hands. For the first twenty days after they enter this wilderness they have no water; during this period, the caravan is obliged to carry water in goat-skins [11], as not a drop is to be found by digging. On this account, about a third part of the camels are employed in carrying water, and even with this quantity the camels are often left for three or four days without any. They never use mules in this part of the journey; they neither find the *sheh* [12], nor the thorny plant so common in the deserts of Africa.

The country on the borders of this desert, to the right and left, is inhabited by roving Arabs, at the distance of three or four days from the track which the caravan pursues; and is said to be partly plain, and in part hilly, with a little grass, and a few shrubs; when the cattle of these Arabs have consumed what grows in one spot, their owners remove to another. The caravan, though it generally consisted of about 400 men well armed, seeks its route through the most unfrequented part of the desert, from a dread of the attacks of the Arabs. The hottest wind is that from the east-south-east, and is called *Esshume* [13]; the coldest is that which blows from the west-north-west. To alleviate the great drought which travellers feel in the desert, they have recourse to melted butter. [14]

Footnote 11: (return) These goat-skins, when containing water, are called by the Arabs *kereb*, or *ghireb*, plur. *kerba*, or *ghirba*, sing.

Footnote 12: (return) The *sheh* is the wormseed plant, the thorny plant here alluded to is the wild myrtle.

Footnote 13: (return) *Esshume*, or the hot wind. For a particular description of this extraordinary wind, see Jackson's Account of the Empire of Marocco, &c. &c. 2d or 3d edition, page 283 and 284.

Footnote 14: (return) This is old butter kept several years in a *matamore*, or subterraneous cavern. It is called by the Arabs of the desert, *bûdra*; and much virtue is ascribed to it when it has attained a certain age: a small quantity swallowed, quickly diffuses itself through the system.

[6] After passing this desert of twenty days, they enter a country which varies in its appearance, particular spots being fertile [15] (called El Wah). Here they meet with *sederah* [16], a kind of wild myrtle, in great quantities. This plant is called by the natives, *gylan:* its height is about that of a man; the camels feed upon it. Between these shrubs there is a very small quantity of grass in particular spots. In this part of the desert they meet with extensive strata of stones: though the surface is generally sand, yet at the depth of eight or ten inches, they meet with a yellow or reddish earth; and about four feet deeper, with another kind of earth of various colours, but most commonly of a brownish cast; about five or six feet under this they find water, [7] which springs up very slowly, and at the bottom of this water you meet with a light sand. Sometimes the water is sweetish, frequently brackish, and generally warm. This last desert is about twenty days' journey, and is a vast plain without any mountains. They meet with no Arabs in this part, but the country on the right and left of their route, at the distance of from three to eight days' journey, is inhabited by Arabs, who are governed by their own (*sheiks*) chiefs, and are perfectly independent.

Footnote 15: (return) El Wah. For a full explanation of this term, see Jackson's Account of the Empire of Marocco, 3d edition, p. 283.

Footnote 16: (return) *Sederah*, thorny shrubs of all kinds are so called.

From Akka to Timbuctoo, a journey of forty-three days, they meet with no trees, except the *sederah*, no rivers, towns, or huts. From Draha, which is a country abounding in camels, to Timbuctoo, the charge per camel is from sixteen to twenty-one ducats. [17] That so long a journey is performed at so small [18] an expense, is owing to the abundance of camels in Draha. The caravan generally contains from 300 to 400 men, of whom a great part prefer walking to the uneasy motion of the camels.

Footnote 17: (return)

```
         From Fas to Tafilelt, 20 days, for 11 ducats per
camel.

             Tafilelt to Draha,      6 do.      6 do.     do.

             Draha to Timbuctoo,    48 do.    18-1/2 do.  do.

                                    ---        ----
```

                                                    69 days, for 35-1/2 ducats per
camel
load, which is about the rate of one farthing per quintal per
mile. This does not include the expense of camels for the
conveyance of merchants, servants, &c. or of provisions or
water, but merely of those carrying goods. A full account
of these caravans, and their mode of crossing the Sahara,
will be found in Jackson's Marocco, ch. 13.

Footnote 18: (return) The expense is now (A.C. 1818) smaller, as the ducat, by a coinage which is depreciated, has fallen to 3s. 6d. sterling.

[8]

Situation Of The City Of Timbuctoo.

On the east side of the city of Timbuctoo, there is a large forest, in which are a great many elephants. The timber here is very large. The trees on the outside of the forest are remarkable for having two different colours; that side which is exposed to the morning sun is black, and the opposite side is yellow. The body of the tree has neither branches nor leaves, but the leaves, which are remarkably large, grow upon the top only: so that one of these trees appears, at a distance, like the mast and round top of a ship. Shabeeny has seen trees in England much taller than these: within the forest the trees are smaller than on its skirts. There are no trees resembling these in the Emperor of Marocco's dominions. They are of such a size that the largest cannot be girded by two men. They bear a kind of berry about the size of a walnut, in clusters consisting of from ten to twenty berries. Shabeeny cannot say what is the extent of this forest, but it is very large. Close to the town of Timbuctoo, on the south, is a small rivulet in which the inhabitants wash their clothes, and which is about two feet deep. It runs in the great forest on the east, and does not communicate with the Nile, but is lost in the sands west of the town. Its water is brackish; that of the Nile is good and pleasant. The town of Timbuctoo is surrounded by a mud-wall: the [9] walls are built tabia-wise [19] as in Barbary, viz. they make large wooden cases, which they fill with mud, and when that dries they remove the cases higher up till they have finished the wall. They never use stone or brick; they do not know how to make bricks. The wall is about twelve feet high, and sufficiently strong to defend the town against the wild Arabs, who come frequently to demand money from them. It has three gates; one called Bab Sahara, or the gate of the desert, on the north: opposite to this, on the other side of the town, a second, called Bab Neel, or the gate of the Nile: the third gate leads to the forest on the east, and is called Beb El Kibla. [20] The gates are hung on very large hinges, and when shut at night, are locked, as in Barbary; and are farther secured by a large prop of wood placed in the inside slopingly against them. There is a dry ditch, or excavation, which circumscribes the town, (except at those places which are opposite the gates,) about twelve feet deep, and too wide for any man to leap it. The three gates of the town are [10] shut every evening soon after sun-set: they are made of folding doors, of which there is only one pair. The doors are lined on the outside with untanned hides of camels, and are so full of nails that no hatchet can penetrate them; the front appears like one piece of iron.

Footnote 19: (return) The tabia walls are thus built: They put boards on each side of the wall supported by stakes driven in the ground, or attached to other stakes laid transversely across the wall; the intermediate space is then filled with sand and mud, and beat down with large wooden mallets, (as they beat the terraces) till it becomes hard and compact; the cases are left on for a day or two; they then take them off, and move them higher up, repeating this operation till the wall is finished.

Footnote 20: (return) El Kibla signifies the tomb of Muhamed: in most African towns there is a Kibla-gate, which faces Medina in Arabia.

Population.

The town is once and a half the size of Tetuan [21], and contains, besides natives, about 10,000 [22] of the people of Fas and Marocco. The native inhabitants of the town of Timbuctoo may be computed at 40,000, exclusive of slaves and foreigners. Many of the merchants who visit Timbuctoo are so much attached to the place that they cannot leave it, but continue there for life. The natives are all blacks: almost every stranger marries a female of the town, who are so beautiful that travellers often fall in love with them at first sight.

Footnote 21: (return) That is about four miles in circumference. Tetuan contains 16,000 inhabitants; but, according to this account, Timbuctoo contains 50,000, besides slaves, a population above three times that of Tetuan: now, as the houses of Timbuctoo are more spacious than those of Tetuan, it is to be apprehended that Shabeeny has committed an error in describing the size of Timbuctoo.

Footnote 22: (return) Who go there for the purposes of trade.

INNS, OR CARAVANSERAS.

When strangers arrive they deposit their merchandise in large warehouses called fondacs; and hire as many rooms as they choose, having [11] stables for their camels, &c. in the same place. These fondacs [23] are private property, and are called either by the owner's name, or by that of the person who built them. The fondac, in which Shabeeny and his father lived, had forty apartments for men, exclusive of stables; twenty below and twenty above, the place having two stories. The staircase was within the inclosure, and was composed of rough boards; while he staid, the rooms were constantly occupied by natives and strangers; they hired rooms for three months, for which they paid thirty okiat, or fifteen shillings sterling per month. These fondacs are called Woal [24] by the negroes. The money was paid to the owner's agent, who always lives in the fondac for this purpose, and to accommodate strangers with provisions, &c. At their arrival, porters assisted them and procured every thing they wanted; but when they were settled they hired a man and a woman slave to cook and to clean their rooms, and to do every menial office. Slaves are to be bought at all hours: the slave-merchants keep a great number ready for sale.

Footnote 23: (return) It is probable that Adams, the American sailor, (if he ever was at Timbuctoo,) saw one of these fondacs that belonged to the king, and mistook it for his palace.

Footnote 24: (return) Ten okiat, or drahems, make a Mexico dollar. The name of the king of Timbuctoo, in 1800 A.C. was Woolo. Many of the fondacs are rented of him.

HOUSES.

In the houses little furniture is seen; the principal articles (those of the kitchen excepted) [12] are beds, mats on the floor, and the carpets; which cover the whole room. The rooms are about fourteen feet by ten; the kitchen and wash-house are generally to the right and to the left of the passage; the necessary is next the wash-house. [25]

Footnote 25: (return) Being more convenient for the Muhamedan ablutions.

GOVERNMENT.

Timbuctoo is governed by a native black, who has the title of sultan. He is tributary to the sultan of Housa, and is chosen by the inhabitants of Timbuctoo, who write to the king of Housa for his approbation. Upon the death of a sultan, his eldest son is most commonly chosen. The son of a concubine cannot inherit the throne; if the king has no lawful son (son of his wife) at his decease, the people choose his successor from among his relations. The sultan has only one lawful wife, but keeps many concubines: the wife has a separate house for herself, children, and slaves. He has no particular establishment for his concubines, but takes any girl he likes from among his slaves. His wife has the principal management of his house. The sultan's palace is built in a corner of the city, on the east; it occupies a large extent of ground within an inclosure, which has a gate. Within this square are many buildings; some for the officers of state. The king often sits in the gate to administer justice, and to converse with his friends. There is a small garden within it, furnishing [13] a few flowers and vegetables for his table; there is also a well, from which the water is drawn by a wheel. [26] Many female slaves are musicians. The king has several sons, who are appointed to administer justice to the natives. Except the king's relations, there are no nobles nor any privileged class of men as in Barbary [27]: those of the blood-royal are much respected. The officers of state are distinguished by titles like those of Marocco; one that answers to an Alkaid, *i. e.* a captain of 700, of 500, or of 100 men; another like that of Bashaw. The king, if he does not choose to marry one of his own relations, takes a wife from the family of the chiefs of his council; his daughters marry among the great men. The queen-dowager has generally an independent provision, but cannot marry. The concubines of a deceased king cannot marry, but are handsomely provided for by his successor.

Footnote 26: (return) A wheel similar to the Persian wheel, worked by a mule or an ass, having pots, which throw the water into a trough as they pass round, which trough discharges the water into the garden, and immerges the plants.

Footnote 27: (return) The privileged class of men in Barbary, are the Fakeers; but no one in Barbary is noble but the King's relations, who are denominated shereefs.

REVENUE.

The revenue arises partly from land and partly from duties upon all articles exposed to sale. The king has lands cultivated by farmers who are obliged to supply his household and troops; [14] the surplus after the support of their own families is deposited in matamores [28], these are stores to be used in time of scarcity: the matamores are about six feet deep. The king often gives gold-dust, slaves, &c. to his favorites, but the royal domains are never given. Lands not very fruitful are common pastures. Moors pay no duties; they say they will not bring goods if compelled to pay duty, but the natives must pay; the duties are collected by the king's officers, they are four per cent. upon each article *ad valorem*. At the gate of the desert, goods brought by foreigners pay nothing, but goods brought in by the gate of the Nile, (which is the gate of the Negroes,) pay a tax: another part of the revenue is two per cent, in kind on the produce of the land; but the people of Barbary do not pay even this for what land they cultivate. The property of those who die without heirs goes to the king, but when a foreigner dies the king takes no part of his property; it is kept for his relations. Timbuctoo being a frontier town remits no revenue to Housa; the king of Housa sends money to Timbuctoo to pay the garrison.

Footnote 28: (return) Subterraneous excavations, or rooms in the form of a cone, which have a small opening like a trap-door; when these matamores are full of grain, they are shut, and the air being excluded, the grain deposited in them will keep sound twenty or thirty years. I have been in matamores in West and in South Barbary, that would contain 1000 saas of wheat, or nearly 2000 bushels Winchester measure. They are from six to sixteen feet deep, and of various conical forms.

[15]

ARMY.

The troops are paid by the king of Housa, and are armed with pikes, swords, cutlasses, sabres, and muskets; the other natives use the bow and arrow. At Timbuctoo, in time of war, there are about 12,000 or 15,000 troops, 5000 of which receive constant daily pay in time of peace, and are clothed every year; they are all infantry except a few of the king's household. Sometimes he subsidises the friendly Arabs, and makes occasional presents to their chiefs [29]; these Arabs can furnish him with from 80,000 to 40,000 men.

Footnote 29: (return) Of the Brabeesh clan; see the Map.

ADMINISTRATION OF JUSTICE.

Punishments are the bastinado, imprisonment, and fine. He recollects but one prison. If a native stabs another, he is obliged to attend the wounded man until he recovers; if he dies, the offender is put to death. The offender must pay a daily allowance to the wounded man for his support; if the wound appears dangerous, the culprit is immediately imprisoned; if the wounded man recovers, the offender must pay a fine and suffer the bastinado. There are four capital punishments: beheading, hanging, strangling and bastinadoing to death. Beheading is preferred; it is thus performed: the criminal sits down, and a person behind gives him a blow or push on the back or shoulder, which makes him turn his head, and while his attention is thus employed, the executioner strikes it off. Hanging [16] and strangling are seldom used; and bastinadoing to death, is only inflicted when the crime is highly aggravated. Capital crimes are murder, robbery with violence, and stealing cattle. Small offences, as stealing slaves and other articles, are punished by the bastinado. The landed estates of criminals are never forfeited. [30] The police is so good, that merchants reside there in perfect safety. There are no exactions or extortions practised by government, as in Barbary, nor even any presents asked for the king. A debtor proving his inability, cannot be molested [31]; but to the extent of his means he is always liable; on refusing to pay, he may be imprisoned; but upon proving his insolvency before the judge, he is discharged, though always liable if he should have means at any future time. Watchmen patrole in the [17] night with their dogs; others are stationed in particular places, as the market-place and the *kasserea*, or square, where the merchants have their shops. Guards are placed at the king's palace. Capital crimes are tried by the king: smaller offences by inferior magistrates. The council sit with the king, every man according to his rank; it consists of the principal officers of his household; he asks *their* opinion, but unless they are unanimous, decides according to his own. There are always five or six judges sitting in the king's court for the general administration of justice. The king is understood to have no power of altering the laws: if the council are unanimous, the king never decides against them. [32]

Footnote 30: (return) But go to the next heir.

Footnote 31: (return) This is the written Muhamedan law: the insolvent is always liable, but cannot be arrested or imprisoned whilst he remains insolvent, but continues always liable for the debt if he afterwards becomes solvent. The present Emperor of Marocco has lately published an edict. Hearing that his Jew subjects in London frequently became bankrupts, or made compositions with their creditors, has enacted, that all, persons in his dominions who live by buying and selling, shall pay their just debts; but if unable, their brethren, or relations shall pay their creditors for them. If *they* are unable, the insolvent is to receive a beating every morning at sunrise, to remind him of his defalcation. This law was enacted at Fas in 1817, and since then, I am informed, no bankruptcy has happened in that great commercial city.

Footnote 32: (return) This is a custom derived from Muhamedan governments.

A slave is entirely at his master's disposal, who may put him to death without trial; yet the slave may complain to the council of ill-usage, and if the complaint be well-founded, his master is ordered to sell him. The slaves are always foreign; a native cannot be made a slave. There are three reasons for which a slave may be entitled to freedom: *want of food, want of clothes, and want of shoes*: an old slave is frequently set at liberty, and returns to his own country. The children of slaves are the property of their master. Slaves cannot marry without the consent of their masters. The master of the female slave generally endeavours to buy the male to whom she is attached. [33]

Footnote 33: (return) Many conscientious Muhamedans, in purchasing slaves, calculate how many years' service their purchase money is equal to. Thus, if a man pays a servant twenty dollars a-year for wages, and he gives 100 dollars for a slave, he retains the slave five years, when, if his conduct has been approved, he often discharges him from servitude. The period for liberating slaves in this manner is however quite optional, and admits of great latitude; neither is there any compulsion in the master. I have known instances of a slave being liberated after a few years of servitude; and his master's confidence has been such that he has advanced him money to trade with, and has allowed him to cross the desert to Timbuctoo, waiting for the repayment of his money till his return. This is often the treatment of Muhamedans to slaves! how different from that practised by the Planters in the West India Islands!!!

[18]

SUCCESSION TO PROPERTY.

Upon the decease of a native, the first claim is that of his creditors; the next is that of his widow, who is entitled to the dower [34] promised by her husband to her father, if, not already paid, and to one-eighth of the remainder; the rest is divided among the children. A son's share is double that of a daughter. If they agree, the land may be sold, if not, it must be divided as above. Of lands and houses, nothing is sold till the children arrive at the age of discretion; when each is entitled to his share, the rest being unsold till the others are of age in turn. This age is not fixed at so many years, but [19] the period of discretion is determined by the relations, upon oath, before a magistrate: there is hardly any man that knows his own age. The father may dispose of his property by will, as far as regards the property of his children, but he cannot divest his wife of her rights; if a wife dies without a will, her children succeed. Wills are not written; the guardian appointed by the father takes care of the property of the deceased, and employs in trade, and lends out the money for the benefit of his children. Relations succeed if there are no children; and if there are no relations, the king takes all but the wife's share. The wife's relations are not considered as the husband's relations. Children of concubines inherit equally with those of the wife. If a man have two children by a concubine, she becomes free at his death, otherwise she remains a slave. She is entitled, having children, to an eighth of the property.

Footnote 34: (return) The husband always stipulates to pay the father of his wife a certain sum: this is the Muhamedan dower.

MARRIAGE.

A man agrees to pay a certain price to the father of his wife, and witnesses are called to support the proof of the contract: the girl is sent home, and at night a feast is made by the husband for his male friends; by the wife for her female friends.

Rape is punished by death. Adultery is not punishable by the law, nor is it a ground for divorce. A husband may always put away his wife, but if without sufficient legal ground, [20] he must pay her stipulated dower. Abusive language is a sufficient ground of divorce, but adultery is not. The dower is the price originally agreed upon with the father; and if it has been already paid (which it seldom is), she has no further claim upon the husband, though put away without sufficient ground. Her clothes, jewels, &c. given to her by her relations are her own property. A father generally gives the daughter in jewels, &c. a present double the value of that given him by the husband. A man can have but one wife, but may keep concubines. Seduction and adultery are not cognisable by law. The law says, "a woman's flesh is her own, she may do with it what she pleases." Prostitutes are common. A man may marry his niece, but not his daughter.

The people of Timbuctoo are not circumcised.

TRADE.

Timbuctoo is the great emporium for all the country of the blacks, and even for Marocco and Alexandria.

The principal articles of merchandise are tobacco, kameemas [35], beads of all colours for necklaces, and cowries, which are bought at Fas by the pound. [36] Small Dutch looking glasses, some [21] of which are convex, set in gilt paper frames. They carry neither swords, muskets, nor knives, except such as are wanted in the caravan. At the entrance of the desert they buy rock-salt [37] of the Arabs, who bring it to them in loads ready packed, which they carry as an article of trade. In their caravan there were about 500 camels, of which about 150 or 200 were laden with salt. The camels carry less of salt than of any other article, because (being rock-salt) it wears their sides. They pay these Arabs from twenty to fifteen ounces [38] of Barbary money per load. An ounce of Barbary is worth about *6d.*, and a ducat is worth about *5s.* sterling. They sell this salt at Timbuctoo upon an average at 50 per cent. profit; it is more profitable than linen. They take no oil from Barbary to Timbuctoo as they are supplied from other places with fish-oil used for lamps but not for food; they make soap with the oil. The returns are made in gold-dust, slaves, ivory, and pepper; gold-dust is preferred and is brought to Timbuctoo from Housa in small leather bags. He bought one of these bags of gold-dust and pieces of rings for 90 Mexican dollars, and sold it at Fas for 150. The merchants bring their gold from Timbuctoo in the saddle-bags, in small purses of different sizes [22] one within the other. The bag which Shabeeny purchased was bought at Housa, where it sells for seven or eight ducats cheaper than at Timbuctoo. On articles from Marocco they make from thirty to fifty per cent. clear profit. Cowries and gold-dust are the medium of traffic. The shereefs and other merchants generally sell their goods to some of the principal native merchants, and immediately send off the slaves, taking their gold-dust with them into other countries. The merchants residing at Timbuctoo have agents or correspondents in other countries; and are themselves agents in return. Timbuctoo is visited by merchants from all the neighbouring black countries. Some of its inhabitants are amazingly rich. The dress of common women has been often worth 1000 dollars. A principal source of their wealth is lending gold-dust and slaves at high interest to foreign merchants, which is repaid by goods from Marocco and other countries, to which the gold-dust and slaves are carried. They commonly trade in the public market, but often send to the merchant or go to his house. Cowries in the least damaged are bad coin, and go for less than those that are perfect. There are no particular market days; the public market for provisions is an open place fifty feet square, and is surrounded by shops. [39] The Arabs sit down on their goods in the middle, till they have sold them. The pound weight of Timbuctoo is about two ounces heavier than the small [23] pound of Barbary, which weighs twenty Spanish dollars; they have also half and quarter pounds; by these weights is sold milk, rice, butter, &c. as well as by the measure. The weights are of wood or iron under the inspection of a magistrate called in Barbary *m'tasseb, i.e.* inspector of weights and measures, and if the weights are found deficient, he punishes the offender immediately; they have also a quintal or cwt. They have a wooden measure called a *m'hoad* [40], equal to the small *m'hoad* of Barbary, where a *m'hoad* of wheat weighs about 24 lb. Both the weights and measures are divided into 1/2, 1/4, 1/8 and 1/16.

Footnote 35: (return) *Kameema* is the Arabic word for the linen called *plattilias*. They are worth 50 Mexico dollars each, at Timbuctoo.

Footnote 36: (return) Called, in Amsterdam, *Velt Spiegels*, and in Timbuctoo, *Murrâih de juah*.

Footnote 37: (return) This salt is bought at Tishet, at Shangareen, and at Arawan, in the south part of Sahara; for which see the Map of Northern and Central Africa, in the new Supplement to the Encyclopædia Britannica, Article *Africa*.

Footnote 38: (return) *Okia* is the Arabic name for this piece of money.

Footnote 39: (return) Similar to the corn-market at Mogodor.

Footnote 40: (return) The *m'hoad* is no longer used in Barbary. There is a *krube*, of which sixteen are equal to a *saa*, which, when filled with good wheat, weighs 100 lbs. equal to 119 lbs. English weight.

MANUFACTURES.

The black natives are smiths, carpenters, shoemakers, tailors, and masons, but not weavers. The Arabs in the neighbourhood are weavers, and make carpets resembling those of Fas and of Mesurata, where they are called telisse [41]; they are of wool, from their own sheep, and camels' hair. The bags for goods, and the tents, are of goats' and camels' hair; there are no palmetto trees in that country. Their thread [42], needles, scissors, &c. come from Fas: most of their [24] ploughs they buy of the Arabs near the town, who are subject to it. Some are made in the town. These Arabs manufacture iron from ore found in the country, and are good smiths. They make iron bars of an excellent quality. They tan leather for soles of shoes very well, but know nothing of dressing leather in oil: the upper leather comes from Fas [43]; their wooden combs [44] and spoons come from Barbary; they have none of ivory or horn. No lead is brought from Barbary; he thinks they have lead of their own. The best shoes are brought from Fas.

Footnote 41: (return) *Telissa*, sing.; *Telisse*, plur.

Footnote 42: (return) To Fas they are brought from England through Gibraltar and Mogodor.

Footnote 43: (return) Leather is also imported from Marocco, and from Terodant in South Barbary.

Footnote 44: (return) Wooden combs are imported from Marseilles to Mogodor.

The country is well cultivated, except on the side of the desert. They have rice, *el bishna* [45], and a corn which *they* call *allila* [46], but in Barbary it is called *drâh*: this requires very rich ground. They make bread of *el bishna*: they have no wheat or barley. Property is fenced by a bank and a ditch. Dews are very heavy. Lands are watered by canals cut from the Nile; high lands by wells, the water of which is raised by wheels [47] worked by cattle, as in Egypt. They [25] have violent thunder-storms in summer, but no rains: the mornings and evenings, during winter, are cold; the coldest wind is from the west, when it is as cold as at Fas. The winter lasts about two months, though the weather is cool from September to April. They begin to sow rice in August and September, but they can sow it at any time, having water at hand: he saw some sowing rice while others were reaping it. *El bishna* and other corn is sown before December. *El bishna* is ripe in June and July; as are beans. *Allila* may be sown at all seasons; it requires water only every eight or ten days. Their beans are like the small Mazagan beans, and are sown in March; the stalk is short, but full of pods. The *allila* produces a small, white, flattish grain.

Footnote 45: (return) *El Bishna*. This is the Arabic name for Indian corn.

Footnote 46: (return) *Allila*, a species of millet.

Footnote 47: (return) A wheel similar to the Persian wheel, as before described in the note, page 13.

PROVISIONS.

Rice is their principal food, but the rich have wheaten flour from Fas [48], and make very fine bread, which is considered a luxury. Bread is also made from the *allila*. They roast, boil, bake, and stew, but make no *cuscasoe*. Their meals are breakfast, dinner, and supper. They commonly breakfast about eight, dine about three, and sup soon after sunset. They drink only water or milk with their meals, have no palm wine or any fermented liquor; when they wish to be exhilarated after dinner, they provide [26] a plant of an intoxicating quality called *el hashisha* [49], of which they take a handful before a draught of water.

Footnote 48: (return) And also from Marocco.

Footnote 49: (return) *El Hashisha*. This is the African hemp plant: it is esteemed for the extraordinary and pleasing voluptuous vacuity of mind which it produces on those who smoke it: unlike the intoxication from wine, a fascinating stupor pervades the mind, and the dreams are agreeable. The *kief* is the flower and seeds of the plant: it is a strong narcotic, so that those who use it cannot do without it. For a further description of this plant, see Jackson's Marocco, 2d or 3d edit. p. 131 & 132.

ANIMALS.

Goats are very large, as big as the calves in England, and very plentiful; sheep are also very large. Cattle are small; many are oxen. Milk of camels and goats is preferred to that of cows. Horses are small, and are principally fed upon camels' milk; they are of the greyhound [50] shape, and will travel three days without rest. They have dromedaries [51] which travel from Timbuctoo [52] to Tafilelt in the short period of five or six days.

Footnote 50: (return) These horses are the desert horse, or the *shrubat er'reeh*. See Jackson's Marocco, 2d or 3d edition, p. 94. to 96.

Footnote 51: (return) These are *El Heirie*, (or *Erragual*), for a particular description of which see Jackson's Marocco, p. 91. to 93.

Footnote 52: (return) A distance of upwards of 1200 British miles.

[27]

BIRDS.

They have common fowls, ostriches, and a bird larger than our blackbird [53]; also storks, which latter are birds of passage, and arrive in the spring and disappear at the approach of winter; swallows, &c.

Footnote 53: (return) The starling.

FISH.

They have many extremely good in the Nile; one of the shape and size of our salmon [54]; the largest of these are about four feet long. They use lines and hooks brought from Barbary, and nets, like our casting nets, made by themselves. They strike large fish with spears and fish-gigs.

Footnote 54: (return) The *shebbel*, a species of salmon, a very delicate fish, but so rich that it is best roasted, which the Arabs do in a superior manner.

PRICES OF DIFFERENT ARTICLES.

Sheep from ten to sixteen cowries. Cowries [55] are much valued, and form an ornament of head-dress even for the richest women; they are highly valued as ornaments. Goats are cheaper than sheep; the best from eight to twelve cowries. Fowls from four to six cowries each. Antelopes are very scarce and dear. Camels from thirty to sixty cowries, according to their size and condition. Ostriches, of which vast numbers are brought to market, are very cheap; the fore-feathers [56] are often carried to Tafilelt and Marocco, the inferiors are thrown away. A good [28] slave is worth ten, fifteen, or twenty ducats of five shillings each; at Fas, they are worth from sixty to a hundred ducats: females are the dearest. Slaves are most valuable about twelve years old. They have fish-oil for lamps, but use neither wax nor tallow for candles. The fish-oil is a great article of trade, and is brought from the neighbourhood [57] of the sea by Genawa [58] to Housa, and thence to Timbuctoo; dearer at Timbuctoo than at Housa, and dearer at Housa than at Genawa.

Footnote 55: (return) Cowries are called *El Uda*, and are sold in Santa Cruz and in South Barbary, at twenty Mexico dollars per quintal.

Footnote 56: (return) Called *Ujuh*.

Footnote 57: (return) Probably from the coast of Guinea, with which Housa carries on an extensive trade.

Footnote 58: (return) *i.e.* Guinea; Genawa being the Arabic name for the coast of Guinea.

DRESS.

The sultan wears a white turban of very fine muslin, the ends of which are embroidered with gold, and brought to the front; this turban [29] comes from Bengala. [59] He wears a loose white cotton shirt, with sleeves long and wide, open at the breast; unlike that of the Arabs, it reaches to the small of the leg; over this a *caftan* [60] of red woollen cloth, of the same length; red is generally esteemed. The shirt (*kumja*) is made at Timbuctoo, but the caftan comes from Fas, ready made; over the caftan is worn a short cotton waistcoat, striped white, red, and blue; this comes from Bengala, and is called *juliba.* [61] The sleeves of the caftan are as wide as those of the shirt; the breast of it is fastened with buttons, in the Moorish style, but larger. The *juliba* has sleeves as wide as the caftan. When he is seated, all the sleeves are turned up over the shoulder [62], so that his arms are bare, and the air is admitted to his body.

Footnote 59: (return) *i.e.* Bengal.

Footnote 60: (return) A *caftan*, or coat, with wide sleeves, no collar, but that buttons all down before.

Footnote 61: (return) It is not the cotton cloth which comes from Bengal that is named *Juliba*, but the fashion or the cut of it.

Footnote 62: (return) The Moorish fashion.

Upon his turban, on the forehead, is a ball of silk, like a pear; one of the distinctions of royalty. He wears, also, a close red skull-cap, like the Moors of Tetuan, and two sashes, one over each shoulder, such as the Moors wear round the waist; they are rather cords than sashes, and are very large; half a pound of silk is used in one of them. The subjects wear but one; they are either red, yellow, or blue, made at Fas. He wears, like his subjects, a sash round the waist, also made at Fas; of these there are two kinds,--one of leather, with a gold buckle in front, like those of the soldiers in Barbary; the other of silk, like those of the Moorish merchants. He wears (as do the subjects) breeches made in the Moorish fashion, of cotton in summer, made at Timbuctoo, and of woollen in winter, brought ready made from Fas. His shoes are distinguished by a piece of red leather, in front of the leg, about three inches wide, and eight long, embroidered with silk and gold.

[30]

When he sits in his apartment, he wears a dagger with a gold hilt, which hangs on his right side: when he goes out, his attendants carry his musket, bow, arrows, and lance.

His subjects dress in the same manner, excepting the distinctions of royalty; viz. the pear, the sashes on the shoulders, and the embroidered leather on the shoes.

The sultana wears a caftan, open in front from top to bottom, under this a slip of cotton like the kings, an Indian shawl over the shoulders, which ties behind, and a silk handkerchief about her head. Other women dress in the same manner. They wear no drawers. The poorest women are always clothed. They never show their bosom. The men and women wear ear-rings. The general expense of a woman's dress is from two ducats to thirty. [63] Their shoes are red, and are brought from Marocco. [64] Their arms and ankles are adorned with bracelets. The poor have them of brass; the rich, of gold. The rich ornament their heads with cowries. The poor have but one bracelet on the leg, and one on the arm; the rich, two. They also wear gold rings upon their fingers. They have no pearls or precious stones. The women do not wear veils.

Footnote 63: (return) Equal to from two to thirty Mexico dollars.

Footnote 64: (return) They are manufactured at Marocco.

[31]

DIVERSIONS.

The king has 500 or 600 horses; his stables are in the inclosure; the saddles have a peak before, but none behind. He frequently hunts the antelope, wild ass, ostrich, and an animal, which, from Shabeeny's description, appears to be the wild cow [65] of Africa. The wild ass is very fleet, and when closely pursued kicks back the earth and sand in the eyes of his pursuers. They have the finest greyhounds in the world, with which they hunt only the antelope [66]; for the dogs are not able to overtake the ostrich. Shabeeny has often hunted with the king; any person may accompany him. Sometimes he does not return for three or four days: he sets out always after sunrise. Whatever is killed in the chace is divided among the strangers and other company present; but those animals which are taken alive are sent to the king's palace. He goes to hunt towards the desert, and does not begin till distant ten miles from the town. The antelopes are found in herds of from thirty to sixty. He never saw an antelope, wild ass, or ostrich alone, but generally in large droves. The ostriches, like the storks, place centinels upon the watch: thirty yards are reckoned a distance for a secure shot with the bow. The king always shoots on horseback, [32] as do many of his courtiers, sometimes with muskets, but oftener with bows. The king takes a great many tents with him. There are no lions, tigers, or wild boars near Timbuctoo. They play at chess and draughts, and are very expert at those games: they have no cards; but they have tumblers, jugglers, and ventriloquists, whose voice appears to come from under the armpits. He was much pleased with their music, of which they have twenty-four different sorts. They have dances of different kinds, some of which are very indecent.

Footnote 65: (return) The *Aoudad*; for a particular description of which, see Jackson's Marocco, Chapter V., Zoology, p. 84.

Footnote 66: (return) The Gazel, or Antelope, outruns at first the greyhound; but after running about an hour the greyhound gains on him.

TIME.

They measure time [67] by days, weeks, lunar months, and lunar years; yet few can ascertain their age.

Footnote 67: (return) The hour is an indefinite term, and assimilates to our expression of a good while; it is from half an hour by the dial to six hours, and the difference is expressed by the word *wahad saa kabeer*, a long hour; and *wahad saa sereer*, a little hour; also by the elongation of the last syllable of the last word.

RELIGION.

They have no temples, churches, or mosques, no regular worship or sabbath; but once in three months they have a great festival, which lasts two or three days, sometimes a week, and is spent in eating and drinking. He does not know the cause; but thinks it, perhaps, a commemoration of the king's birth-day; no work is done. They believe in a Supreme Being and [33] another state of existence, and have saints and men whom they revere as holy. Some of them are sorcerers, and some ideots, as in Barbary and Turkey; and though physicians are numerous, they expect more effectual aid in sickness from the prayers of the saints, especially in the rheumatism. Music is employed to excite ecstasy in the saint, who, when in a state of inspiration, tells (on the authority of some departed saint, generally of Seedy Muhamed Seef,) what animal must be sacrificed for the recovery of the patient: a white cock, a red cock, a hen, an ostrich, an antelope, or a goat. The animal is then killed in the presence of the sick, and dressed; the blood, feathers, and bones are preserved in a shell and carried to some retired spot, where they are covered and marked as a sacrifice. No salt or seasoning is used in the meat, but incense is used previous to its preparation. The sick man eats as much as he can of the meat, and all present partake; the rice, or what else is dressed with it, must be the produce of charitable contributions from others, not of the house or family; and every contributor prays for the patient.

DISEASES.

The winds of the desert produce complaints in the stomach, cured by medicine. They have professed surgeons and physicians. The bite of a snake is cured by sucking the wound. They have [34] the jlob [68] violently, for which sulphur from Terodant in Suse is taken internally and externally. This disorder is sometimes fatal. They are afflicted also with fevers and agues. Bleeding is often successful; the physicians prescribe also purgatives and emetics. Ruptures are frequent and dangerous; seldom cured, and often fatal. They tap for the dropsy. He never heard of the venereal disease there. Head-aches and consumptions also prevail. The physicians [69] collect herbs and use them in medicine.

Footnote 68: (return) Probably the itch, called El Hack in Barbary.

Footnote 69: (return) The physicians have a very superior and general knowledge of the virtues of herbs and plants.

MANNERS AND CUSTOMS.

The nails and palms of the hands are stained red with henna [70], cultivated there: the Arabs tatoo their hands and arms, but not the people of Timbuctoo. These people are real negroes; they have a slight mark on the face, sloping from the eye; the Foulans have a horizontal mark; the Bambarrahees a wide gash from the forehead to the chin. Tombs are raised over the dead; they are buried in a winding-sheet and a coffin: the relations mourn over their graves, and pronounce a panegyric on the dead. The men and women mix in society, and visit together with the same freedom as in Europe. [35] They sleep on mattresses, with cotton sheets and a counterpane; the married, in separate beds in the same room. They frequently bathe the whole body, their smell would otherwise be offensive; they use towels brought from India. At dinner they spread their mats and sit as in Barbary. They smoke a great deal, but tobacco is dear; it is the best article of trade. Poisoning is common; they get the poison from the fangs of snakes, but, he says, most commonly from a part of the body near the tail, by a kind of distillation. Physic, taken immediately after the poison, may cure, but not always; if deferred two or three days, the man must die: the poison is slow, wastes the flesh, and produces a sallow, morbid appearance. It causes great pain in the stomach, destroys the appetite, produces a consumption, and kills in a longer or shorter time, according to the strength of constitution. Some who have taken remedies, soon after the poison, live 8 or 10 years; otherwise the poison kills in 4 or 5 days. Physicians prescribe an emetic, the composition of which he does not know.

Footnote 70: (return) A decoction of the herb henna produces a deep orange die. It is used generally by the females on their hands and feet: it allays the violence of perspiration in the part to which it is applied, and imparts a coolness.

NEIGHBOURING NATIONS.

There are no Arabs between Timbuctoo and the Nile; they live on the other side [71], and would not with impunity invade the lands of [36] these people, who are very populous, and could easily destroy any army that should attempt to molest them. The lands are chiefly private property. The Foulans are very beautiful. The Bambarrahs have thick lips and wide nostrils. The king of Foulan is much respected at Timbuctoo; his subjects are Muhamedans, but not circumcised. [72] They cannot be made slaves at Timbuctoo; but the Arabs steal their girls and sell them; not for slavery, but for marriage.

Girls are marriageable very young; sometimes they have children at ten years old.

Footnote 71: (return) North of the town.

Footnote 72: (return) All true Muhamedans are circumcised, so that they must partake of Paganism if uncircumcised.

[37]

JOURNEY

From

TIMBUCTOO TO HOUSA.

Shabeeny, after staying three years at Timbuctoo, departed for Housa: and crossing the small river close to the walls, reached the Nile in three days, travelling through a fine, populous, cultivated country, abounding in trees, some of which are a kind of oak, bearing a large acorn [73], much finer than those of Barbary, which are sent as presents to Spain. Travelling is perfectly safe. They embarked on the Nile in a large boat with one mast, a sail, and oars; the current was not rapid: having a favourable wind, on his return, he came back in as short a time as he went. The water was very red and sweet. [74] The place where they embarked is [38] called Mushgreelia; here is a ferry, and opposite is a village. As the current is slow, and they moored every night, they were eight or ten days sailing down the stream to Housa. They had ten or twelve men on board, and when it was calm, or the wind contrary, they rowed; they steered with an oar, the boat having no rudder. He saw a great many boats passing up and down the river; *there are more boats* [75] *on this river between Mushgreelia and Housa than between Rosetta and Cairo on the Nile of Egypt.* A great many villages are on the banks. There are boats of the same form as those of Tetuan and Tangiers, but much larger, built of planks, and have ribs like those of Barbary; instead of pitch or tar, they are caulked with a sort of red clay, or bole. The sail is of canvas of flax (not cotton) brought from Barbary, originally from Holland; it is square. They row like the Moors, going down the stream.

Footnote 73: (return) Called El Belûte. These acorns are much prized by the Muhamedans, and are considered a very wholesome fruit.

Footnote 74: (return) The word hellue, in Arabic, which signifies literally, sweet, here implies that the water was pure and good.

Footnote 75: (return) See Jackson's Marocco, page 314, 2d or 3d edition.

There is a road by land from Timbuctoo to Housa, but on account of the expense it is not used by merchants: Shabeeny believes it is about 5 days' journey. If you go this way, you must cross the river before you reach Housa. They landed at the port of Housa, distant a day and a half from the town; their merchandise was carried from this port on horses, asses, and horned cattle; the blacks dislike camels; they say, "*These are the beasts that carry us into slavery.*"

[39]

The country was rich and well cultivated; they have a plant bearing a pod called mellochia, from which they make a thick vegetable jelly. [76] There is no artificial road from Timbuctoo to the Nile; near the river the soil is miry. Shabeeny travelled from Timbuctoo to Housa in the hot weather when the Nile was nearly full; it seldom falls much below the level of its banks; he travelled on horseback from Timbuctoo to the river, and slept two nights upon the road in the huts of the natives. One of the principal men in the village leaves his hut to the travellers and gives them a supper; in the mean time he goes to the hut of some friend, and in the morning receives a small present for his hospitality. [77]

Footnote 76: (return) The pod of the mellochia, which grows near Sallee and Rabat, is of an elongated conical form, about two inches long.

Footnote 77: (return) This is a common custom in West and South Barbary; they always clear a tent for the travellers.

THE RIVER NEEL OR NILE.

The Neel El Kebeer [78], (that is, the Great Nile,) like the Neel Masser or Nile of Egypt, is fullest [40] in the month of August, when it overflows in some places where the banks are low; the water which overflows is seldom above midleg; the banks are covered with reeds, with which they make mats. Camels, sheep, goats, and horses, feed upon the banks, but during the inundation are removed to the uplands. The walls of the huts both within and without are cased with wood to the height of about three feet, to preserve them from the water; the wells have the best water after the swelling of the river. The flood continues about ten days; the abundance of rice depends on the quantity of land flooded. He always understood that the Nile empties itself in the sea, the salt sea or the great ocean. There is a village at the port of Housa where he landed, the river here is much wider than where he embarked, and still wider at Jinnie. He saw no river enter the Nile in the course of his voyage. It much resembles the Nile of Egypt, gardens and lands are irrigated from it. Its breadth is various; in some places he thinks it narrower than the Thames at London, in others much wider; at the landing place they slept in the hut of a native, and next morning at sunrise set off for Housa, where they arrived in twelve hours through a fine plain without hills; the country is much more populous than between Timbuctoo and the Nile. Ferry boats are to be had at several villages.

Footnote 78: (return) Properly Enneel. El is the article; but when it precedes a word beginning with a letter called a labial, it takes the sound of that letter. This error is committed throughout a book, lately published, entitled Specimens of Arabic Poetry, by J.D. Carlyle, Professor of Arabic in the University of Cambridge, 2d edition p. 53, Abdalsalam, instead of Abdassalum; p. 59, Ebn Alrumi, instead of Ebn Arrumi; and p. 65, Alnarhurwany, for Annarhurwany, &c. &c.

[41]

HOUSA.

They did not see the town till they came within an hour from it, or an hour and a half; it stands in a plain. Housa is south-east [79] of Timbuctoo, a much larger city and nearly as large as London. He lived there two years, but never saw the whole of it. It has no walls; the houses are like those of Timbuctoo, and form irregular lanes or streets like those of Fas or Marocco, wide enough for camels to pass with their loads. The palace is much larger than that of Timbuctoo; it is seven or eight miles in circumference and surrounded by a wall; he remembers but four gates, but there may be more; he thinks the number of guards at each gate is about 50; it is in that part of the town most distant from the Nile. The houses are dark coloured and flat roofed. He thinks Cairo is about one-third larger than Housa; the streets are much wider than those of Timbuctoo; the houses are covered with a kind of clay of different colours but never white. They have no chalk or lime in the country.

Footnote 79: (return) Rather south-east by east.

GOVERNMENT.

If the king has children, the eldest, if a man of sense and good character, succeeds; otherwise, one of the others is elected. The grandees of the court are the electors. If the eldest son [42] be not approved, they are not bound to elect him; he has, however, the preference, and after him the other sons; but the choice of the council must be unanimous, and if no person of the royal line be the object of their choice, they may elect one of their own body. The members of the council are appointed by the king; he chooses them for their wisdom and integrity, without being limited to rank: the person appointed cannot refuse obedience to the royal mandate. The council consists of many hundreds. The governor who controls the police lives in the centre of the town.

THE ADMINISTRATION OF JUSTICE

Is very similar to that of Timbuctoo, except that the king is perfectly despotic; and though he consults his council, he decides as he thinks proper. The governor administers justice in small affairs; but, in important cases, he refers the parties to the king and council, of which he is himself a member. No torture, is ever inflicted. The governor employs a great number of officers of police at a distance from the town. If robberies are committed, the person robbed must apply to the chief of the district, who must find or take into custody the offender, or becomes himself liable to make compensation for the injury sustained. [80]

Footnote 80: (return) This is also the law in West Barbary. When a robbery is committed, the district where it has been committed is made liable for double the amount; the half goes to the person robbed, and the other half to the treasury. The good effects of this law is admirable, insomuch that it has almost annihilated robbery: but when one has actually been committed, the energy and exertion of every individual is directed to discover the depredator, and they seldom fail to discover him. The fear of the penalty also makes them very cautious who they admit among them; and very inquisitive respecting the character and vocation of all, strangers in particular, who sojourn in their country!!

[43]

LANDED PROPERTY.

They have a class of men whose peculiar business it is to adjust all disputes concerning land; the office is hereditary; *the offender* pays the compensation, and also the fees of these officers; *the innocent* pays nothing. When lands are bought, these officers measure them. There is a plant resembling a large onion, which serves as a land-mark; if these are removed, (which cannot be easily done without discovery) reference is had to the records of the sale, of which every owner is in possession; they express the sum received; the quantity, situation, and limits of the land. These are given by the seller, and are written in the language and character of the country, very different from the Arabic. The same letters are used at Timbuctoo. They write from right to left. The character [81] was perfectly unintelligible to Shabeeny. Children, whose father is dead, succeed to the same portion of their [44] grandfather's property as their father would, had *he* out outlived *his* father, though there are other issue of the grandfather. The rules of succession are the same as at Timbuctoo.

Footnote 81: (return) Possibly the ancient Carthaginian character.

Persons of great landed property, of which there are many, employ agents or stewards; they let the lands, and the rents are paid sometimes in kind, and sometimes in gold-dust and cowries. Houses are let by the month. He paid four Mexico dollars per month; but a native would not have paid above two for the same house. A man who has five Mexico dollars [82] a month, is esteemed in easy circumstances; those, however, who have 30 or 40 per month, are common.

Footnote 82: (return) Ten dollars worth of rice is sufficient for the daily food of a man a twelve-month.

REVENUES.

The king has 2 per cent. on the produce of the land. The revenues arise from the same sources as at Timbuctoo, but are much larger. Foreign merchants pay nothing, as the Housaeens think they ought to be encouraged. The revenue is supposed to be immense.

ARMY.

He cannot precisely tell the number of troops, but believes the king can raise 70,000 to 80,000 horse, and 100,000 foot. The horses are poor and small, except a few kept for the king's own [45] use. He has no well-bred mares. Their arms are the same as at Timbuctoo; the muskets, which are matchlocks, are made in the country. They are very dexterous in throwing the lance. Gunpowder is also manufactured there; the brimstone is brought from Fas; the charcoal they make; and he believes they prepare the nitre. [83] Their arrows are feathered and barbed; the bows are all cross-bows, with triggers; the arrows, 20 to 40 in a quiver, are made of hides, and hang on the left side. The king never goes to war in person. The soldiers have a peculiar dress; their heads are bare; but the officers have a kind of turban; the soldiers have a shirt of coarse white cotton, and yellow slippers; those of the officers are red. Some have turbans adorned with gold. They carry their powder in a leather purse; the match, made of cotton, is wound round the gun; they have flint and steel in a pouch, and also spare matches.

Footnote 83: (return) The saltpetre and brimstone are probably derived from Terodant in Suse, where both abound.

THE TRADE

Is similar to that of Timbuctoo; in both places foreign merchants always employ agents, or brokers, to trade to advantage; a man should reside sometime before he begins. Ivory is sold by the tooth; he bought one, weighing 200 lb. for five ducats (1£. 5s.); he sold it in Marocco for 25 ducats, per 100 lb.; it is now [84] worth 60.

Footnote 84: (return) A.D. 1795.

[46]

The king cannot make any of his subjects slaves. They get their cotton from Bengala. [85] They have no salt, it comes from a great distance, and is very dear. Goods find a much better market at Housa than at Timbuctoo. There are merchants at Housa from Timboo, Bornoo, Moshu, and India; the travelling merchants do not regard distance. From Timboo and other great towns he has heard, and from his own knowledge can venture to assert, that they bring East India goods. Gold-dust, ivory, and slaves are the principal returns from Housa. The people of Housa have slaves from Bornoo, Bambarra, Jinnie, Beni Killeb [86] (sons of dogs), and Beni Aree (sons of the naked); they are, generally, prisoners of war, though many are stolen when young, by people who make a trade of this practice. The laws are very severe against this crime; it requires, therefore, great cunning and duplicity; no men of any property are ever guilty of it. The slave stealers take the children by night out of the town, and sell them to some peasant, who sells them to a third, and so from hand to hand, till they are carried out of the country; if this practice did not exist, there would be few slaves for the Barbary market. Beyond the age of fourteen or fifteen, a slave is hardly saleable in Barbary. Few merchants [47] bring to Housa above two or three slaves at a time; but there are great numbers of merchants continually bringing them. His own slave was a native of Bambarra, and was brought very young to Timbuctoo. Slaves are generally stupid; but his, on the contrary, was very sensible; he understood several languages, particularly Arabic; he bought him as an interpreter; he would not have sold publicly for above twenty ducats; but he gave 50 for him; his master parting with him very reluctantly. He bought two female slaves at Housa, at 15 ducats each. [87] The value of slaves has since then doubled in Barbary; he does not know the present [88] price at Timbuctoo. At Timbuctoo not ten slaves in the hundred bought there, are females; when bought, the merchant shuts them up in a private room, but not in chains, and places a centinel at the door: when the confidence of any of them is supposed to be gained, they are employed as centinels. Housa having a great trade, is much frequented by people from Bambarra, Foulan, Jinnie, and the interior countries.

Manufactures and husbandry are similar to those at Timbuctoo.

Footnote 85: (return) Bengal, or the East Indies.

Footnote 86: (return) Properly Ben Ekkilleb, or Hel Ekkileb, i.e. the canine-race. These are described to be swift of foot and low of stature, having a language peculiar to themselves.

Footnote 87: (return) About the 1790th year of the Christian era.

Footnote 88: (return) In the year 1795.

CLIMATE.

The hot winds blow from the east; the summer is hotter than in Marocco, and hotter at [48] Timbuctoo than at Housa. The cold winds are from the west: the morning fog is great. He never saw it rain at Housa, in the course of two years; he says it never rains there. Scarcity is never known. A considerable part of their provisions is brought from the banks of the Nile; the river, when overflowing, never reaches above half way from its common channel towards Housa. They have excellent wells in their houses, but no river near the town.

ZOOLOGY.

He saw no camels at Housa, but heard, they use them to fetch gold, and cover their legs with leather, to guard them from snakes. They have dogs and cats, but no scorpions or snakes in their houses. Lice, bugs, and fleas abound. He saw no wild animals or fowl in the neighbourhood of Housa.

DISEASES.

Physicians agree with the patient for his cure. No cure no pay. The prevailing diseases are colds and coughs.

RELIGION.

The same as at Timbuctoo; the poorer classes, as in most countries, have many superstitious notions of spirits, good and bad, and are alarmed by dreams, particularly, the slaves, some of whom cannot retain their urine in the night, as he thinks, from fear of spirits, they take them [49] often upon trial when they buy them, and if they have this defect, a considerable deduction is made in the price. A man possessed by a good spirit is supposed to be safe amidst 10,000 shot. A man guilty of a crime, who in the opinion of the judge is possessed by an evil spirit, is not punished! He never heard of a rich man being possessed.

PERSONS.

They are of various sizes, but the tallest man he ever saw was at Housa. The city being very large, he seldom had an opportunity of seeing the king, as at Timbuctoo. He saw him but twice in two years, and only in the courts of justice; he was remarkable for the width of his nostrils, the redness of his eyes, the smoothness of his skin, and the fine tint of his perfectly black complexion.

DRESS.

Like that of Timbuctoo, their turbans are of the finest muslin. The sleeves of the soldiers are small, those of the merchants wide. The former have short breeches, the latter long. The officers dress like the merchants, each according to his circumstances. The caftan is of silk, in summer, brought from India; instead of the silk cords worn by the king of Timbuctoo, the king of Housa wears two silk sashes, three fingers broad, one on each shoulder; they are richly adorned with gold; in one hangs his [50] dagger, and when he rides out, his sword in the other; he wears not the silk pear in his turban, as does the king of Timbuctoo. The front of his turban is embroidered with gold.

BUILDINGS.

The houses are like those at Timbuctoo, but many much larger. They have no wind or water-mills, but they have stone mills, turned by horses.

MANNERS.

They never bow. An inferior kisses the hand of a superior; to an equal he nods the head, gives him his hand and asks him how he does. The women do the same.

The general body are honest and benevolent, the lower class is addicted to thieving. They are very careful of children, to prevent their being stolen. Snakes do not frequent cultivated lands, so that animals are not there in danger from them. The people of Timbuctoo and Housa resemble each other in their persons and in their manners. They castrate bulls, sheep, and goats, but never horses. Supper is the principal meal. They do not use vessels of brass or copper in cookery; they are all of earthenware. At sunset the watchmen are stationed in all parts of the town, and take into custody all suspected or unknown persons. They have lamps made of wood and paper; the latter comes from Fas. Women of respectability are attended by a slave [51] when they walk out or visit, which they do with the same freedom as in Europe. The women ride either horses or asses, they have no mules; the men commonly prefer walking, they are strong and seldom sensible of fatigue, which he attributes to their having a rib more than white men. Some bake their own bread, others buy it, as in England. They make leavened bread of allila [89] and bishna; the cattle-market is within the city, in a square, appropriated to this purpose. There are a great many rich men, some by inheritance, others by trade. Every morning the doors of the rich are crowded with poor, the master sends them food, rice, milk, &c. They have names for every day. They make their own pipes for smoking, the tubes are of wood. They have songs, some with chorus, and some sung by two persons in alternate stanzas. They have the same feasts once a quarter as at Timbuctoo. The king has but one wife, but many concubines. The favourite slaves of the queen of Housa are considered as superior to the queen of Timbuctoo.

Footnote 89: (return) Millet and Indian corn.

GOLD.

The ground where it is found is about sixteen miles from Housa. They go in the night with camels whose legs and feet are covered to protect them against snakes, they take a bag of sand, and mark with it the places that glitter with gold; [52] in the morning they collect where marked, and carry it to refiners, who, for a small sum, separate the gold. There are no mountains or rivers near the spot, it is a plain without sand, of a dark brown earth. Any person may go to seek gold; they sell it to the merchants, who pay a small duty to the king. The produce is uncertain; he has heard that a bushel of earth has produced the value of twelve ducats, three pounds sterling, of pure gold. They set out from Housa about two o'clock in the afternoon, arrive about sun-set, and return the next day seeking for gold during the whole night.

LIMITS OF THE EMPIRE

Beyond Timboo, on the north side of the Nile, are very extensive. Afnoo is subject to the king of Housa, no slaves can be made from thence. Darfneel is near Afnoo; the latter is on the north side of the river, nearer to its source, and a great way from Timbuctoo. No Arabs are found on the banks of the Nile. He supposes the circumference of the empire to be about twenty-five days' journey; has heard that many other large towns are dependent upon it, but does not remember their names.

The neighbouring countries are Bambarra, Timboo, Mooshee, and Jinnie; all negroes. He has heard of Bernoo [90] as a great empire.

[53]

On the 31st of March, 1790, Shabeenee gave further information, in the presence of Lord Rawdon [91], Mr. Stuart, and Mr. Wedgewood. Mr. Wedgewood proposed the questions, and Mr. Dodsworth interpreted. The following is some of the information, omitting what has been noticed already.

Between Timbuctoo and Housa, there is a very good trade. Timbuctoo is tributary to the king of Housa. The imports into Timbuctoo [92] are spices, corn, and woollens from Barbary, and linens from the sea-coast.

Footnote 90: (return) Ber Noh, or Bernoh, *i.e.* the country of Noah, is said by the Africans, to be the birth-place of the patriarch Noah.

Footnote 91: (return) Now the Marquis of Hastings.

Footnote 92: (return) For a more detailed account of the imports to Timbuctoo, see Jackson's Account of Marocco, &c.

The written character is very large, perhaps half an inch long. The empire is divided into provinces; the provinces into districts. The king appoints the governors of both; but the son of the deceased governor is understood to have the preference.

They make their pottery by a wheel, but do not glaze it. The wheel turns upon a pivot placed in a hole in the ground: at top and bottom are two pieces of wood like a tea-table; the lower, which is largest, is turned by the foot, and the upper forms the vessel. When they make a large pot, they put on the top a larger piece: the pots are dried in the sun or burnt in the fire. The iron mines are in the desert; the iron is brought in small pieces by the Arabs, who melt and purify it. They cannot cast iron. [54] They use charcoal fire, and form guns and swords with the hammer and anvil. The points of their arrows are barbed with iron; the crossbows have a groove for the arrow. No man can draw the bow by his arm alone, they have a kind of lever; the bow part is of steel brought from Barbary, and is manufactured at Timbuctoo. They do not make steel themselves.

They inoculate for the small-pox; the pus is put into a dried raisin and eaten. "*Rooka Dindooka*" is a kind of oath, and means, by God. They believe only one God. After dinner they use the Arabic expression, El Hamd Ulillah; praise to be to God. [93]

They believe the immortality of the soul, and that both men and women go to paradise; that there is no future punishment; the wicked are punished in this world. Happiness, after death, consists in being in the presence of God. They are not circumcised. A divorce may take place while a woman is pregnant, but she cannot marry again till delivered. As soon as a woman is divorced, midwives, women brought up to that profession, examine her to see whether she is pregnant.

Footnote 93: (return) This is the Arabic, or Muhamedan grace after meat; the grace before meat is equally sententious, viz. Bismillah, i.e. in the name of God.

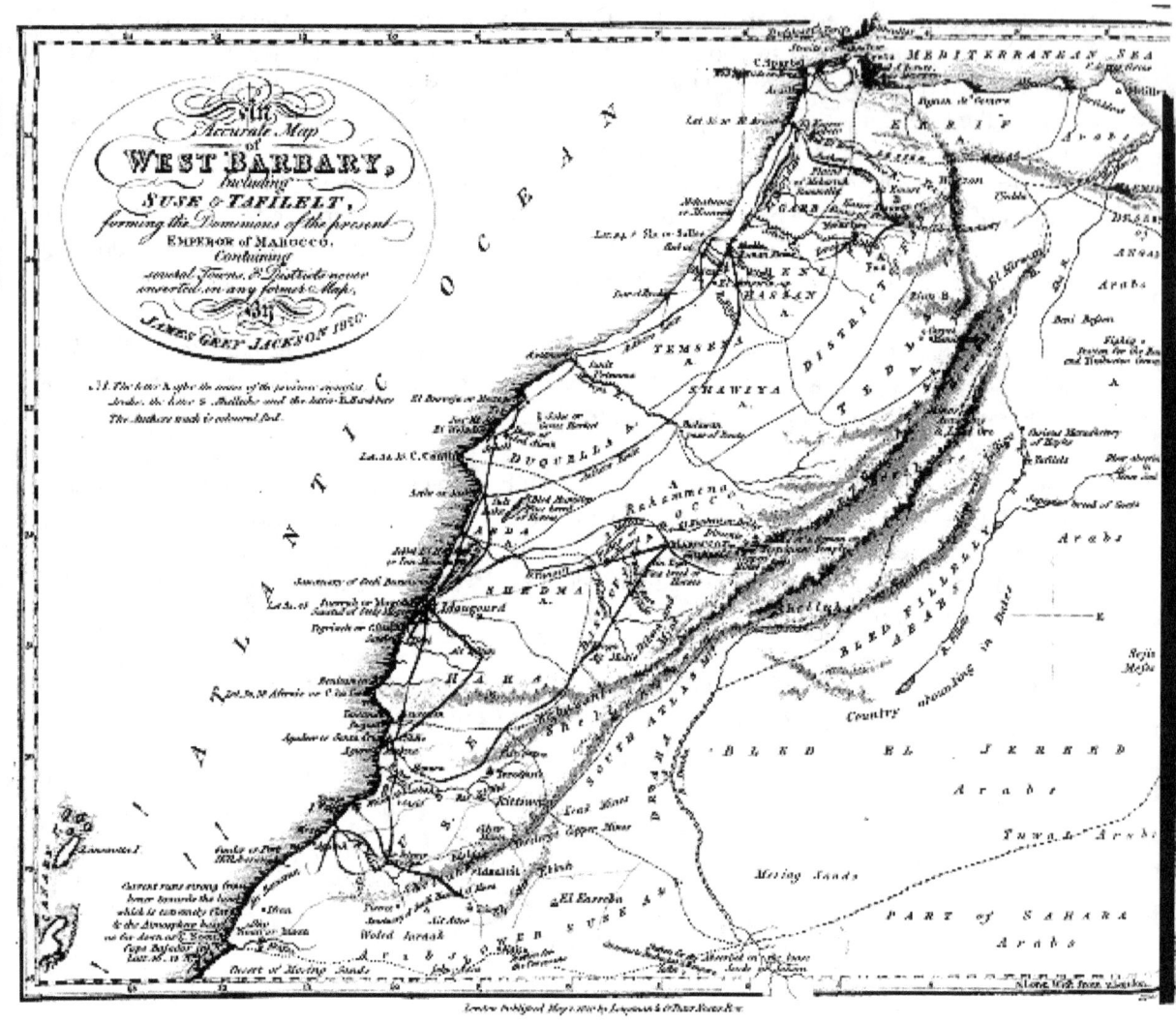

Larger format

[55]

LETTERS

CONTAINING

AN ACCOUNT OF JOURNIES

THROUGH VARIOUS PARTS OF

WEST AND SOUTH BARBARY,

AT DIFFERENT PERIODS,

PERFORMED PERSONALLY BY J.G.J.

LETTER I.

On the opening of the Port of Agadeer, or Santa Cruz in Suse, and of its Cession by the Emperor Muley Yezzid, to the Dutch.

TO JAMES WILLIS, ESQ.

(Late British Consul for Senegambia) Eversholt, near Woburn, Bedfordshire.

Mogodor, 28th February, 1792.

The emperor has consented to the proposition of the Dutch government, to open the port of Agadeer, or Santa Cruz, in the province of Suse, to the commerce of that nation; and I have finally resolved to establish a house there, so soon as the sultan Yezzid's order respecting that port shall reach the hands of Alkaid Aumer ben Daudy, the governor of this port. There are various political intrigues in agitation, to deter me from going personally to establish the commerce of this most desirable and long-neglected [56] port of Santa Cruz. The governor anticipates a considerable diminution in the treasury of Mogodor; and the merchants of this place anticipate a great diminution of the various articles of produce of this fine country, seeing that the principal articles of exportation from the empire of Marocco are produced in the province of Suse, and in the neighbourhood of Santa Cruz.

The stream of commerce will, therefore, necessarily be converted from Mogodor to Santa Cruz. The merchants of Fas also, who have their establishments and connections at Timbuctoo, and in other parts of Sudan, will resort to Santa Cruz in preference to Mogodor, for all European articles calculated for the markets of Sudan, the former port being in the neighbourhood of the desert, or Sahara, and at a convenient distance from Akka in Lower Suse, the general rendezvous of the akkaba, (or accumulated caravans,) destined for the interior regions of Africa or Sudan. This akkaba starts annually for Timbuctoo, consisting of 2000 or 3000 camels, loaded with merchandise from Fas, Tetuan, Sallee, Mogodor, Marocco, Tafilelt, Draha, and Terodant. The port of Santa Cruz is hence aptly denominated *Beb Sudan*, i.e. the gate or entrance of Sudan. [57] The port of Santa Cruz was formerly farmed by the emperor [94] Muley Ishmael, to some European power, for 50,000 dollars a-year, as I have been informed; others say it was purchased of him by his own Jewish subjects, for the purposes of trade. However this may have been, no advantage was ever taken of the favourable opportunity then offered, of opening and securing to Europe an extensive and lucrative trade with the various countries of Sudan or Nigritia.

I can account for this omission only by supposing that the interior of Africa was then less known than even it now is; and that the merchants then established at Santa Cruz, had there sufficient advantages in commerce to engage their attention, without examining into this immense undiscovered mine of wealth!

Footnote 94: (return) Great-grandfather of Muley Soliman, the present emperor, who is denominated Soliman ben Muhamed ben Abdallah ben Ismael.

[58]

LETTER II.

The Author's arrival at Agadeer or Santa Cruz.--He opens the Port to European Commerce.--His favourable Reception on landing there.--Is saluted by the Battery.--Abolishes the degrading Custom that had been exacted of the Christians, of descending from on Horseback, and entering the Town on Foot, like the Jews.--Of a Sanctuary at the Entrance of the Town, which had ever been considered Holy Ground, and none but Muhamedans had ever before been permitted to enter the Gates on Horseback.

TO THE SAME.

Santa Cruz, 7th March, 1792.

The emperor's [95] letter ordering the port of Santa Cruz to be opened to the Dutch, having reached Mogodor, and having received my instructions from Webster Blount, Esq. Dutch consul-general to this empire, to act as agent for him at that port, until my appointment be ratified and confirmed by the States General, of which he informs me there is no doubt, I proceeded hither in the Snell Zee Post, Dirk Morris, master; and after being becalmed off (Affernie) Cape de Geer, I arrived here the third morning after my departure from Mogodor. I sent my horses by land; and on our approach to the [59] shore, I discovered them approaching the mountain on which Santa Cruz stands. Soon after we came to anchor in the road, the boats came off, and the battery, which is situated about half-way up the mountain on the western declivity, saluted me with 8 guns, (the Muhamedans always saluting with an even number.) This compliment being unexpected, we were about half an hour preparing to return it, when we saluted the battery with 9 guns. The captain of the port received me with great courtesy, and was ordered by the bashaw El Hayanie, governor of

Santa Cruz, to pay the most unqualified attention to my wishes. I landed amidst an immense concourse of people, assembled on the beach to witness the re-establishment of their port, most of whom were without shoes, and very ill clad.

Footnote 95: (return) See specimens of Arabic epistolary correspondence, Appendix, Letter 9th.

The most hearty exclamations of joy and approbation were manifested by the people when I landed; a merchant was come to establish, once more, that commerce by which the fathers of the present generation had prospered; and their sons appeared to know full well the advantages that again awaited their industry, which for 30 years had not been exercised. I mounted my horse on the beach, amidst the general acclamations of the people, and ascended the mountain, on the summit of which is the town. On my arrival at the gate, I was courteously received by the bashaw's sons; who, however, informed me that the entrance of Santa Cruz was [60] ever considered holy ground, and that Christians, during its former establishment, always descended and entered the town on foot, intimating at the same time that it was expected I should do the same. I had been before cautioned by Mr. Gwyn, the British consul at Mogodor, not to expostulate at this request, as it would certainly be required of me to conform to ancient usages. But I knew too well the disposition of the people, and the great desire that pervaded all ranks to have the port established; I therefore turned my horse, and told the bashaw's sons, that I was come, with the blessing of God, to bring prosperity to the land, to make the poor rich, and to improve the condition and multiply the conveniences of the opulent; that I came to establish commerce for *their* advantage, not for mine; that it was indifferent to me whether I returned to Mogodor or remained with them. The sons of the bashaw became alarmed, and entreated me, with clasped hands, to wait till they should report to the bashaw my words and observations. I consented, and soon after they returned with their father's earnest request that I should enter a-horseback: old customs, said the venerable old bashaw when, immediately afterwards, I met him in the street; old customs are abolished, enter and go out of this town a-horseback or a-foot, we desire the prosperity of this port, and that its commerce may flourish; *All the people of Suse hail you as their deliverer, God has sent you to us to turn the desert into* [61] (jinen afia) *a fruitful garden; come, and be welcome, and God be with you.*

I was conducted to the best house in the town, a house which belonged to our predecessor, Mr. Grover; and I was informed, that if any demur had been made by the bashaw respecting my entrance through the sanctuary or holy ground, it might have caused an immediate insurrection; so anxious and impatient were all ranks of people for the new establishment of this eligible port of Suse.

The privilege thus established, of riding in and out of the town, I continued; and I procured it immediately afterwards for all Christians! even masters of ships and common sailors.

[62]

LETTER III.

The Author makes a Commercial Road down the Mountain, to facilitate the Shipment of Goods.-- The Energy and Liberality of the Natives, in working gratuitously at it.--Description of the Portuguese Tower at Tildie. --Arab Repast there.--Natural Strength of Santa Cruz, of the Town of Aguzem, and the Portuguese Spring and Tank there.--Attempt of the Danes to land and build a Fort.--Eligibility of the Situation of Santa Cruz, for a Commercial Depot to Supply the whole of the Interior of North Africa with East India and European Manufactures.--Propensity of the Natives to Commerce and Industry, if Opportunity offered.

TO THE SAME.

Santa Cruz, 20th March, 1792.

The road up the mountain of Santa Cruz was so dangerous and impassable, that I undertook to repair it; accordingly, I agreed with a Shilluh to make it safe and convenient for transporting goods for shipment; and such was the eager desire of the people for the establishment of the port, that hundreds brought stones and assisted gratuitously in the construction of this road; so that what would have cost in England thousands of pounds, was here completed for a few hundred dollars.

The natives of this long-neglected territory were too acute not to perceive the field of wealth that was thus opened to their industry; they were convinced, from the traditions of their [63] fathers, of the incalculable benefits that would arise from a commercial reciprocity; and they were determined to cultivate the opportunity that was now offered to put them in possession of those commercial advantages which their fathers had enjoyed before: the benefits of which they had often related to their children, when they talked of the prosperity and riches of the country during the reign of Muley Ismael, when this port was before open to foreign commerce. Agreeably to these well-founded anticipations, the genial influence of commerce began, soon after my arrival, to manifest itself throughout all ranks and denominations of men; *the whole population visibly improved in their apparel and appearance; new garments were now becoming common, and were every where substituted for the rags and wretchedness before witnessed on landing here.*

About four miles east of Santa Cruz, in a very romantic valley surrounded by mountains, are found the ruins of a Portuguese tower. *Tildie,* which is the name of this place, abounds in plantations of the most delicious figs, grapes of an enormous size and exquisite flavour, citrons, oranges, water-melons, walnuts, apricots in great abundance, and peaches, &c. &c.

I invited a party of Arabs to accompany me to this delightful retreat, where we dined: the Arabs killed two sheep; one they roasted whole on a wooden spit, made on the spot; the other they baked whole in an oven made for the purpose, [64] in the following manner: A large hole was dug in the ground; the inside was plaistered with clay; after which they put fire in the hole till the sides were dry; they then put the sheep in, and the top was covered by clay in the form of an arch, fashioned and constructed by the hand only; they afterwards made a large trough round this temporary oven, and filled it with wood, to which they set fire. The sheep was about three hours preparing in this manner, and it was of exquisite flavour; the roasted mutton also was equally well flavoured. No vegetables were served with this repast; for I had desired that the fare should be precisely according to their own custom; I therefore declined interfering with the arrangement of the food. This mode of cooking is in high estimation with travellers. These people never eat vegetables with their meat. When they see Europeans eat a mouthful of meat, and then another of vegetables, they express their surprise, observing that the taste of the vegetables destroys the taste of the meat; and *vice versa*, that the taste of the meat destroys the flavour of the vegetables!

The town of Santa Cruz, built on the summit of a branch of the Atlas, by the Portuguese, is enclosed by a strong wall, fortified with bastions mounting cannon; it is about a mile in circumference. Half way down the mountain, on the western declivity, opposite the sea, stands a battery, which defends the town, towards the north, south, and west, at the foot of the mountain. [65] Westward, on the shore of the sea, stands a town, called by the Shelluhs, (the natives of this country,) Agurem. There is a copious spring of excellent water at Agurem, built and ornamented by the Portuguese, when they had possession of this country, and called by them *Fonté*, which name the town still retains, and is so called by Europeans. The royal arms of Portugal are seen, carved in stone, over the tank. Santa Cruz is supplied with spring-water from here, having none but rain-water in the town, which is collected in the rainy season, and preserved in subterraneous apartments, called mitferes [96], one of which is attached to every respectable house, and contains sufficient for the consumption of the family during the year. The natural position of Santa Cruz is extremely strong, perhaps not less so than Gibraltar, though not on a peninsula; and it might, in the hands of an European power, be made impregnable with very little expense; it might also be made a very convenient and most advantageous depot for the establishment of an extensive commerce with [66] the whole of the interior of North Africa. An attempt of this kind was made about forty or fifty years since, by the Danes, who anchored with several ships, and landed a mile south of Agurem; and with stones, all ready cut, and numbered, erected on an eminence [97], by the dawn of the following day, a battery of twelve guns. But by a stratagem of the bashaw El Hayanie, who at that time was bashaw of Suse, they were rendered unable to retain possession of their fort; their plans were accordingly disconcerted, and the adventurers retreated, and returned to their ships.

Footnote 96: (return) The mitfere under my house at Santa Cruz, contained, when full, four hundred pipes of water. At the termination of the rainy season in March, it was generally about two-thirds full, supplied from the flat roof or terras during the rainy season. There was always much more than we could consume, accordingly great quantities were distributed among the poor, about the close of the season, or the autumn previous to the next rainy season.

Footnote 97: (return) Called Agadeer Arba.

At the south-east extremity of the wall of Santa Cruz there is a round battery, which protects the town from west to east; and might be made to protect the valley to the east of the mountain. This battery, with a little military skill, might be made to protect every access to the town, not protected by the battery before mentioned, which is situated about half way up the western declivity of the mountain, and which commands or secures the fonte, or spring, against an attack from any hostile force.

[67]

LETTER IV.

Command of the Commerce of Sudan.

TO THE SAME.

Santa Cruz, May 5, 1792.

If Great Britain were to purchase the port of Santa Cruz of the emperor, for a certain annual stipend, we should be enabled to command the whole commerce of Sudan, at the expense of Tunis, Tripoli, Algiers, and Egypt; not at the expense of Marocco, because an equivalent, or what the emperor would consider as such, would be given in exchange for it; and we should then supply all those regions with merchandise, at the first and second hand, which they now receive through four, five, and six. We should thus be enabled to undersell our Moorish competitors, and thus draw to our commercial depot, all the gold-dust, gold-bars, and wrought-gold, gum-sudan, (commonly called in England, Turkey gum-arabic), ostrich feathers, and other articles the produce of Sudan; besides the produce of Suse, viz. gum-barbary, sandrac, euphorbium, and ammoniac, almonds, olive oil, wine, &c., together with the richest fruits of every kind. These we should take in barter for our manufactures.

[68]

The road of Santa Cruz is very safe, and the best in the empire of Marocco; it is defended from the fury of the tremendous gales that visit this coast in December and January, and which invariably blow from the south, by a projection of land that extends gradually from the river Suse to cape Noon, very far westward into the ocean. During my residence of several years at this summit of Atlas, not one ship was wrecked or lost; there is plenty of water, and good anchorage for ships of the line.

A thousand European troops, directed by a vigilant and experienced captain, might take the place by a *coup de main*; and the natives, (after a proper explanation and assurance that trade was the object of the capture,) would probably become allies of the captors, and would supply in abundance all kind of provisions. They esteem the English, and denominate them their brothers. [98] They sorely regret the loss of trade occasioned by the emperor's restrictions, and would gladly promote the cultivation of commerce if they had an opportunity. They have been from time immemorial a trading generation.

Footnote 98: (return) *N'henna û l'Ingleez Khowan*, they say, "we and the English are brothers."

[69]

LETTER V.

FROM MR. WILLIS TO MR. JACKSON.

My dear sir,

I have this moment received your favour, dated yesterday, and am extremely sorry I had not the pleasure of seeing you before your departure. We might have taken a farewell dinner together. You will most highly oblige me by communicating to me all the intelligence you can collect concerning the interior of Africa, more especially of Timbuctoo; its trade, government, geographical situation, and the manners and customs of its inhabitants. If you could send me too, any of its products or manufactures, which may appear to you curious or interesting, or may serve to shew the state of knowledge and civilisation in the country, and the progress they may have made in the arts, in manufactures or commerce, you will confer upon me a singular favour; the expense of which I will readily repay, and which I shall be happy to return whenever I can be of use to you. If ever this region of Africa, which excites so strongly our curiosity, should be laid open to us, you are, of all the men with whom I am acquainted, the best qualified, and the most likely to lead the way to this important discovery. I request you to favour me with your correspondence; let me hear from you as frequently [70] as possible, without ceremony, and as one who wishes to be considered as an old friend. When peace returns, I shall certainly take my station in Senegambia [99], where we may then be fellow-labourers in the same vineyard. There is no news yet of Park; perhaps you would like to know how he proceeds; and as I expect to hear of him by the return of my ship, I will inform you, if you wish it; and, in short, will keep up a regular correspondence on my part, if you will do the same on your's. Pray, in what ship do you go? Perhaps, if you would give me encouragement, I might venture into a little commercial speculation to Santa Cruz. I heartily wish you a pleasant voyage, health, and success; and am, with great regard,

My dear Sir,

Very truly your's,

J. WILLIS.

August 12,1796.

Footnote 99: (return) Mr. James Willis had the appointment of consul at Senegambia, and was then waiting an opportunity of proceeding thither.

[71]

LETTER VI.

FROM THE SAME TO THE SAME.

My dear sir,

I duly received your letter from Gibraltar, and have made known to Government the expediency of sending a person to Marocco, to oppose the influence of the French and Spaniards; but I cannot yet say with certainty whether the measure will be adopted or not; if it should, you may rely upon my attention to your interest. I have given your name to the secretary of state, and have spoken of you with that distinction, which I think, without any flattery, your qualifications justly deserve.

Peace still appears to be at a great distance, since the late negociations; yet, as nothing is so uncertain as an event of this kind, it may come upon us, (as the last peace did) like a thief in the night, when we least expect it. You will have, I have no doubt, frequent opportunities of procuring information concerning Timbuctoo, and other places in the interior of Africa. Your knowledge of the language, customs, and commerce of that continent, give you advantages which few possess upon this ground; and I assure you, every kind of information will be greedily received here, concerning those regions; especially that which [72] relates to their commerce, civilisation, customs, geography, and language.

I request as a favour that you would write me as often as possible; exclusive of the interest I take in all that relates to the politics and commerce of Africa, (particularly of the interior,) to hear of your own individual welfare, will give me the sincerest pleasure.

I remain, my dear Sir,

Your's very sincerely,

J. WILLIS.

No. 67. Harley-street, London,
2d February, 1796.

We have no letters from Mr. Park, since he left the river Gambia; but we have heard from others, that he had proceeded in safety above two-thirds of the journey. We expect soon to hear of his return. If he succeeds, his fame and fortune will be worthy of envy.

[73]

LETTER VII.

Emperor's March to Marocco.--Doubles the Customs' Duties of Mogodor.--The Governor, Prince Abd El Melk, with the Garrison and Merchants of Santa Crux, ordered to go to the Court at Marocco.--They cross the Atlas Mountains.--Description of the Country and Produce.-- Dangerous Defile in the Mountains through which the Author passed.--Chasm in the Mountain.-- Security of Suse from Marocco, originating in the narrow Defile in the Mountains of Atlas.-- Extensive Plantations of Olives.--Village of Ait Musie.--Fruga Plains.--Marocco Plains.--Fine Corn.--Reception at Marocco, and Audience with the Emperor.--Imperial Gardens at Marocco.-- Prince Abd El Melk's magnificent Apparel, reprobated by the Sultan.--The Port of Santa Cruz, shut to the Commerce of Europe, and the Merchants ordered to Mogodor.--The Prince banished to the Bled Shereef *or Country of Princes, viz., Tafilelt, of the Palace at Tafilelt.--Abundance of Dates.--Face of the Country. --Magnificent Groves of Palm or Date-trees.--Faith and Integrity of the Inhabitants of Tafilelt.--Imperial Gardens at Marocco.--Mode of Irrigation.--Attar of Roses, vulgarly called Otto of Roses (Attar being the Word signifying a Distillation.)--State of Oister Shells, on the Top of the Mountains of Sheshawa, between Mogodor and Marocco, being a Branch of the Atlas.--Description of the Author's Reception on the Road from Marocco to Mogodor.--Of the Elgrored, or Sahara of Mogodor.*

TO JAMES WILLIS, ESQ.

Santa Cruz, March 15, 1797.

When the emperor Soliman proceeded from Fas with a numerous army to the south, he doubled the export and import duties at Mogodor, [74] viz., from six to twelve per cent., payable in kind. Those of Santa Cruz remained as before, but so soon as his imperial majesty reached Marocco, he sent orders for the prince Abd El Melk, who is his nephew and governor of Santa Cruz, with the garrison, together with the merchants, to proceed to Marocco; accordingly we all departed, the prince having first engaged a revered (fakeer) saint to accompany the army across the Atlas mountains, the fastnesses of which it appeared no army would be permitted to pass, without the protection of this fakeer. We departed about noon, and passed through the plains of the Arab province of Howara [100], a very fine country; we pitched our tents at sunset, near a sanctuary, where we had all kinds of provisions sent to us, in great abundance: we continued our journey the following morning through the plains, and about the middle of the day we reached the foot of Atlas.

This country abounds in extensive plantations of olives, almonds, and gum trees; some plants of the (*fashook*) gum ammoniac are here discovered. Vines producing purple grapes of an enormous size and exquisite flavour: (*dergmuse*) the Euphorbium plant is discovered in rocky parts of the mountains; and great abundance of worm-seed and stick-liquorice. [101] The indigo plant (*Enneel*) [75] is found here; as are also pomegranates, of a large size and a most exquisitely sweet flavour, and oranges. Ascending the Atlas, after five hours' ride, we reached a table-land, and pitched our tents near a sanctuary. The temperature of the air is cooler here, and the trees are of a different character; apples, pears, cherries, walnuts, apricots, peaches, plums, and rhododendrums, were the produce of this region. The next morning at five o'clock, the army struck their tents, and after ascending seven hours more, we met with another change in vegetation. Leguminous plants began to appear; pines of an immense size, ferns, *the belute*, a species of oak, the acorn of which is used as food, and is preferred to the Spanish chesnut; elms, mountain-ash, *seedra* and *snobar*, the two latter being a species of the juniper. After this we passed through a fine campaign country of four hours' ride: we were informed that this country was very populous; but our fakeer and guide avoided the habitations of men. We now began again to ascend these magnificent and truly romantic mountains, and in two hours approached partial coverings of snow. Vegetation here diminishes, and nothing is now seen but firs, whose tops appear above the snow; the cold is here intense; and it is remarkable, that, the pullets' eggs that we procured in the campaign country just described, were nearly twice the size of those of Europe. Proceeding two hours further, we came to a narrow pass, on the east side of [76] which was an inaccessible mountain, almost perpendicular, and entirely covered with snow; and on the west, a tremendous precipice, of several thousand feet in depth, as if the mountain had been split in two, or rent asunder by an earthquake: the path is not more than a foot wide, over a solid rock of granite. Here the whole army dismounted, and many prostrated in prayer, invoking the Almighty to enable them to pass in safety; but, however, notwithstanding all possible precaution, two mules missed their footing, and were precipitated with their burdens into the yawning abyss. There is no other pass but this, and that of Belawin, which is equally dangerous for an army; so that the district of Suse, which was formerly a kingdom, might be defended by a few men, against an invading army from Marocco of several thousands, by taking a judicious position at the southern extremity of this narrow path and tremendous precipice, which is but a few yards in length. Proceeding northward through, this defile, we continued our journey seven hours, (gradually descending towards the plains of Fruga, a town of considerable extent, distant about fifteen miles from the mountains.) Proceeding two hours further, making together nine hours' journey, the army pitched their tents, and we encamped on another table-land, on the northern declivity of Atlas, at the entrance of an immense plantation of olives, about a mile west of a village, called Ait Musie, [77] a most luxuriant and picturesque country. The village of Ait Musie contains many Jews, whose external is truly miserable; but this appearance of poverty is merely political, for they are a trading and rich people, for such a patriarchal country. The olive plantations at this place, and in many other parts of this country, do honour to the agricultural propensity of the emperor Muley Ismael, who planted them. They cover about six square miles of ground; the trees are planted in right lines, at a proper distance; the plantation is interspersed with openings, or squares, to let in the air. These openings are about a square acre in extent.

Footnote 100: (return) migration from this tribe attacked and took the city of Assouan, in Egypt, some years ago. Vide Burckhardt's Travels in Nubia.

Footnote 101: (return) This root abounds all over Suse, and is called by the natives *Ark Suse, i.e.* the foot of Suse: the worm-seed is called sheh.

In travelling through the various provinces of South and West Barbary, these extensive plantations of olives are frequently met with, and particularly throughout Suse. It appeared that they were all planted by the emperor Muley Ismael, whose indefatigable industry was proverbial. Wherever that warrior (who was always in the field) encamped, he never failed to employ his army in some active and useful operation, to keep them from being devoured by the worm of indolence, as he expressed it. Accordingly wherever he encamped, we meet with these extensive plantations of olive trees, planted by his troops, which are not only a great ornament to the country, but produce abundance of fine oil. The olive plantations at Ras El Wed, near Terodant in Suse, are so extensive, that one may travel from the rising to the setting sun [78] under their shade, without being exposed to the rays of the effulgent African sun.

We remained encamped at Ait Musie [102] three days, amusing ourselves by hawking with the prince's falconer, and hunting the antelope. Early in the morning of the fourth day, we descended the declivity of the Atlas, and travelling eight hours, we reached the populous town of Fruga, situated in the same extensive plain wherein the city of Marocco stands. From this village to Marocco, a day's journey, the country is one continued corn-field, producing most abundant crops of wheat and barley, the grain of which is of an extraordinary fine quality, and nearly twice the size of the wheat produced at the Cape of Good Hope.

Footnote 102: (return) Here the prince sent couriers to the emperor, to announce his approach.

On our approach to the metropolis, the emperor sent the princes that were at Marocco to welcome the prince Abd El Melk. They were accompanied by 100 cavalry, who saluted our prince with the Moorish compliment of running full gallop and firing their muskets. These princes, who were relations of Abd El Melk, son of Abd Salam, shook hands with him respectively, and then kissed their own. This is the salutation when friends of equal rank meet. We entered the city of Marocco at the *Beb El Mushoir*, which is the gate situated near the palace and place of audience, towards the Atlas mountains. The next day I had an audience of the emperor, [79] who received me in (the *Jenan En neel*) the garden of the Nile, a small garden adjoining the palace, containing all the fruits and plants from the Nile [103] of Egypt. The (*worde fillelly*) Tafilelt-rose grows in great luxuriance in this garden, resembling that of China; the odour is very grateful and strong, perfuming the air to a considerable distance. This is the rose, from the leaves of which the celebrated (*attar el worde*) *i.e.* distillation of roses is made, vulgarly called in Europe, *otto* of roses.

Footnote 103: (return): This orthography, *Nile*, has been imported from France; with the French it is pronounced as we pronounce Neel; and this is the intelligible pronunciation in Africa.

The emperor declared the port of Santa Cruz to be shut; and that no European merchant of any nation should continue there. He gave me my choice, either to quit the country, or establish a house at Mogodor. I entreated a short time to consider which I should choose, which was readily granted.

The prince Abd El Melk was magnificent in his apparel, the Emperor dressed very plain; these were two incompatible propensities, the latter had probably heard of the prince's extravagance in this respect, and chose to moralise with him by comparing his own parsimonious and plain apparel to *his* costly attire; and insinuating that the iron buckle to his belt answered every purpose of a gold one, reprimanded the prince for the extravagance and vanity of his wardrobe, and acquainted his Highness that the port of [80] Santa Cruz should no longer remain open to European commerce. The prince remained some days after this notification at Maroco; an annual stipend was allowed him and he was sent to (the *Bled Shereef, i.e.* the country of princes, viz.) Tafilelt, and had apartments allotted him in the Imperial Palace at that place, which is very magnificent and extensive. It is built of marble collected for the most part from the *Kaser Farawan* or ruins of Pharaoh, an ancient city now in ruins, contiguous to the sanctuary of Muley Dris Zerone, east of the city of Mequinas, on the western declivity of the Atlas; this marble was transported across the mountains of Atlas on camels, a distance of fifteen journies to Tafilelt. The inhabitants of this part of Bled Eljereed live principally on dates, which abound so in this country that the fruit of one plantation is commonly sold for 1000 dollars, producing 1500 camel load of dates, or 4500 quintals; there are thirty-five species of this rich fruit, of which the *butube* is unquestionably the best and the most wholesome; it is rich, of a fine flavour, and sweet as honey: the *buscré* is also good; but so dry and full of saccharine matter that it resembles a lump of sugar. Undoubtedly if this country were in the hands of Europeans they would extract sugar, perhaps as much as 150 lb. from a camel load of dates weighing 300 lb. The *adamoh* is the date that is imported to this country; it is the best for keeping, but at Tafilelt they use it only for the cattle, considering it an unwholesome kind and heavy of digestion. The country [81] from the eastern declivity of Atlas to Tafilelt, and to the eastward of Tafilelt, even unto Seginmessa is one continued barren plain of a brown sandy soil impregnated with salt, so that if you take up the earth it has a salt flavour; the surface also has the appearance of salt, and if you dig a foot deep, a brackish water ooses up. On the approach, to within a day's journey of Tafilelt, however, the country is covered with the most magnificent plantations and extensive forests of the lofty date, exhibiting the most elegant and picturesque appearance that nature, on a plain surface, can present to the admiring eye. In these forests there is no underwood, so that a horseman may gallop through them without impediment. Wheat is cultivated near the river, and honey is produced of an exquisite quality. The faith and honour of the (filelly) inhabitants of Tafilelt is proverbial; a robbery has not been known within the memory of man; they use neither locks nor keys, having no need of either!

Having had my audience of leave of the Emperor, I prepared to proceed to Mogodor, but before I describe the country through which we passed thither, it may not perhaps be uninteresting to give some account of the Imperial gardens at Marocco, which are three, the *Jenan Erdoua*, the *Jenan El Afia*, and the *Jenan En. neel*: the last is confined to plants brought from the Egyptian Nile. The *Jenan El Afia*, and the *Jenan Erdoua*, contain oranges, citrons, vines, [82] figs, pomegranates, water and musk melons, all of exquisite flavour. The orange and fig trees are here as large as a middling sized English oak. Roses are so abundant at Marocco that they grow every where, and have a most powerful perfume, insomuch that one rose scents a large room; all other flowers are in abundance, and many that are nursed with care in English hot-houses are seen in the Marocco plains growing spontaneously. These gardens, as well as others throughout the country, are watered by the Persian or Arabian wheel, with pitchers fixed to it, which discharge the water into a trough or tank; as the pitchers rise and turn over their contents into this tank, the water is communicated to the garden and inundates the plants. Departing from Marocco to Mogodor, the first day's journey is through the plains of Sheshawa, a fine campaign country abounding in corn;

the mountains of Sheshawa, which are higher than any in Great Britain, have strata of oyster and other shells at the top of them. We encamped at the foot of these mountains; I had the curiosity to examine the depth of these strata of shells, and found them several feet deep, and extending all the way down the mountains. The rivers Sheshawa and Wed Elfees water these plains. The next day's journey brought us to a sanctuary, where we met very good entertainment, that is, such as the country affords, plenty of good provisions and hospitable treatment. [83] The next evening we encamped at a place called *Dar El Hage Croomb*, a very picturesque situation, where we were hospitably entertained; the Sheik coming to drink tea with me, related the history of his ancestors and traced his descent through many generations of warriors, whose dextrous management of the lance was the burden of the story. The next day, after travelling about six hours, we arrived at the extremity of the productive country, and entered *El Grored*, or the desert of sandy hills, which divide the rocky peninsula of Mogodor, from the cultivated land; this Sahara consists of loose sand-hills very fatiguing to the horses, and although not more than three miles in width, we were an hour and a half in crossing them, before we entered the gate of Mogodor.

[84]

LETTER VIII.

FROM MR. WILLIS TO MR. JACKSON.

My Dear Sir, Harley-Street, London,
12th December, 1797.

I thank you warmly for your intelligence concerning the interior of Africa, and beg you will continue to favour me with all the information you can collect upon this subject. Mr. Park has been almost as far as Jinnie, but did not reach Timbuctoo; he is now on his way to England, in an American ship, via America. We are anxious for his arrival, which may be expected in the course of the present month; and all the Africani are extremely curious to hear the detail of his most interesting journey, which we hope will produce some authentic knowledge, of a considerable part of those regions, that have hitherto baffled all the ardour and energy of European enquiry, though they have always excited the curiosity of the most eminent and enlightened men, both in past and present times.

I thank you also for the commercial intelligence you have sent me.

Do you know whether the emperor of Marocco has any collection of books? If he has, probably some ancient books, of great value, might be found among them.

[85]

I should consider it as a very great obligation if you could procure, and send me any book or manuscript in the character and language of Timbuctoo. We are informed that, besides the Arabic, they have a character of their own, perfectly different.

I remain, my dear Sir, Sincerely your's,
J. WILLIS.

Extract of a Letter to Mr. Jackson, from His Excellency
J.M. Matra, British Envoy to Marocco, &c.

Tangier, November 8, 1797.

I have not yet received any answer from Sir Joseph Banks to the letter from you, which I sent to him. Should you be able to obtain any information from Timbuctoo [104], or of the interior of this country, which would gratify one's curiosity, I will be very thankful for a slice of it.

I am ever, dear Jackson, Most faithfully your's,
JAMES M MATRA.

Footnote 104: (return) All *my information* respecting Timbuctoo, will be found in Jackson's Account of Marocco, Chapter XIII.

[86]

LETTER IX.

Custom of visiting the Emperor on his Arrival at Marocco.--Journey of the Merchants thither on that occasion.--No one enters the imperial Presence without a Present.--Mode of travelling.--The Commercio.--Imperial Gardens at Marocco.--Audience of the Sultan.--Amusements at Marocco.--Visit to the Town of Lepers.--Badge of Distinction worn by the Lepers.--Ophthalmia at Marocco.--Its probable Cause.--Immense Height of the Atlas, east and south of Marocco.--Mode of visiting at Marocco.--Mode of eating.--Trades or Handicrafts at Marocco.--Audience of Business of the Sultan.--Present received from the Sultan.

TO JAMES WILLIS, ESQ.

Mogodor, 1788.

The emperor having departed from Mequinas where he passed the winter, to Marocco, his summer residence, it becomes an incumbent duty for all loyal subjects, to pay their respects to him. All the bashaws of provinces, south of the river Morbeya, which divides the northern part of his dominions from the southern, as well as all the alkaids or governors of towns and districts under the authority of the bashaws of the provinces, are expected to show their loyalty, by obtaining permission to present themselves to the imperial presence; when they give an account of the state of the district which they respectively [87] govern. The bashaw of each province communicates with the emperor, and determines which of the alkaids [105] shall have the honour of presenting themselves. On these occasions, that is, when the emperor comes to Marocco, it is customary for the merchants of Mogodor to perform the journey to the metropolis [106] of the south, and to present his imperial majesty with a present; indeed, it is not the etiquette of this court for any one to demand an audience (which the lowest subject in the realm may claim) without being prepared to present something; so that the poor may have an audience by presenting half a dozen eggs, or any similar trifle, such as some fruit or flowers; but no one enters the imperial presence (*khawie*, as they term it, *i. e.*) empty-handed. The routine is this: The European merchants, together with the house of Guedalla and Co., who are native Jews, are called *el commercio;* the commercio, therefore, solicit the honour of presenting themselves to the emperor, to offer their congratulations on his arrival; this is acceded to, and the minister, who is denominated the *talb cadus*, a term designating a man who disperses orders and communications to every one, writes a letter to the commercio, [88] expressive of the emperor's disposition to see them, and requesting them to repair to his presence: a guard is given by the alkaid of Mogodor, and a present *ought* to be selected of such articles as are not to be bought at the markets of the country. A present consisting of such articles, previously ordered from Europe, and judiciously selected, is better calculated to gratify the emperor, than ten times the value injudiciously collected. The merchants accordingly prepared themselves to proceed to Marocco; some rode mules, some horses, for there are no carriages in this country; and every individual had his tent and servants with him. We travelled three days through a fine country, and reached the city of Marocco the fourth day, in the afternoon, travelling eight hours each day, at the rate of four miles an hour. On our approach to the city, we sent an express to the *talb cadus*, who, by the imperial order, appropriated the emperor's garden, *jinnen el afia*, for our reception, the pavilion in which was appropriated to our service; we preferred, however, in this delightful climate, sleeping in our tents, which we were permitted to pitch in this beautiful garden. We dined in the *coba*, or pavilion. The (*talb cadus*) minister paid us a visit, to say that the emperor requested we would take the following day to rest from our journey, and at eight o'clock on the following morning, he would receive us; the present was accordingly prepared, which was carried by [89] four-and-twenty men; every article (the bulky ones excepted) being enveloped in a Barcelona silk handkerchief. The emperor was in the (*m'ushoir*) place of audience, on that side of the city which faces the mountains of Atlas. At our presentation we did not prostrate ourselves, but bowed, in the European manner; the emperor said, bono el commercio, a Spanish phrase which he uses in interviews with Europeans, and which is equivalent to his saying, you are welcome, merchants. To this we replied, *Allah iberk amer seedi,* God bless the life of my master. The emperor asked if we were recovered from the fatigue of our journey, and was quite affable; he then said, communicate with the effendi [107], and whatever you want shall be granted to you; for I am disposed to encourage and (*amel el k'here*) to do good to my merchants. The master of the audience then came to us, and signified that we might depart; we made our obeisance, and returned to our habitation. This was the audience of introduction, which is always short; the second audience is for business; and the third is the audience of departure. We remained encamped in the imperial garden a fortnight before we had another audience; in the mean time we amused ourselves in riding about the country, and in visiting some of the most respectable inhabitants, among whom was [90] the *cadus*, who has a noble mansion, replete with every convenience, and a garden in the centre of it. The rooms of this house were long and narrow, with a pair of high doors in the centre of the room, through which alone the light is admitted; the floors were paved with small glazed tiles, about two inches square, very neatly fitted, and of different colours; the walls were the same, a mode of building which in this warm climate imparts a grateful coolness; the ceilings are painted in the Araberque style, with brilliant colours. The roofs are of terras, and flat, having an insensible declivity, just sufficient to give the rain that falls a course, which falling into the pipes, is received in the (*mitfere*) a subterraneous cistern, which supplies the family with water the whole year, till the rainy season returns again.

Footnote 105: (return) In each province, or bashawick, there are several alkaids or governors of districts.

Footnote 106: (return) The city of Fas is the metropolis of the north, as Marocco is of the south. Mequinas is the court town of the north, and resembles the Hague, where few reside but such as are employed in the service of the crown.

Footnote 107: (return) This word was used by the seed, or emperor, in the presumption that it is understood by Europeans; but *cadus* is the Arabic term.

There is near to the walls of Marocco, about the north-west point, a village, called (*Deshira el Jeddam*) i.e. the Village of Lepers. I had a curiosity to visit this village; but I was told that any other excursion would be preferable; that the Lepers were totally excluded from the rest of mankind; and that, although none of them would dare to approach us, yet the excursion would be not only unsatisfactory but disgusting. I was, however, determined to go; I mounted my horse, and took two horse-guards with me, and my own servant. We rode through the Lepers' town; the inhabitants collected at the doors of their habitations, [91] but did not approach us; they, *for the most part*, showed no external disfiguration, but were generally sallow; some of the young women were very handsome; they have, however, a paucity of eyebrow, which, it must be allowed, is somewhat incompatible with a beauty; some few had no eyebrows at all, which completely destroyed the effect of their dark animated eyes. They are obliged to wear a large straw hat, with a brim about nine inches wide; this is their *badge of separation*, a token of division between the clean and unclean, which when seen in the country, or on the roads, prevents any one from having personal contact with them. They are allowed to beg, and accordingly are seen by the side of the roads, with their straw hat badge, and a wooden bowl before them, to receive the charity of passengers, exclaiming (*attanie m'ta Allah*) "bestow on me the property of God;" (*kulshie m'ta Allah*) "all belongs to God!" reminding the passenger that he is a steward of, and accountable for the appropriation of his property; that he derives his property from the bounty and favour of God. When any one gives them money, they pronounce a blessing on him; as (*Allah e zeed kherik*) "may God increase your good," &c. The province of Haha abounds in lepers; and it is said that the Arganic [108] oil, which, is much used in food throughout this picturesque province, promotes this loathsome disease!

Footnote 108: (return) This oil, which is excellent, and generally used for frying fish, should be thus prepared, according to the learned Doctor Barata, who was pensioned physician to the *Commercio* of Mogodor, by which preparation it becomes perfectly wholesome, and deprived of any leprous or other bad quality: Take a quart of Argan oil, and put in it a large onion cut in slices; when it boils add a piece of crumb of bread, equal in size to an onion, then let it boil a few minutes more, take it off, let it cool, and strain the oil through a sieve, and bottle it for daily use.

[92]

The chain of Atlas, east of Marocco, continually covered with snow, gives a pleasant coolness to the air of the city, in the summer season, particularly in the morning and evening; the coolness is generally said, however, to produce ophthalmia. [109] These mountains are immensely high, and their magnitude makes them appear not more than five miles from the city. It is, however, a day's journey to the foot of them, after which the ascent is so gradual, that it takes two days more to reach the snow. This part of the chain of Atlas, east of the city of Marocco, is seen at sea, twenty miles west of Mogodor, which latter place is about 120 miles from Marocco; it is 35 miles from the city of [93] Marocco to the foot of Atlas; and it is two days' journey from the foot of Atlas to the snow, which constantly covers the summit of these immense mountains. They are thus seen at a distance of 245 miles:

```
    20 miles from land at sea.
   120     do.    Mogodor to Marocco.
    35     do.    Marocco to the foot of
                     the mountains.
    70     do.    the foot of Atlas to the snow.
   ---
Seen at 245 miles distance.
   ---
```

Footnote 109: (return) Ophthalmic disorders prevail among the Jews of Marocco, but are seldom seen among the Moors. The Jews live in great filth at Marocco; the dung-hills and ruins are in some places as high as the houses. The Muhamedan doctrine does not allow the Moors to neglect personal cleanliness, which, among these people, is a cardinal virtue; and this, I presume, is the cause of their being, in a great measure, exempt from ophthalmia, whereas the Jews, on the contrary, are generally affected with it.

In this calculation, the direct distance in the ascent of the mountain, is less than the travelling distance; but without taking notice of the distance from the border of the snow to the summit of this lofty mountain, which is said to be another day's journey, the one may balance the other: we may therefore calculate 70 miles as the direct longitudinal distance, although I am persuaded it is much more from the foot to the summit of that part of the Atlas which is visible at sea.

H.T. Colebrooke, Esq., in a paper inserted in the Asiatic Transactions, vol. xii. asserts, that it requires an elevation of 28,000 feet, for an object to be visible at the distance of 200 geographical miles; now 245 English miles are [94] equal to 211-1/2 geographical miles; consequently, if Mr. Colebrooke be correct, the summit of Atlas, east of Marocco and Dimenet, which is seen at a distance of 211-1/2 geographical miles, must be 29,610 feet high, or above five miles and a half.

Again, the chain of Atlas in Lower Suse, which lies east of Elala, and which is constantly covered with snow, is situated three days' journey, horse travelling, east-south-east from Elala, in Lower Suse; Elala is three days' journey from Santa Cruz, horse travelling, making together 180 miles: add for distance from the foot of the Elala mountains to the snow, 60 miles, and the Atlas in Lower Suse will be seen at the distance of 240 miles, or 207 geographical miles.

```
   Thus, from Santa Cruz to the     }
foot of the Atlas mountains, in the} 180 miles.
district of Elala, in Lower Suse   }

   Add for distance from the foot   }
of the Elala mountains to the      }   60
snow                               }
                                       ---
   So that the Atlas in Lower Suse, }
being seen at a distance of         }  240
```

Or 207 geographical miles, must have an altitude of 28,980 feet.

On the north side of the city of Marocco is a gate called *Beb El Khummes*, and near it is held, every Thursday, a market called soke *El Khummes*; at which immense quantities of horses, camels, mules, asses, oxen, sheep, goats, wheat and barley are sold; oils, gums, almonds, dates, raisins, figs, bees' wax, honey, skins, [95] &c. &c. &c.; also, slaves, male and female. Such a horse as would cost in London 50*l.*, sells here for 50 dollars; a good mule sells for the same, viz. 50 dollars; a bull, 12 dollars; a cow, 15 dollars; sheep, a dollar and a half, each; a goat, a dollar. Very fine large grained wheat, which increases one-fifth in the grinding, sells at one dollar per saa, or about half a dollar per Winchester bushel. The slaves are conducted through the market by the auctioneer (*delel*), who exclaims, occasionally, (*khumseen reeal aal zeeada*, i.e.) "50 dollars on the increase," till he finds no one will advance; when he goes to the owner and declares the price offered; the owner then decides if he will sell or not; if he sells, the money is paid immediately, but if not, he takes his slave away with him, and tries him again the next market-day, or waits in expectation that this wretched article of trade will rise in value.

A stranger passing through Marocco would consider it an irregular miserable town; but the despotic nature of the government induces every individual to secrete or conceal his opulence; so that the houses of the gentry are surrounded with a shabby wall, often broken or out of repair, at a considerable distance from the dwelling house, which does not appear, or is invisible to the passenger. Some of these houses are very handsome, and are furnished with couches, circular cushions to sit on, and other furniture, in all the luxury of the East. When a [96] visitor or a guest enters one of these houses, slaves come in with perfumes burning, in compliment to the visitor. Coffee and tea are then presented in small cups, having an outer cup to hold that which contains the liquor, instead of a saucer; the sugar being first put into the pot. The coffee or tea being poured out, already sweetened with sugar, a negro boy generally takes his station in one corner of a spacious room, pours out the liquor, and sends it to the guests by another boy. The tea table is a round stand, about twelve inches from the ground, at which the tea boy sits down on a leather cushion, cross legged.

When dinner is served, the food is in a large dish or bowl, on a round stand, similar to that above described; three, four, or more sit round it; a servant comes to the company with a ewer and napkin; each person wash their right hand, and eat with their fingers; in the higher circles, rose-water is used instead of plain; if soup is served, they eat it with wooden spoons; in this respect the emperor himself sets them the example, who reprobates the use of the precious metals with food.

When the Moors sit down to eat; high and low, rich and poor, (for I have partaken of food with all ranks, from the prince to the plebeian,) they invariably invoke God's blessing, previous to the repast, and offer thanks at the conclusion. Their first grace is, invariable, short, and comprehensive; *bis'm illah*, "In the name of God." [97] The after grace is, *El Ham'd û littah*, "Praise be to God."

A very excellent dish is generally eaten in this country, called *cuscasoe*; it is made with flour, granulated into particles the size of a partridge shot, which is, put over a steamer, till the steam has sufficiently passed through it, so as to produce the effect of boiling; it is then taken off, broken, and returned to steam a second time; in the meantime, a chicken or some meat is boiling in the saucepan, under the steamer, with onions, turnips, and other vegetables; when the *cuscasoe* has been steamed a second time, it is taken off, coloured with saffron, and mixed with some butter, salt, and pepper, and piled up in a large round bowl or dish, garnished with the chicken or meat and vegetables. This is a very nutritious, wholesome, and palatable dish, when well cooked. It is in high estimation with the Arabs, Moors, Brebers, Shelluhs, and Negroes. When they sit down to eat, each person puts his fingers into the dish before him; and in respectable society, it is remarkable how dextrously they jerk the food into their mouths, which never come into contact with their hands; so that this mode of eating is scarcely objectionable, certainly not obnoxious, as some travellers have represented it; but who probably had associated with the lower ranks of society, who, indeed, are not particular in these observances.

All kind of trades are carried on at Marocco: [98] jewellers, goldsmiths, blacksmiths, coppersmiths, tanners, &c. &c.; but that which is the most honourable, is a shoe-maker, because Muhamed himself was one. At Mequinas they make excellent shoes, of leather impervious to water, for 1*s*. 8*d*. per pair.

The time now approached for our audience of business, and we had represented to the *Talb Cadus*, that the export duties on some articles were too heavy, viz. on wax, almonds, and olive oil; also on certain imports, viz. iron, steel, and Buenos Ayres hides; but no diminution was obtained, except in the duty of bees' wax. The emperor gave hopes of an exportation of grain, and desired us to write to Europe for ships to come and load wheat, barley, Indian corn, caravances, beans, lentils, and millet. We were favourably received; the emperor asked several questions respecting Europe, and informed us we should return to Mogodor in a few days. Three days after this audience we were ordered to meet the emperor in the *Jenan En neel*, where we had our audience of leave, and the emperor gave each of us a fine horse, chosen by ourselves out of his own stable; and we took our leave and departed for Mogodor the following evening. We slept encamped under the magnificent and lofty date trees, in the neighbourhood of the city, the first night.

[99]

LETTER X.

FROM MR. WILLIS TO MR. JACKSON.

My dear Sir Harley-street, London,,
September 10, 1798.

I write to acknowledge the receipt of your favour. I know no man better qualified than yourself for the station of an African consul; and really think, that to assist you in obtaining such a post, is to render service to my country, as well as to yourself. Your information concerning the interior of Africa, and especially concerning Timbuctoo, appears to me to be more accurate, authentic, and extensive than that of any other person I have met with; considerably more so than that of any of the correspondents of the African association. Mr. Park, of whose return you are informed, has brought home no addition to the stock of our knowledge of that important place; though I think his geographical communications are highly valuable, particularly as they regard the river and course, &c. of the Niger. This celebrated river will, I think, in time be the channel of communication between Europe and the interior of Africa. It seems to penetrate into that continent, in its widest and most interesting part; if it should be navigable through its entire course, we might hereafter make it the instrument of the most important discoveries, and the channel of the most valuable commerce. I [100] shall be much obliged to you for information concerning this river, particularly as to its termination. I suspect it discharges itself into some interior sea or vast lake, like the Caspian; unless, like the Burrampooter, after various and extensive windings, it may return towards its source, and fall into the Atlantic.

You will have heard of the landing of a French army in Egypt, under Buonaparte; the French are enterprising, and if they should penetrate from the eastward, while we advance from the west, the interior of the African continent may at length be laid open.

I remain, my dear Sir, Your's sincerely,
J. WILLIS.

LETTER XI.

FROM THE SAME TO THE SAME.

My dear Sir, Harley-street, London,
June 10.1800.

I did not receive, till the 22d November, your favour, dated 1st September last, for which I beg you to receive my best thanks. I have transmitted an extract of it to Lord Moira, Sir Joseph Banks, and to a friend of mine, who is a member of parliament, and has great influence with his majesty's ministers; in order that he may lay it before the secretary of state, in such a manner as to draw his attention to it in the most impressive and effectual manner; but I much fear that the pressure of the war, and its consequent effects; the arrangements of finance, &c. will preclude their immediate support to objects which they consider as of very subordinate importance. The time is certainly highly favourable for the cultivation of the friendship of the emperor, and of other Muhamedan sovereigns; now that the British arms have preserved the principal empire of the Moslems, by the victory at Aboukir, and the defense of Acre; in consequence of which, Egypt has been recovered, and one of the sacred gates of the Caaba again opened to the Mussulmen. This appears to be an event of [102] the highest consideration to the Muhamedans of Africa, since it is by Grand Cairo, that the western pilgrims communicate with Mecca.

I suppose you have received the narratives, published by Park and Browne, of their respective journies and discoveries in the interior of your continent; they have done much, but much more still remains to be done; and above all, the discovery of Timbuctoo and its commercial relations.

There is a captain Wild, now either at Tunis or Algiers, preparing himself for this journey, (as I am informed,) a man of intrepidity, judgment, and enterprise; whom Sir Joseph Banks writes me, he hopes to engage in the employment of the African association.

I assure you that I consider you, as the only European that possesses any substantial and interesting information concerning that part of interior Africa, which we are most solicitous to investigate; and, therefore, set a high value upon whatever you are so good as to communicate. I am also of opinion, that your plans may very probably be adopted by administration, when the return of peace shall leave their minds at liberty to attend to it.

[103]

LETTER XII.

FROM THE SAME TO THE SAME.

My dear Sir, Harley-street, London,
5th May, 1801.

I wrote you at considerable length on the 1st of June last, and assure you that none of your letters, received prior to that date, have remained unanswered. I have now to acknowledge the receipt of your several favours, and beg you to accept my best thanks, for your very curious and valuable present of the gold ring from Wangara, which has been shown to several persons of great distinction, and even to the king himself. *It is universally considered as a great curiosity*; and I have taken care to make it known that you are the person to whom I am indebted, for the first *Wangarian* jewel that has ever been seen in England. I have also shown your letter, containing your judicious opinions upon the course of the Niger [110], and other geographical points, to Sir Joseph Banks and Major Rennell; and have invariably represented you to them, and to others, as the person possessing eminently the best information concerning the interior of Africa; an object which draws at present the earnest attention, both of the learned and the great, and which [104] our late victories in Egypt, render more peculiarly interesting.

Footnote 110: (return) See Jackson's account of Marocco, last chapter.

I think, with you, it is probable there is a communication by water between Jinnie and Egypt; but I should rather imagine there is some large lake or Mediterranean sea, like the Caspian, for instance, into which the Niger may discharge itself from the west, and a branch of the Nile from the east. This idea seems to reconcile the opinions of ancient geographers, with those resulting from modern discoveries. If we should be able to effect the complete conquest of Egypt, and to retain that kingdom, much light will probably soon be acquired upon these interesting subjects.

[105]

LETTER XIII.

Journey from Mogodor, to Rabat, to Mequinas, to the Sanctuary of Muley Dris Zerone in the Atlas Mountains, to the Ruins of Pharaoh, and thence through the Amorite Country to L'Araich and Tangier.--Started from Mogodor with Bel Hage as my (Tabuk) *Cook, ana Deeb as my* (Mûle Lukkerzana) *Tent Master.--Exportation of Wool granted by the Emperor.--Akkermute depopulated by the Plague.--Arabs, their Mode of hunting the Partridge.--Observations respecting the River Tansift.--Jerf El Eûdie, or the Jews' Pass.--Description of Saffy, and its Port or Road.--Woladia calculated to make a safe Harbour.--Growth of Tobacco.--Mazagan described.--Azamor the Abode of Storks.--Saneet Urtemma a dangerous Country.--Dar El Beida, Fedalla, and Rabat described.--Mausoleum of the Sultan Muhamed ben Abd Allah at Rabat.--Of Shella, a Roman Town.--Of the Tower of Hassan.--Road of Rabat.--Productive Country about Rabat.--Salee.--The People inimical to Christians.--The Dungeon where they confined Christian Slaves.--Ait Zimurh, notorious Thieves.--Their Mode of Robbing.--Their Country disturbed with Lions.--Arrival at Mequinas.--Some Account of that City and its imperial Palace.--Ladies of*

Mequinas extremely beautiful.--Arrival at the renowned Sanctuary of Muley Dris Zerone.-- Extraordinary and favourable Reception there by the Fakeers of the Sanctuary.--Slept in the Adytum.--Succour expected from the English in the Event of an Invasion by Bonaparte.-- Prostration and Prayer of Benediction by the Fakeers at my Departure from the [106] Sanctuary.--Ruins of Pharaoh near the Sanctuary.--Treasures found there.--Ite Amor.--The Descendants of the Ancient Amorites.--Character of these People.--Various Tribes of the Berebbers of Atlas.--El Kassar Kabeer.--Its Environs, a beautiful Country.--Forest of L'Araich.-- Superior Manufacture of Gold Thread made at Fas, as well as Imitations of Amber.--Grand Entry of the British Ambassador into Tangier.--Our Ignorance of African Matters.--The Sultan's Comparison of the Provinces of his Empire to the various Kingdoms of Europe.

TO JAMES WILLIS, ESQ.

Dear Sir, Tangier,
8th August, 1801.

My journey to meet His Excellency James M. Matra, the British ambassador to the Court of Marocco, was undertaken principally to obtain permission to ship a large quantity of wool which I had in my possession, the exportation of which had been recently prohibited. I thought I could not select a more seasonable time than when our ambassador was at court; accordingly, I started from Mogodor (the morning after I dispatched two vessels for Europe) on the 4th June last, at four o'clock, P.M. My journey was first to Rabat; thence, across the country, to Fas and Mequinas; thence to the renowned and revered sanctuary of Muley Dris Zerone, on the declivity of the mountains of Atlas, east of Mequinas; thence to *Kassar Farawan* (the ruins of Pharaoh), and through the warlike province of the Ait Amor, to L'Araich, Arzilla, and to Tangier.

[107]

I took with me two of the finest horses in the country, to ride alternately. Two mules and three camels carried my baggage, tents, &c. Muhamed of Diabet, commonly called *Deeb*, I engaged as tent-master; this is the man that astonished Aly Bey El Abassy, when he shot the fish in the river, as recorded by that interesting traveller. I engaged a most excellent fellow as cook, a man who had performed many journies in a similar capacity with the princes; he was acquainted with the roads, the country, and the character of the people; the camel-drivers and muleteers completed our party. We arrived at Tela at nine o'clock in the evening, being a journey of five hours. We remained at Tela the whole of the following day, and started on the 6th June at seven o'clock; arrived, at ten o'clock, at Akkermute, a town in ruins, in the plains west of *Jebbel El Heddeed* (the iron mountains), which was depopulated by the plague about fifty years since. Passing through the plains of Akkermute, towards the river Tensift, we saw a party of Arabs hunting partridges; we did not stop to see this novel sport, but I was informed that the dogs were directed by the huntsmen to the spot where the birds settled, which roused them; they then pursued them again, and after rousing them several times without intermission, the birds become fatigued and exhausted by continual flying, and the dogs then run them down and seize on them. [108] In six hours from Akkermute, at four o'clock, P.M., we reached the river Tensift, which brings its water from the Atlas, east of Marocco, meandering through the plains and passing about three miles north of that city.

We pitched our tents under the walls of the (*Luksebba*) castle, on the south bank of the river.

We started the next morning at six o'clock, and travelling through a fine country, we came to a narrow pass on the declivity of a lofty mountain called Jerf El Eudie, a most picturesque country, and arrived at the port of Saffy at eleven o'clock. Saffy has no harbour, but a road where ships are obliged to put to sea whenever the south-wind blows; the town was fortified when in possession of the Portuguese, and is situated in a declivity between two hills, so that during the rainy season the waters come down so rapidly that they sometimes overflow the lower apartments of the houses and commit considerable damage. On the 8th June we started from Saffy at nine o'clock, and arrived at the sanctuary of Seedi Cuscasoe at five o'clock, P.M.; and proceeding on, we reached El Woladia at nine, and pitched our tents. This place might be made a secure harbour for the whole British navy, by blowing up a rock which impedes the narrow passage at the entrance of a long and extensive bay. From hence we started at half-past five o'clock in the morning; we proceeded northwards along the coast till eleven o'clock, when we reached the beautiful and abundant [109] valley, the Woolga; travelling on through the country, leaving the sea to the left, we arrived at six o'clock at the Douar, (an encampment of Arabs,) called *Woled Aisah, i.e.* "Sons of Jesus," situated in the productive province of Duquella. The environs of the Douar of Woled Aisah abound in plantations of tobacco, of a superior quality, equal to the Havannah. The next morning, viz. on the 10th June, we struck our tents at six o'clock, and travelling three hours we arrived, at nine, at the *Jerf el Saffer* (the Yellow Cliff): three hours more brought us to Tet, and an hour more to Mazagan, which we reached at one o'clock. Mazagan is the Portuguese name; the Moorish name is El Burreja. This is a very strong place, having several stout bastions; there is a magnificent (*mitfere*) cistern of water, built by the Portuguese, supported by many pillars of great strength of the Tuscan order. The water in the neighbourhood of Mazagan is very salubrious; this country is full of springs. The inhabitants have a good healthy colour, very different from the inhabitants of the plains of the province of Duquella, which being supplied by water from wells only, of from 100 to 200 feet deep, have a sallow and sickly appearance. It may, in Europe, appear extraordinary that the quality of water should produce such a manifest difference in the complexion of the inhabitants, but when we consider that these people drink no wine, spirits, or malt liquor, the paradox will immediately vanish. After viewing [110] the mitfere, or cistern, and batteries at Mazagan, we mounted at four o'clock, and arrived at Azamor at seven o'clock P.M., pitched the tents in a large spacious fondaque, or caravansera, in the centre of the town. We were annoyed during the night by thousands of storks, the cluttering of whose bills would not permit us to sleep. This town is in the centre of a beautiful country. On the 11th June, at noon, we pursued our journey, and reached Sancet Urtemma at eight o'clock P.M. This is a dangerous country, infested with robbers, who, from the undulating face of the country, have many modes of escape; we, therefore, retired into a solitary retreat, and lay on our arms, without sleep, all night. At six o'clock next morning, being the 12th June, we started, and arrived at Dar el Beida at twelve. Here I was hospitably entertained by the agents of the Spanish house of the Cinquo Gremos of Madrid, who were established here for the purpose of shipping corn to Spain. We left Dar el Beida, at half-past three, and reached Fedalla at half-past seven. This is a fine productive country, abounding in grain as well as Dar el Beida. On the 13th we started at four o'clock, and reached El Mensoria at seven; stopped and dined, mounted at ten A.M. and arrived at Rabat at seven o'clock, P.M. after a journey from Mogodor, of 80-1/2 hours of actual travelling, or 242 English miles. [111]

Footnote 111: (return) Calculated at the rate of three miles an hour, including stoppages and refreshments.

[111]

Rabat is the largest town on the coast of the empire, it is walled round; its circumference is about four miles; an aqueduct conveys abundance of water to the town from a distance of several miles. The mausoleum of the sultan Muhamed, father to the present sultan Soliman, is in the town of Rabat, it is a neat building, surrounded by a colonade; here is a lamp continually burning, and a *muden* [112], who is a fakeer, is continually proclaiming the omnipotence of God, and that Muhamed is the prophet. "*La Allah, ila Allah, wa Muhamed rassul Allah.*" There is a very strong battery towards the sea, at the mouth of the river, which is bomb proof. The city wall is high, and is strengthened by several bastions mounting cannon: towards the land, about a mile from Rabat, there is a spring, reported to have been discovered by the Romans, and near it is the Roman town of Shella, which none but musulmen are permitted to enter. In it are said to be the tombs of two sultans, but most probably of Roman generals. Kettles or pans of coins are continually found by the people who dig the ground at this place, and the coins found are Roman. Some European travellers enhanced the price of these coins so much, by their eagerness to purchase them, that they offered more than double their intrinsic value, so that the Jews imitated them so well that they [112] deceived even these antiquaries. There are several mosques in this town, but that which attracts particularly the notice of travellers, is the *sma Hassan, i.e.* the tower of Hassan, situated about a mile from Shella, on the south banks of the river Buregreg, so called from its being in the province of Beny Hassan, it is an old tower built in a superior manner by an architect of Grenada, the same that built the tower at Marocco, called *Jamaa Lifenar*, one at Timbuctoo, and that at Seville; it is about 200 feet high, perfectly square, and a person may ride up to the top on horseback, having a gradual ascent, and seven chambers one above the other: the cement with which it is made is so hardened that no pickaxe can destroy it. It was represented to the sultan Muhamed that the apartments in this tower were the haunts of vice and immorality, and the sultan ordered the floor or terras, by which visitors ascend, to be broken; it was found, however, impossible to destroy it, wherefore the workmen were ordered to desist, and the entrance was blocked up with loose stones. This tower I ascended with my friend the Comte de Fourban, nephew to the duke de Crillon, who conducted the famous siege of Gibraltar, and whose machinations were so admirably defeated by the immortal governor of that garrison, General Elliott, Lord Heathfield. The Comte had ruined his constitution by being immolated in a dungeon in France, during the reign of Robespierre, where he remained during [113] fifteen months, oftentimes seated on steps in water up to his ankles. The Comte was a very generous and liberal man, an emigrant French nobleman, protected by the British consul at the court of Morocco. The disorder contracted by ill usage and confinement in prison, brought on a disease which, after applying various remedies to no purpose, carried him off, and he died at Rabat. The house of the French consul and those of some other European consuls who formerly resided here, are conveniently situated on the southern banks of the river Buregreg, which divides Rabat from Salee. Ships of one hundred tons, that do not draw much water, may pass the bar and load close to these houses; but larger vessels must come to anchor in the offing, and take in their cargoes by boats. The country about Rabat and Salee is wonderfully abundant in all the finest grain, leguminous plants, fruits, vegetables, and cattle; the orange, lemon, Seville, or bitter orange, and citron plantations are here very extensive and extremely productive. Several ships might be loaded here with oranges in October and November, before the gales of the latter half of December and the month of January set in. One hundred fine large oranges may be had for a drahim, a silver coin worth 6d. sterling. The orange plantations of Rabat are of incalculable extent; the trees are as large as a middling-sized oak; the vineyards and cotton plantations are likewise most abundant; and nothing can exceed the good quality of the grapes, [114] figs, oranges, citrons, apricots, peaches, and water-melons; the quality of the latter is peculiarly *sweet*, they are called *Dilla Seed Billa*; the seed of which might be advantageously transported to our new colony, the Cape of Good Hope. The vineyards of Rabat are very extensive; the vines are cultivated in the Arabian system, on the ground, which is a light sandy soil: the immense numbers of turtle-doves that are in these vineyards is such, that a bad sportsman cannot fail killing a dozen or two at every shot; they rise just before you in thousands, and the foulahs, or vine cultivators, express their gratitude to the Christians who go to shoot them. These birds, from being unmolested, are so tame and so abundant, that they destroy an incalculable quantity of the best fruit.

Footnote 112: (return) The muden is the man who ascends the tower of the Mosque and announces prayer.

On the 14th, the Comte de Fourban accompanied me, and we crossed the river, in the ferry, to visit Salee. The inhabitants of this town are inimical to Christians: we viewed the subterraneous cavern where the Sallee rovers formerly confined their Christian slaves: it resembled a mitfere or large subterraneous granary; it had two grates to let in the air; it appeared perfectly dry, but no one was in it. The Comte observed that it was far preferable to the prison where he was confined in France, during the reign or usurpation of Robespierre. The air of Salee and Rabat, and the adjacent country, is strongly perfumed, morning and evening, with the sweet [115] odour of the orange-flower, of which they make immense quantities of delectable comfits.

On the morning of the 15th, we pursued our journey to Mequinas, passing through a very fine country, inhabited by a Kabyl of Berebbers, called Ait Zemurh. We halted, at four o'clock P.M. at a circular Douar of these Berebbers, in a fine campaign country. The next morning, at five o'clock, we struck the tents, and proceeded through a dangerous country, infested by artful robbers, and the occasional depredations of the lion and other wild beasts, whose roaring we heard at a distance. We saw several square buildings, which our guides informed us were built by the Berebbers, for the purpose of destroying the lion. The patient hunter will conceal himself in one of these buildings, which are about five feet by seven, and will wait whole days for an opportunity to get a shot at the lion: these noble beasts are here said to be the largest in all Africa. After travelling this day ten hours, we pitched our tents at another circular encampment of the Zimurite [113] Berebbers. These people drive in stakes and place thorny bushes round their encampment, eight feet high, and fill up the entrance every night with thorns, as the fiercest lions of Africa abound in the adjacent forests, and sometimes attack their habitations, accordingly they keep a large fire all night to [116] deter the lions and other wild beasts from approaching. About two hours after midnight, my grey horse, who was an old campaigner, neighed and awoke us; this gave the alarm, and my people were presently on the alert, and perceived two men approaching our tents, crawling naked along the ground, which was of the same colour with their bodies. We did not wish to take them, fearing that the people of the Douar would espouse the cause of their countrymen, but my people gave the alarm, and exclaimed "*Erd abellek asas*," i.e. "Be watchful, guards!" We then saw these marauders jump up, and run away as fast as they could; keeping watch the rest of the night: we were advised to take no notice of this circumstance. The people of Ait Zimurh are professed robbers: they would not allow us to pitch our tents *within* their circular encampment, a privilege universally granted to strangers and travellers. I thought this very unhospitable; being totally different from any thing I had ever before witnessed in this country, where hospitality generally exceeds all bounds. I have no doubt that the people of the Douar were in league with the robbers; I considered my escape, the next day, when I was apprised of the danger of the country I had confided in, quite providential, and I have no doubt but these people would delude any one that would trust to their honour: they reminded me of the ancient Africans, as described by Sallust, in the wars of Jugurtha.

Footnote 113: (return) The Zimurites, or Ait Zimure, are probably the descendants of the Zemarites: for which see 1 Chron. i. 16.

[117]

We struck our tents at five o'clock, and travelled very fast to get out of these treacherous habitations; for we learned that, the preceding night, Alkaid L'Hassan Ramy, a Negro captain of the emperor's army, passed this Douar, and was robbed of his bridles, saddles, and tent equipage, with which the thieves made off, without being discovered. I afterwards met Alkaid L'Hassan Ramy at Mequinas; and he appeared quite astonished that I should have escaped being robbed at the above Douar, calling the whole Kabyl a set of lawless thieves. On the 17th, we started at five o'clock, and arrived at Mequinas at nine o'clock, performing the journey from Rabat to Mequinas in twenty-two hours, being sixty-six miles. The city of Mequinas is the court-town of the northern division of the empire: the imperial palace at this place is above two miles in circumference. At the corners are erected (*Coba's*) square buildings or pavilions, containing one room up stairs, where the emperor frequently transacts business. This palace was built by the sultan Muley Ismael: it is very neat, and consists for the most part of moresque architecture; the marble columns and other decorations were brought from (*Kasser Farawan*) the ruins of Pharaoh, about a day's journey to the eastward. There is a superior garden of choice fruit within the wall which surrounds the palace, and in the latter are many elegant apartments, ornamented *À-la-mauresque*. The ladies of Mequinas are so extremely handsome, that I cannot [118] say I saw one plain young woman, although I visited several families; nay, I can say, without offense to truth, that I did not see one that was not comely and handsome. I was most hospitably entertained wherever I went. On the 18th June, at eight o'clock A.M. we started for Fas; when we had approached the latter city, we met a messenger, with the prince Muley Abdsalam's secretary, from the emperor to his excellency J.M. Matra, the British ambassador to the court of Marocco, who informed me that his excellency had just terminated his embassy, had waited for my arrival two days, and was on his return to Tangier. Presuming, therefore, that the ambassador had negociated my business for me, I turned to the north-east, travelled all day without halting, till eight o'clock in the evening, when we arrived at the renowned sanctuary [114] of Muley Dris Zerone, on the declivity of North Atlas; a most magnificent, beautiful, and picturesque country, abounding in all the necessaries and luxuries of life. This sanctuary was never before, nor since, visited by any Christian. It was here that the standard of Muhamed was first planted in North-western Africa, by the fakeer and prince Muley Dris, the founder. A favourable combination of circumstances, of which I availed myself, enabled me to procure not only an asylum, but a most hospitable and kind reception and entertainment in [119] this renowned sanctuary; and I actually slept in the *Horem* or Adytum itself, which honour I obtained by a present, appropriated to the circumstance, and sent to the chief fakeer of the sanctuary, accompanied with some observations expressed in a manner which was agreeable to the holy fraternity. When I entered the *Horem* of this renowned sanctuary, where I slept alone, its silence reminded me of the silence of death, which formed one of the ancient mysteries of Egypt. The chief of the fakeers met me in the portico, and cordially shook hands with me, calling me his brother. At this time there was a rumour that Bonaparte was preparing to invade the country; and indeed he had intimated as much, the English were therefore courted; it was even hoped and expected by the emperor that they would in such an event become his allies, and give him succour. The next morning, I gave the fakeer some wax candles accompanied with observations emblematical of the present, which was so favourably received, that no less than nine saints prostrated themselves at the place of prayer, which is at the entrance of the town, as I passed out to pursue my journey, uttering with audible voices a (*fâtha*) prayer of benediction, invoking on me the protection of Almighty God, and a blessing on the English nation; also that God would avert every danger from the embassy, and restore them in safety to their native land. I am perfectly aware that, in recording [120] this extraordinary circumstance, persons who have visited this country, and have remarked the rancour that generally exists with the lower orders against Christians, may doubt my veracity, so unprecedented a circumstance it is for a Christian to be admitted into a *Horem*! the most respected also and the most sacred in the empire! My answer to such is, that the circumstance is so incredible, that I should not have presumed to lay it before the British public, if I had not two most respectable witnesses, *now living* in West Barbary, who can and will corroborate my report; these two men are Bel Hage, a Muselman, who had been the prince's cook, and who officiated as mine during the journey, and Muhamed, commonly called Deeb, of Diabet, a village near Mogodor, the same man whose dexterity Aly Bey, in his travels, alludes to, when he shot a fish in the river near Mogodor.

Footnote 114: (return) The town, in the centre of which stands the sanctuary, contains about 5000 inhabitants.

Half an hour's journey after leaving the sanctuary of Muley Dris Zerone, and at the foot of Atlas, I perceived to the left of the road magnificent and massive ruins; the country for miles around is covered with broken columns of white marble, the ruins appeared to be of the Egyptian, and massive style of architecture. There were still standing two porticos, about thirty feet high and twelve feet wide, the top of which was one entire stone. I attempted to take a view of these immense ruins, which have furnished marble for the imperial palaces at [121] Mequinas and at Tafilelt; but I was obliged to desist, seeing some persons of the sanctuary following the cavalcade. Pots and kettles of gold and silver coins are continually dug up from these ruins. The country, however, abounds in serpents, and we saw many scorpions under the stones that my conductor Deeb turned up. These ruins are said by the Africans to have been built by one of the Pharaohs: they are called "*Kasser Farawan*" i.e. the ruins of Pharaoh. [115] Here begins the territory of the [122] Brebber Kabyl, the Amorites or Ite-amor, said to be the descendants of the ancient [116] Amorites, whose country was situated east of Palestine. These people retain their ancient warlike spirit, but they are a faithless tribe, and intolerable thieves, unlike the other Kabyles (who are, at least, faithful to one of their own Kabyl); but these marauders are exceedingly mistrustful of their own brethren, so that their habitations consist of two or three tents only, in one encampment; and even these are sometimes at variance with each other. The lamentable result of this [123] mistrustful and marauding spirit, is wretched and universal poverty. Their country is a succession of gentle undulating hills, without trees or plantations of any kind. The late sultan Muhamed used to compare the provinces or races of men in his empire, to the nations of Europe, the English he called warriors, the French faithless, the Spaniards quiet and inoffensive, the Romans, i.e. the people of Italy, treacherous, the Dutch a parsimonious and trading people; the other powers of Europe, having no consul at Marocco, nor merchants in the country, are known only by name: accordingly, in allusion to the warlike spirit of the English, he would call the Ait Amor, "the English of Barbary;" Temsena, the French; Duquella, the Spanish; Haha, the Italians; and Suse, the Russians. When the sultan Muhamed began a campaign, he never entered the field without the warlike Ait Amor, who marched in the rear of the army; these people received no pay, but were satisfied with what plunder they got after a battle; and accordingly, this principle stimulating them, they were always foremost on any contest, dispute, or battle. They begin the campaign almost in a state of nudity, and seldom return to their homes without abundance of apparel, arms, horses, camels, and money; but this property quickly disappears, and these people are soon again reduced to their wonted misery and nudity, and become impatient for another campaign of plunder. When [124] the present sultan, Soliman, came from Mequinas, in the year of the plague (1799), a division of his army passed near Mogodor, and the encampments of the Ait Amor, or Amorites occupied the whole of the country from the river to the Commerce Garden, a distance of three miles. It is very probable that some other of the tribes bordering on Palestine, may have emigrated in remote times, and may have taken their abode on the Atlas mountains. There are above twenty (kabyls) tribes of [117] Berebbers occupying the mountains of Atlas, as Ait-Girwan, Zian, Ait-Ziltan, Ait-Amor, Ait-Ebeko, Ait-Kitiwa, Ait-Attar, Ait-Amaran, and many more whose names I do not now recollect. We travelled seven hours through the Amorite country, and pitched our tents in the north part of the plains of Msharrah Rummellah. Fire being lit, the Moors sat round to warm themselves, and confidently animadverted on the prosperity that would necessarily attend our journey, after having met with such a hospitable and favoured reception at the renowned sanctuary before mentioned.

Footnote 115: (return) In reply to those learned sceptics who have studied books; but not men, and the manners of different countries; who believe nothing but what they have seen; and who say that Pharaoh never came so far west; I reply, that our knowledge of African history is extremely imperfect. In fact, we now know as certainties, various articles of which no record is to be found in any ancient writer; for the affairs of Africa, which, of late, have so deservedly excited the attention of the learned, were as little known to the ancients as they are to the moderns; insomuch that not a word is to be found in any ancient record or history extant, of those curious astronomical representations, the Zodiacs, which adorn the ceilings of the temples in *Egypt*, nor of the paintings which cover the silent and solemn repositories of their dead. Even the royal sepulchres, surpassing all the efforts of art hitherto known, in brilliancy of colours and decorative sculptures, are recorded by no historian! Neither in any history, *known to Europe,* is there any allusion to the Egyptian custom of placing books, i.e. rolls of manuscript, in the mummy coffins with the bodies of the deceased. For much of the knowledge collected respecting Africa, we are indebted to the catacombs of Egypt, and we must not hope to know much more, whilst our ignorance of the Arabic language is so manifest; we must travel far out of the precincts of Greek and Latin lore, before we shall procure correct histories of African affairs! Our knowledge of Hebrew, in Europe I apprehend, is almost as much confined and as imperfect as that of Arabic! By the assistance, however, of the latter, what store of learning might we not expect from complete Arabic translations of many of the Greek and Latin authors, *viz.* of the *complete* works of Livy, Tacitus, and many others. I recollect conversing with Abdrahaman ben Nassar, bashaw of Abda, (a gentleman deeply versed in Arabian literature,) about the close of the last century, who mentioned circumstances, which gave me reason to suppose that there is extant a complete Arabic translation of Livy as well as of Tacitus, as the bashaw assured me there was, and that he had read them, and they were to be found in the recondite chests of the Imperial library at Fas, in which it is more than probable that there are many valuable transcripts in Arabic of ancient authors, quite lost to erudite Europe! A knowledge of the Arabic language in this country is so indispensable, and is held in such high estimation, that every one who does not understand it, is denominated *ajemmy, i.e.* barbarian or European.--St. Paul in the same spirit says, I Corinth. ch. xiv. v. 11., "He that speaketh unintelligibly, is unto us a barbarian."

Footnote 116: (return) See Genesis, xv. 16. Deuteron. xx. 17. Judges, i. 34.

Footnote 117: (return) Some persons consider several tribes of these Berebbers to be colonies of the ancient Phenicians.

On the morning of the 20th June, we struck our tents at six o'clock, and pursued our journey to L'Araich, and soon entered the territory that belongs to the agriculturists of El Kassar Kabeer, a beautiful country not unlike that of Ait-Amor [125] in appearance, but bearing the evidences of agricultural industry. Here we discovered magnificent and extensive plantations of olives, immense citron-trees, orange-groves, and spacious vineyards, peaches, apricots, greengages, and walnuts were also the produce of this country, besides excellent wheat of a large and long transparent grain like amber, yielding, when ground into flour, from fifteen to twenty per cent. increase, in quantity. Anxious now to overtake His Excellency the ambassador, for the purpose of being present at his entry into Tangier, we accelerated our pace, with a view of coming up with him at L'Araich. We arrived at the forest of L'Araich at dusk, and travelled through it all night till five o'clock next morning.

Having travelled incessantly twenty-three hours without halting, being much fatigued, I desired Deeb to take a little rest with me in an adjacent field, and we sent on Bel Hage with the baggage to L'Araich, to wait our arrival at the ferry. We pursued our journey at seven o'clock, and entered the town at nine. On reaching the ferry, Bel Hage introduced a courier, who had been dispatched to me from Fas, by a friend of mine, who informed me how much he, and many of my Moorish friends had been disappointed, that I did not enter that city, where I understood preparations had been made for my entertainment, in the odoriferous gardens of the merchants of Fas. The courier brought me a present of gold wire and gold [126] thread, of the manufacture of Fas, and some gold ornaments of filligrane work from Timbuctoo, of the manufacture of Jinnie. It is more than probable that the Fasees learned the art of manufacturing gold thread from the Egyptians: it is much superior to that which is imported into Barbary from Marseilles. The ladies ornament their cambric dresses with it, and the Fas gold-thread never loses its colour by washing, but the French does; the Fas gold thread wears also much better, and is more durable; the change of colour may possibly originate from the great proportion of alloy in the gold of the French manufacture, whereas that of Fas, according to an imperial edict, must be of a certain fineness, approaching to pure gold; the gold wire of which it is made being first assayed by the (*M'tasseb*) supervisor of manufactures. Great quantities of gold thread are used in the elegant shawls and sashes of silk and gold made at Fas, the better kind of which are reserved for princes and bashaws, in which they use, as before observed, the Fas thread only. They manufacture also at Fas, a very correct imitation of amber-beads, impossible to be discriminated by the best judges, but by rubbing the artificial amber, and then applying it to a bit of cotton; the latter does not adhere, but the natural amber attracts the cotton as a magnet does iron; and this is the discriminating criterion whereby to distinguish them.

[127]

But, to return to our journey, we found the ambassador had passed the preceding day, we therefore crossed the river, and travelled on till nine o'clock at night, when, after being a-horseback thirty-four hours, refreshed only by two hours' sleep, we came up with the ambassadors, Cafila, and guard, in a fine open campaign country, half-way between Tangier and Arzilla; and soon after I received a courier from Sir Pieter Wyk, Swedish consul-general to the empire residing at Tangier, with a very friendly invitation to his house and table, which being the first offer and from a sincere and worthy friend, I with pleasure accepted it, and returned the express immediately. On the morning of the 22d June, I breakfasted at five o'clock with the ambassador, and, discussing with him my business, I learned that he had terminated it to my satisfaction. We started together at seven o'clock, and moved slowly on towards Tangier, it having been ordered by the emperor, that the English ambassador's entry into that town should be marked with every possible honour and attention. An hour before we reached Tangier, the governor, with the whole garrison, came out to salute and greet the ambassador, the cavalry running full gallop, and firing their muskets, as is the custom with them in all rejoicings. At half-past eleven the cannon of Tangier began to announce the ambassador's arrival, and continued, not a royal salute, but every gun in Tangier was discharged; and at twelve o'clock we entered the gates.

[128]

LETTER XIV.

Result of the British Embassy.

FROM HIS EXCELLENCY J.M. MATRA TO MR. J.

Dear Jackson;
Old Fez,
Sunday night, June 14, 1801.

After a most unpleasant and tedious negotiation of nine days, I have just finished my business. I march off early to-morrow morning, and am much employed in packing up, translating, and copying of papers.

The letter I solicited for you is just brought to me, mixed with Mr. Foxcroft's business, and the provision for the shipping in Mogadore; but the Talb promises to bring me a separate one very early in the morning, when I will inclose it to you.

Through the interest of Muly Abdel-melk-ben Driss, the orders were some time since sent to Mogadore, to reduce your new duty to the old standard of Seedi Muhamed.

I have been treated by the emperor like a prince, and with a friendly personal attention I had no idea of; but my business has been marvellously tormented. Of that, as we are to meet soon, I will say no more. I am half dead.

God bless you.
J. MATRA.

[129]

LETTER XV.

European Society at Tangier.--Sects and Divisions among Christians in Muhamedan Countries counteracts the Propagation of Christianity, and casts a Contempt upon Christians themselves.-- The Cause of it.--The Conversion of Africa should be preceded by an Imitation of the divine Doctrine of Christ among Christians themselves, as an Example eligible to follow.

TO JAMES WILLIS, ESQ.

It is not only the duty, but it is the manifest policy of Christians who reside in Muhamedan countries, to preserve that peace and harmony that is so often inculcated by our divine Master: there should be no followers of Paul or of Apollos, of the Pope or of Luther, but Christians altogether should forget sects, and become followers of Christ, by practising his divine and luminous doctrine. This principle, strictly adhered to, would have greater effect in propagating the Christian doctrine, than the united efforts, however arduous, of all the missionaries in Africa. We should first begin by reforming the manners of those Christians who are established in

Muhamedan countries, holding responsible situations, so as to show the Muhamedans, by their harmony and good will, the advantages of the benign influence of the great Christian principle, "Love thy neighbour as thyself." Until the disgraceful animosity lamentably prevalent between the Catholic and Protestant, [130] the Lutheran, Calvinist, and other sects of Christians be annihilated, it cannot be expected by any reasonable and reflecting mind, that essential progress can be made in the propagation of Christianity in Africa, at least in the Muhamedan part of it. We must purify our own actions, and set a laudable example of chaste and virtuous conduct, as a prelude to the conversion of the people of this continent. The Africans, viz. the Arabs, Berebbers, Shelluhs, Moors, and Negroes are, *generally* speaking, shrewd, acute, discerning races of men; and it cannot be supposed by any but insane enthusiasts, that the doctrines of Christ can be propagated in those countries, until an example be set for their imitation better than their own practice, and more conformable to the true Christian doctrine than any that has hitherto been offered for their imitation.

Tangier is the residence of the consuls-general of all the nations of Europe, who send occasionally ambassadors to the Court of Marocco; and these gentlemen generally act as envoys or ministers, as well as consuls. The English, French, Dutch, American, Spanish, Portuguese, Swedish, and Danish consuls reside here, some with their families, some without. I had not been long here before I perceived that the Moors of Tangier manifested an extraordinary contempt for Christians, the general respect which is shown to them at Mogodor, is unknown here. The reason is evident: the families of these [131] gentlemen were at variance with each other, and the respective ladies did not visit one another. This circumstance was too well known to the Moors, and materially contributed to create among those people that contempt for the Christians, which, perhaps, is due to all, whatever be their *professed* doctrines, who have not charity enough, in the correct acceptation of the word, to maintain harmony in their own community. I was shocked to see so many amiable families at variance. I will not declare if it was pride, ambition, or contention for pre-eminence that produced this want of harmony; but it is most certain, that Christians, whose destiny it is to reside among Muhamedans, should have more than ordinary care to preserve that philanthropic disposition to each other, which carries with it a high recommendation, particularly in a country like *West Barbary*, where the gate of every tent is open to the largest, most disinterested, and unqualified hospitality, and where the sheik of every douar considers it his first and indispensable duty to provide food and rest to the needy traveller, and to the stranger at his gate.

[132]

LETTER XVI.

Diary of a Journey from Tangier to Mogodor, showing the Distances from Town to Town, along the Coast of the Atlantic Ocean; useful to Persons travelling in that Country.

TO THE SAME.

Mogodor, 1801.

If you should ever come to this country, and have occasion to travel through it, the following journal of a journey from Tangier to Mogodor may be of service to you, in ascertaining the distances from one port to another, &c.

```
Departed from Tangier for Mogodor,
July 15, 1801, at 9 o'clock, A.M.              Hours.

Arrived at Arzilla, at 7, P.M.                   10

Mounted at 7, A.M.; arrived at L'Araich,
at 2, P.M.                                        7

Started at 5, A.M.; arrived at Ras Doura,
at 3, P.M.                                       10

Mounted at 6, A.M.; travelled three hours;
came to a plain, level country, and arrived
at Sallée, at 10 o'clock, P.M.                   16

Crossed the river in the ferry, and remained
at the French Consul's Hotel, at
Rabat, three days. Mounted at 9; arrived
at El Mensoria, at 9, P.M.                       12
[133]
Mounted at 6, A.M.; arrived at Dar El
Beida, at half-past 2, P.M.                      8-1/2

Proceeded without halting, and arrived at
the Douar of Woled Jeraar, at 9, P.M.
and pitched our tents                            7

Mounted at 5, A.M.; arrived at Azamore,
at 7, P.M.                                       14

Mounted at 7, A.M.; travelled southward,
leaving Mazagan to the right, and arrived
at the Douar of Woled Aisah, at
1 o'clock, P.M. and pitched our tents            6

Departed at 7, A.M.; arrived at El Woladia,
at 6, P.M.                                       11

Mounted at 8; arrived at Saffy, at 5            9

Started at 1, P.M.; rode six hours to the
river Tansift; slept at the Sanctuary
```

```
near the river                              6

Rose at midnight, struck the tents, and
mounted at 1 o'clock, A.M. arrived at
the Sanctuary of Seedi Buzurukton, at
11                                         10

Dined, slept, and started again at 4
o'clock, P.M. and entered Mogodor at
half-past 7 o'clock                       3-1/2

                                          ----
                                          130
```

Average rate of travelling, (including
stoppages,) three miles per hour, 390
miles in 130 hours.

[134]

LETTER XVII.

An Account of a Journey from Mogodor to Saffy, during a Civil War, in a Moorish Dress, when a Courier could not pass, owing to the Warfare between the two Provinces of Haha and Shedma.-- Stratagem adopted by the Author to prevent Detection.--Danger of being discovered.-- Satisfaction expressed by the Bashaw of Abda, Abdrahaman ben Nassar, on the Author's safe Arrival, and Compliments received from him on his having accomplished this perilous Journey.

TO THE SAME.

Mogodor, 1802.

Having arranged all my affairs, I awaited an opportunity to depart for England. A Spanish vessel was lying at the port of Saffy, nearly ready to sail, bound to Cadiz; but how to reach the former port was the difficulty; the provinces of Shedma and Haha, through which I must necessarily pass, were at war against each other, and an army of several thousand men were encamped at Ain el Hajar, a spring near the road, between Mogodor and Saffy; so that all communication was cut off, insomuch that it was dangerous, even for a courier, to attempt to pass from one port to the other. I was extremely anxious to reach Europe, and I determined to go to Saffy by land. I accordingly sent for a trusty Arab, whose character for fidelity I [135] had often before proved. I asked him if he would undertake to conduct me to Saffy. He required a day to consider of it. He then resolved to attempt it, provided I would adopt the dress of an Arab, and accompany him: I agreed; and we started from Mogodor at 4 o'clock; P.M. We passed into a convenient recess, to change my dress, which being done, we mounted our horses and rode away; we had not gone two hours, before some scouts of the army came galloping towards us. Billa (my trusty guide, who was a native of Shedma, and a man of considerable influence in that province) and his friend rode off with speed to meet them, and having satisfied them that we were about business relating to the army, they returned, and Billa's friend joining me, we inclined our steps towards the sea, whilst Billa kept guard at a distance; and, reaching a convenient and solitary retreat, we halted there till dark; when retracing our steps for a few miles, it was concerted that I should pass as a wounded man retiring from the army to have my wounds examined and dressed. Billa was so well acquainted with the roads, and all the bye-passes of the country, that, travelling fast over the plains, not on the roads, we soon reached to the northward of the encampments of Shedma. We passed several straggling parties from the army, who saluted us with (*Salem u alikume*) "Peace be to you;" to which we replied ("*Alikume assalam*") "To you peace;" and Billa added [136] "*Elm'joroh*," i.e. a wounded man. In the old bed of the river Tansift, now full of bushes of white broom, I narrowly escaped being discovered: as the day was breaking, a party of Arabs suddenly turned a corner, and I had just time to cover my mouth and chin with my (*silham*) cloak, before they gave the salutation, or they would have discovered me (being without a beard) to be a Christian; we passed the river, however, perfectly safe, and were then soon in the province of Abda, when all danger was at an end; we entered the town of Saffy, at two o'clock in the afternoon. The Bashaw of Abda, *Abdrahaman ben Nassar*, a renowned warrior, who had been at the head of an army of 60,000 horse, in opposition to the Emperor, Muley Soliman, received me with his accustomed urbanity and hospitality, and asked me if I had come to Saffy through the air, or by sea. I replied, I had come by neither, but by land. "How is it possible," said he, "that you could come by land, when even a courier could not pass. Did you meet with no impediment?--you astonish me: but praise be to God, that you have arrived safe, and you are welcome."

[137]

LETTER XVIII.

Journey to the Prince Abd Salam, and the Khalif Delemy, in Shtuka.--Encamped in his Garden.-- Mode of living in Shtuka.--Audience of the Prince.--Expedition to the Port of Tomie, in Suse.-- Country infested with rats.--Situation of Tomie.--Entertainment at a Douar of the Arabs of Woled Abbusebah.--Exertions of Delemy to entertain his Guests.--Arabian Dance aud Music.--Manner and Style of Dancing.--Eulogium of the Viceroys and Captains to the Ladies.--Manners of the latter.--Their personal Beauty.--Dress.--Desire of the Arabs to have a Commercial Establishment in their Country.--Report to the Prince respecting Tomie.--Its Contiguity to the Place of the Growth of various Articles of Commerce.--Viceroys offer to build a House, and the Duties.-- Contemplated Visit to Messa.--Nature of the Country.--Gold and Silver Mines.--Garden of Delemy.--Immense Water-melons and Grapes.----Mode of Irrigation.--Extraordinary People from Sudan at Delemy's.--Elegant Sword.--Extensive Plantations.--The Prince prepares to depart for Tafilelt.

TO THE SAME.

Santa Cruz, June 7, 1794.

I received a letter from the [118] Prince Muley Abdsalam, who lately went from Santa Cruz to the Khalif of Suse, Alkaid Muhamed ben Delemy, whose castle is in Shtuka. The prince wished to see me on some commercial business that had [138] been suggested to him by the khalif or viceroy. We (that is, Signor Andrea de Christi, a native of Italy, and a Dutch merchant established at Santa Cruz, and myself) prepared our tents and servants, and departed for Shtuka early in the morning. We passed through a fine campaign country, occupied by a tribe of the Woled Abbusebah Arabs, and arrived, late at night, at (*Luksebba*) the castle of Delemy, who was also sheik of an emigration of the Arabs called Woled Abbusebah, and of another emigration of Arabs called Woled Deleim, who had taken up their abodes in Shtuka. When we arrived, our reception was in the true style of Arabian hospitality. Delemy had prepared and had pitched tents in a large garden adjoining his castle, wherein we resided. Our own tents were pitched in the Mushoir, or place of audience, a spacious plain, enclosed by a wall, where the sheik gave audience to the various kabyls of Suse. The following day we had an audience of the prince, who requested me to accompany Delemy to a port of Suse, which had been formerly frequented by European ships, which took in water there, and ascertain if it were a port convenient for a commercial establishment. The name of this seaport was called Tomie by the Portuguese, who formerly had an establishment there; but by the Arabs, *Sebah Biure*, i.e. the Seven Wells, because there were seven wells of excellent water there: three of them, however, when we visited this port, were [139] filled up and useless. We left Delemy's castle in the afternoon, about two or three o'clock, and we went at a pace called by the Arabs *el herka* [119], over a plain country infested with rats, and the haunts of serpents, our horses continually stumbling over the rat-holes. We were, to the best of my recollection, about four hours going. We found Tomie, an open road, not altogether calculated to form an advantageous commercial establishment. Its situation with respect to the sea being somewhat objectionable. We sat down near one of the wells, and after Delemy and his guards had amused themselves with (*lab el borode*) running full gallop and firing, we drank Hollands till we became gay. The sun had just set, when we mounted our horses to return. After an hour's *herka*, we approached a douar of the Woled Abbusebah Arabs, who, seeing their sheik, came forward and kissed his stirrups, entreating him to pass the night with them, which, it appeared, would have been contrary to the etiquette of Arabian hospitality to refuse. Delemy, therefore, asked us if we would consent to sleep there; and, apologising for not conducting us to our own beds that night, again intimated, that it was, in a manner, incumbent on him, not to refuse. We, therefore, consented to stop. This noble-spirited Arab, anxious to entertain us, and justly conceiving that the beds and [140] habits of these Arabs were very different from what we had been accustomed to, sought to beguile the time, and accordingly endeavoured to engage some ladies belonging to the douar to dance, but they positively declined dancing before Christians. Delemy expostulated with them, representing the propriety of doing so, before the prince's guests; but the ladies apologised, by declaring that their splendid dancing dresses were not made up. Delemy, however, with the true energy of an Arab, was determined that he would make our abode here as pleasant as possible, and desirous also to show us the spirit of Arabian dancing, he went himself, accompanied by two of his friends, to a douar, at some miles' distance, and, after much persuasion, he prevailed on six young ladies to come and dance. In about two hours, the sheik returned, and informed us, that knowing that beds in the desert would not suit our customs, he had engaged some young girls to amuse us with dancing during the night, assuring us at the same time that they excelled in that graceful art, and he had no doubt they would amuse us. The tents were cleared and lighted; two sheep were killed, and the *cuscasoe* was preparing, when the ladies arrived. The music consisted of an instrument similar to a flageolet, (*tabla*) a kettle-drum, and a sort of castanets of steel, an *erbeb*, or fiddle with two strings, played with a semicircular bow. The tunes were gay and sprightly, and the damsels tripped along on the [141] light fantastic toe in a very superior and elegant style. They danced without men; advancing gently at first, apparently without taking the foot off the ground, but gradually advancing; after which they performed some steps similar to those in the Spanish bolera; and, turning round on the toe, they danced a most elegant *shawl* dance, equal to what was danced at the Opera in London by Parisot, but without the horizontal movement, or any motion that could offend the chastest eye. This unique national dance was encouraged from time to time by the approbation of twelve captains of the viceroy's guard, warriors of fame in arms, who were Arabs of the Woled Deleim, and who were seated in a circle, with us, round the dancers, expressing their delight and gratification in witnessing such superior grace and elegance, exclaiming--

"Afakume el Arabe, makine fal el Arabe,

El Hashema, u zin, u temara, fie el Arabe."

"Bravo, O Arabs! there is none equal to the Arabs:

Excellent is the modesty, beauty, and virtue of the Arabs."

Footnote 118: (return) Elder Brother of the present Emperor of Marocco, Muley Soliman.

Footnote 119: (return) A pace similar to that which European cavalry go when charging.

These eulogiums were not lost on the ladies, who increased the spirit of the dance. When this amusement had continued about three hours, the cuscasoe, meat, and vegetables were brought in, as a supper. The Moors ate plentifully; but the abstemious Arabs ate very little; the ladies partook of sweet cakes and dates; they very seldom chew meat, but when they do, they [142] think it gross to swallow it, they only press the juices from the meat, and throw away the substance. The manners of these damsels were elegant, accompanied with much suavity and affability, but very modest and unassuming withal: indeed, they were all individuals, as I afterwards learned, belonging to respectable and ancient Arab families, who could not resist the exhortations of their sheik to amuse and entertain his guests. The manners of these Arabs, their elegant forms, sparkling black eyes, long black eye-lashes, which increased the beauty of the eye, adding character to the countenance, seemed to make an indelible impression on the whole party. The ladies wore robes of Indian muslin, girdles of gold thread, interwoven with silk of the Fas manufacture; and their shawls of silk and gold were displayed in various elegant devices. We were given to understand by Delemy's captains, on our return to the sheik's castle, that we had been entertained with extraordinary honours: we certainly were highly gratified, and my friend Signor Andrea declared he had never seen better dancing at Venice, his native place. Among the

Arabs was an old man of ninety, who appeared very desirous of an European establishment at Tomie. He related several anecdotes of his life; and, among others, the money he had gained, by purchasing goods of vessels which came forty or fifty years before to Tomie for water, with which he said he used to exchange gums and almonds, feathers and ivory, for linens, [143] cloths, and spices. I am disposed to think these vessels were Portuguese; for this coast is but little known to the English. The ladies having returned home, we prepared to leave this douar early in the morning; and with no small regret did I quit this abode of simple and patriarchal hospitality; a pleasing contrast was here formed to the dissipation and pleasure of civilised life--to the life of fashionable society, where the refinements of luxury have multiplied their artificial wants beyond the proportion of the largest fortunes, and have brought most men into the class of the necessitous, inducing that churlish habit of the mind, in which every feeling is considered as a weakness, which terminates not in self, unlike those generous sympathies of the Arabs, where every individual seems impelled to seek, as they express it, (*ê dire el khere fie nes*) "to do good to men." The effect of luxury, dissipation, and extravagance, (where the fortune is not large enough to support them,) tends to render man selfish upon principle, and extinguishes all genuine public spirit, that is, all real regard to the interests and good order of society; substituting in its place, the vile ambition and rapacity of the demagogue, which, however, assumes the name of patriotism. This contrast between the temperance and sobriety of these Bedouin or primitive Arabs, and the luxury and dissipation of civilised life, was the more remarkable, when we observed among this rude people such extraordinary and mutual exercise of benevolence, manly and open presence, honesty and [144] truth in their words and actions.--On our return to Delemy's castle, in Shtuka, the Prince asked me, what observations I had made respecting Tomie; I told his Royal Highness that it was an open roadstead, and not a convenient place for ships to lie. The Prince appeared pleased at this report; but Delemy had rendered to Muley Abdsalam so many essential services, that the latter could not, in courtesy, refuse him any thing. When Delemy found that my report to the Prince did not realise his expectations, offers were made to me, supported by every possible encouragement, to form a commercial establishment at Tomie, which, as was observed, being advantageously situated for trade, being in the neighbourhood of the gum, almond, and oil countries, would offer advantages to the merchants which they could not expect at Santa Cruz, or Mogodor. Accordingly, I was urged to send to Europe for ships, with assurances that the duty on all imports, as well as exports, should be only two per cent. *ad valorem.* A house was offered to be built for me, according to any plan I might choose to suggest, free of expense. The people were desirous of having a commercial establishment in their country, and would have done any thing to accomplish this object. The extensive connections which I had throughout Suse, Sahara, and even at Timbuctoo, would have facilitated my operations; but my connections in England were not such as to enable me to engage advantageously in this enterprise, I was obliged, therefore, though reluctantly, to decline it, although, if otherwise [145] situated, I might have realised an independent fortune in two or three years at Tomie, besides having a most favourable opportunity of opening a trade with Timbuctoo, and other territories of Sudan.

I now felt a strong inclination to visit the port of Messa, which was reported to have been about two centuries before, a considerable port of trade, and the capital of Suse, when that country was a separate kingdom, and the state-prisoners were banished to Sejin-messa [120], (commonly called Segelmessa in the maps;) as the state prisoners of Marocco have been from time immemorial, and are to this day sent to Tafilelt, which territory lies contiguous to, and west of Sejin-messa. We started for Messa in the morning, and reached the town in the afternoon. Delemy sent a strong guard with me for protection, with an injunction to his friend the *fakeer* of Messa, to treat me as his friend and guest, and to do whatever he could to gratify my curiosity in every respect. The country about Messa is very picturesque, and productive: the river also abounds with romantic scenery, it has a sandbar at its entrance to the ocean, which is dry at low water; but it was once navigable several miles up, as was reported to me. On the south bank of the river, about two miles from the sea, is a gold-mine, in the territory of a tribe hostile [146] to Delemy, but the influence of the Fakeer, who is held in reverential awe, enabled us to examine it without danger. What they told us was the entrance, was filled with immense large pieces of rock-stone; and I was informed, that when the Christians left the place, (the Portuguese, no doubt,) they placed these stones at the entrance of the mine, to prevent the natives from getting access to it. In the bed of the river, near the sea, is a mine of silver; the ore is in very small particles, like lead-coloured sand, intermixed with mud. I sent a small quantity of this to England to be analysed; and it produced, as I was informed, just enough to pay the expenses of analysation. I sent also several specimens of gold and silver ore, which I collected in various parts of Suse; but I apprehend that sufficient attention was not paid to them, and they also scarcely paid for the analysation. I sent also to the Honourable Mr. Greville, brother to the late Earl of Warwick, a great many basaltick and other stones, collected in the mountains of Barbary, which that gentleman considered valuable. After remaining two days at Messa, I returned to Shtuka. I was again urged to form an establishment at Tomie; but, limited as my connection was in England, I did not feel competent to the undertaking, and was obliged, reluctantly indeed, but finally, to decline it.

Footnote 120: (return) Sejin Messa signifies the prison of Messa.

The garden of Delemy, where we encamped, is stocked with very fine vines from the mountains [147] of Idautenan, [121] a mountainous and independent country, a few miles north of Santa Cruz; these grapes were of the black or purple kind, as big as an ordinary-sized walnut, and very sweet flavoured, as much superior to the finest Spanish grapes, as the latter are superior to the natural grown grapes of England. Large pomegranates, exquisitely sweet, the grains very large, and the seed small, brought from Terodant; figs, peaches, apricots, strawberries, oranges, citrons of an enormous size, water-melons, weighing fifty pounds each, four of which were a camel load, together with culinary vegetables of every description. This garden was watered by a well, having what is called a Persian wheel, worked by a horse, having pots all round the perpendicular wheel, which, as they turn round, discharge their contents into a trough, which communicated to the garden, and laid the beds under [148] water. This is the general mode of irrigation throughout west and south Barbary, as well as in Sudan.

Footnote 121: (return) The mountains of Idautenan divide the province of Haha from Suse: they are exempt from *Ska u Laskor*, that is, two per cent. on live stock, and 10 per cent. on produce which is the regular impost on the country. They are a brave race of Shelluhs, inhabiting a table-land in the mountains that is a perfect terrestrial paradise. There is but one person in Europe besides myself who has ever been in this country. Sheik Mûluke, the sheik of Idautenan, is a generous noble-spirited independent character. When an emperor dies, the sheik sends Muley Ismael's firman, emancipating the district from all impost or contribution to the revenue, for some military service rendered by this district to the ancestor of Ismael, and the succeeding emperors invariably confirm their emancipation of Idautenan.

The Prince was very anxious to be of service to Delemy, who had ingratiated himself with the former, by signalising himself in feats of arms. He had been also a main pillar to the throne, and I sincerely regretted that the combination of circumstances did not permit me to accept the liberal and advantageous offers made to me.

Delemy's renown had spread far to the south, even unto Sudan: from the latter country he was visited by some people, who wore circular rings of pure gold, through the cartilage of the nose. The rings were two or three inches in diameter; and when these people ate, they turned them up over the nose. Delemy had received a present, from some king of Sudan, of a very elegant sword, ornamented with diamonds, rubies, and emeralds, he showed me this sword, which was evidently manufactured in Europe; he told me, he had been offered 5000 dollars for it; but he had been informed that it was worth double that sum.

I was invited by the Khalif of Suse to visit the immensely extensive plantations of olives at Ras el Wed, near Terodant, through which a man may proceed a whole day's journey without exposure to the sun: also he offered to accompany me to the eastern part of Shtuka, where the produce of bitter and sweet almonds is equally abundant, and the plantations equally extensive with those of the olive at Ras el Wed; but I had [149] seen plantations of both on a smaller scale at Ait-Musie, Fruga, and other parts of this empire; and therefore the sight would have been no novelty, except in extent. I understood these plantations were on the same plan and principle with those I had seen, leaving at certain distances, square openings, to admit the air, for the better promotion of the growth and increase of the fruit and produce of the trees.

The Prince was preparing to depart through Draha, and Bled el Jereed, to Tafilelt; and we had our audience of leave previous to his departure.

[150]

LETTER XIX.

Journey from Santa Cruz to Mogodor, when no Travellers ventured to pass, owing to civil War and Contention among the Kabyles.--Moorish Philanthropy in digging Wells for the Use of Travellers.--Travelled with a trusty Guide without Provisions, Tents, Baggage, or Incumbrances.--Nature of the Warfare in the Land. Bitter Effects of Revenge and Retaliation on the Happiness of Society.--Origin of these civil Wars between the Families and Kabyles.--Presented with Honey and Butter for Breakfast.--Patriarchal Manner of living among the Shelluhs compared to that of Abraham.--Aromatic Honey.--Ceremony at Meals, and Mode of eating.--Travelled all Night, and slept in the open Air;--Method of avoiding the Night-dew, as practised by the Natives.--Arrival at Mogodor.

TO THE SAME.

Santa Cruz, April 7, 1795.

The province of Haha was in arms; caffilahs, and travellers could not pass; but it was expedient that I should go to Mogodor. Men of property in this country, influenced by a philanthropic spirit, often expend large sums in digging wells in districts, through which caffilahs pass, on their road from one country to another. I knew one of these philanthropists who was at Santa Cruz, and who had recently benefited the province of Haha, by having dug a well in the Kabyl of Benitamer, a mountainous district in [151] Haha; I sent for him, and as he was under obligations to me for various services I had rendered to him and his family, he consented to accompany me to Mogodor, through the disturbed province of Haha; and he assured me, that his influence throughout that province was such, that, by travelling quick, and without any baggage, tents, or incumbrances, he did not doubt of conducting me safe to Mogodor. I agreed to go with him, without servants, tents, or bedding, being determined to reconcile myself, under present circumstances, to the accommodation the country might afford. We started from Santa Cruz at sun-set; travelling through Tamaract, to the river Beni Tamur. We continued our journey till we arrived, at the dawn of day, at the foot of immense high mountains, called Idiaugomoron. Here my companion and guide L'Hage Muhamed bu Zurrawel, pointed out to me two castellated houses, about two miles distant from each other; the family-quarrels of these people had produced such animosity, that the inhabitants of neither house could with safety go out, for fear of being overpowered and killed by those of the other; so that wherever they went, they were well armed, but dared not go far. These two families were preparing for a siege, which often happens in this province. Thus the inhabitants of one house attack another, and sometimes exterminate or put to death the whole family, with their retainers. The province of Haha was thus in a state of the most lamentable [152] civil war, originating from these family-quarrels and domestic feuds. The heathen and anti-christian principle of revenge and retaliation, is here pursued with such bitter and obstinate animosity, that I have known instances of men relinquishing their vocation, to go into a far country to revenge the blood of a relation after a lapse of twenty years, and pursue the object of his revenge, for some murder committed in his family, perhaps forty or fifty years before.

To a British public, blessed with the benign influences of the Christian doctrine, it is perhaps necessary that I should elucidate this retaliative doctrine by an example:--Two men quarrel, and fight; they draw their kumäyas (curved daggers about 12 inches long), which all the people of Haha wear, as well as all the clans or kabyles of Shelluhs; and if one happens to give his antagonist a *deadly* wound, it becomes an indispensable duty in the next of kin to the person killed or murdered, (though perhaps it can hardly be termed a murder, as it is not committed, like an European duel, in cold blood, but in the moment of irritation, and at a period when the mind is under the influence of anger,) to seek his revenge by watching an opportunity to kill the survivor in the contest. If the former should die, his next of kin takes his place, and pursues his enemy, whose life is never safe; insomuch that, whole kabyles, when this deadly animosity has reached its acme, have been known to quit their country and emigrate into the Sahara; for when [153] the second death has been inflicted, it then becomes the incumbent duty of the next of kin of the deceased to seek his revenge: they call this justifying blood. This horrible custom has the most lamentable influence on the happiness of human life; for there will sometimes be several individuals seeking the life of one man, till this principle, pervading all the ramifications of relationship and consanguinity, produces family-broils, hostility, and murder, *ad infinitum!!* We stopped at a friend of L'Hage Muhamed, who presented us with honey and butter, thin shavings of the latter being let to fall into a bowl of honey for breakfast. This bowl was served up with flat cakes kneaded without leaven, and baked on hot stones; these are converted from corn into food in less than half an hour; they are in shape similar to our crumpets or pancakes. We were pressed by this Shelluh to stay and dine with him, which being agreed to, he sent a shepherd to his flock to kill a fat young kid, which was roasted with a wooden spit, before the vital heat had subsided, which was very tender, and of an exquisite flavour. The bread or cakes above described appear to be similar to what the women kneaded for the guests in the patriarchal ages: indeed, the customs of these people, as well as those of the Arabs, is precisely the same as they were in the patriarchal ages, and which are delineated in the 18th chapter of Genesis, 1st to the 8th verse.

[154]

The honey of this province is very fine: it has an aromatic flavour, derived from the wild thyme and other aromatic herbs on which the bees feed. Among these people every meal is preceded with a washing of their hands with water, which is brought round for the purpose in a brass pan; each guest dips his right hand in the pan, and a napkin is presented to wipe them; they then break the bread, and, after saying grace, which is universally this,--*bismillah*, i.e. "in the name of God," each guest takes a bit of bread, dips it in the honey and butter, and eats it. It is reckoned uncourteous or vulgar to bite the bread; therefore the piece broken off is sufficient for a mouthful, so that there is nothing that should offend a delicate appetite in this antique mode of eating. We remained several hours with our hospitable Shelluh friend; and we departed, after taking a little sleep, at four o'clock in the afternoon. Travelling all night, we arrived, at the dawn of day, at a large house in Idaugourd; the Shelluh to whom it belonged brought us carpets, and we slept under the wall of his house till the sun arose. The people of this country prefer sleeping in the open air to a room, and they have an excellent mode of securing themselves from the heavy dews of the night, by covering their heads and faces with a thin woollen hayk or garment, which they throw over their heads and faces. When I have had the Arabs of Sahara (who have conducted the caffilahs from Timbuctoo) at my house at Santa Cruz, I gave them a long narrow room, 48 feet long, which [155] was called (*beet assuda*) the apartment of Sudan, to sleep in; but they invariably came out at night, and placed their carpets and mats, as beds, outside of the room, and slept under the balustrade, in preference to the confinement, as they called it, of a room.

We rose at sun-rise, passed through the picturesque district of Idaugourd and the Woolja, and entered Mogodor at four o'clock, P.M.

[156]

AN ACCOUNT

OF THE

RISE, PROGRESS, AND DECREASE

OF

THE PLAGUE

That ravaged Barbary in 1799;

**FAITHFULLY EXTRACTED FROM
LETTERS WRITTEN BY THE HOUSE OF JAMES JACKSON
AND CO., OR BY JAMES G. JACKSON,
MERCHANTS AT MOGODOR,**

**TO THEIR CORRESPONDENTS IN EUROPE, DURING THE
EPIDEMY.**

Fragments respecting the Plague.

When the Emperor's army proceeded from Fas to Marocco in the summer of 1799, a detachment of which passed by Mogodor, consisting of 20,000 horse and 10,000 foot, it had the plague with it; so that, wherever it passed, the plague uniformly appeared three days after its arrival at the respective douars near which it encamped; those who died were buried in the tents, and the people of the provinces knew little about it.

A large *akkaba* [122], consisting of upwards of 1700 camels, arrived 23d August, 1799, at Akka [157] from Timbuctoo, laden with gum-sudan, ostrich-feathers, and gold dust, which had brought also many slaves; this *akkaba* had deposited its merchandize at Akka, till the plague should disappear and the country become healthy; as the people of that territory, unlike Muhamedans in general, will hold no communication with the infected, nor will they admit any one from these parts.

Footnote 122: (return) An *akkaba* is an accumulated caravan.

Mogodor, April 31, 1799.

A violent fever now rages at Fas: some assert it to be the plague, but that is Moorish report, and little to be depended on; the European consuls at Tangier, and the Spanish ambassador, who, having terminated his embassy, has lately left Mequinas, mention it as an epidemical disorder.

May 20. The small-pox rages violently throughout this country, and is of a most virulent kind: its origin is ascribed to the famine that has of late pervaded this country, and which was produced by the incredible devastation of the devouring locusts; the dregs of olives, after the oil had been extracted, has been the only food that could be procured by many thousands.

Mogodor, June 14, 1799.

Various reports reach us daily from *the city of Marocco*, respecting the epidemy that prevails there, some say 200 die, some say 100, others [158] limit the daily mortality to 50, in a population, according to the imperial register, of 270,000.

When any *light* rain falls, as is the case at Marocco at this season of the year, the mortality increases. Mr. Francisco Chiappe, an Italian merchant, is just arrived from Marocco, and is performing quarantine, by his own desire, at the Emperor's garden. [123] This gentleman reports, that the greater portion of the people die of fear, from hunger, or bad food, or from the small-pox, which latter has raged at Marocco the last month or two; but he had not been able to ascertain, so various were the reports, whether it was the plague or not. The emperor's army, a division of which passed through this country, and encamped at the river, about two miles south of this port, had the distemper with it. We have been assured, that the soldiers who died, were immediately buried within the tents, so that, by this stratagem, the mortality was not perceived by the public; it was apprehended that, if the mortality were known, the kabyls, through which the army passed from Mequinas to Marocco, would not have supplied the troops with provision. This detachment consisted of 20,000 horse and 10,000 foot. No disorder has yet appeared here, nor in the adjacent provinces of Shedma and Haha.

Footnote 123: (return) A garden in the province of Haha, five miles from Mogodor, that was presented to the European merchants by the late sultan, Seedy Muhamed ben Abdallah.

[159]

July 5. We dispatched the Spanish brig yesterday; but she is still at anchor in the road, waiting for passengers, who fly from hence with precipitation, from fear of the fever or plague, which prevails at Fas and at Marocco, and which, it is reported, has made its appearance at the port of Saffy. We have, however, nothing of the kind here yet, though we expect we shall not escape the general scourge.

July 13. The epidemy in the interior provinces has greatly augmented, insomuch, that the demand for linen to bury the dead rapidly increases, and the stock is almost exhausted. This article has risen to an unprecedented price. All the relatives of L'Hage Abdallah have fallen victims to the epidemy. This gentleman is consequently in possession of very considerable property; and (if he be not also carried off) there will be no fear of our recovering the debt he owes you.

We cannot ascertain if the disorder prevails in the outer town, and in the Jews' quarter, or not; it is certain, however, that eight or ten die daily of the small-pox, and as many more of fevers and other disorders, as report proclaims.

July 25. We are so much engaged in making arrangements against the epidemy, which is now confidently reported to us to be the plague, of a most deadly species, that we have only time to refer you to the captain of the Aurora, to whom we have communicated every particular, and who [160] is extremely anxious to be off for England. The deaths in this town, which contained a population of 10,000, according to the imperial register, are from forty to fifty each day.

Aug. 1. As the plague now rages violently here, no one thinks of business or the affairs of this world; but each individual anticipates that he will be next called away. I send the inclosed, to be forwarded to Mr. Andrea de Christo, at Amsterdam, to announce to him the sudden death of his partner, Mr. J. Pacifico, who is lately dead of the plague. I paid him a visit a few hours before his death; I met there Don Pedro de Victoria, who was smoking a segar; he offered me one, and urged me to smoke it. I believe that the smoke of tobacco is anti-pestilential; this, added to the precaution of avoiding contact, and inhalation of the breath of the person infected, appears to be quite sufficient to secure a person from infection.

Aug. 1. (Translation of a letter to Mr. Andrea de Christi, merchant at Amsterdam.) We are sorry that the subject of this letter is so melancholy. All our domestics have left us; the plague rages so violently here, that the daily mortality is from sixty to seventy, among which we are sorry to announce the death of your partner, Mr. J. Pacifico, who died two days since.

August 23. The best gum is selling at Akka for six dollars a quintal: they will not bring it here, fearing the infection. A large Brazil ship has been wrecked off Cape Noon, [161] her cargo, consisting for the most part of silks and linens, is estimated at half a million of dollars. The Arabs of Sahara convert the most beautiful lace into bridles for their horses, by twisting it; and superior silk stockings are selling at Wedinoon at a dollar per dozen pair. The plague is rapidly diminishing from 100 deaths to 20 or 30 per day. Meeman Corcoes is dead, as well as most of the principal tradesmen of Marocco and Fas; whole families have been swept off, and there is none left to inherit their property. Immense droves of horses, mules, and cattle of every description stray in the plains without owners.

September 5. The plague continues to decrease; and in another month we expect to be quite free from it. Signor Conton died this morning of the epidemy; yesterday afternoon he was apparently quite well, and paid me a visit. He wished me to shake hands with him, which I declined, alleging as an excuse, that I would dispense with that custom till the plague should pass over. He drank a glass of wine, and appeared cheerful and in good health. I have had fixed in my dining room, a table that extends from one end to the other. I walk or sit on one side of the table, my visitors on the other. I am only cautious to avoid personal contact. All the houses of the other merchants are closely barricaded or bolted. A fumigating pot of gum [162] sandrac stands at the entrance of my house, continually burning, which diffuses an agreeable perfume, but is not, as I apprehend, an antidote to the epidemy.

October 1. We have to apprise you of the decease of L'Hage Abdallah El Hareishy, most of whose relations are dead. His brother is the only one of the family besides himself that remains: he has inherited considerable property, and thence will be enabled to pay your bill on him in our favour.

October 29. The plague appears to have ceased in this town. All the merchants have opened their houses; but the disorder continues in the provinces, from whence there is little or no communication with the town. The kabyls seem to be wholly engaged in burying their dead, in arranging the affairs of their respective families, in dividing the property inherited by them, and in administering consolation to the sick.

Nov. 11. The plague having committed incalculable ravages throughout this country, had put a stop to all commerce, which now begins to revive, in proportion as that calamity subsides. Linens are selling to great advantage, a cargo would now render 60 per cent. profit, clear of all charges.

Nov. 29. The deadly epidemy that has lately visited us, and which at one period carried off above 100 each day, has now confined its [163] daily mortality to two or three; some days none. When, however, the Arabs of Shedma, and the Shelluhs of Haha come to town, and bring the clothes of their deceased relations for sale, the epidemy increases to three, four, and five a day; then, in three or four days, it declines again to its former number, one, two, or three. We have reason to expect, that, before the vessels which we expect from London shall arrive, the plague will have subsided entirely.

Mogodor, Dec. 12. 1799. The plague or mortality of this town is now reduced to three or four weekly.

OBSERVATION.

After the plague had subsided, a murrain attacked the cattle, and great numbers of all kinds died; so that they became reduced in the same proportion as the race of man had been reduced before.

Letter from His Excellency James M. Matra to
Mr. Jackson.

Gibraltar, 28th Oct. 1799.

Dear Jackson;

Within a few days of each other, I received your packets of the 21st of September, and 8th instant. Their inclosures are of course [164] taken care of. Your letter about Soke Assa was received, and sent home to government ages ago.

I never could understand the drift of the people either at Tangier or Mogodor, in asserting that my report of the plague was political. God knows, that our politics in Barbary are never remarkable for refinement: they are, if any thing, rather too much in the John Bull style; and the finesse they gave me such credit for, was absolutely beyond my comprehension, as I never could discover what advantage a genuine well-established plague in Barbary could be to our country. Of its existence I had not the shadow of doubt, for more than eight months before it was talked of; and when Doctor Bell was going that way, I begged of him to be particular in his enquiries, which he, as usual, neglected. When John Salmon [124] was up, he was *very particular*, and *I* of course was laughed at. *Here* I saw politics, and told all the gentlemen, that when Salmon [125] arrived at Tariffa, then, and not till then, we should have the plague in Barbary; and just so it turned out.

Footnote 124: (return) John Salmon was Spanish envoy to the emperor of Marocco, and was at this time up at Fas, *i.e.* on his embassy.

Footnote 125: (return) Arrived at Tariffa, and so secured his admission into Spain on his return from his embassy.

[165]

I am confident, if my advice had been taken, the disease might have been checked in the beginning; for it was almost three quarters of a year confined to *old* Fas. I wrote in the most pressing manner to Ben Ottoman [126], who never believed me. A few days before he was seized with it, he wrote me a melancholy letter for advice, and pathetically lamented that he had not listened to me in time; and I suppose that even Broussonet [127] believed me when he embarked. I hope your opinion that it diminishes with you will prove well founded; but I fear its ravages are only suspended by the great heats; besides, you should recollect that people cannot die twice, and with a population so diminished, you must not expect so many as formerly on your daily dead-list. Mrs. M., who desires her remembrance to you, is well, but barring plague, would rather be at Tangier than Gibraltar; so would I.

Ever truly thine,
J. MATRA.

Footnote 126: (return) The emperor's prime-minister, or *talb cadus* at that time.

Footnote 127: (return) Dr. Broussonet, French consul. This gentleman was intendant of the botanical garden at Montpelier: he, with another doctor embarked for Europe just as the plague began to appear at Mogodor in the year 1799.

[166]

Some Account of a peculiar Species of Plague which depopulated West Barbary in 1799 and 1800, and to the Effects of which the Author was an eye-witness.

From various circumstances and appearances, and from the character of the epidemical distemper which raged lately in the south of Spain, there is every reason to suppose, it was similar to that distemper or plague which depopulated West Barbary; for, whether we call it by the more reconcileable appellation of the epidemy, or yellow fever, it was undoubtedly a plague, and a most destructive one; for wherever it prevailed, it invariably carried off, in a few months, one-half, or one-third, of the population.

It does not appear how the plague originated in Fas in the year 1799. [128] Some persons, who were there at the time it broke out, have confidently ascribed it to infected merchandise imported into that place from the East; whilst others, of equal veracity and judgment, have not scrupled to ascribe it to the locusts which had infested West Barbary during the seven preceding years, the destruction of which was followed by the (*jedrie*) small-pox, which pervaded [167] the country, and was generally fatal. The *jedrie* is supposed to be the forerunner of this species of epidemy, as appears by an ancient Arabic manuscript, which gives an account of the same disorder having carried off two-thirds of the inhabitants of West Barbary about four centuries since. But however this destructive epidemy originated, its leading features were novel, and its consequences more dreadful than the common plague of Turkey, or that of Syria, or Egypt. Let every one freely declare his own sentiments about it; let him assign any credible account of its rise, or the causes that introduced so terrible a scene. I shall relate only what its symptoms were, what it actually was, and how it terminated, having been an eye-witness of its dreadful effects, and having seen and visited many who were afflicted, and who were dying with it.

Footnote 128: (return) See the Author's observations, in a letter to Mr. Willis, in Gentleman's Magazine, February, 1805.

In the month of April, 1799, a dreadful plague, of a most destructive nature, manifested itself in the city of Old Fas, which soon after communicated itself to the new city. This unparalleled calamity, carried off one or two the first day, three or four the second day, six or eight the third day, and increasing progressively, until the mortality amounted to two in the hundred of the aggregate population, continuing *with unabating violence*, ten, fifteen, or twenty days; being of longer duration in old than in new towns; then diminishing in a progressive proportion from one thousand a day to nine hundred, [168] then to eight hundred, and so on until it disappeared. Whatever recourse was had to medicine and to physicians was unavailing; so that such expedients were at length totally relinquished, and the people, overpowered by this terrible scourge, lost all hopes of surviving it.

Whilst it raged in the town of Mogodor, a small village, *Diabet*, situated about two miles south-east of that place, remained uninfected, although the communication was open between them: on the *thirty-fourth day*, however, after its first appearance at Mogodor, this village was discovered to be infected, and the disorder raged with great violence, making dreadful havock among the human species for *twenty-one* days, carrying off, during that period, one hundred persons out of one hundred and thirty-three, the original population of the village, before the plague visited it; none died after this, and those who were infected, recovered in the course of a month or two, some losing an eye, or the use of a leg or an arm.

Many similar circumstances might be here adduced relative to the numerous and populous villages dispersed through the extensive Shelluh province of Haha, all which shared a similar or a worse fate. Travelling through this province shortly after the plague had exhausted itself, I saw many uninhabited ruins, which I had before witnessed as flourishing villages; on making enquiry concerning the population of these dismal [169] remains, I was informed that in one village, which contained six hundred inhabitants, four persons only had escaped the ravage. Other villages, which had contained four or five hundred, had only seven or eight survivors left to relate the calamities they had suffered. Families which had retired to the country to avoid the infection, on returning to town, when all infection had apparently ceased, were generally attacked, and died; a singular instance of this kind happened at Mogodor, where, after the mortality had subsided, a corps of troops arrived from the city of Terodant, in the province of Suse, where the plague had been raging, and had subsided; these troops, after remaining three days at Mogodor, were attacked with the disease, and it raged exclusively among them for about a month, during which it carried off two-thirds of their original number, one hundred men; during this interval the other inhabitants of the town were exempt from the disorder, though these troops were not confined to any particular quarter, many of them having had apartments in the houses of the inhabitants of the town.

The destruction of the human species in the province of Suse was considerably greater than elsewhere; Terodant, formerly the metropolis of a kingdom, but now that of Suse, lost, when the infection was at its acme, about eight hundred each day; the ruined, but still extensive [170] city of Marocco [129], lost one thousand each day; the populous cities of Old and New Fas diminished in population twelve or fifteen hundred each day [130], insomuch, that in these extensive cities, the mortality was so great, that the living having not time to bury the dead, the bodies were deposited or thrown altogether into large holes, which, when nearly full, were covered over with earth. All regulations in matters of sepulture before observed were now no longer regarded; things sacred and things prophane had now lost their distinction, and universal despair pervaded mankind. Young, healthy, and robust persons of full stamina, were, for the most part, attacked first, then women and children, and lastly, thin, sickly, emaciated, and old people.

Footnote 129: (return) I have been informed that there are still at Marocco, apartments wherein the dead were placed; and that after the whole family was swept away the doors were built up, and remain so to this day.

Footnote 130: (return) There died, during the whole of the above periods, in the city of Marocco, 50,000; in Fas, 65,000; in Mogodor, 4500; and in Saffy, 5000; in all 124,500 souls!

After this violent and deadly calamity had subsided, we beheld a general alteration in the fortunes and circumstances of men; we saw persons who before the plague were common labourers, now in possession of thousands, and keeping horses without knowing how to ride them. Parties of this description were met wherever we went, and the men of family called [171] them in derision *el wuratu*, the inheritors. [131] Provisions also became extremely cheap and abundant; the flocks and herds had been left in the fields, and there was now no one to own them; and the propensity to plunder, so notoriously attached to the character of the Arab, as well as to the Shelluh and Moor, was superseded by a conscientious regard to justice, originating from a continual apprehension of dissolution, and that the *el khere* [132], as the plague was now called, was a judgment of the Omnipotent on the disobedience of man, and that it behoved every individual to amend his conduct, as a preparation to his departure for paradise.

Footnote 131: (return) *Des gens parvenus*, as the French express it; or upstarts.

Footnote 132: (return) The good, or benediction.

The expense of labour at the same time increased enormously [133], and never was equality in the human species more conspicuous than at this time; when corn was to be ground, or bread baked, both were performed in the houses of the affluent, and prepared by themselves, for the very few people whom the plague had spared, were insufficient to administer to the wants of the rich and independent, and they were accordingly compelled to work for themselves, performing personally the menial offices of their respective families.

[172]

Footnote 133: (return) At this time I received from Marocco a caravan of many camel-loads of bees-wax, in serrons containing 200 lbs. each; I sent for workmen to place them one upon another, and they demanded one dollar per serron for so moving them.

The country being now depopulated, and much of the territory without owners, vast tribes of Arabs emigrated from their abodes in the interior of Sahara, and took possession of the country contiguous to the river Draha, as well as many districts in Suse; and, in short, settling themselves, and pitching their tents wherever they found a fertile country with little or no population.

The symptoms of this plague varied in different patients, the variety of age and constitution gave it a like variety of appearance and character. Those who enjoyed perfect health were suddenly seized with head-aches and inflammations; the tongue and throat became of a vivid red, the breath was drawn with difficulty, and was succeeded by sneezing and hoarseness; when once settled in the stomach, it excited vomitings of black bile, attended with excessive torture, weakness, hiccough, and convulsion. Some were seized with sudden shivering, or delirium, and had a sensation of such intense inward heat, that they threw off their clothes, and would have walked about naked in quest of water wherein to plunge themselves. Cold water was eagerly resorted to by the unwary and imprudent, and proved fatal to those who indulged in its momentary relief. Some had one, two, or more buboes, which formed themselves, and [173] became often as large as a walnut, in the course of a day; others had a similar number of carbuncles; others had both buboes and carbuncles, which generally appeared in the groin, under the arm, or near the breast. Those who were affected [134] with a shivering, having no buboe, carbuncle, spots, or any other exterior disfiguration, were invariably carried off in less than twenty-four hours, and the body of the deceased became quickly putrified, so that it was indispensably necessary to bury it a few hours after dissolution. It is remarkable, that the birds of the air fled away from the abode of men, for none were to be seen during this calamitous period; the [174] hyænas, on the contrary, visited the cemeteries, and sought the dead bodies to devour them. I recommended Mr. Baldwin's [135] invaluable remedy of olive oil, applied according to his directions; several Jews, and some Muselmin [136], were induced to try it, and I was afterwards visited by many, to whom I had recommended it, and had given them written directions in Arabic how to apply it: and I do not know any instance of its failing when persevered in, even after the infection had manifested itself.

Footnote 134: (return) *M'drob* is an idiom in the Arabic language somewhat difficult to render into English; it is well known that the Muhamedans are predestinarians, and that they believe in the existence of spirits, devils, &c.; their idea of the plague is, that it is a good or blessing sent from God to clear the world of a superfluous population--that no medicine or precaution can cure or prevent it; that every one who is to be a victim to it is (*mktube*) recorded in the Book of Fate; that there are certain Genii who preside over the fate of men, and who sometimes discover themselves in various forms, having often legs similar to those of fowls: that these Genii are armed with arrows: that when a person is attacked by the plague, which is called in Arabic *l'amer*, or the destiny or decree, he is shot by one of these Genii, and the sensation of the invisible wound is similar to that from a musquet-ball; hence the universal application of *M'drob* to a person afflicted with the plague, i.e. he is shot; and if he die, *ufah ameruh*, his destiny is completed or terminated (in this world). I scarcely ever yet saw the Muselman who did not affirm that he had at some time of his life seen these Genii; and they often appear, they say, in rivers.

Footnote 135: (return) Late British Consul in Egypt.

Footnote 136: (return) Muselman, sing.: Muselmin. plur.

I have no doubt but the epidemy which made its appearance at Cadiz, and all along the southern shores of Spain, immediately as the plague was subsiding in West Barbary, was the same disorder with the one above described, suffering, after its passage to a Christian country, some variation, originating from the different modes of living, and other circumstances; for nothing can be more opposite than the food, dress, customs, and manners of Muhamedans and Christians, notwithstanding the approximation of Spain to Marocco. We have been credibly informed, that it was communicated originally to Spain, by two infected persons, who went from Tangier to Estapona, a small village on the opposite shore; who, after eluding the vigilance of the guards, reached Cadiz. We have also been assured that it was communicated by some infected persons who landed in Spain, from [175] a vessel that had loaded produce at L'Araiche in West Barbary. Another account was, that a Spanish privateer, which had occasion to land its crew for the purpose of procuring water in some part of West Barbary, caught the infection from communicating with the natives, and afterwards proceeding to Cadiz, and spread it in that town and the adjacent country.

It should be observed, for the information of those who may be desirous of investigating the nature of this extraordinary distemper, that, from its character and its symptoms, approximating to the peculiar plague, which (according to the before mentioned Arabic record) ravaged and depopulated West Barbary four centuries since, the Arabs and Moors were of opinion it would subside after the first year, and not appear again the next, as the Egyptian plague does; and agreeably to this opinion, it did not re-appear the second year: neither did St. John's day, or that season, affect its virulence; but about that period there prevails along the coast of West Barbary, a trade-wind, which, beginning to blow in the month of May, continues throughout the months of June, July, and August, with little intermission. It was apprehended that the influence of this trade-wind, added to the superstitious opinion of the plague ceasing on St. John's day, would stop, or at least sensibly diminish the mortality; but no such thing happened: the wind did set in, as it invariably does, about St. John's day; the disorder, however, increased [176] at that period, rather than diminished. Some persons were of opinion, that the infection maintained its virulence till the last; that the decrease of mortality did not originate from a decrease of the *miasma*, but from a decrease of population, and a consequent want of subjects to prey upon; and this indeed is a plausible idea; but admitting it to be just, how are we to account for the almost invariable fatality of the disorder, when at its height, and the comparative innocence of it when on the decline? for *then*, the chance to those who had it, was, that they would recover and survive the malady.

The old men seemed to indulge in a superstitious tradition, that when this peculiar kind of epidemy attacks a country, it does not return or continue for three or more years, but disappears altogether, (after the first year,) and is followed the seventh year by contagious rheums and expectoration, the violence of which lasts from three to seven days, but is not fatal. Whether this opinion be in general founded in truth I cannot determine; but in the spring of the year 1806, which was the seventh year from the appearance of the plague at Fas in 1799, a species of influenza pervaded the whole country; the patient going to bed well, and, on rising in the morning, a thick phlegm was expectorated, accompanied by a distressing rheum, or cold in the head, with a cough, which quickly reduced those affected to extreme weakness, but was seldom fatal, continuing from three to seven days, with more or less violence, and then gradually disappearing.

[177]

During the plague at Mogodor, the European merchants shut themselves up in their respective houses, as is the practice in the Levant; I did not take this precaution, but occasionally rode out to take exercise on horseback. Riding one day out of the town, I met the Governor's brother, who asked me where I was going, when every other European was shut up? "To the garden," I answered.--"And are you not aware that the garden and the adjacent country is full of (*Jinune*) departed souls, who are busy in smiting with the plague every one they meet?" I could not help smiling, but told him, that I trusted to God only, who would not allow any of the *Jinune* to smite me unless it were his sovereign will, and that if it were, he could effect it without the agency of *Jinune*. On my return to town in the evening, the beach, from the town-gate to the sanctuary of

Seedi, [137] Mogodole was covered with biers. My daily observations convinced me that the epidemy was not caught by approach, unless that approach was accompanied by an inhaling of the breath, or by touching the infected person; I therefore had a separation made across the gallery, inside of my house, between the kitchen and dining parlour, of the width of three feet, which is sufficiently wide to prevent the inhaling the breath of a [178] person. From this partition or table of separation I took the dishes, and after dinner returned them to the same place, suffering none of the servants to come near me; and in the accounting-house, I had a partition made to prevent the too near approach of any person who might call on business; and this precaution I firmly believe to be all that is necessary, added to that of receiving money through vinegar, and taking care not to touch or smell infectious substances.

Footnote 137: (return) A sanctuary a mile south-east of the town of Mogodor, from whence, the town receives its name.

Fear had an extraordinary effect in disposing the body to receive the infection; and those who were subject thereto, invariably caught the malady, which was for the most part fatal. At the breaking out of the plague at Mogodor, there were two medical men, an Italian and a Frenchman, the latter, a man of science, a great botanist, and of an acute discrimination; they, however, did not remain, but took the first opportunity of leaving the place for Teneriffe, so that the few Europeans had no expectation of any medical assistance except that of the natives. Plaisters of gum ammoniac, and the juice of the leaves of the *opuntia*, or *kermuse ensarrah*, *i.e.* prickly pear, were universally applied to the carbuncles, as well as to the buboes, which quickly brought them to suppuration: many of the people of property took copious draughts of coffee and Peruvian bark. The *Vinaigre de quatre voleurs*, was used by many, also camphor, smoking [179] tobacco, or fumigations of gum Sandrac; straw was also burned by some, who were of opinion, that any thing which produced abundance of smoke, was sufficient to purify the air of pestilential effluvia.

During the existence of the plague, I had been in the chambers of men on their death-bed: I had had Europeans at my table, who were infected, as well as Moors, who actually had buboes on them; I took no other precaution than that of separation, carefully avoiding to touch the hand, or inhale the breath; and, notwithstanding what may have been said, I am decidedly of opinion that the plague, at least this peculiar species of it, is not produced by any infectious principle in the atmosphere, but caught solely by touching infected substances, or inhaling the breath of those who are diseased; and that it must not be confounded with the common plague of Egypt, or Constantinople, being a malady of a much more desperate and destructive kind. It has been said, by persons who have discussed the nature and character of the plague, that the cultivation of a country, the draining of the lands, and other agricultural improvements, tend to eradicate or diminish it; but, at the same time, we have seen countries depopulated where there was no morass, or stagnate water for many days' journey, nor even a tree to impede the current of air, or a town, nor any thing but encampments of Arabs, who procured water from wells of a great depth, and inhabited plains so extensive [180] and uniform, that they resemble the sea, and are so similar in appearance after, as well as before sun-rise, that if the eye could abstract itself from the spot immediately surrounding the spectator, it could not be ascertained whether it were sea or land.

I shall now subjoin a few cases for the further elucidation of this distemper, hoping that the medical reader will pardon any inaccuracy originating from my not being a professional man.

Case I.--One afternoon, I went into the kitchen, and saw the cook making the bread; he appeared in good health and spirits; I afterwards went into the adjoining parlour, and took up a book to read; in half an hour the same man came to the door of the room, with his eyes starting from his head, and his bed-clothes, &c. in his hands, saying, "open the gate for me, for I am (*m'dorb*) smitten." I was astonished at the sudden transition, and desired him to go out, and I would follow and shut the gate. The next morning he sent his wife out on an errand, and got out of bed, and came to the gate half-dressed, saying that he was quite recovered, and desired I would let him in. I did not, however, think it safe to admit him, but told him to go back to his house for a few days, until he should be able to ascertain that he was quite well; he accordingly returned to his apartments, but expired that evening, and before day-break his body was in such a state, that his feet were actually putrified. His wife, by attending on him, [181] caught the infection, having a carbuncle, and also buboes, and was confined two months before she recovered.

Case II.--L'Hage Hamed O Bryhim, the old governor of Mogodor, had twelve or more children, and four wives, who were all attacked, and died (except only one young wife); he attended them successively to the grave, and notwithstanding that he assisted in performing the religious ceremony of washing the body, he never himself caught the infection; he lived some years afterwards, and out of the whole household, consisting of wives, concubines, children, and slaves, he had but one person left, which was the before-mentioned young wife: this lady, however, had received the infection, and was confined some time before she recovered.

Case. III.--Hamed ben A---- was smitten with the plague, which he compared to the sensation of two musket balls fired at him, one in each thigh; a giddiness and delirium succeeded, and immediately afterwards a green vomiting, and he fell senseless to the ground; a short time afterwards, on the two places where he had felt as if shot, biles or buboes formed, and on suppurating, discharged a foetid black pus; a (*jimmera*) carbuncle on the joint of the arm near the elbow was full of thin ichor, contained in an elevated skin, surrounded by a burning red colour; after three months' confinement, being reduced to a skeleton, the disorder appeared to have exhausted itself, and he began to recover his [182] strength, which in another month was fully reestablished. It was an observation founded on daily experience, during the prevalence of this disorder, that those who were attacked with a nausea at the stomach, and a subsequent vomiting of green or yellow bile, recovered after suffering in various degrees, and that those who were affected with giddiness, or delirium, followed by a discharge or vomiting of black bile, invariably died after lingering one, two, or three days, their bodies being covered with small black spots similar to grains of gun-powder; in this state, however, they possessed their intellects, and spoke rationally till their dissolution.

When the constitution was not disposed, or had not vigour enough to throw the miasma to the surface in the form of biles, buboes, carbuncles, or blackish spots, the virulence is supposed to have operated inwardly, or on the vital parts, and the patient died in less than twenty-four hours, without any exterior disfiguration.

Case IV.--It was reported that the Sultan had the plague twice during the season, as many others had; so that the idea of its attacking like the small-pox, a person but once in his life, is refuted: the Sultan was cured by large doses of Peruvian bark frequently repeated, and it was said that he found such infinite benefit from it, that he advised his brothers never to travel without having a good supply. The Emperor, since the plague, always has by him a sufficient quantity of quill bark to supply his emergency.

[183]

Case V.--H.L. was smitten with the plague, which affected him by a pain similar to that of a long needle (as he expressed himself) repeatedly plunged into his groin. In an hour or two afterwards, a (*jimmera*) carbuncle appeared in the groin, which continued enlarging three days, at the expiration of which period he could neither support the pain, nor conceal his sensations; he laid himself down on a couch; an Arabian doctor, applied to the carbuncles the testicles of a ram cut in half, whilst the vital warmth was still in them; the carbuncle on the third day was encreased to the size of a small orange; the before-mentioned remedy was daily applied during thirty days, after which he resorted to cataplasms of the juice of the (*opuntia*) prickly pear-tree, (*feshook*) gum ammoniac, and (*zite el aud*) oil of olives, of each one-third; this was intended to promote suppuration, which was soon effected; there remained after the suppuration a large vacuity, which was daily filled with fine hemp dipped in honey; by means of this application the wound filled up, and the whole was well in thirty-nine days.

Case VI.--El H--t--e, a trading Jew of Mogodor, was sorely afflicted; he called upon me, and requested some remedy; I advised him to use oil of olives, and having Mr. Baldwin's mode of administering it [138], I transcribed it in [184] the Arabic language, and gave it to him; he followed the prescription, and assured me, about six weeks afterwards, that (with the blessing of God) he had preserved his life by that remedy only; he said, that after having been anointed with oil, his skin became harsh and dry like the scales of a fish, but that in half an hour more, a profuse perspiration came on, and continued for another half hour, after which he experienced relief: this he repeated forty days, when, he was quite recovered.

Footnote 138: (return) Mr. Baldwin observed, that, whilst the plague ravaged Egypt, the dealers in oil were not affected with the epidemy; and he accordingly recommended people to anoint themselves with oil every day as a remedy.

Case VII.--Moh--m'd ben A---- fell suddenly down in the street; he was conveyed home; three carbuncles and five buboes appeared soon after in his groin, under the joint of his knee, and arm-pits, and inside the elbow; he died in three hours after the attack.

Case VIII.--L.R. was suddenly smitten with this dreadful calamity, whilst looking over some Marocco leather; he fell instantaneously; afterwards, when he had recovered his senses, he described the sensation as that of the pricking of needles, at every part wherein the carbuncles afterwards appeared: he died the same day in defiance of medicine.

Case IX.--Mr. Pacifico, a merchant, was attacked, and felt a pricking pain down the inside of the thick part of the thigh, near the sinews; he was obliged to go to bed. I visited him the next day, and was going to approach him, but he exclaimed, "Do not come near for although I know I have not the prevailing [185] distemper, yet your friends, if you touch me, may persuade you otherwise, and that might alarm you; I shall, I hope, be well in a few days." I took the hint of Don Pedro de Victoria, a Spanish gentleman, who was in the room, who, offering me a sagar, I smoked it, and then departed; the next day the patient died. He was attended during his illness by the philanthropic Monsieur Soubremont, who did not stir from his bed-side till he expired; but after exposing himself in this manner, escaped the infection, which proceeded, as he thought, from his constantly having a pipe in his mouth.

Case X.--Two of the principal Jews of the town giving themselves up, and having no hope, were willing to employ the remainder of their lives in affording assistance to the dying and the dead, by washing the bodies and interring them; this business they performed during thirty or forty days, during all which time they were not attacked: when the plague had nearly subsided, and they began again to cherish hopes of surviving the calamity, they were both smitten, but after a few days' illness recovered, and are now living.

From this last case, as well as from many others similar, but too numerous here to recapitulate, it appears that the human constitution requires a certain miasma, to prepare it to receive the pestilential infection.

General Observation.--When the carbuncles or buboes appeared to have a blackish rim round [186] their base, the case of that patient was desperate, and invariably fatal. Sometimes the whole body was covered with black spots like partridge-shot; such patients always fell victims to the disorder, and those who felt the blow internally, showing no external disfiguration, seldom survived more than a few hours.

The plague appears to visit this country about once in every twenty years [139]: the last visitation was in 1799 and 1800, being more fatal than any ever before known.

Footnote 139: (return) This opinion is confirmed by the plague, being now (1820) in Marocco just twenty years since the last plague. 65,000 persons have been lately carried off by this disease in the cities of Old and New Fas.

Observations respecting the Plague that prevailed last Year in West Barbary, and which was imported from Egypt; communicated by the Author to the Editor of the Quarterly Journal of Literature, Science, and the Arts, edited at the Royal Institution of Great Britain, No, 15, published in October, 1819.

His Majesty's ship, which was lying in the port of Alexandria, when Colonel Fitzclarence passed through Egypt, from India, on his way to England, convoyed to Tangier a vessel which had on board two of the sons of Muley Soliman, emperor of Marocco; on their arrival at Tangier, the princes immediately landed and proceeded to their father at Fas; but it was discovered by the governor or alkaid of Tangier, that during the passage some persons had died; and [187] accordingly the alkaid would not suffer any of the passengers to land, except the princes, until he should have received orders from the Emperor how to act; he accordingly wrote to Fas, for the imperial orders, and in the mean time the princes arrived, and presented themselves to the emperor: the latter wrote to the alkaid, that as the princes had been suffered to land, it would be unjust to prohibit the other passengers from coming ashore also. He therefore ordered the alkaid to suffer all the passengers, together with their baggage, to be landed, and soon afterwards the plague appeared at Fas, and at Tangier. Thus the contagion which is now ravaging West Barbary was imported from Egypt. It does not appear that the mortality is, or has been, during its acme at Fas, any thing comparable to what it was during the plague that ravaged this country in 1799, [140] and which carried off more than two-thirds of the population of the empire.

Footnote 140: (return) It has been asserted by a physician who has lately written, *Observations on contagion, as it relates to the plague and other epidemical diseases*, reviewed in article 20th of the *British Review*, and *London Critical Journal*, published in May last, that I have asserted that the deaths during the prevalence of that disorder in West Barbary in 1799, amounted to 124,500; but on a reference to my account of Marocco, Timbuctoo, &c., 2d or 3d edition, note, page 174, it will appear, that this mortality was that of two cities, and two sea-ports only, viz., the cities of Fas and Marocco, and the ports of Saffy and Mogodor; the mortality, however, was equally great in the imperial cities of Mequinas and Terodant, and in the sea-port towns of Tetuan, Tangier, Arzilla, L'Araich, Salee, Rabat, Dar el Bieda, Azamore, Mazagan, and Santa Cruz, or Agadeer; and considerably greater among the populous and numerous encampments of the Arabs, throughout the various provinces of the empire; not to mention the incredible mortality in the castles, towns, and other walled habitations of the Shelluh province of Haha, the first province, travelling from the shores of the Mediterranean, where the people live in walled habitations, the seaports excepted.

[188]

Whence proceeds this difference? Is it a different species of plague, and not so deadly a contagion? Or is it because the remedy of *olive* oil, applied and recommended generally by me, and by some other Europeans during the plague of 1799, is now made public and generally administered? This is an inquiry well deserving the attention of scientific men. And His Majesty's ministers might procure the information from the British consul at Tangier, or from the governor of Gibraltar: perhaps the truth is, that the contagion is of a more mild character.

With regard to the remedy of olive oil applied [141] internally, I should, myself, be disposed to doubt its efficacy unless M. Colaço, the [189] Portuguese consul at L'Araich, is competent to declare, *from his own knowledge and experience*, that this remedy has been administered effectually by him to persons having the plague, who did not *also use the friction with oil*. I say, till this can be ascertained, I think the remedy of oil applied *externally*, should not be forsaken; as *it has been proved during the plague in Africa, in 1799, to be infallible*, and therefore indispensable to people whose vocation may lead them to associate with, or to touch or bury the infected. For the rest, such persons as are not compelled to associate with the infected, may effectually avoid the contagion, however violent and deadly it may be, by avoiding contact. I am so perfectly convinced of this fact, from the experience and observation I have made during my residence at Mogodor, whilst the plague raged there in 1799, that I would not object to go to any country, although it were rotten with the plague, provided my going would benefit mankind, or serve any useful purpose; and I would use no fumigation, or any other remedy but what I actually used at Mogodor in 1799. I am so convinced from my own repeated and daily experience, that the most deadly plague is as easy to he avoided by strictly adhering to the principle of avoiding personal contact and inhalation, and the contact of infectious substances, that I would ride or walk through the most populous and deeply-infected city, as [190] I have done before, without any other precaution than that of a segar in my mouth, when, by avoiding contact and inhalation, I should most assuredly be free from the danger of infection!!

Footnote 141: (return) Mr. Colaço, having lately observed that oil was used externally to anoint the body, as a preservative against the plague; conceived the idea of administering this simple remedy *internally* to persons already infected; numerous experiments were made by this gentleman, who administered from four to eight oz. olive oil at a dose; and out of 300 individuals already infected, who resorted to this remedy, only twelve died.

When these precautions are strictly observed, I maintain, (in opposition to all the theoretical dogmas that have lately been propagated) that there is no more danger of infection with the plague, than there is of infection from any common cold or rheum.

[191]

JOURNEY FROM TANGIER TO RABAT

THROUGH THE PLAINS OF SEBOO,

To accompany Dr. Bell, in Company with the Prince Muley
Teib and an Army of Cavalry.

Officiated as Interpreter between the Prince and Dr. Bell.--Description of Food sent to us by the Prince.--The Plains of M'sharrah Rummellah, an incomparable fine and productive Country.-- The Cavalry of the Amorites,--their unique Observations on Dr. Bell.--their mean Opinion of his Art, because he could not cure Death.--Passage of the River Seboo on Rafts of inflated Skins.-- Spacious Tent of Goat's Hair erected for the Sheik, and appropriated to the Use of the Prince.-- Description of the magnificent Plains of M'sharrah Rummellah and Seboo.--Arabian Royalty.-- Prodigious Quantity of Corn grown in these Plains.--Matamores, what they are.--Mode of Reaping.--The Prince presents the Doctor with a Horse, and approves of his Medicines.--The Prince and the Doctor depart south-eastwardly, and the Author pursues his Journey to Rabat and Mogodor.

I happened to be at Tangier when the (*shereef*) prince Muley Teib was collecting an army to join that of the emperor, which was on the banks of the river Morbeya, (see the map of West Barbary, p. 55,) in Shawiya. Doctor Bell, who had then recently arrived from Gibraltar, to attend the prince, whose lungs were affected, was to accompany his Royal Highness; and, as I had nothing to detain me [192] in Tangier, and was going to Rabat, I engaged to accompany the doctor, and offered to officiate as interpreter between him and the prince till our arrival at Rabat; after which I should leave him, and proceed to Mogodor. The Doctor readily assented to my proposition, because it is considered more respectable in this country, where the Jews are reprobated and despised, to have for an interpreter a Christian; the prince also, when he heard that I had thus offered my services, expressed himself much gratified, and I received a very polite message from him. The next day we started from Tangier, in the morning at ten o'clock. The army halted east of Arzilla, in the plains: the prince sat down under the shade of a tree to dinner, Dr. Bell and myself under another tree, about 100 yards distant. The Prince sent us a capon stewed *à-la-mauresque* with saffron, the exquisite flavour of which proved that he had an excellent cook with him. We departed in half an hour; and the tents were pitched at sunset, in a campaign country, between Arzilla and L'Araich. The Ait-Amor or Amorites who formed a part of this army, a wild, uncontrolled race of Berebbers, saw the attention that was paid by the shereef to the doctor, and after dinner they were determined to see what sort of a fellow this doctor was, whom the shereef treated so familiarly. They galloped their high-mettled horses up to the doctor; and stopping short to examine him, made a reflection on him and returned. The [193] doctor observed the wild and tattered appearance of these excellent horsemen. There was nothing evil-minded in them; but their observations were remarkable. The Doctor wore powder, a custom unknown in this country: one party would say, "He has got lime in his head to kill the vermin;" another would observe that "He was old or grey-headed." The Doctor was fond of his bottle, and some said *skurren bel akkaran*, i.e. "The [142] son of a cuckold is drunk." Others would bawl out, *Wa Tebeeb washka't dowie elmoot*, i.e. "O, doctor, canst thou cure death?" To which he replied, "No."--"Then," returned they, "thou art no doctor!" On the following morning at sun-rise we proceeded, and reached L'Araich at twelve o'clock; we did not enter the town, but dined in the plains, and proceeding afterwards out of the main road, we directed our course south-east, till we reached a most beautiful and very extensive plain, called M'sharrah Rummellah. This plain was covered with numerous and immense flocks of sheep and horned cattle, and is many times more extensive than Salisbury plain. We pitched our tents near a very extensive and populous douar of Arabs. We departed the next morning at sun-rise, and reached the plains of the river Seboo about two o'clock in the afternoon; which plains are a continuation of those of M'sharrah Rummellah; the [194] army were engaged the remaining part of the day and the whole night crossing the river Seboo, on rafts made of inflated cow-hides, covered with planks and straw. The river is here about twenty yards wide, but very deep and rapid; the Arabs had a long and spacious sheik's tent pitched for the reception of the prince, about forty feet long and fifteen wide, somewhat similar to the hull of a ship reversed, having the long side open to the sun. These tents are the palace of the sheik of the Arabs, and are erected on great occasions only, such as that of the emperor, or a prince passing through their territory. The plains of M'sharrah Rummellah are one hundred and fifty British miles in circumference, perfectly flat, without a stone, a tree, a hedge, or a ditch; with the majestic river Seboo passing through the centre of the plain. The soil of this territory, which, in the hands of Europeans, might be made a terrestrial paradise, is a rich, productive, decomposed vegetable earth, which extends, as we perceived from various chasms, to the depth of several feet from the surface. It produces incredible quantities of the finest wheat, of a hard grain, very large and long, clear as amber, and yielding a prodigious increase of flour, so that a saa of wheat [143] produces a saa and a sixth of flour. The prince, Muley Teeb, seated on [195] an eminence in this spacious tent, resembled what we should imagine the patriarch Abraham to have been, entertaining his friends; or Saul upon his throne, with his javelin in his hand. He had twelve lanciers, six on each side of him in a row, standing with their lances erect, the Prince having one in his hand. It appears that this is the Arabian etiquette; and the Arabs appeared much gratified that the prince had personified their sheik, with all the paraphernalia of royalty. His Royal Highness whose mind seemed moved with the beauty of this country, sent for the Doctor and myself, and asked us if we had ever seen such a country before. We frankly confessed we had not. The prince smiled, and said, that the (*sehell*) plain we were on, although extremely populous, and full of douars, could grow seventeen times as much corn as the inhabitants could consume; that there was then corn enough in the matamores [144] of this plain, to supply (*El garb kamel*) the whole of El garb, i.e. the country north of the river Morbeya. [145]

Footnote 142: (return) Intoxication is a damnable vice with these people; and when they remark drunkenness, they invariably add an opprobrium to the observation.

Footnote 143: (return) A saa of wheat is little less than two Winchester bushels. The wheat is very heavy, and this measure weighs 100 lb., equal to 119 lb. English.

Footnote 144: (return) The matamores are subterraneous depositories for corn, in which they preserve the wheat sound and good thirty years; but when a matamore is once opened, it is expedient to consume the corn immediately, otherwise it contracts what is called the matamore twang. These depositories are indispensable in countries exposed to drought, scarcity, or locusts, and *should be adopted in our colony of South Africa*. The art of constructing them is very peculiar, and I devoted some time in learning it.

Footnote 145: (return) See the map of West Barbary.

[196]

We took our leave of the Prince, who appeared much gratified with the hospitable entertainment of the Arabs, and with their patriarchal style of living, and sent us an enormous dish of cuscasoe, coloured with saffron.

Encamped in the centre of this plain, when the sun had set, and the twilight came on, we could have imagined ourselves in the midst of the ocean. Not a cloud was in the sky, nor a hill on the land, to intercept the uniformity of the horizon; the moon shone so bright, that we could read by its light, and the universal novelty of the scene resembled enchantment.

On this rich land they use no dung: they reap the corn about a foot from the ground, and burn the stubble. The produce is greater even than that of the *new-dyke land*, on the banks of the river Ems, in North Holland. The allotments of land are ascertained by a large stone, placed at each corner of the square, when the reapers reach these stones, they desist from proceeding or reaping the corn of other proprietors. We rose early in the morning, and found the air of this terrestrial paradise strongly perfumed with millions of odoriferous flowers, that were growing spontaneously throughout the plains. Walking with Dr. Bell through the Prince's camp, we saw a beautiful grey horse. The doctor admired it. I recommended him to ask the Prince for it, he was not acquainted with the customs of this country, and ridiculed my observation. "If you wish to have [197] that horse, Doctor," said I, "I will engage that the Prince will get it for you. I represented immediately to His Royal Highness, that the Doctor had taken a liking to the horse, and would wish to buy it. Not buy it," said the Prince; "he will receive it as a present from me. Tell him, he deserves seven horses for the benefit he has done me: all doctors that I have heretofore had have taken twenty-four hours to give me ease; he relieves me in one. Tell him so," said the prince, "and that he (*massab ala genibuna*) is in the number of my dearest friends. (*e jeek elkhere attibib u asselem*), Good be with you, doctor, and peace be with you." Thus ended the negociation for the horse. I found afterwards that it belonged to a sheik of the Arab province of Beni Hassen, who regretted parting with it, but the Prince gave him the value of it, and much courtesy withal. We struck our tents next morning at eleven o'clock, and, travelling southward, the Prince received an express from the Emperor to join his imperial army forthwith: accordingly the Prince and his doctor departed south-east, and I took leave of them, and pursued my journey to Rabat. p. 198

[198]

OF

THE EXCAVATED RESIDENCES

OF THE

INHABITANTS OF ATLAS:

THE

ACEPHALI, HEL SHUAL, AND HEL ELKILLEB:

The Discovery of Africa not to be effected by the present System of solitary Travellers; but by a grand Plan, with a numerous Company; beginning with Commerce, as the natural Prelude to Discovery, the Fore-runner of Civilization, and a preliminary Step, indispensable to the Conversion of the native Negroes to Christianity.

The inhabitants of the snowy or upper regions of the Atlas live, during the months of November, December, January, February, and half of March, in caves or excavations in the mountains; the snow then disappears, and they begin to cultivate the earth.

I have repeatedly heard reports of the (*Helel Killeb*, [146]) dog-faced race; of the (*Hel Shual*,) tailed race; and of the race having one eye, [147] [199] and that in the breast. It is extremely difficult to ascertain the origin of these reports, which are so involved in metaphor that the signification is not intelligible to Europeans; their existence is not doubted, however, in Africa. Of the *Hel El Killeb* some ignorant people affirm that the Almighty transformed one of the tribes of the Jews into these people, and that these are their descendants; others report them to be a mongrel breed, between the human and ape species; their strength is said to be very great. The Africans assert with considerable confidence, which is corroborated, that the Hel Shual have a tail half a cubit long; that they inhabit a district in the Desert at an immense distance south-east of Marocco; that the Hel El Killeb [148] are in a similar direction; that the latter are diminutive, [200] being about two or three cubits [149] in height; that they exclaim *bak, bak, bak*, and that they have a few articulate sounds, which they mutually understand among themselves; that they are extremely swift of foot, and run as fast as horses. The Arimaspi of Herodotus are called by the Arabs *Hel Ferdie*, these are represented by the Arabs of the Desert as living at the foot of the lofty mountains of the Moon, near Abyssinia: the male and female are equally without hair on their head, having large chins and nostrils, like the ape species; they are said to have a language of their own; their costume is a *jelabea*, [150] and a belt, without shoes or head dress; their country is said to abound in gold. It is "a consummation devoutly to be wished," that our knowledge of Africa should increase so as to enable us to unravel the mystery of these doubtful reports, to ascertain the degree of credit that is due to these mysterious traditions. These desiderata, however, can hardly be expected, whilst the present injudicious plans for [201] the discovery of Africa are persevered in. We must, if we desire to discover effectually the hidden recesses and reported wonders of this continent, adopt plans and schemes very different from any that have hitherto been suggested; we must adopt *a grand system upon an extensive scale*, a system directed and moved by a person competent to so great an undertaking. The head or director of such an expedition should be master of the general travelling and trafficking language of Africa, the modern Arabic: he should moreover be acquainted with the character of the people, their habits, modes of life, religious prejudices, and fanaticism. A grand plan, thus directed, could hardly fail to secure the command of the commerce of Africa to Great Britain. Then the discovery of the inmost recesses would follow the path of commerce, and that continent, which has baffled the researches of the moderns as well as of the ancients, would lay open its treasures to modern Europe, and civilisation would be the natural result. Then would be the period to attempt the conversion of the Negroes to Christianity; and the standard of peace and good will towards men might be successfully planted on the banks of the *Nile El Kabeer*, or *Nile Assudan*, the Great Nile, or Nile of Sudan, or Nigritia, commonly called the Niger.

Footnote 146: (return) Apollonius Rhodius calls these people [Greek: ημικυγες êmikuges] or half-dogs.

Footnote 147: (return) The ingenious author of Philosophic Researches concerning the Americans, speaking of a race which appear to resemble the Acephali of Herodotus, or the race of men having one eye, and that in their chest, says, "There is in Canibar a race of savages who have hardly any neck, and whose shoulders reach up to their ears. This monstrous appearance is artificial, and to give it to their children they put enormous weights upon their heads, so as to make the vertebræ of the neck enter, if we may so say, the channel bone, (clavicule.) These barbarians, from a distance, seem to have their mouth in the breast; and might well enough, in ignorant and enthusiastic travellers, serve to revive the fable of the Acephali, or men without heads." (See Larcher's Notes on Herodotus's Melpomene, cap. 191.)--Saint Augustin, whose veracity is scarcely to be doubted, declared in his thirty-third sermon, intituled *"A ses Frères dans le Désert"--Avoir vu en Ethiopie des hommes et des femmes sans tête avec des grands yeux sur le poitrine.*

Footnote 148: (return) We have heard of a pig-faced lady; if there is such a person, there might also be a pig-faced gentleman, and these might generate a pig-faced race; and if a pig-faced race, why not a dog-faced race?

Footnote 149: (return) Seven Cubits make four English yards.

Footnote 150: (return) The best description I can give of a *jelabea* is this: Take a large sack and cut a hole in the bottom, big enough to admit the head; then cut the two bottom corners off to admit the arms: this garment will then resemble the *jelabea*.

[202]

CAUTIONS

TO BE USED IN TRAVELLING.

Danger of travelling after Sun-set.--The Emperor holds himself accountable for Thefts committed on Travellers, whilst travelling between the rising and the setting Sun.--Emigration of Arabs.-- Patriarchal Style of living among the Arabs; Food, Clothing, domestic Looms, and Manufactures.--Riches of the Arabs calculated by the Number of Camels they possess.--Arabian Women are good Figures, and have personal Beauty; delicate in their Food; poetical Geniuses; Dancing and Amusements; Musical Instruments; their Manners are courteous.

Travellers in West and South Barbary should never be out after sun-set: it is not safe to travel in many parts of the country during the night. The emperor holds himself accountable for thefts committed between the rising and the setting sun; so that, if a traveller be robbed of property, the value should be ascertained, and an application being made to the bashaw of the province where the robbery was committed it will be restored forthwith; but if there be any demur, an application should be made to the Emperor, personally, if possible, but if not, by letter; and the district is immediately ordered to pay double the loss, one half to the person robbed, and the other half to the Imperial treasury. [203] These robberies, however, rarely occur; for the bashaws of the provinces and the alkaids of the douars feel it a duty incumbent on them to protect all travellers and strangers; so that they would, in the event of a robbery being committed, expose themselves to a severe reprimand from the emperor, and an intimation that they were, by suffering such irregularity, incompetent to their situation, and would be liable to a heavy fine, or a discharge from their office, for *neglect of vigilance*, which, in this country, is considered *very reprehensible.*

Travelling through the province of Suse, I once witnessed the emigration of an extensive douar of Arabs, amounting to about 200 families. They were just leaving their habitation, where they had been encamped only a few months: it was a fine grazing country; the camels, horses, mules, asses, oxen and cows, were all laden with the tents and baggage of these wanderers. On enquiring the cause of this emigration, I was told that the inhabitants were infested with musquitoes and fleas to such a degree, that they had all unanimously resolved to emigrate to another place, which they had fixed upon, and that they would reach it by night. These wandering Arabs, without any fixed habitation, are of a restless, ungovernable spirit: they never cultivate the earth, as do the Arabs of the plains of Marocco, but live, for the most part, on camels' milk, occasionally killing a camel or a goat for food; grazing their [204] camels in the adjacent country: they live in the true Patriarchal style, and seek the means of supplying all their wants within themselves. To effect this purpose, they barter a few of their camels for wool, and thus supply themselves with that article for clothing, which is made in every (*keyma*) Arab tent, by the women, at their own respective looms; each female being the manufacturer for her own family. The cloth is wove in pieces of seven cubits long and about two and a half broad, of the natural colour of the wool: these pieces of cloth are afterwards converted into cloaks, mantles, and tunics. Those who choose to indulge in the luxury of dress, by wearing linen, or turbans, send a few goat-skins, collected from the goats that have served them occasionally for food, to Mogodor, or Marocco, or barter them with some Jews for linen or shoes, and thus supply all their wants; so that their resources considerably exceed their wants, for some of them have several thousand camels which cost them nothing. These animals browse on the bushes in the environs of their habitations, and are continually increasing and multiplying. They never kill any animal for food until full grown: this custom, from which the Arab never departs, is manifestly calculated to increase property, which, being invested in camels, is transportable, without trouble or expense, wherever they choose.

The Arabs are gay and cheerful; the brow of care is rarely seen among them. The more children [205] they have, the greater the blessing. They turn their hands in early youth to some useful purpose: so soon as they can walk they attend the camels, or are put to some domestic occupation; thus forming a useful link in the chain of their patriarchal society. The independence of these Arabs is depicted in their physiognomy; they are oppressed by no cankering care, no anxiety, no anticipation of distress. The food and clothing of the Arab is always at hand; fuel is not required in this warm country; and a glass of cool water is all that is desired to allay the thirst. This simple and abstemious mode of living is congenial to the human constitution; accordingly they enjoy uninterrupted health: sickness is so uncommon with them that to be old and to be sick are synonymous terms. They think one cannot happen without the other. Some of the women of these people, whilst young, are extremely delicate, handsome, and have elegant figures. They account it gross to swallow food, that would, they say, fatten them like their Moorish neighbours; they therefore masticate it only. Their physiognomy is very interesting and animated; their features are regular; large black expressive eyes; a ready wit, poetic fancy, expressing themselves in poetic effusions, in which, from constant habit, some of them have become such adepts, that they with facility speak extempore poetry; those who are unable to converse [206] in this manner are less esteemed. Their evening amusements consist in dancing and music, vocal and instrumental. Generally, throughout all the Arab provinces, but particularly in Suse, among the Mograffra Arabs, the Woled Abbusebah, and Woled Deleim, the whole country is in a blaze of light of a summer's evening; music, dancing, and rejoicing, is heard in every direction. Their music consists of a kettle-drum, a flute or reed, similar to what Homer describes as the instrument of the ancient shepherds, a rhabeb or two-stringed fiddle, played with a semicircular bow, a tamboureen, and brass castanets. They play in precise time; and the ladies arrange themselves at the entrance of the sheik's tent. It is pleasant to observe the beauty of their fine-formed feet, uninjured by tight shoes, and free from corns and all excrescences. They dance some dances barefooted, making very short steps, scarcely raising the foot from the ground, in a peculiar manner. They have elegant and circular ankles; and their light motions fascinate the eyes of the spectators and the admiring strangers, who occasionally exclaim, (*Allah éhrduh alikume ia Elarb*) "the protection of God be upon you, O Arabs!" (*makine fal Elarb,*) "there are none comparable to the Arabs!" They have a very elegant shawl-dance: in the management of the shawl they display singular grace, and practise elegant figures, sometimes concealing their faces, sometimes [207] showing their brilliant eyes through an opening in the shawl. The manners of these ladies is courteous, but chaste; perfectly modest, but without reserve; and the other sex pay them courteous attention.

[208]

ABUNDANCE OF CORN

PRODUCED IN

WEST BARBARY.

Costly Presents made by Spain to the Emperor.--Bashaw of Duquella's weekly Present of a Bar of Gold.--Mitferes or Subterraneous Depositories for Corn.

The empire of Marocco, west of the Atlas, during the reign of Seedi Muhamed ben Abdallah, father of the present Emperor Soliman, was one continued corn-field. At that time the exportation was free to all parts of the world. It is impossible to conceive the abundance produced in this prolific land, none but those who have actually seen the standing corn in the ear, and have seen it reaped, can form any correct idea of its prodigious increase. The plains of Rahamena, of Shawiya, of Temsena, of Abda, and Duquella, those immense plains of M'sharrah Rummellah, of Ait-Amor, and many others, form each, separately, extensive fields of corn, farther than the eye can reach. To give an idea of the quantity produced in the plains near Dar El Beida, it will be sufficient to say, that 250 sail of ships, from 150 to 700 tons, were loaded at that port in one year of Seedy Muhamed's reign. At the other ports on the shores of the Atlantic, viz. at Arzilla, L'Araich, Mcheduma, Rabat, [209] Azamor, Mazagan, Saffy, and Mogodor, were shipped a quantity, almost equal in proportion to what was shipped at Dar-El-Beida, so that the duties at one dollar per fanegue, of 80 lb. weight on the exportation of wheat, barley, Indian corn, caravances, beans, and seeds, in one year, according to the imperial registers, amounted to 5,257,320 Mexico dollars. [151] Besides which, presents to an incalculable amount were made from time to time by Spain and Portugal, particularly by the former, to keep the Emperor in good humour, and to prevent him from prohibiting the exportation of grain, of which however there was little chance, as his Imperial Majesty was always diligent in the accumulation of treasure, and let no opportunity pass of encouraging the agriculture of his dominions. This system gave general occupation to the Arabs, or agriculturists, and enriched them so universally, that the diffusion of wealth among them, produced other incalculable sources of revenue, insomuch that it was customary for Muhamed Ben Amaran, Bashaw of Duquella, to present to the Emperor at Marocco, every Friday, (the Muhamedan sabbath), as he returned home from the mosque, a massive bar of pure gold of Timbuctoo, valued at some thousand dollars; which [210] was considered as the fee by which he held his bashawick. The Arabs who are the agriculturists of the before-mentioned plains, besides the corn exported, lay up immense quantities in subterraneous caverns, constructed by a curious process, well deserving the attention of the colonists of South Africa; these repositories are called mitferes [152], they are constructed in a conical form, and will contain from 200 to 2000 quarters of corn. [153] It is expedient, in their construction, to exclude the atmospheric air; and the soil, in which they are constructed, should be essentially conservative, the air being never changed, is constantly of the same temperature, very dry, and not subject to the variations of humidity, which affect the external air: this, with other necessary precautions being observed, they will preserve the corn twenty or thirty years perfectly sound. In countries, (like that of the Cape of Good Hope,) subject to drought, inundations, or locusts, these mitferes, or catacombs are indispensable, as they preserve corn as a reserve stock, in the event of scarcity, or famine, produced by any of the before mentioned calamities, or providential visitations. It is more [211] than probable that this singular art of constructing mitferes, was derived in ancient times from the catacombs of Egypt, and that Joseph might have preserved Pharaoh's corn [154] upwards of seven years, in similar magazines. The Emperor Seedi Muhamed, who possessed considerable talent, and had a perfect knowledge of the disposition and character of his subjects, used to say in the (*em'shoer*,) place of audience, before all the people, in the latter part of his reign:--"You complain of my decrees; but when I am departed from this world, you shall seek for one day of Seedi Muhamed's reign, but you shall not find it." This prediction has been literally verified throughout the respective reigns of his sons Muley Yezzed, and Muley El Hesham, and even his son the present Emperor has often manifested an anti-commercial system, and has accordingly (probably by the advice of the Fakeers belonging to the divan) prohibited the exportation of most articles of clothing, and provision, such as wool, Fas manufactures, corn, olive oil, raisins, &c. [155]

Footnote 151: (return) Barley and wheat imported from different ports of England and from the Continent into London (which is more than is imported into Great Britain) in 1818, was 6,179,330 quintals or saas of Barbary, which are equal to 7,415,390 fanegues $.

Footnote 152: (return) Genesis, xli. 9.--"And Joseph gathered corn as the sand of the sea very much."

Footnote 153: (return) I descended into a mitfere in the Arab province of Duquella, and remained there whilst the Arab explained to me the mode of constructing them; this was near the douar of Woled Aisah (see the map): it had just been emptied, and produced 3450 saas or quintals.

Footnote 154: (return) Genesis, xli. 48.

Footnote 155: (return) The result of this anti-commercial system is, that corn is dearer than it was during the exportation. Many millions of acres of the finest and most productive land lies fallow for want of a market for its produce; indeed, the produce has sometimes been so low for want of a market, that I have known instances of the corn having been left standing, not being worth the expense of reaping. Now this prohibition undoubtedly will appear to many intelligent readers bad policy in his Imperial Majesty, but it is nevertheless consistent policy. The *sine qua non* of the court of Marocco is to keep the inhabitants poor. It is asserted by the political economists of this country, that the Arab should not have more than sufficient to feed and clothe him; every thing beyond this turns to evil, and is an incentive to rebellion: the superflux, they maintain, should go to (*Beit el melh d'el muselmen,*) the Muselman treasury.

A wine company, consisting of gentlemen of practical experience in that branch of business, might form a most beneficial establishment at [212] Santa Cruz, whither the grapes of Edautenan are brought to market, and other grapes from the Arab countries, of exquisite quality and flavour, infinitely superior in richness, size, and flavour to those of Spain and Portugal, or any part of Italy; indeed, I have no hesitation in declaring, (without fear of contradiction,) that this country produces the finest grapes, oranges, and pomegranates in the world, and in the greatest abundance. I have myself tasted at Marocco, at a Hebrew Rabbi's table, excellent imitations of burgundy, claret, champagne, madeira, and rhenish, or old hock, all the produce of grapes reared in the plains of that city, and in the adjacent mountains. The port of Santa Cruz, if purchased of the Emperor by the English, would, besides securing the trade to Sudan, and the interior of Africa, supply the London market with abundance of all these excellent wines.

[213]

DOMESTIC SERPENTS OF MAROCCO.

Every house in Marocco has, or ought to have, a domestic serpent: I say ought to have, because those that have not one, seek to have this inmate, by treating it hospitably whenever one appears; they leave out food for it to eat during the night, which gradually domiciliates this reptile. These serpents are reported to be extremely sagacious, and very susceptible. The superstition of these people is extraordinary; for rather than offend these serpents, they will suffer their women to be exposed during sleep to their performing the office of an infant. They are considered, in a house, emblematical of good, or prosperity, as their absence is ominous of evil. They are not often visible; but I have seen them passing over the beams of the roof of the apartments. A friend of mine was just retired to bed at Marocco, when he heard a noise in the room, like something crawling over his head, he arose, looked about the room, and discovered one of these reptiles about four feet long, of a dark colour, he pricked it with his sword, and killed it, then returned to bed. In the morning he called to him the master of the house where he was a guest, and telling him he had attacked the serpent, the Jew was chagrined, and expostulated with him, for the injury he had done him: apprehensive that evil would visit him, he intimated to his guest, that he hoped he would leave his house, as he feared the malignity of the serpent; and he was not reconciled until my friend discovered to him that he had actually killed the reptile.

MANUFACTURES OF FAS.

Superior Manufacture of Gold-thread.--Imitation of precious Stones.--Manufactory of Gun-barrels in Suse.--Silver-mine.

The manufactures of West Barbary, are of various kinds. They excel, in the city of Fas, in the manufacture of woollens, cottons, silks, and gold-thread. The wool and cotton are made into *hayks*, which are pieces of cloth five feet wide, and about three and a half, or four yards long, used to throw loosely over the dress, when they go out into the external air: it resembles the Roman toga, and when *tastefully adjusted*, gives an elegance to the Moorish costume. These *hayks* are manufactured in most of the private families of Fas; the women employ themselves about them, and sell them to the merchants. They are sometimes made of cotton mixed with silk, and also altogether of silk. They make also pieces of silk of various bright colours, called *bulawan*; the sky-blue, dark-blue, scarlet, and yellow, are vivid colours, produced by their mode of dying the silk before it is manufactured. They manufacture their silks from *Bengal raw silk*, which they call *emfitla*. The *bulawan* is striped, or chequered, [215] pink, blue, yellow, scarlet, and green: it resembles what is called, in England, Persian, but it is much stronger, and more [156] durable, though equally light. The silk sashes, called *hazam*, are made in large quantities, and are deserving of imitation in Europe; they are very substantial, but of the same superior colours with the *bulawan*. They are made generally half a yard wide, and three yards long: these sell at Fas, from two to fifty dollars each. The superior kind made for the ladies of the *horam* [157], or emperor's seraglio, for the ladies of the bashaws, and for those of the great and opulent, are intermixed with a beautiful gold-thread, much superior to any that is manufactured in Europe, insomuch, that the gold-thread imported from Leghorn and Marseilles is used only in such *hazams* as are made for exportation to Sudan, Draha, or Bled-el-Jereed, but those made for the great and opulent, for home consumption, are manufactured with the gold thread of the Fas manufacture. Whether these expert artificers learned the mystery of gold beating, and gold wire drawing, by which they obtain gold-thread, from the Egyptians, I am not competent to say; [216] but *they* say they derived it in ancient times from the Arabs, as well as the art of cutting, polishing, and setting precious stones. They make a composition in imitation of amber, which cannot, by the keenest eye, be distinguished from the natural amber, the latter, however, by [158] friction attracts cotton, but the manufactured amber does not; this is the only criterion by which they ascertain the true from the false amber. They also compose artificial stones with equal sagacity; the topaz, the emerald, and the ruby they imitate to perfection. The wool with which they make shawls almost equal in appearance to those of Kashmere, is procured from the sheep of the province of Tedla, and is finer than the Spanish Merino. They might manufacture shawls of goats' hair, equal to those of Kashmere, from the goats of the eastern declivity of the Atlas, whose hair is like silk: these goats are called (*el maize Felelley*,) i.e. Tafilelt goats. [159] There can be no doubt, if our intercourse with Marocco had not been impeded by a general [217] ignorance of the language of that country, that we might long since have received from the manufacturers of Fas, shawls of Tafilelt goat-hair, equal to the finest of the Kashmere manufacture. There is a very extensive manufactory of red woollen caps at Fas, the contexture of which is well deserving investigation. There is also a manufactory of gun locks and barrels; the former appear to have reached the acmé of the art, the latter are not so good as those which they procure from Europe: so that a Spanish or an English barrel, and a Fas lock, is considered a complete gun. Such articles of manufacture as require a complication of machinery and power to produce they import from Europe, except only when the market is bare, and then necessity compels them to attempt their construction. The (*hayk Filelly,*) i.e. Tafilelt hayk, is a fine elegant woollen cloth, thin as a muslin. The Emperor Seedi Muhamed ben Abdallah patronised this manufacture of his native country, and never wore any other. The art of manufacturing leather is carried to great perfection at Mequinas: shoes of the thinnest leather are there made impervious to water. The manufactures at Marocco and Terodant are similar to those of Fas, with the exception of that of gold-thread, and the cutting and polishing of precious stones. The preparation of leather at Marocco surpasses any thing known in Europe: lion and tiger skins they prepare white as snow, and soft as silk. There are two plants that grow in the Atlas [218] mountains, the leaves of which they use in the manufacture of leather; they are called *tizra*, and *tasaya*. Whether these render the leather impervious, I am not competent to say; every inquiry that I have made at Marocco respecting this beautiful manufacture, has been unsatisfactory. I have always found the manufacturers very guarded, and extremely jealous; but I have often thought that two or three of our leather manufacturers, well versed in their art, and withal of penetrating minds, might contrive to extract the secret from them. In the mountains of Idaultit, in Lower Suse, they have iron-mines, and they make gun-barrels and gun-locks equal to what are made at Fas. The temptations to agriculture, however, are such, that sufficient only for the consumption of their own *kabyl* are manufactured; which is done rather from a principle of self-defense, and from the *amor patriæ*, than with a view to gain. The silver from the mines of Elala, comes to the Santa Cruz market pure, and in round lumps, weighing about two ounces each. I have bought it for its weight in Spanish dollars; but it is generally taken to the Mint for sale. Ores of gold from the mines of South Barbary, and silver dust from the bed of the river at Messa, collected personally by me, I sent to England to be assayed: the person who got them assayed, reported, that the metal yielded was scarcely sufficient to pay the charges of assaying; so that the speculation was abandoned.

Footnote 156: (return) The spirit of avarice does not sufficiently prevail to induce the manufacturer to make imperfect articles for the purpose of sale only. Moreover, they are restrained from deception by an officer, who inspects the quality of manufactures, and does not suffer an imperfect article to be sold.

Footnote 157: (return) This word is called by Europeans *haram* or seraglio; but haram thus applied, is a barbarism: it signifies *vicious*. Horam is the correct pronunciation: it signifies a place of safety, that admits of no intrusion.

Footnote 158: (return) Thales, the chief of the seven wise men of Greece, detected the existence of electricity in amber about 600 years before the Christian era. He was the first who observed *attraction* to be the distinguishing property of amber; and he was so forcibly struck with this singular discovery, that he was almost led to suppose that it possessed animation. The term electricity is derived from the Greek word [Greek: ηλεκτρον], amber. See Remarks on Electricity and Galvanism, by M. La Beaume, p. 29.

Footnote 159: (return) There was a breed of these goats on the island of Mogodor, kept there by the emperor's orders. This island is the state-prison of the empire.

[219]

ON THE STATE OF SLAVERY

IN MUHAMEDAN AFRICA.

The state of slavery in this country is very different from that which is experienced by the unfortunate men who are transported from Africa to work under our Christian brethren in the West India islands. No man, who is sufficiently erudite to read the Koran can be (*abd*) a slave in a Muhamedan country. It is incumbent on a good mûselman to give such his liberty, that the propagation of the (*Deen el Wâsah* [160]) mûselman faith, be not impeded. A man who has served his master faithfully [161] seven years, sometimes gets liberated. This liberation, however, is not compulsory; but conscientious mûselmen, of good moral character, often adopt this enlarging system. I have, however, met with many Moors, who, on offering liberty to their slaves, the latter have declined it, preferring to continue in obeisance; a clear proof that their servitude is not very severe. All slaves, without exception, are brought to this country from the various territories of Sudan, by the akkabars, kaffilas, or caravans, that traverse Sahara. They are all pagans or idolaters (from the interior regions). They are worth from ten to twenty dollars at Timbuctoo; and at Marocco and Fas [220] they sell for, from seventy to one hundred dollars. They are received into the Moorish families as domestic servants, and soon forget their idolatrous superstitions, and become (nominally at least) Muhamedans. After which, many learn to read the Koran, and becoming observers of ablution and prostration, often procure their liberation, for if any one should neglect to liberate such a slave, his brethren in Muhamed will urge him to it, as a good and charitable work, becoming a true, mûselman. [162]

Footnote 160: (return) So called by Muhamedans: *literally* means the liberal of *wide doctrine*, alluding to that of the Arabian Prophet.

Footnote 161: (return) Jeremiah, xxxiv. 14.

Footnote 162: (return) The etymology of *muselman* is, a man of peace; from *salem*, peace.

The man who wrote the letter from Timbuctoo, giving his master at Mogodor an account of Mungo Park, having visited Kabria, which letter I read, and reported its contents on my arrival in England from Mogodor, about the year 1807, to my Lord Moira (now the Marquis of Hastings), to Sir Joseph Banks, and to Sir Charles Morgan, was a liberated negro of Seed el Abes Buhellel, a Fas merchant, whose father had an establishment at Timbuctoo. When Buhellel liberated this negro, he had such confidence in him, that he advanced to him, on his own personal credit, goods to a considerable amount, with which he crossed Sahara, and took them to Timbuctoo for a market. It were to be desired, for the sake of *humanity*, that our West-India planters would take a lesson on this subject from the Moors, whose conduct, in this particular, is worthy of imitation.

[221]

THE PLAGUE OF LOCUSTS.

Their incredible Destruction.--Used as Food.--Remarkable Instance of their destroying every Green Herb on one Side of a River, and not on the other.

In the autumn of 1792, (Jeraad) locusts began to appear in West Barbary. The corn was in ear, and therefore safe, as this devouring insect attacks no hard substance. In (the *liahli*,) the period of heavy rains comprised between the forty longest nights, *old style*, they disappeared; so that one or two only were seen occasionally: but so soon as the *liahli* had passed, the small young green locust began to appear, no bigger than a fly. As vegetation increased, these insects increased in size and quantity. But the country did not yet seem to suffer from them. About the end of March, they increased rapidly. I was at (*Larsa Sultan*) the emperor's garden, which belongs to the Europeans, and which was given to the merchants of Mogodor by the emperor Seedi Muhamed ben Abdallah, in the kabyl of Idaugourd, in the province of Haha, and the garden flourished with every green herb, and the fruit-trees were all coming forward in the productive beauty of spring. I went there the following day, and not a green leaf was to be seen: an army of locusts had attacked it during the [222] night, and had devoured every shrub, every vegetable, and every green leaf; so that the garden had been converted into an unproductive wilderness. And, notwithstanding the incredible devastation that was thus produced, not one locust was to be seen. The gardener reported, that (*sultan jeraad*) the king of the locusts had taken his departure eastward early in the morning; the myriads of locusts followed, so that in a quarter of an hour not one was to be seen. The depredations of these devouring insects was too soon felt, and a direful scarcity ensued. The poor would go out a locusting, as they termed it: the bushes were covered; they took their (*haik*) garment, and threw it over them, and then collected them in a sack. In half an hour they would collect a bushel. These they would take home, and boil a quarter of an hour; they would then put them into a frying-pan, with pepper, salt, and vinegar, and eat them, without bread or any other food, making a meal of them. They threw away the head, wings, and legs, and ate them as we do prawns. They considered them wholesome food, and preferred them to pigeons. Afterwards, whenever there was any public entertainment given, locusts was a standing dish; and it is remarkable that the dish was always emptied, so generally were they esteemed as palatable food.

A few years after the locusts appeared, I performed a journey from Mogodor to Tangier. [223] The face of the country appeared like a newly ploughed field of a brown soil; for it was completely covered with these insects, insomuch that they had devoured even the bark of the trees. They rose up about a yard, as the horses went on, and settled again; in some places they were one upon another, three or four inches deep on the ground; a few were flying in the air, and they flew against the face, as if they were blind, to the no small annoyance of the traveller. It is very remarkable, that on reaching the banks of the river [163] Elkos, which we crossed, there was not, on the north side of that river, to my great astonishment, one locust any where to be seen; but the country was flourishing in all the luxuriance of verdure, although the river was not wider than the Thames at Windsor. This extraordinary circumstance was accounted for by the Arabs, who said that not a locust would cross the river, till (*sultan jeraad*) the king of the locusts should precede and direct the way.

Footnote 163: (return) See the Map of the empire of Marocco.

[224]

ON THE INFLUENCE

OF THE

GREAT PRINCIPLE OF CHRISTIANITY

ON THE MOORS.

(Mat. vii. 12.)

Of the Propagation of Christianity in Africa.--Causes that prevent it.--The Mode of promoting it is through a friendly and commercial Intercourse with the Natives.--Exhortation to Great Britain to attend to the Intercourse with Africa.--Danger of the French colonizing Senegal, and supplanting us, and thereby depreciating the Value of our West-India Islands.

That it is a Christian duty to attempt, by lenient measures, to propagate the Christian religion among the Idolaters and Muhamedans of Africa, I think cannot be doubted; but this propagation will not spread to any considerable extent until, (in that country,) the morals of Christians in general shall approach nearer than they actually do to the standard of Christian perfection. It is, however, most certain that there never was a more promising, or a more favourable opportunity of subverting paganism in Africa, and establishing Christianity on its ruins, than at this present period; and I think the best method to effect this desirable purpose is through the medium of commerce, which must, in that continent, necessarily precede science and civilisation. It is well known, by all men of penetration who have [225] resided in Muhamedan countries, that the principles of the religion of Muhamed are not so repugnant to Christianity as many, nay, most persons have imagined. Various causes, however, tend to increase the hostility that exists between the two religions. First, it is augmented by the fakeers, and by political men, who are ever active in bringing to their aid superstition and enthusiasm, to increase the hostility. Secondly, it is augmented by the very little intercourse which they have with Christians, originating, for the most part, in our ignorance of the Arabic language, an ignorance which has been lamented by the emperor [164] Seedy Muhamed ben Abdallah himself. Thirdly, the hostility of these two religions is augmented by a very ancient tradition, that the country will be invaded by the Christians, and converted to Christianity, that this event will happen on a Friday (the Muhamedan sabbath), during the time that they are at the (*silla dohor*) prayers at half past one o'clock, P.M.; so that [226] throughout the empire they close the gates of all the towns on this day, at this period of time, till two o'clock, P.M.: when the prayers are over, and the people go out of the mosques, the gates are again thrown open. This tradition, which is universally believed, acts on the minds of the whole community, and fans the embers of hostility already lighted between Christians and Muhamedans, bringing to the recollection of the latter the hostile intentions of the former to invade and take their country from them, when an opportunity shall offer. On the other hand, what tends to reconcile the two creeds is, the influence that European commerce, and the principles of the Christian doctrine, have had on the muselmen of Africa. This influence extends as far as the commerce with Europeans extends. Wherever the Europeans negociate with the Moors, the great principle of the Christian doctrine is known and discussed,--that principle which surpasses every doctrine propagated by the Grecian philosophers, or the wise men of the East,-- that truly noble, liberal, and charitable principle, "Do as you would be done by," influences the conduct of the better educated muselmen who have had long intercourse and negociations with Christians; and they do not fail to retort it upon us, whenever *our conduct* deviates from it. Thus, the minds of muselmen, wherever European commerce flows, are tinctured with this great principle of the Christian doctrine. And, to an accurate observer of [227] mankind, it will appear that this principle, from its own intrinsic beauty, has in many superseded the muselman retaliative system of morality, originating in the Mosaic law,--"An eye for an eye, and a tooth for a tooth." For I have heard muselmen, in their individual disputes with one another, advance this precept as a rule of conduct. If, therefore, this divine principle be recognised by muselmen, who have had intercourse and commercial negociations with Europeans, in defiance of the obstacles to this doctrine suggested by the fakeers and political men; what might we not expect from the due cultivation of an extensive commerce, upon a grand national scale, with this interesting continent? Might we not expect a gradual diffusion of the principles of Christianity among the muselmen, as well as among the pagans and idolaters, of Africa? I would venture to assert, that in the event of the British government engaging, with energy and determination, to cultivate a commercial intercourse and extensive connection with Africa, that the negroes, and possibly even the Muhamedans, might gradually be converted to Christianity. This event would take a long time to accomplish, but its gradual progress, most probably, would be more rapid than was the progress of Muhamedanism during the life of the Arabian prophet.

Footnote 164: (return) When this Emperor, for the purpose of satisfying his people that he administered retributive justice, ordered two teeth of an English merchant to be drawn, he repented so much of what he had done, that he offered to make any amends that the merchant might require, expressing his wish that he had an English consul with whom he could converse colloquially, without the inconvenience of an interpreter; and for this purpose the Emperor, after granting him considerable favours, urged him to accept of the British consulship; adding, that he himself would secure him the appointment, and that he would then refuse nothing, but whatsoever the English should ask of him, they should have.

Associations have been formed in this philanthropic country, through the medium of extensive subscriptions, for the civilisation of [228] Africa, and the abolition of the slave trade: the greatest merit is due to the individuals who have subscribed to such institutions; their motives have been unexceptionable, but we grossly deceive ourselves, and the whole is an illusion! The French, as it were, have taken the staff out of our hands; and whilst we are in vain endeavouring to abolish the trade in slaves, *by the capture of slave-ships at sea* [165], they are insidiously cultivating the growth of cotton, coffee, sugar, indigo, and other colonial produce, on the banks of the Senegal river; insomuch that if we shall continue thus supinely to disregard their important African agricultural operations, the result in a few years will probably be, that they will be able to undersell us in West-India produce, in the markets of continental Europe; for they can cultivate, with free negroes at Senegal, colonial produce at considerably less expense than our West-India cultivation. The voyage, also, is not half the distance; so that the continental market for the sale of West-India produce will be shortly supplied from Senegal, from whence it [229] is more than probable that colonial produce will be imported to Europe at little more than half the expense of importing it from the West Indies: thus Great Britain may be driven out of the market for colonial produce, except for what may be sufficient for her own domestic supply.

Footnote 165: (return) Many naval officers concur in thinking, that to suppress the slave trade, by interrupting the ships, would employ all the navy of Great Britain; and entail a war-expense on the nation; besides the enormous expense that will be necessarily incurred by the various commissions dispatched to Sierra Leone, Havannah, &c. &c. for the adjudication of slave-causes. To which may be added, our expensive presents to Spain and Portugal, to induce those powers to coalesce in the abolition; which there is too much reason to apprehend will be evaded by the subjects of those powers.

This has been a favourite scheme of the French, who have now begun to taste the fruits of it: they have had it in view and in operation *ever since we gave them possession of Senegal*. It was the system of her late Emperor, Bonaparte, suggested to him by the arch and brilliant genius of Talleyrand, to indemnify the loss of St. Domingo.

Moreover, the French, who are cultivating the territory of Senegal with indefatigable industry, will be, in a few years, not only able to supply the continental markets of Europe with colonial produce, but they will become masters of North Africa, establish another Ceuta at the African promontory of the Cape de Verd, and, in the event of a war, annoy incalculably our East-India trade, and enhance the price of East-India produce in the British dominions; whilst they will, by the aid of the Americans, who will be always ready to assist them, form a depot for East-India goods at the Cape de Verd, and from thence introduce them into Africa and France, to the almost total exclusion of Great Britain. If we are to prevent these events from taking place, we must adopt different measures from what we have adopted; we must [230] move in a very different sphere from that in which we have been accustomed to move; we must be much more energetic, more vigilant, and more active than we have been, with respect to African matters. It is presumed that these suggestions are well deserving the consideration of His Majesty's ministers. May they view with the eye of an eagle and the wisdom of the serpent the insidious encroachments that are thus making on our colonial markets!!

The Africans, by which term I mean the natives, viz. the Moors, the Arabs, the Berebbers, the Shelluhs, and the Negroes, (not the Jews, who, although numerous in this country, yet, as they are and have been ever since their Theocratical Government, a distinct race, and their customs and manners well known, I do not include them in the term Africans, although from their birth they are entitled to the appellation,)--the Africans, I say, are seldom met with in closed rooms, but are constantly in the open air, transacting their business in *dwarias*, which are detached rooms, or apartments, with three sides, the fourth being supported by pillars; this custom of living continually in or exposed to the external air renders them strong and healthy, wherefore their bodies, by an *antiperistasis*, have the natural heat repelled and kept within, increasing by this action their appetite for food, which is always strong. They live in a frugal manner, seldom eating but of one food: the prevailing dish throughout North [231] Africa is cuscasoe, a granulated paste, cooked by steam, and garnished with vegetables, and chickens, or mutton; this is a very nutritive, palatable, and wholesome dish. They are not incumbered at their meals with a variety of dishes; but a large bowl, or spacious plate, is introduced on a round table, supported by one pillar, like the *Monopodia* of the ancients, rather larger than the bowl or dish, and about six inches high. Half a dozen Moors sit round this repast, on cushions or on the ground, cross-legged; a position which they remain in with perfect ease and pliability from custom and the loose dress they wear. When the company have seated themselves, a slave or a servant comes round to the guests, to perform the ceremony of (*togrêda*) washing of the hands; a brass bason or pan, which they call *tas*, is brought round to all the company, the slave holding it by his left hand, while, with the right hand, he pours water on the hands of the guests from a (*garoff*) pitcher, in the form of an Etruscan vase, having (*zeef*) a towel thrown over his shoulder to dry their hands. This ceremony is performed before and after meals. The master of the feast, before they begin to eat, pronounces (*Bismillah*) the grace before meat, which signifies, "In the name of God;" after the repast, he says (*El Ham'd û lillah*) "Praise be to God." Each guest eats with the fingers of his right hand, none ever touching the food with their left. If a piece of meat, or a joint of a fowl or chicken is to be [232] divided, two of the guests take hold of it, and pull it till it is divided. This is somewhat repugnant to an European's ideas of delicacy; but if we consider that the hands are previously washed, and that they never come in contact with the mouth in decent or respectable society, there is not so insuperable an objection to this way of eating as might otherwise appear. Each person in eating the granulated flour or cuscasoe, puts his two fore-fingers into the dish before him, and by a dextrous turn of the hand converts the quantity taken up into the form of a ball, which he, with a peculiar dexterity, jirks into the mouth. The Africans never drink till they have done eating; when dinner is over, a large goblet, or *poculum amicitiæ*, of pure water is passed round, and each person drinks copiously; the washing is then repeated, and the repast is terminated. Afterwards coffee is introduced, without milk: the cup is not placed in a saucer, nor do they hand you a spoon, for the sugar is mixed in the coffee-pot; the cup is presented in an outer cup of brass, which preserves the fingers from being burned. They use no bells in their tents; but the slaves or servants are called by the master when wanted, one generally standing in the corner of the tent to superintend the others. The pipe is sometimes introduced after the coffee, but this is by no means a general custom, except among the negroes. The pipe is of rose-wood, of jasmin, or of rhododendrum wood: great quantities of the latter are conveyed [233] across the Sahara, for pipe-tubes for the negroes of Timbuctoo, and other territories of Sudan, bordering on the Nile el Abeed, or Nile of the Negroes (Niger).

Passing through this territory of encampments, when travellers are disposed to sleep at a douar, one of the party presents himself at the confines of the encampment, and exclaims (*Deef Allah*)

"The guest of God." The sheik of the douar is immediately apprised of the circumstance; and after investigating the rank of the travellers, he enquires if they have tents with them; if they have not, he has his own or (*kheyma deâf*) the guest's tent appropriated for the travellers. If they have their own tents, which persons of respectability generally have, the sheik comes and directs the servants where to pitch them; the camels and mules are disburdened, and the sheik declares (*atshie m'hassub alia*) "For all this baggage I hold myself accountable." Europeans travelling in this country generally follow their own customs: accordingly, among the English, tea is ordered; a most delectable refreshment after a fatiguing journey on horseback, exposed to the scorching rays of the African sun. If the sheik and a few of his friends are invited to tea, which these Arabs designate by (*elma skoon û el hadra*) hot water and conversation, they like it very sweet, and drink half-a-dozen cups at least. Nothing ingratiates travellers with these people so much as distributing a few lumps of sugar among [234] them: sugar, honey, or any thing sweet, being with these Arabs emblematical of peace and friendship. Some of the women of the Arabs are extremely handsome; in all the simplicity of nature "when unadorned adorned the most." To fine figures they unite handsome profiles, good and white teeth, and large, black, expressive, intelligent eyes, like the eyes of a gazel; dark eye-brows, and dark long eye-lashes, which give a peculiar warmth and softness to the eye. They concern themselves little about time, and will sometimes come to converse after midnight with the Europeans. When the guard of the tent informs them they cannot go in, that the Christian is a-bed and undressed, they are not less astonished than we are to see them sleeping in the open air at night, on the ground, with their clothes on. When candles are brought into the tent at night, the servant wishes the company a good evening: he says "*M'sah elkhere*," the literal meaning of which is "*Good be with you this evening*;" which salutation it is courteous to return, even to a slave; and if any one, however great his rank, were not to return it, he would be considered a bad muselman, a disaffected and inhospitable barbarian. The morning salutation is (*Alem Allah sebak*,) "May your morning be accompanied with the knowledge of God;" or, (*Sebah el khere*, or *sebahk b'elkhere*) "Good morning to you," or "May your morning be good." Equals meeting, touch hands, and then each kisses his own respectively; they [235] then say, (I now speak of the middle order of society,) "And how are you, and how have you been: how long it is since I saw you! and how are you, and how are your children; (*ûhel Dar'kume*,) and the people of your family, how are they, certainly you are well:" and so they will go on, sometimes for a quarter of an hour, repeating the same thing. If an inferior meets a superior, he kisses his hand or his garment and retires, when there is a greater disparity of rank, the inferior kisses the stirrup of the superior; or prostrates himself if the superior is a prince, a fakeer, or a bashaw.

Another salutation among respectable individuals is, by each placing his right hand on his heart, indicating that part to be the residence of the friend!

The Jews of this country retain the customs of their ancestors more pure and unmixed than those in other countries.

When a Jew dies he is interred the same day, or the day after at farthest. The female relations and the friends of the deceased assemble round the corpse, and utter bitter lamentations, tearing their faces and their hair in a most woeful manner; they disfigure their faces with their finger-nails, till they bleed, and during the whole time keep stamping or moving their legs, beating time, as it were, with their feet; these lamentations are continued, with occasional intermission, till the body of the deceased is carried away for interment. The performers [236] of these bitter lamentations appear to have all the marks of hideous grief inscribed on their faces, but most of them feel no real concern; some of the girls, young and handsome, near akin to the deceased, are ambitious to disfigure themselves, and they lacerate their pretty faces most lamentably. The more wounds these bear on their cheeks the greater is their grief considered to be. But the corpse being removed the mourners regale themselves with *Mahaya*, or African brandy, and make up for their lamentations, by converting their bitter strains into conviviality.

There is a strange resemblance between this custom and that practised by the inhabitants of New Zealand; insomuch that we might imagine the latter to be one of the lost tribes of this extraordinary people. It is true that we have no record of such a perfection of navigation as to enable us to conjecture how a tribe of Jews could reach New Zealand: but many things remain in great obscurity even in this enlightened age; and we have had no historical record transmitted to us from the ancients of many extraordinary discoveries that recently have been made in Egypt.

[237]

INTEREST OF MONEY.

Application of the Superflux of Property or Capital.

In this country the law allows no interest of money; the consequence is, that the country is overwhelmed with usurers, who exact, generally, an oath of secrecy, and lend money on pledges of valuable and convertible merchandise: the interest paid on these negociations is most exorbitant; I have known five, six, eight, ten, and even twelve per cent, per month paid for the use of money! There is no paper money in this country; but a bank might be established at Mogodor, for the convenience of internal trade: the *sine qua non* of the bank should be, AN ADEQUATE CAPITAL. The advantages that would necessarily result from an establishment of this kind are incalculable; the paper of a bank, *thus established*, would be current in a short time, UNDER JUDICIOUS AND INTELLIGENT MANAGEMENT, in all the territories of Sudan, through the heart of Africa, through Bambâra, Timbuctoo, Houssa, Cashna, Wangara, Bernôh, Fas, and Marocco, and various other countries. The immense advantages of the carriage of paper through the Desert and [238] through Sudan, *convertible* into cash at every commercial city, port, or district in a country like this, would greatly facilitate the operations of commerce; this must be evident to every political economist acquainted with the nature of commercial negociations in Africa.

The superflux of coin, consisting principally of Mexico dollars, and doubloons, (over and above the quantum necessary for the circulating medium of commercial negociations,) is either buried under ground by the owner, or converted into jewels for the ladies of his family; there is a general propensity to these subterraneous hordes; the bulk of the people, the lower classes in particular, have an idea that they will enjoy in the next world what they save in this; which opinion is not extraordinary, when we consider how many cases there are, wherein we see the sublimest capacity prostrate at the shrine of an *early imbibed* superstition. Many of these erring philosophers, therefore, attentive to the accumulation of riches, retire from this sublunary world with an immense immolated treasure, wherewith to begin, as they imagine, their career in the world to come!

"We," they say, "convert our superflux to jewels and costly apparel for our females, and we have the gratification of seeing them well apparelled and agreeably ornamented. Moreover, a great part of our possessions is appropriated to the sacred rites of hospitality, which [239] you Christians know not how to practise; for you worship the idol of ostentation; you invite your friends to dinner; you incur an intolerable and injudicious expense, and provide a multiplicity of dishes to pamper their appetites, sufficient for a regiment of muselmen; when nature and national beings, which men were born to be, require only one dish. Moreover, your sumptuous entertainments are given to those only who do not want; therefore is it an ostentatious and a wanton waste! We, on the contrary, that is to say, every good Muselman, gives one-tenth of his property to the poor; and moreover much of his substance is appropriated to the support, not of the rich and independent, who do not want it, but to (*deefan*) strange guests who journey from one country to another; insomuch that, with us, a poor man may travel by public beneficence and apt hospitality from the shores of the Mediterranean to the borders of Sahara, without a fluce [166] in (*hashituh*) the corner of his garment. [167] A traveller, however poor he may be, is never at a loss for a meal, several meals, and even for three days entertainment, wherever he travels through our country; and if any man were to go to a douar in any of the Arab provinces of our Sovereign's [240] empire, and not receive the entertainment and courtesy of a brother, that douar would be stamped with a stigma of indelible disgrace! Pardon us, therefore, if we say, you have not such hospitality in your country, although the great principle of (*Seedna Aisa*) our Lord Jesus, is charity." [168] I should, however, observe that this hospitality is shown almost exclusively to Muhamedans.

Footnote 166: (return) A fluce is a copper coin, one hundred of which are equal to sixpence English.

Footnote 167: (return) In the corner of his garment:--The Africans have no pockets; they carry their money in the corner of their garment, and tie it with a knot to secure it.

Footnote 168: (return) The Muhamedans acknowledge Jesus Christ to have been a Prophet that worked miracles; the indelible proof of his mission.

Respecting women and horses, speaking of the treatment of them in England, they remark, that "England is a paradise for women, who are there exalted beyond the fitness of things; and it is (*gehennum*) a hell for horses, for those poor ill-treated animals in the hackney coaches and carts, need only to be seen to be pitied; the hard blows which they receive from their cruel masters are calculated to impress our minds with an opinion that we are in a land of barbarians, whereas you call yourselves a civilised people: You say you are such; your actions deny the fact, and we judge by actions, not by words or self-commendations. When, therefore, you pride yourselves on your superiority and civilisation the whole is a delusion; and when we hear you set forth these absurd pretensions, we are compelled to commiserate our common race, and to exclaim, Alas, poor human nature!" This is the verbatim [251] reply that a very intelligent but irritated Muselman made to my animadversions on the absurdity of burying treasure. This gentleman's father had been ambassador from the Emperor of Marocco to Great Britain, and to France; and had seen much of French, Spanish, and English manners, among the higher orders of society in those countries.

Too much cannot be said in commendation of this generous, open-hearted philanthropy of the Arabs, here described: but the intelligent reader will understand, that it applies particularly to the Arabs, or cultivators of the plains, in the empire of Marocco; and, in its large and unlimited extent, to the Bedouin or roving Arabs of the Sahara, and of Lower Suse, from whose (*kabyles*) clans, the Arabs cultivators are early emigrations; almost all of them having their original stock in the Sahara. It is also confined, almost exclusively, to Muhamedans, and does not, like the divine doctrine of Jesus Christ, with universal benevolence embrace all mankind, without distinction of party, sect, or nation;--a doctrine which has lately been put in considerable practice in our own country, by institutions supported by voluntary subscriptions for the destitute, for foreigners in distress, and for negroes; by institutions in aid and support of all needy persons labouring under sickness, or having need of surgical aid; by institutions for the encouragement of industry, for the refutation of vice and immorality; [242] by institutions that reflect immortal honour on this country, and cast a lustre on the respective individuals who have contributed to all these heart-approving institutions, which are calculated to afford relief to almost every description of suffering humanity!!

Itinerant (*tebeebs*) doctors travel through the country to administer to the sick; which, however, are seldom found. They carry over their shoulders a leathern bag, containing their surgical apparatus, which consists of a lancet, a scarifying knife, and a caustic knife, or knife for burning: they scarify the neck, the forehead, or the wrists. The caustic knife is an instrument of very general application. They convert all gun-shot and other wounds, as well as sores, into burns, by heating the knife in the fire, and gently touching the circumference of the wound with it. This produces acute pain; but the Africans bear pain heroically: they say that this method prevents inflammation and festering. They perform, by caustic, extraordinary cures. I imagine this method would not agree with an European body, pampered with a variety of high food and luxurious living.

The inhabitants of this country break their fast with (*el hassûa*) barley-gruel; they grind the barley to the size of sparrow-shot, this they mix with water, and simmer over a slow fire two or three hours. This food is esteemed extremely wholesome, and is antifebrile. The [243] Emperor takes this before he drinks tea in a morning: his father, Seedi Muhamed ben Abdallah, also, who drank none but fine hyson tea, never would drink that beverage till he had first laid a foundation of *el hassûa*.

The Arabs and Shelluhs, with whom *el hassûa* is generally used, urge its salubrity, by reporting that a physician alighted in a strange country, and when he arose in the morning, after performing his matins, he seated himself with some of the inhabitants, and, conversing, asked them how they lived, and with what food they broke their fast? "With *el hassûa*," was the reply: "Then," rejoined

Esculapius, (*Salam û alikume*,) "Peace be with you; for if you eat *el hassûa* in the morning you have no need of a doctor:" and he immediately departed.

When I established the port of Santa Cruz, and opened it to European commerce, the gratitude and hospitality of the Arabs and Shelluhs of the province of Suse, was demonstrated in every way: so rejoiced were they to see their port, after an inactivity of thirty years, again re-established. If I rode out to visit any part of the country, the women, on my approach to a douar, would come out to a great distance with bowls of milk on their heads; others with bowls of honey, with thin scrapings of butter in them, and bread or cakes [169], similar to pancakes, [244] baked in five minutes, on stones heated with the embers of charcoal. These greetings I received by tasting every bowl of milk, and dipping a bit of bread in the honey and eating it. The milk thus presented is emblematical of peace and amity; the honey of welcome: to refuse eating or tasting what is thus presented, is considered, among this patriarchal people, a great breach of good manners, an inexcusable want of courtesy, which they say none but a *kaffer* [170] would commit. They would then say, *Birk eeaudee, birk attajar u straha*, "Alight, I pray thee, alight, merchant! and rest yourself."

Footnote 169: (return) See a similar custom in Genesis, xxiii. 5--8.

Footnote 170: (return) Kaffer is the Arabic term for Infidel. All the idolatrous Negro nations are, by Muhamedans, denominated Kaffer, (or Caffres). Sing. Kâffer--plural Kaffer.

In these halcyon days, these grateful people never knew when to cease offering presents. They sat on the ground in the refulgent meridian sun, and when I dismounted to walk to the shade of a tree, to partake of their hospitality, they would exhort me to shun the shade, (*lie ê drab'k elbird*) for fear it should give me cold. These Bedouin [171] Arabs of Suse and Sahara [245] are the descendants of the ancient Arabs, whose bold and figurative language is the same that was spoken in Arabia twelve centuries ago, in the time of Muhamed.

Footnote 171: (return) The Arabs of the vast plains of the empire of Marocco, who live in douars, or encampments, are emigrations from the original stock or clan in Sahara; who are the pure or Bedouin Arabs. Being established in the beautiful and productive plains of West and South Barbary, they soon forget their Bedouin customs, change their wandering, plundering habits, and become cultivators, and stationary; for the immense produce of their labour in these plains, which require no dung, nor any preparation but the plough, soon rewards their industry, so as to determine them to continue this new mode of life.

Passing early one morning by a douar, in the territory of Howara, [172] I was invited to join a party to hunt the wild boar. The plains of Howara, between the city of Terodant and Santa Cruz, abound with boars: we started, in a few hours, seven of these animals, two of which were taken and killed. The dogs best calculated for this sport are what they call *sereet telt*, or the third race of greyhounds, which is a very strong dog. One of these, I observed, attacked the boars by the nape of the neck, and never left his hold till the other dogs came up to the attack: although the boar would toss him about in all directions, he never left his hold. The Arabs of Suse are very dextrous and active at this sport: they hunt with javelins; some have guns, which they fire when opportunity offers, but they never expend their powder and shot (*batâl*) vainly, as they express it, but always make sure of their mark. I could not but admire this celebrated (*slogie*) greyhound; [246] which the Arab to whom it belonged observing, insisted on my taking it home to Santa Cruz, adding, that whenever I wished to hunt, to let him know, and he would accompany me. I offered him a present of money for the dog, which is what I never had refused before in the provinces north of Suse; but he declined the offer, saying he was more than recompensed already by the establishment of the port of Santa Cruz. "Myself, my family, my kabyl," said he, "hail you as a father; (*e moot alik*) they will die in your cause." No favour could have equalled that of re-establishing the commerce of Agadeer. These circumstances serve to show what reception might be expected from these people, if the British Government would negociate with the Emperor for the purchase of the port of Agadeer, or Santa Cruz, preparatory to the establishment of a commerce with Timbuctoo, and other regions of Sudan.

Footnote 172: (return) In the 815th year of the Hejira, an emigration from the Howara Arabs attacked, took possession of, and destroyed the city of Assouan, in Egypt.

[247]

PLAN

FOR THE

GRADUAL CIVILISATION OF AFRICA.

On the Commercial Intercourse with Africa, through the
Sahara and Ashantee.

To cultivate an extensive commercial intercourse with Africa, I have already observed, that the best method, the simplest, and that which is, from contingent circumstances, the most likely to succeed, is the plan which I have pointed out in the following prospectus. I shall now offer several reasons why this plan is superior to any other hitherto suggested.

The riches of the Arabs of Sahara generally, as well as of that part which I have contemplated as a convenient spot for establishing a colony, and for opening a communication with Sudan, consists exclusively in camels. The independence of a man is there ascertained by the number of camels he possesses; it is not said, how many thousand dollars has he? or, what quantity of gold does he possess? or, what land has he? but, how many camels does he own? The master of these, aptly denominated, ships of the Desert, is urged by interest to let on hire his camels, as [248] the master of a ship of the ocean is urged by interest to seek freight for his ship. And it is observed, that the ferocious appearance among the Arabs, (which is too often assumed,) subsides in proportion to the intercourse they have with merchants, who negociate with them for the transport of their goods. Thus, at the *depôts* for camels between the cultivated country and the Desert, viz. at *Akka, Tatta, Ufran,* and *Wedinoon*, the ferocity of the Arabs is greatly lost in the commercial spirit and endeavour to let their camels on hire to the merchants. The Mograffra, the Woled Abbusebah, and the Tejakant Arabs, therefore, who possess the Sahara, from the shores of the Atlantic to the confines of Timbuctoo, would act in concert with the colony, and would have a joint interest in promoting their commercial views. The Brabeesh Arabs who receive, occasionally, tribute from Timbuctoo, would also find it expedient to promote the commerce of Sudan, and the prosperity of Timbuctoo; both which would necessarily be united to their own interest, and would provide a demand for their camels.

If the profits of this commerce, when once established and secured to the British, were to be cent. per cent., the whole would remain a bonus to the colony. There would be no shereef of Fezzan, or bashaw of Tripoli, to take their share of the profits, in any shape, in exchange for the privilege of being suffered to pass through their country. But, on the contrary, the Arabs [249] of the Mograffra and other tribes would find it so evidently their interest and advantage to be friendly with us, that we might absolutely have the entire command of the Desert, from the shores of the Atlantic to the city of Timbuctoo, which would eventually throw such a weight of power into our hands, as to make even that city itself, in a manner, tributary to us.

A plan of this kind should be executed *upon a grand national scale*, and be pursued with discretion and perseverance.

An attempt to penetrate to Timbuctoo, through Ashantee, and establish a commerce through that country, might meet with temporary success; but I apprehend that we should labour under the same inconveniences, and be subject to the same arbitrary imposts and exactions, whether in the shape of duties, part of the profits, or otherwise, as we should, by opening a communication through Tripoli. There would be a present or douceur to the king of Ashantee; others to the princes of the adjoining territories; and, finally, (taking the character of this king to be as represented by the late traveller in that country, Mr. Bowdich), might we not reasonably anticipate that, on the first dispute respecting the division of the profits, the king of Ashantee would order all the English out of his country, and, to terminate the dispute, plunder them of their property? But, perhaps the establishment of a colony in Ashantee, *conjoined* to one in Sahara, might not be objectionable. We [250] should then have two routs to the grand emporium of central Africa: if one failed, the other would remain open for our countrymen to recover their property and to return by; and thus, in establishing a commercial intercourse with the interior of Africa, through two routes, we should secure, at the same time, our retreat, by one of them, and not remain at the mercy of the barbarous king of Ashantee, or any other African potentate, who might be urged, from jealousy or avarice, to sacrifice our people, when once he had them in his power!

[251]

PROSPECTUS OF A PLAN

FOR FORMING A

NORTH AFRICAN OR SUDAN COMPANY

To be instituted for the purpose of establishing an extensive Commerce with, and laying open to British Enterprise, all the Interior Regions of North Africa.

OBJECTS OF THE SOCIETY.

1st. To lay open the interior regions of North Africa to British enterprise--to supply those vast and unexplored countries with British manufactures, with East-India goods, and with colonial produce.

2dly, To encourage our manufactories, by opening a new market calculated to improve the revenue of the country, to provide employment for the labouring poor, and to enrich the mercantile community; *the genial influence of which sources of prosperity will necessarily diffuse itself through all classes.*

3dly, To facilitate, through the medium of commerce (*the only medium by which it can possibly be effected*), the exploration of the interior regions of Africa, (*which have remained to this day a sealed book, notwithstanding the many adventurous expeditions that have been undertaken,*) by opening a communication with the natives [252] of that vast and little-known continent, and by calling to our aid the co-operation of the native chiefs, by holding out to them the benefits which they will derive from commercial intercourse as a reward for their assistance and exertions in promoting this desirable Object.

For these purposes it is proposed--

That the funds to be raised be one hundred thousand pounds, in shares of one hundred pounds each. Ten shares to constitute a director.

The spot proposed to be fixed on as the point of communication, and commercial depôt, between Great Britain and the interior of Africa is safe and healthy: it will afford a *direct communication with Timbuctoo and the interior regions of Sudan*, without being subject to the uncertainty of securing the favour and protection of the various sultans and sheiks of the respective territories of the interior, through which the merchants and traders may pass--a measure which would have been indispensable in every plan that has hitherto been suggested for the discovery of those interesting regions.

The plan now to be adopted, on the contrary, will be subject to none of those impediments and uncertainties; but the merchants and travellers will pass through territories where they need fear no hostility, but will be received with hospitality and attention by the natives, who will give them every assistance and accommodation in their progress through their country.

[253]

Connected with this plan, a school for instructing the British youth in African Arabic, so as to initiate them in the rudiments of that language previously to their departure for Africa, might be established, under the direction of James Grey Jackson, professor of African Arabic, &c.

The present scheme has been many years in contemplation, but no favourable opportunity of making it thus public having hitherto occurred, it is now offered to the public, in consequence of the energies lately manifested by France and by America for African colonisation, and also by Holland.

The projectors, for the honour of their own country, are anxious that Great Britain may not, through supineness, suffer this important discovery to be wrested from her by any foreign power, but that she should *at least share the glory* due to this important achievement, the completion of which would *immortalize the prince who should cherish it to its maturity*.

Capitalists, and gentlemen resident in Great Britain, desirous of further information on this subject, may address themselves to James Grey Jackson, whose residence, at any time, may be known at Messrs. Longman, Hurst, Rees, Orme, and Brown, London.

TO THE BRITISH PUBLIC.

London, 31st March, 1819.

The above plan is ingenuously, liberally, and disinterestedly submitted to the consideration of [254] British capitalists and merchants of respectability. The advantages to be derived from such an establishment as is here contemplated, if not evident to Great Britain, is clearly visible to Holland, to France, and to America.

The projector, therefore, without mentioning the offers that have been made to him by a foreign maritime power, and *without courting* the suffrages of British merchants in support of this plan, has it in contemplation, (*provided no attention is paid to it in England,*) to lay this eligible scheme open to a foreign power. If, therefore, the projector should accept employment in this undertaking from a foreign power, it will be in the conviction, that *it is more to the interest of mankind in general, and to Europe in particular*, that this plan for opening an *extensive, lucrative, and beneficial commerce with Africa*, (which would necessarily lead to its civilisation,) should be known to, and adopted by, *a foreign power*, than that this vast and little-known continent should, (to the indelible disgrace of civilised Europe,) *still continue to remain* an useless and an undiscovered country to the present generation!

James Grey Jackson

Appendix to the foregoing Prospectus, being an Epitome of the Trade carried on by Great Britain and the European States in the Mediterranean, indirectly with Timbuctoo, the Commercial Depôt of North Africa, and with other States of Sudan.

Marseilles, Genoa, Leghorn, and other commercial ports of France and Italy, as well as of [255] Spain, send to Algiers, Tunis, Tripoli, and Egypt, *for the markets of Sudan*, manufactured silks, damask, brocade, velvets, raw silk, combs of box and ivory, gold-thread, paper, manufactured sugar, cochineal, and various other merchandise.

Great Britain sends to the Barbary ports in the Mediterranean, and to Mogodor on the Atlantic Ocean (which are afterwards conveyed to Timbuctoo), for distribution at the several markets of Sudan--

East India Goods, viz.--Gum benjamin, cassia, cinnamon, mace, nutmegs, cloves, ginger, black pepper, Bengal silk, China silks, nankeens, blue linens, long cloths, and muslins (mulls).

West India Produce.--Pimento, tobacco, coffee, cocoa, and manufactured sugar.

Linens.--Dimities, plattilias, creas, rouans, Britannias, cambrics, and Irish linens.

Hardware.--Iron nails, copper ditto, brass ditto, sword blades, dagger ditto, guns, gunpowder, knives, &c. &c.

Cloths.--Superfine, of plain brilliant colours, not mixtures, and cassimeres. And various other articles of merchandise.

Immense quantities of salt are also sent to Timbuctoo, which is for the most part collected at the mines of Tishet and Shangareen, (see the map of northern and central Africa, in the New Supplement to the Encyclopaedia Britannica,) through which the caravan would pass to Timbuctoo.

[256]

The following are the articles purchased by the Moors and Arab traders, and are the returns brought back to Barbary from Sudan; viz.

Gold dust, and trinkets of pure Wangara gold, of various fashions, of the manufacture of Housa and Jinnie.--*B'Kore Sudan* (fumigation of Sudan), a kind of frankincense highly esteemed by the Africans. Ostrich feathers (the finest in the world). Elephants' Teeth. *Korkidan*, so called by the Arabs, being the horns of the rhinoceros: these are a very costly article, and are in high estimation among the muselmen, for sword-hilts and dagger-handles. *Guza Sarawie* (Grains of Paradise). Gum Copal Assafoetida, and a great variety of drugs for manufacturing uses, and various roots for dyeing. Ebony. Camwood. Sandal wood. Indigo, equal to that of Guatimala: to which may be added, the command of the gum trade of Senegal.

All the foregoing merchandise being first landed at Alexandria, Tripoli, Tunis, Algiers, and Tetuan, and other Barbary ports in the Mediterranean, *as well as at Mogodor on the western coast of Africa*, are afterwards sold to the Muhamedan merchants, who sell them with a very good profit to other Moors. These goods frequently go through three, four, and five hands, before they reach the consumer in Sudan, subject to a profit gained by each holder of from twenty to thirty per cent.; the last purchaser, who conveys them through the Desert, however, [257] expects, and generally obtains, from fifty to sixty per cent. profit on them, to which he considers himself entitled, from the fatigue and privations of his passage through the Desert, during a journey through a country, for the most part barren, of above fifteen hundred miles in length; through various kingdoms and principalities, subject to a charge for (*statta*) convoy at the exit and entrance of each respective state or district on each side of the Sahara, as well as in the Sahara itself.

But, according to the plan here suggested to the commercial community, all these various articles, instead of passing through five several hands, would now pass through only two hands, viz. through those of the shippers in England, and those of their agents established on *the western coast of Africa*, who would sell them directly to the Timbuctoo trader, which latter, instead of having several principalities and kingdoms to pass through (at the exit from each of which, as well as at the entrance of them, he would have a charge for protection or convoy, called *statta*, levied on the goods), would have no convoy-charge, or statta, to pay; he would have but ten hundred, instead of fifteen or sixteen hundred miles to go, being about two-thirds of the distance of the road from Tunis or Tripoli, through Fezzan, to Timbuctoo.

N.B. There is an immense bank near the contemplated depôt, or port (abounding in fish, which now supplies the *wahs*, or cultivated [258] spots in the desert, as well as the territories on the southern confines thereof), which produces fish sufficient to supply the whole of the interior of Africa, as well as the shores of the Mediterranean, &c. &c.

Letter from Vasco de Gama, in elucidation of
this Plan.

Sir,

The Society of Encouragement for National Industry in France, has granted prizes for various discoveries in the arts and sciences; but I wish government, or some society of our own country, would offer a liberal prize for the best mode of colonising Africa, and for meliorating the condition of the inhabitants of that vast and little known continent. A well-digested plan for the discovery of this continent might be followed by the most desirable events. The efforts of the African Association have, to say the least, been lamentably disastrous; little good can be anticipated from the efforts of solitary or scientific travellers in a country where science is not cultivated, and where the travellers know little or nothing of the [173] general language of [259] Africa, or of the manners and dispositions of the natives.

Footnote 173: (return) The general language of North Africa is the Western Arabic, with a knowledge of which language, a traveller may make himself intelligible wherever he may go; either in the negro countries of Sudan, in Egypt, Abyssinia, Sahara, or Barbary.

A knowledge therefore of the *African Arabic* appears indispensable to this great undertaking; and it should seem that a commercial adventurer is much more likely to obtain his object than a scientific traveller, for this plain reason,--because it is much easier to persuade the Africans that we travel into their country for the purposes of commerce and its result--*profit*, than to persuade them that we are so anxious to ascertain the course of their rivers!

Accordingly, it was aptly observed by the Negroes of Congo, when they learned that Captain Tuckey came not to trade nor to make war; *"What then come for? only to take walk and make book?"*

I do not mean now to lay down a plan for the colonisation of Africa, or for opening an extensive commerce with that vast continent, but I would suggest the propriety of the method by which the East India Company govern their immense territories. *I would wish to see an African Company formed on an extensive scale, with a large capital.* I am convinced that such a company would be of more service to the commerce of this country than the present India trade, where the natives, *without being in want* of our manufactures, surpass us in ingenuity. But the Africans, on the contrary, *are in want* of our manufactured goods, and give immense sums for them. According to a [260] late author, who has given us the fullest description [174] of Timbuctoo [175] and its vicinity, a *Plattilia* is there worth fifty Mexico dollars, or twenty *meezens of gold*, each meezen being worth two and a half Mexico dollars; *a piece of Irish linen* of ordinary quality, and measuring twenty-five yards, is worth seventy-five Mexico dollars; and a quintal of *loaf sugar* is worth one hundred Mexico dollars. Now if we investigate the parsimonious mode of traversing the Desert, we shall find that a journey of 1500 English miles is performed from Fas to Timbuctoo at the rate of forty shillings sterling per quintal, so that loaf sugar (a weighty and bulky article) can be rendered from London at Timbuctoo through Tetuan and Fas, including the expense of a land-carriage of 1500 miles at about 6£. per quintal, thus:

	s.	d.
Refined sugar on board in London for per cwt.	70	0
Duty on importation in any part of Marocco, ten per cent.	7	0
Freight, &c. five per cent.	3	6
Land carriage across the Desert on camels to Timbuctoo	40	0

Footnote 174: (return) See new Supplement to the Encyclopedia Britannica, article Africa, page 98.

Footnote 175: (return) See the account of Timbuctoo appended to Jackson's account of Marocco, published by Cadell and Davies, London, Chap, 18.

[261]

So that if 100 lb. of loaf sugar rendered, at Timbuctoo cost 120*s*. 6*d* and sells there for 100 Mexico dollars at 4*s*. 6*d*. each, or for 22£. 5*s*. there will result a profit of 270 per cent.

The profit in fine goods, such as the linens before mentioned, is still more considerable, not being subject to so heavy a charge for carriage. The immense quantity of [176] gold dust and gold bars that would be brought from Timbuctoo, Wangara, Gana, and other countries, in exchange for this merchandise, would be incalculable, and has, perhaps, never yet been contemplated by Europeans!!--In the same work, above quoted, 3d edition, page 289, will be found a list of the various merchandise exportable from Great Britain, which suit the market of the interior of Africa or Sudan: and also a list of the articles which we should receive in return for those goods.

Footnote 176: (return) The Kings, David and Solomon, extracted from Africa to enrich the temple of Jerusalem upwards of 800,000,000£. sterling, a sum sufficient to discharge the national debt; see Commercial Magazine for May 1819, page 6.; which is eight times as much gold as the mines of Brazil have produced since their discovery in 1756. See Commercial Magazine for the same month, page 44.

Plans to penetrate to the mart of Timbuctoo (which would supply Housa, Wangara, Gana, and other districts of Sudan with European merchandize) have been formed; but if a treaty of commerce were made with any of the Negro kings, these plans would be subject to various impediments.

[262]

The goods, in passing through hostile territories, (these sovereigns living in a state of continual warfare with each other,) would be subject to innumerable imposts; *it would therefore be expedient to form a plan whereby the goods should reach Timbuctoo through an eligible part of the Desert*: but some persons who have been in the habit of trading for gum to *Portandik*, have declared the inhabitants of Sahara to be a wild and savage race, untractable and not to be civilised by commerce, or by any other means. This I must beg leave to contradict: the Arabs of Sahara, from their wandering habits, are certainly wild, and *they are hostile to all who do not understand their language*; but if two or three Europeans capable of holding colloquial intercourse with them, were to go and establish a factory on their coast, and then suggest to them the benefit *they would derive*, being the *carriers* of such a trade as is here contemplated, their ferocity would be transferred forthwith into that virtue in the practice of which they so eminently excel all other nations, *hospitality*; and the most inviolable alliance might be formed with such a people. I speak not from the experience of books, but from an actual intercourse, and from having passed many years of my youth among them.

An advantageous spot might be fixed upon [263] on the western coast, in an independent district, where our alliance would be courted, from which the Kafila [177] or Akkaba would have to pass through only one tribe with perfect safety, and subject to no impost whatever; neither would they be subject to any duty on entering the town of Timbuctoo, as they would enter at the *Beb Sahara*, or gate of the Desert, which *exempts them* from duty or impost.

Footnote 177: (return) Caravan.

That civilisation would be the result of commerce, and that the trade in slaves would decrease with the increase of our commerce with these people, there can be little doubt; and, independent of the advantages of an extensive commerce, the consolation would be great to the Christian and to the Philosopher, of having converted millions of brethren made in the perfection of God's image, and endowed with reason, from barbarism to civilisation, if not to Christianity!!!

Let us hope, then, that some of the intelligent readers of your luminous and interesting pages will direct their attention to this great national object, and produce ah eligible and well-digested plan for the cultivation of a mutual intercourse *through the medium qf commerce with Africa*, and for the civilisation of that hitherto neglected continent.

Vasco De Gama.

Eton, 28th May, 1819.

[264]

On Commercial Intercourse with Africa.

(TO THE EDITOR OF THE MONTHLY MAGAZINE.)

Sir,

The plan of your correspondent, for opening a commercial intercourse with the interior of Africa, appears to me so direct and simple, that I am only surprised it has not been thought of before. The Moors are the merchants of Africa; the chain of communication that runs from the states of Barbary to the negro kingdoms, and from the shores of the Atlantic Ocean to the Red Sea. To judge of the humanity of these people from the accounts of shipwrecked sailors, whom they have dragged into slavery, and then liberated for money, would be not less fallacious than to estimate the character of the English nation from the plunderers of the wrecks on their coast. From such accounts, the name of Moor has inspired us with horror; and Park's detention at the camp of Ali, one of their chiefs, has contributed to confirm it. Park, however, so far from endeavouring to conciliate his captors, endeavoured, by his own confession, to appear as contemptible as possible in their eyes; and yet, with this disadvantage, the greater part of the miseries he endured proceeded from the climate and the irritation of his own mind.

The Arabs of Sahara are the carriers of merchandize throughout North Africa, and the Moors are in the constant habit of selling gum to the French on the Senegal. The French say [265] they are perfidious; but they give no proof of it that I have seen. I have met with a French traveller, who owns that his countrymen deceive them either in the weight or measure of the gum they purchase.

Bruce found a friend in every Moorish merchant, and integrity and intelligence in all. And where should these qualities be found in a country like the interior of Africa, in which learning has no place but among merchants?

So much for the proposed carriers of English goods to Timbuctoo. Now for the road. The fertile parts of Africa are hot and humid, unwholesome and dangerous; and the kings are often at war with each other. Park experienced both these evils; and the wonder was, not so much that he perished on his second journey, as that he returned from his first. The Desert is dry and heathful. It is sprinkled with fertile spots, which form a succession of known resting-places, and the distance between each requires a certain number of days to travel. The Moors are at home in Sahara; and, when they go long journeys, the fertile spots are their inns. The road from the coast of Sahara is also the shortest that has yet been pointed out to Timbuctoo.

If the means of executing the plan appear sufficient, it is not necessary to say any thing in favour of the object. the exchange of British manufactures for gold, speaks for itself. But there is no time to be lost. The French settlement of Galam is advantageously situated for commerce with Timbuctoo: a Frenchman has [266] already travelled from Galam to that city, I believe on a commercial speculation, and he has returned safe.

Catherine Hutton.

Impediments to our Intercourse with Africa.

When we consider the maritime strength of Great Britain; her command of the ocean; the vicinity to Europe of West Barbary, one of the finest countries in the world; the rich and valuable produce which is cultivated in this country;--when we consider that our garrison of Gibraltar is in its vicinage, and but a few hours' sail from it, we are naturally astonished that our communication with this country is so limited. That we have less commercial communication with Barbary, than we have with countries that do not open to us any thing like the commercial advantages that this country offers, though they are thousands of miles from us. It appears relevant, therefore, to inquire, whence originates this impeded intercourse? There are two great impediments to our free intercourse with Sudan through Marocco: viz., a general ignorance of the Arabic language, as spoken in the latter country; and the repugnancy of the Muhamedan religion to that of Christ. With respect to the first of these impediments, it is remarkable that this learned language is so little known in Europe,--this language, the most prevalent in the world, a language which [267] is spoken or understood almost without intermission from the western shores of Africa on the Atlantic ocean, to the confines of China,--a language understood, wherever Muhamedans are to be found, throughout all the populous and commercial regions of Africa, from the Western Ocean to the Red Sea, and from the Mediterranean to the country of Kaffers, [178] in the vicinage of the Cape of Good Hope. With respect to the second of these impediments, the repugnancy of the Muhamedan religion to that of Christ, it may justly be observed, that this is not really so great as we are apt to imagine; the moral principles of Muhamedans being not unlike those of the former Christians, being in fact a composition of Hebrew and Christian morality. They acknowledge Jesus Christ to be a prophet, and tell us, that, in this respect, they are on the safe side, as we impute no Divine authority to Muhamed. But a most violent repugnance to Christians has been propagated by the (*Fakeers*) Muselmen saints, or holy men. They have industriously circulated the belief of an old superstitious prediction which they have on record, viz. that the Christians will invade the Muhamedan countries, take their cities and towns, and establish the Christian religion [268] on the ruins of that of Muhamed, and take possession of the country. These reports, propagated, as before observed, by the (*Fakeers*) Muhamedan saints, among the lower orders, have kindled a high degree of rancour and animosity, (equal to that which the Catholics formerly indulged towards their protestant brethren,) which will never be extinguished until a friendly alliance and extensive commercial intercourse be established with them; which alone can soften this rancour and animosity into peace and amity. This animosity has been increased also by the rancorous anti-christian disposition manifested towards these people by the writings of Roman catholic priests and others. [179] If these uncharitable opinions of each other could be eradicated, the blessings that would result to the Africans would be incalculable; a reciprocal exchange of good offices might pave the way to purchase of the Emperor of Marocco the port of Agadeer or Santa Cruz, aptly denominated, from its contiguity to the Sahara (*Beb Sudan*) "the gate of Sudan," which, in the hands of the English, would be the key to the whole of the interior of Africa, and an effectual link in our chain of communication [269] with the interior of that undiscovered continent; it would moreover secure to us the entire commerce of those extensive and populous regions, to the exclusion of our Moorish competitors of Cairo, Alexandria, Tripoli, Tunis, Algiers, and other ports of Barbary, who supply the people of Sudan with European merchandise at the fourth, fifth, and sixth hand.

Footnote 178: (return) *Kaffer (or Caffre)* is an Arabic word which signifies infidels or unbelievers (in Muhamed); the very name has been given by Muhamedans, and therefore it is to be presumed that the Muhamedans approximate the countries contiguous to the Cape.

Footnote 179: (return) See Martin Martinius. Abraham Ecchellensis. Maccarius, Theolog. Polemic. Peter Cevaller. Robert de Retz, translator of the Koran. See also the support of this assertion in Jackson's Account of the Empire of Marocco, enlarged edition, published by Cadell and Davies, Strand, from p. 196. to 208.

The abolition of the slave-trade cannot be effected until we shall have substituted some commerce with the Negro countries, equivalent at least, or that shall be more than equivalent to it, otherwise the negro sovereigns of Sudan will never be induced to relinquish so great a source of profit. Every naval officer in His Majesty's service knows, that if we were to have thirty sail of the line continually off the coast of Guinea, it would not be sufficient to annihilate this abominable traffic, or to deter people from embarking in a trade that yields such extraordinary profits. This being admitted, as it certainly will be by every intelligent man, it follows, that the system now in operation by the British government for the abolition of the slave-trade, will be attended only with an unnecessary expense to this country, without the possibility of effecting the desired object; but, on the contrary, judging from recent events, there is every reason to presume, that this detestable commerce will increase, as it has continued to increase, these last two or three years, in spite of all our operations to prevent it; the Spaniards alone [270] having imported into the island of Cuba more slaves in 1818 and 1819, than in the four preceding years. The result has been, that that island has produced, in 1819, more than double the produce of the former year; their waste lands, accordingly, are in progressive cultivation, and, if they go on thus improving, that island, in a few years hence, will produce coffee and sugar sufficient for the supply of all the markets of Europe.

Finally, Slavery will never give way to any thing but civilisation; the civilisation of Africa can never be accomplished but through a great and extensive commercial intercourse, a commerce that will *enrich the negroes, and enable them, by a supply of arms, to contend with and gain an ascendancy over their Muhamedan oppressors*, who want no other pretext for attacking them, than that of their being idolaters, which idolatry, it is asserted, authorises the Muselman to make them slaves. Thus, *the abolition of slavery must depend on the Africans themselves*; and although it is in our power to supply them with the means for *their emancipation*, yet it is absurd to suppose that we can effect it by our naval operations. If all the great sovereigns of Europe were to agree to make the trading in slaves piracy, they would not prevent it. We cannot emancipate them; *that only can be accomplished by their own energy*, awakened in them by commercial intercourse, and its accompanying civilisation.

[271]

Much might be done if all the African societies were to unite their interest, knowledge, and abilities for this desired object. If the African Company would unite their energies with the African Association, and with the African Institution, such an union would promote the civilisation of the African continent, and the conversion of the Negroes to Christianity.

ARCHITECTURE OF THE MOSQUES.

The architecture of this country is of the Gothic character. The mosques are built somewhat like our churches: the body of the mosques are covered with green glazed tiles; the steeples are invariably an exact square, the sides being ten or twelve feet, not tapering as those of Coventry, but the top having the same dimensions as the base. At the top is erected a smaller square, with a flag-staff similar to a gallows, to which is suspended every day at noon, a white flag, the signal of preparation for prayers; but on Fridays, the Muhamedan Sabbath, a dark-blue one is substituted for the same purpose. Some of the mosques are paved with white and black chequered marble, some are tessellated pavements, consisting of white, blue, and green glazed tiles, about two inches square, a very pretty mode of paving, extremely clean, and has a very cool appearance; others are terrassed, which is lime and small stones beaten down [272] with wooden mallets. They excel in the art of making terras. The houses are all flat roofed, so as to resist the heaviest rains: the declivity of the terrasses is so imperceptible, that it is just sufficient to give the rains a tendency to the great conduit or pipe that leads to the mitfere underneath the house, which is underground, and has a terras bottom, impervious to the water. Here is collected water sufficient for the family or household during the year; the lime that washes into the mitfere from the terrassed roof, purifies the water, and preserves it from worms and other insects. They have no ornaments in their mosques; but the place where the Mufti or Fakeer reads prayers, is covered with mats or carpets; the rest of the floor is bare, and the respective individuals prostrate themselves on the bare floor, or on an antelope's or *Elhorreh* [180] skin, or the skin of a lion or tiger, prepared in a superior manner by the tanners at Marocco, the leather of which is made soft as silk, and white as snow.

Footnote 180: (return) For a description of this curious animal, see Jackson's Marocco, page 83, Chapter on Zoology.

The bodies of the dead are never laid in the mosques or near them, but are invariably carried out of the town, to some coba [181] in the vicinity. [273] The bodies of the dead are washed, and covered with lawn, and placed on an oblong wooden machine, resembling a box without a cover, called a *kiffen;* it has four legs about six inches long, to uphold it from the ground, and two horizontal projections at each end, to place on the shoulders of four men, generally the nearest relations of the deceased, who thus carry the body to the grave, chanting with the whole company, amounting sometimes to some hundreds, *La Allah, ila Allah wa Muhamed Rassule Allah,* "There is no God but God, and Muhamed is the prophet of God." This repetition may appear extraordinary to the English reader; but let it be observed that the Muhamedans never use the pronoun for the name of the Omnipotent, but invariably the noun. The body is taken out of the bier, and laid in the ground, the face upwards, without any coffin or box, the legs towards Mecca, and then covered with earth, so that it might, at the resurrection, rise with its eyes towards (*El Kaaba*) Muhamed's mausoleum. No money is paid for the ground, nor is any expense paid for a monument: a stick or a stone stands erect at the head, and another at the feet. If the deceased [274] lived a moral, inoffensive, and exemplary life, the public, at its own expense, oftentimes erects (*kaba*) a cubical building with a dome at the top to the departed, and he is thence denominated (*fakeer*) a saint.

Footnote 181: (return) A coba is a cubical building, about forty or fifty feet square, having a dome on the top, inhabited by a fakeer; the ground adjacent to this building is consecrated for the dead, but is never inclosed. The living reverence the dead by never, riding over these grounds; but travellers, in passing stop and repeat a fatha. When the ground has been consecrated to the dead, and the *coba* has an inhabitant, who must be a sanctified person, he immediately assumes the name of fakeer or priest, and the building, and cemetery attached to it, becomes a *zowia* or sanctuary.

The palaces of this country generally consist of a perfect square wall, containing from two to forty acres of land, or more; for the imperial palace at Mequinas covers about two square miles of ground. At each corner of the square is a cubical building, with an angular top, of green glazed tiles, having four windows, one in each side; in the centre of the square is the palace, surrounded by a colonnade one or two stories high. The pavement is either tessellated or of chequered marble; some of the walls of the rooms are also tessellated with arabesque, borders, the ceilings are painted with gay colours, viz. scarlet, sky-blue, green, yellow, and orange, in arabesque, and some of them are very elegant. The houses of the opulent are diminutive imitations of the palaces. The house of (*the Talb Câduse*) the minister of the Sultan Seedi Muhamed ben Abd Allah at Marocco, is a building, elegantly neat. Abd Rahamen ben Nassar's house at Mogodor, is well deserving the investigation of an European architect, and his magnificent new house at Saffee, is a model of a particular style of architecture. Some of the houses of the princes and the military at Mequinas are handsome buildings, and many of [275] the houses of the opulent merchants at Fas, who have their commercial establishments at Timbuctoo, and other countries of Sudan, are extremely neat and truly unique, having beautiful gardens in the interior, ornamented with the choicest and most odoriferous flowers and shrubs; with fountains of running water, clear as crystal, delectable to behold in this warm climate, and such as are not to be seen in any part of Europe.

[276]

FRAGMENTS, NOTES,

AND

ANECDOTES;

Illustrating the Nature and Character of the Country.

NTRODUCTION.

In recording the following Anecdotes and Fragments the naked truth is stated, without the embellishments of language, or the labour of rhetoric, which the wiser part of mankind have always approved of as the most instructive way of writing; and all such as are acquainted with books will readily agree with me, that many authors stretch, even to the prejudice of truth, from an affectation of elegance of style.

The following facts, therefore, will form the materials for a history, rather than a history itself.

The study of the *language and customs of the Arabs is the best comment upon the Old Testament*. The language of the modern Jews is little to be regarded; their dispersion into various nations, having no fixed habitation, being *wholly* [277] addicted to their own interest, their conformation to the respective customs of the various nations through which they are dispersed; have caused them, in a great measure, to forget their ancient customs and original language, except what is preserved in the Bible and in the exercise of their religion. Whereas the Arabs have continued in the constant possession of their country many centuries, and are so tenacious of their customs and habits, that they are, at this day, the same men they were three thousand years ago. Accordingly, many of their customs, at this day, remind us of what happened among their ancestors in the days of Abraham.

Trade with Sudan.

1795, June 14th. Two (*Akkabas*) accumulated caravans of Gum Sudan, called in England "Turkey [182] Gum Arabic," have reached the Arab encampment of Dikna, not far from the northern confines of the Sahara; and will be at Santa Cruz, in the province of Suse, in a fortnight.

Footnote 182: (return) This gum is conveyed from Sudan to Alexandria, in Egypt; there it is shipped off for Smyrna, or Constantinople, and from thence imported into England.

Wrecked Ships.

A large ship, supposed to be Spanish, bound to Lima, has been wrecked near Cape Noon; [278]the cargo consists of lace, silks, linens, superfine cloths, and is estimated by the Jews, at Wedinoon, to be worth half a million of dollars.

Wrecked Ships on the Coast.

Extract of a Letter from James Jackson, and Co.
at Mogodor, to their correspondents in London.
January, 1801.

The wine and dollars per the Perola de Setubal, wrecked on the coast of Suse, have been recovered from the Arabs, by Alkaid Hamo, the governor of Santa Cruz; and we have just received them safe by a boat. If this vessel had been wrecked on the coast of Cornwall, it is more than probable that the cargo would have been plundered. We have presented the governor with twenty dollars, for his extraordinary energy, exertions, and great merit in the recovery of the whole of this property.

The Prosperous, Captain Driver, a southwhaler, was wrecked near Cape Noon, in 1790; the crew was redeemed by me, and brought to my house at Santa Cruz, after being upwards of two years in captivity in the Desert: and I sent them all from Santa Cruz to Mogodor on mules, where, after remaining about two months, the Bull-dog sloop of war came down from Gibraltar for them, and they were sent off to her by the imperial order. p. 279

[279]

Wrecked Sailors.

English seamen that are so unfortunate as to be wrecked on the coast of Sahara, are generally better treated than the French, Italian, or Spanish, because there is a greater probability of a ransom; and because it is well known that the English admit no slaves in their own country.

Timbuctoo Coffee.

Coffee grows spontaneously in the vicinage of Timbuctoo, *south of the Nile Elabeed.* I sent a quantity to Mr. James Willis, formerly Consul for Senegambia: it was of a bitter taste, which is the general character of this grain before it is improved by cultivation.

Sand Baths.

The Arabs bury the body erect in sand, up to the chin, as a remedy for several disorders, particularly syphilis.

Civil War common in West Barbary.

In the provinces of Haha and Suse, particularly in the mountainous districts, intestine wars frequently prevail: kabyl against kabyl, village against village, house against house, family against family. In these lamentable wars, which [280] so continually disturb the peace of society, retaliation is considered an incumbent duty on every individual who may have lost a relation, so that the embers of hostility are thus incessantly fanned; and this lamentable revenge pervades whole clans, to the utter destruction of every humane and philanthropic propensity, converting the human race to a degradation below the beasts of the field.

Policy of the Servants of the Emperor.

The Bashaws, and others holding responsible situations in the empire, are continually purchasing a good name and good report at court, by courtesy to and by feeing the ministers of the Emperor to report favourably of them, whenever opportunity may offer. Incredible sums are sometimes expended in this way.

El [183] *Wah El Grarbee, or the Western Oasis.*

The prince, Muley Abd Salam, elder brother of the reigning Emperor, Muley Soliman, purchased, on his return from the pilgrimage to Mecca, a domain in (Santariah [184]) the Oasis of Ammon [281] or Siwah, as a retreat; and being appointed by his father Seedi Muhamed, viceroy of the province of Suse [185], he was enabled to give succour to the Shelluhs, inhabitants of that province, on their pilgrimage to Mecca, and to entertain them with the comforts of hospitality on their passage through the Desert. This was the more agreeable to these Shelluhs, because, after passing a long journey of some thousands of miles through Sahara, they reached, at Santariah, not only a territory yielding every comfort and necessary of life, but a country wherein their own prince had authority, and wherein their own native language is spoken and understood.

Footnote 183: (return) In the Lybian Desert there are three *Wahs* (or *Oasises*, as we call them): the greater, called *El Wah El Kabeer*; the lesser, called *El Wah Segrer*; and the Oasis of Ammon, called *El Wah El Grarbie*, i. e. the Wah of the West.

Footnote 184: (return) The Wah of the West is also called by the Mograbines *Santariah*.

Footnote 185: (return) See the map of West Barbary.

When this prince's father, the emperor Seedi Muhamed died [186], the prince Abdsalam engaged Alkaid Hamed ben Abdsaddock, late governor of Mogodor, to go to Santariah, and sell this domain for him; which he accordingly did. It is more than probable that the Shelluhs of Siwah are an *emigration* from Suse.

Footnote 186: (return) About twenty-eight years since.

Prostration, the etiquette of the Court of Marocco.

An ambassador from Great Britain was sent to the court of Marocco, during the reign of Seedi [282] Muhamed, father of the present emperor, Soliman. On his arrival at Fas, (where the court was at that time held,) the (*Mule M'shoer*) Master of the Audience, who was the (*Sherreef*) Prince Muley Dris, came up to the ambassador and informed him, that it was customary for all persons coming into the imperial presence to take off their shoes, and to prostrate themselves. To these ceremonies the ambassador objected, alleging that he was received by the king his master with his shoes on; and that he presumed the Emperor, on a proper representation being made to him, would not exact from him greater obedience than he paid to his own sovereign. The master of the audience reported the interpretation of the ambassador's remarks to his imperial master. The emperor paused, and (insinuating that the ambassador was somewhat presumptuous in placing a Christian king on a par with a Muselman emperor) commanded the prince to dismiss the ambassador for that time, till the following day. In the interim, the Emperor urged the master of the audience to make diligent inquiry how the Christians conducted themselves in the act of prayer before the Almighty God; and whether they then uncovered their feet, and prostrated themselves, as Muhamedans did. The morning following, the master of audience procured the necessary information respecting this point, and acquainted the Emperor that the English Christians, like [283] the Jews, prayed erect; but that they uncovered their heads, and bowed at the name of Jesus of Nazareth. "Go, then," replied the emperor, "and let the ambassador be presented to me without uncovering his feet, and without prostration; for I cannot require more obeisance from a foreigner, than he himself pays to Almighty God."

Massacre of the Jews, and Attack on Algiers.

In the year 1806, when Algiers was attacked by the Arabs of the mountains, and by the inhabitants of the plains, the Jews of the city were massacred. It was suggested to the present Emperor of Marocco that a favourable opportunity now offered to subdue Algiers, and add it to the empire: but the Emperor replied, "That it was wiser to secure and keep together all those provinces that his father had left him, than to endeavour by *uncertain and expensive* warfare to extend his dominions, by invading a neighbouring nation."

Treaties with Muhamedan Princes.

Treaties of peace and commerce between the Muselmen princes and Christian powers, are regarded by the former no longer than it is expedient to their convenience. Muselmen respect [284] treaties no longer than it is their apparent interest so to do. When an ambassador once expostulated with his imperial majesty for having infringed on a treaty made, an emperor of Marocco replied --"Dost thou think I am a Christian, that I should be a *slave* to my word?"

Berebbers of Zimurh Shelleh.

This kabyl of Berebbers inhabit the plains west and south-west of Mequinas. They are a fine race of men, well-grown, and good figures; they have a noble presence, and their physiognomy resembles the ancient Roman. The laws of hospitality, however, are disregarded among them: they will plunder travellers who sojourn with them, whenever they have an opportunity.

The European Merchants at Mogodor escape
from Decapitation.

The late emperor, Muley Yezzid, proceeded from Mequinas to Marocco, with an army of thirty thousand cavalry, to take the field against the rebellious Abdrahaman ben Nassai, bashaw of the province of Abda, acting conjointly with the bashaw of the province of Duquella, who had collected an army of eighty thousand men, of which fifty thousand were horse. The [285] Emperor, on his arrival at Marocco, was exasperated against the kabyls of the south; and was informed that the merchants of Mogodor had supplied his rebel subject, Abdrahaman, with ammunition. Enraged at this report, which the exasperated state of his mind prompted him to believe, he issued an order to the Governor of Mogodor, implicating the greater part of the European merchants of that port of high treason, and ordered their decapitation. This order was brought by one Fenishe, a relation of Tahar Fenishe; who had been, some years before, ambassador from Marocco to the court of St. James's. The Governor, however, suspecting that the order had been issued in a moment of irritation, delayed its execution, in the hope that it might be countermanded; or, in hope that the result of a battle would render it unnecessary to be put in execution.--Soon afterwards, news arrived at Mogodor that the two armies had met, had fought, and the Emperor had vanquished his antagonists, who had more than double his force, but was himself dangerously wounded. This induced the governor still further to delay the execution; having now ascertained that the order was obtained by a stratagem of malicious and ill-disposed people. The next day news came that the Emperor suffered extremely from a ball in the upper part of the thigh, which the surgeons could not extract. The Emperor, in a fit of [286] frenzy, from pain or passion, took his (*kumaya*) dagger, cut open the wound to the ball, and expired soon after. Thus were the merchants of Mogodor saved providentially from an untimely death.

The Emperor Muley Yezzid's Body disinterred.

When the united armies of Abda and Duquella were vanquished and dispersed by the Imperial troops, in the neighbourhood of Marocco, the report became general that the Emperor was wounded. It is asserted that several men in ambush had orders to wait their opportunity to fire at the Emperor, when he should approach; and when the Emperor did approach the bush wherein these men lay concealed, they all fired. It appears, however, that only one shot had effect. The Emperor finding himself wounded, instead of being discouraged, was reanimated to the combat, and entered into the midst of it; a soldier by his side observed to him, that he was wounded, and whilst expressing his hope that it was not dangerous, the Emperor, with one stroke of his sabre, cut off his head! Even after the death of this redoubted warrior, the people trembled, doubting the truth of his decease. Abdrahaman went personally to Marocco and had the body disinterred to ascertain the fact, suspecting that the report of his death might be a stratagem; but having ascertained it, he returned [287] to Saffy, and his brother Muley Esslemmah was immediately proclaimed by Abdrahaman. Doubts of the Emperor's death still pervaded the minds of men: it was reported that he had been seen in the Atlas Mountains, in Draha, in Suse. At length a person somewhat resembling him in person, appeared between Wedinoon and Ait Bamaran (see the map): the panic took; and men from all parts of the country, who had known the Emperor, hastened to Wedinoon to ascertain the fact. Many who were too curious were shot by order of this pretender, to prevent the possibility of their returning to give notice of the imposture. The immense number of persons who now believed him to be Yezzid was incalculable; his party increased and multiplied, and he soon had thousands of followers who supported his cause. The infatuation of the vulgar and the bulk of the community was astounding; for the renowned Muley Yezzid, like his Majesty George IV., was the first horseman in his empire, and the most accomplished gentleman: whereas Buhellesa [187], for so he was called in derision, was so bad a horseman that he generally rode a mule.

Footnote 187: (return) So called from his generally riding a mule, with a large stuffed saddle, rising high before and behind, covering the whole of the mule's back, and forming a very secure seat. This enormous and ponderous saddle-mattras is called *Hellesa*; and as the Pretender rode on it, he was called *Bû Hellesa*; that is the father of a *Hellesa*.

[288]

This man was reported to be an adept in the occult sciences; and it was both reported and credited, that the occult art enabled him to multiply corn and provision for the army to any quantity he might want. I was established at Santa Cruz, which was three days' horse-travelling from Buhellesa's standard; the (*Shereef*,) Prince Abdsalam, brother to Yezzid, was then resident there, and Viceroy of Suse. It was the Prince Abdsalam's desire to destroy this pretender; for his army and followers exceeded now thirty thousand men, the Prince sent to Muhamed ben Delemy, khalif of Suse, and sheik of the Duleim Arabs, whose castle was about thirty miles south of Santa Cruz. Delemy and the Prince were sworn friends: the latter proposed to him to give battle to

Buhellesa, and so prevent the empire from being usurped. Neither Delemy nor the Prince had funds to raise an army; so that neither of them knew what steps to take. *Delemy, however, with the true spirit of a Bedouin Arab, supported his friend in his adversity,* and promised to exert himself to counteract the operations of the arch-hypocrite Buhellesa. Collecting the sheiks of the various kabyls of Suse, he made an energetic harangue to them; and discussed with them the expediency of their uniting together, to repel the impostor. The sheiks were all loyal, and well affected to Muley Abd Salam; whose government of Suse, by his khaliff Delemy, added to [289] the hospitalities with which the Prince entertained the people of Suse at his domain, the *Wah el Grabie,* or the Oasis of Ammon, called *Santariah,* ingratiated Muley Abd Salam so much in their favour and esteem, that they all unanimously (*passed l'âad* [188]) joined hands, and determined, each individually, to raise his respective kabyl to support the cause of Muley Abd Salam. In a short time they raised an army among themselves of ten thousand horse, and determined to attack Buhellesa, so soon as he should begin to move forwards, and before he should reach Terodant, in his way to Marocco; for there he had a strong party, which would augment his forces. The hero Delemy, who was as valiant a soldier as Muley Yezzid himself, and as expert and dextrous in the management of the horse, determined therefore, with less than half the force of his antagonist, to attack him, before he should be able to gather more strength. The army of the sheiks joined, and proceeded towards Wedinoon. At night they learned that Buhellesa, with an army of 22,000 men, mostly horse, having [290] been apprised of Delemy's preparations and movements, had proceeded through Ait Bamaran towards Shtuka, and that he intended to attack Delemy's castle. On hearing this, the army halted for an hour, and returned towards Shtuka again. In the morning they came up with Buhellesa, who was encamped about four hours south of Delemy's castle. The march of Delemy's troops, all hardy warriors and men of valour, was so rapid, that Buhellesa was taken by surprise. The battle lasted seven hours; during which Delemy's brother was wounded and unhorsed, in the midst of the enemy's troops: but being unknown, and in a similar dress with the rest, he recovered himself by the assistance of some friends, sent to him by his brother the khalif, and was enabled to rejoin his own troops. Buhellesa was so hard pressed, that he made his retreat into a house. on being attacked there, his pistol missed fire, and he was overcome. They immediately cut off his head and his arms, when his army dispersed, most of them making the best of their way to Wedinoon. That same night, the man of Shtuka, who first attacked Buhellesa, was dispatched with his head and feet to Muley Abd Salam, at Santa Cruz.

Footnote 188: (return) The *L'aad* of the Arabs is a joining of hands, without Shaking: the palms of the right hands of the parties coming in contact with each other, and the thumbs over each other. This is a solemn obligation among them; a calling God to witness their resolution of mutual assistance, offensive and defensive; a swearing to stand by each other till death; an obligation that nothing can dissolve; such a pledge, that if a man were to break it, he would be execrated and rejected from society!

The reported approach of Buhellesa, with so strong a force, had urged me to ship all the property I could collect; and I was on the beach early the following morning, directing the [291] shipment of my property; when taking a ride along the beach, I met an Arab, with a basket before him, and a foot sticking out of it. "*Salam u alik,*" I exclaimed, "And what have you got there?"--"*Alik Salam,*" said the Arab, "I have got Buhellesa's head and feet here: I killed him myself; and the khalif Delemy has sent me with them to the Prince. Dost thou think the Prince will reward me?"--

"Certainly," said I, "for such an essential service." The Prince gave the Arab one hundred duckets [189]; the guns were fired; and the head and feet were hung over an embrasure of the round battery, facing the south. Thus terminated the career of Buhellesa.

A short time after this, I was on a visit to Delemy, and he accompanied me to the field of battle; which was an undulating plain, not unlike that of Waterloo: and the house to which Buhellesa made his escape, was not unlike the hotel de la Belle Alliance on the plains of Waterloo, having, however, a flat roof.

Footnote 189: (return) Worth 5*s.* each, but equal to 100*l.*, or more, in that country.

Shelluhs: their Revenge and Retaliation.

A Shelluh, of the province of Suse, had been a servant in the house of Mr. Hutchison, [292] British Consul at Mogodor fifteen years; but it happened to be twenty years since a relation of his, in Suse, had been killed, to whom he was the next of kin but one: but the next of kin dying, it devolved upon him to seek retaliation; no opportunity, however, having occurred, he determined to go to Suse to fulfil this his calling. Now above twenty years had elapsed since the death or murder of the relation of Bel Kossem, the Consul's servant. This man, foregoing the eligibility of his place, apprised the Consul of his intention to leave him. Mr. Hutchison, who esteemed him not a little for his long and faithful services, was astonished to hear of his determination to depart; and, apprehending that he might want an increase of pay, he offered to increase it: but Bel Kossem told him that an imperious duty devolved on him to revenge the blood of his ancestor. Accordingly he received his wages, and departed forthwith for Suse. A few months afterwards he found an opportunity of killing his enemy, which being done, it was expected that this Shelluh would now return to Mogodor, and resume his place again; but by a parity of reasoning, it devolved to the next of kin of the man recently killed to seek revenge for his murdered relation, but Bel Kossem, to avoid the like fate, went into a distant country. This duty of revenging death, is rigidly pursued among the Shelluhs, so that one murder often produces ten, or even twenty deaths; each revenging his relation or next of kin.

[293]

Travelling in Barbary.

It is extremely difficult, whilst travelling in this country, to ascertain from the natives the distance of any (*douar*) encampment of Arabs: the general answer to such a question is (*wahud saa*), "an hour," but this is a very indefinite term, being used for a distance from two to twelve miles, or more; therefore, as these people have no definite notions of time or distance, the only way of ascertaining distances, is by knowing the rate at which the caravan goes, which is a regular pace, and consulting your watch; by this means, the distance of any journey, however long, may be accurately ascertained.

Anecdote displaying the African Character, and
showing them to be now what they were anciently,
under Jugurtha.

A Muhamedan was sent to prison, for having killed a man; and after remaining there some time, it was expected that the Emperor's order would come to have him shot, or to have his right hand cut off, with which it was presumed he killed his enemy. A friend of the prisoner, willing to liberate him, that he might escape the punishment that awaited him, engaged a person well acquainted with the prison to procure his enlargement; accordingly he promised him a sum of [294] money, if he would effect this purpose. It was agreed that the money should be paid. The liberator was then to prove to the man advancing the money, that he had accomplished his purpose. The night in which his liberation was to be attempted was fixed on; ropes were ready to enable the prisoner to escape over the prison-wall. In the mean time the next of kin of the man who had been murdered, sought the blood of the prisoner, and was persuaded by the man that had engaged to liberate the prisoner, that the latter was not in prison, that he had made his escape, but that the former would undertake to put him in his power, so as to enable him to accomplish his revenge. This was agreed to, and accordingly a sum of money was paid as a remuneration for the service. All matters were arranged, and the person who paid the money was desired to be on the rock, near the prison, outside of the town wall, at two o'clock in the morning, and there he would find his enemy. The person who made the first engagement was directed to be at the same spot at three o'clock. In the mean time the liberation was effected at two o'clock, and the prisoner was informed that his friend would meet him under the rock at three o'clock, to conduct him to a place secure from discovery. Soon after two o'clock, the next of kin to the person whom the prisoner had killed came and plunged a dagger into his heart; [295] afterwards came the other man, and saw the body of his friend, whom he recognized. On expostulating with the liberator, the latter replied, "I have executed my engagement to liberate your friend; I am entitled to my reward: what has happened to him since his liberation is no concern of mine; see you to that. But I should inform you, that soon after his liberation, I saw a man approach, and fearing that I was discovered, I ran and hid myself under a rock. In a short time I returned and found your friend weltering in his blood. When I approached him, he had just time before he expired to name to me his murderer, who, he said, was the next of kin to the man he had himself killed."--Note, The Shelluhs consider it a duty incumbent on them, each, individually to revenge the blood of their family; that they are bound to seek the murderer, if possibly he can be found. Such is their invariable attention to this principle of revenging blood for blood, that I have known instances of men who have relinquished eligible appointments, to go into distant countries, several years after a murder has been committed, to revenge the death of a relation, after becoming, by intervening death, the next of kin of the murdered person.

The lamentable effects of this fatal retaliation is such, that one death often produces twenty murders, and afterwards involves whole kabyls in intestine wars.

[296]

It is remarkable, that the more duplicity they use in these horrid transactions, the more merit is ascribed to the agent; who is praised in proportion to the extent of his ingenuity, or duplicity, as was the case with the liberator above mentioned.

Every Nation is required to use its own Costume.

The Jews in West and South Barbary, have a predilection for the European costume, in preference to their own, the former being respected, the latter not: moreover the character of a *merchant* is highly respected by the Moors, and the European dress is a kind of passport to a man as such. One day, the Emperor seeing in the place of audience, at a great distance, a gentleman, apparently an European ambassador, ordered the master of the audience to go and see who he was, and what nation he represented; but it being discovered that he was a Marocco Jew, his scarlet and gold dress was torn from him, and a *burnose*, (a large black cloak, the costume of the Jews of the lower order,) was put over him, when he was buffetted and kicked out of the place of audience. The Emperor was exasperated at this circumstance, which he considered a vain deception: he ordered his secretary to write to all the ports in his dominions, to desire that Jews should wear the *burnose*, that Christians only should wear the European costume, and Moors [297] and Arabs theirs; so that thus every individual might be known by their respective dress. On this occasion, an opulent Hebrew merchant at Mogodor felt so much the insults he was exposed to, from wearing the Jewish costume, that he actually paid several thousand dollars to obtain the privilege he had formerly enjoyed, which, in consequence of his being an opulent man, and a foreign merchant, was granted to him.

The name of this gentleman would here be mentioned to gratify the curious; but as it might give umbrage to his family, and as the intention here is only to describe the character and manners of the country, there is, I conceive no necessity for stating personalities.

Ali Bey (El Abassi), Author of the Travels under that Name.

This extraordinary character visited Marocco about the year 1805 or 1806. He pretended to be a native of Aleppo, called in Arabic *Hellebee*, and was known by the name of Seed Hellebee, which signifies "the gentleman of Aleppo." Europeans, as well as himself, since his return to Europe, have converted this name into Ali Bey, of the family of the Abassides. This gentleman possessed abilities of no ordinary degree, he was supplied with money in abundance by the Spanish government. He had not been long at [298] Mogodor, when his munificence began to excite the suspicion of the governor, as well as the admiration and applause of the populace. Adopting the costume of the country, he professed himself to be a Muselman; and as a pretext for not speaking the [190] Arabic language, he pretended that he had gone from Aleppo, the place of his nativity, to England when very young, and had forgotten it. He had, as he declared, considerable property in the Bank of England. Being desirous of collecting all the information possible respecting the country, he procured two young Spanish renegado musicians, who played on the guitar, and sung Arabic airs and songs, with which he affected to be highly delighted, these musicians, however, served his purpose in another way; for, being apprehensive of creating suspicion by direct enquiries, he prevailed on these renegadoes to procure the information he desired, by giving them from time to time several questions to which they procured direct answers, as reported by the natives.

Footnote 190: (return) He afterwards learned the Arabic language, and I believe spoke it tolerably well when he quitted this country and proceeded to Mekka.

One day he gave a *fête champêtre* at (*L'arsa Sultan*), the [191] Sultan's garden, situated near a [299] very picturesque rivulet, and contiguous to springs of excellent water, which being collected in a large tank, was conveyed by an aqueduct, which extended the length of the garden, to immerge or irrigate the various beds of flowers and plants. On his return home, as he was crossing the river near the village of Diabet, a Shelluh shot a large fish as it was passing the shallows, Seed Hellebee, or Seed Ali Bey admired the dexterity of the Shelluh, (who, from his quickness, was nicknamed Deib, i.e. the fox,) and desired him to take the fish to his house at Mogodor, which he accordingly did, and received from Ali Bey's secretary a handful of dollars. This Shelluh was a keen sportsman, and seldom or never missed his shot: he generally accompanied me in my shooting excursions, and he told me this circumstance himself, adding, that Ali Bey was such a liberal man, that, where any other gentleman gave a dollar, he gave a handful. It was in this manner that Ali Bey purchased his popularity.

Footnote 191: (return) This garden is in the province of Haha, about five miles S.S.E. of Mogodor, and belongs to the European Commerce, to whom it was presented by the Late Emperor Seedi Muhamed ben Abdallah.

The governor of Mogodor, Alkaid Muhamed ben Abdsaddock now began to suspect, not only the faith of this *soi disant* Muhamedan, but that he had some design unavowed; and desirous of ascertaining to what nation of Christendom he belonged, the governor engaged Monsieur Depras, a respectable French merchant of Mogodor, who understood several languages, to ascertain if he was a Frenchman, and if not, who and what [300] he was. The governor, in order to enable M. Depras to converse with Ali Bey, invited them both to tea; this introduction being effected the next day, Depras called on Ali Bey, and conversed with him during an hour in the French language, which he spoke so well, that the former thought there was no doubt of his being a Frenchman. But soon after this, the Spanish Consul was announced, and being introduced, Seed Ali Bey changed his discourse to Spanish, which he also spoke so correctly, that Depras now altered his opinion, and conceiving him to be a Spaniard, took his leave. He then reported to the governor what he had seen and heard, that he spoke French and Spanish so fluently, that he really did not know whether he was a Frenchman or a Spaniard.

Ali Bey continued to live in a most sumptuous and costly style, and afterwards resolved to visit Marocco. On his journey thither, he was particularly inquisitive respecting the population, produce, names and residencies of the (sheiks) chiefs of Haha and Shedma, through which provinces he passed. On his arrival at Marocco, he still continued his magnificent establishment and sumptuous mode of living; distributing money to the people bountifully, on the most trifling occasions, which mode of conduct procured him universal popularity among the lower orders. This soon excited the suspicions of Alkaid Bushta, the governor of Marocco, who ingenuously [301] informed him, that such liberality was fit only for a Christian country, and that he was mistaken if he flattered himself that it would be tolerated at Marocco, and actually desired him to adopt a different and a more parsimonious system, if he wished to be quiet; alleging, that his munificence exceeded that of his Imperial Majesty, which was highly indecorous; but afterwards finding little attention was paid to his injunction, he published a decree throughout the city, that any one that should be found asking for, or receiving money from Ali Bey, should have a very severe bastinado! After residing some time at Marocco, he expressed a desire to visit the Atlas mountains, which appear a few miles east of Marocco, but which are, in fact, a whole day's journey; their immense size and height making them to appear so much nearer than they really are. Ali Bey apprehending the hostility of Alkaid Bushta, he procured an imperial order to visit the Atlas, but Bushta opposed it, and would not, he said, permit him, he being governor of Marocco, without having himself directly from the Emperor a permission to that purpose. He then represented to the Emperor the impolicy of allowing him to go and examine that country; and the imperial order was immediately countermanded.

People now began to imagine that he was an agent of Bonaparte; and their suspicion that he was a Christian spread far and near. It was discovered [302] also that he had corns on his feet, excrescences unknown to Muselmen, whose shoes are made tight over the instep, and loose over the toes, so that the latter being unconfined and at liberty, they never have corns.

Notwithstanding all these suspicions, the courtesy and suavity of the manners of Ali Bey had such influence on the imperial mind, that Muley Soliman gave him a beautiful garden to reside in, wherein there was a (*kôba*) pavilion. Ali Bey, finding his influence considerable, erected with architectural taste several edifices, suited, as he thought, to the imperial *gusto*, in which he succeeded so well that his Imperial Majesty, when he returned the next year to Marocco, resided almost exclusively in one of the pavilions which he had erected.

The splendour of the imperial favour did not however continue long; for Ali Bey began now to be suspected by the Emperor himself, and it was bruited that his renegadoes had acted treacherously towards him.

Ali Bey's knowledge of astronomy was peculiarly gratifying to the Emperor. He could not altogether withdraw from him his attention. The Emperor urged him to take unto himself a wife, and become an useful member of society; but Ali objected, alleging various motives for refusing. He was however at length prevailed on to comply with the imperial injunction, and the Emperor gave him a young girl to marry. It was [303] anticipated that his new wife was a political one, and would betray him to be an uncircumcised dog. The wife, however, became extremely attached to him, and no information could be procured from her to favour the plot that had been laid for him. Various suspicions having increased respecting him, the Emperor finally resolved that he should quit his territory; and an order was issued that himself, his wife, and slaves should be escorted to the port of L'Araich, and there embark for Europe. When the military guard, however, had reached the port of L'Araich, the boat being ready, Ali Bey was desired to embark, when, not suspecting any stratagem, the boatmen pushed off, leaving his disconsolate wife on the beach, bewailing his abrupt departure. The lady appeared deeply affected with this sudden and unexpected separation; and jumping out of the litter tore her dishevelled hair, and distributed it to the winds, and with loud shrieks, which pierced the air, demonstrated to him how sorely she lamented his premature departure, and violent separation. His principal slave was sold, by order of the Emperor's minister, to Seed Abdel'mjeed Buhellel, a merchant of Fas, who was lately in London, and the money was given to his wife.

During his residence at Fas, he predicted an eclipse, and, having foretold to the people of that city, that it would happen at such a time, they waited for the event with considerable curiosity. [304] Now his knowledge of futurity had spread abroad with demonstrations of amazement; the eclipse happened precisely at the time he had predicted, which established his fame as an (*alem min alem*), a man wiser than the wise.

During the latter part of his residence in West Barbary, a report prevailed that Bonaparte was preparing an immense army to invade and subjugate the country. Ali Bey was not only suspected to be his secret agent, but some persons were even ridiculous enough to declare that he was Bonaparte himself in disguise; and accordingly he was denominated *Parte*, for they would not add *Bona*, as that word signifies good, in the *lingua franca* of Barbary, and Bonaparte, they said was not good, but a devil incarnate; so they called him Parte. Last year I met in London the Moor who had purchased Ali Bey's slave, and he told me that his son by the before-mentioned wife lives at Fas; that he is a very amiable and intelligent youth, about fifteen or sixteen years of age; and that he is very poor, and would have starved, but for the charity and protection of the highly respected fakeer of the city of Fas, Muley Dris, under whose roof he resides, and is indebted to him for protection and patronage. This man would be an acquisition to the African Association, and means might be adopted to engage him in their service to explore Sudan.

[305]

The Emperor's Attack of Diminet, in the Atlas.

The emperor Seedi Muhamed ben Abdallah levied a powerful army, and took the field against Diminet, in the mountains of Atlas, east of Marocco. The people of Diminet, and the territory of Berebbers, east of that country, had also levied a strong force to defend themselves. The Diminets were taken by surprise; for they had not had intimation of an attack from Marocco. The Emperor himself, with a few attendants disguised in the Berebber dress, advanced a few miles ahead of the army. A party of mountaineers had received orders from their sheik, (when the latter was informed that the Emperor's army was coming against them,) to seek the Emperor, and endeavour to kill him. They mistook the Emperor and his party for Berebbers, as His Majesty spoke the language correctly, and had in the early part of his life lived among them. "Where is the Emperor's guard?" the mountaineers enquired; "for we are in search of them: we hear he is coming to attack us, in our inaccessible mountains; but we will be beforehand with him, and dispatch him before he reaches us. Dost thou know where he is, or where his guard is." "We do know," replied the Emperor; "for, about an hour behind us, we passed a few men on horseback, among whom was the Emperor; but the army is a long way behind: if you make speed, you will soon pass him, and it will be an easy matter for you to put the whole party [306] to the sword, for they are not a dozen altogether." The Berebbers, elated with this news, communicated from a party whom they mistook for brethren of the neighbouring kabyl, rode off at speed to seek their enemy, and in a short time found themselves surrounded by the Emperor's army, who were scattered about in ambush. These Berebbers were all secured, and were threatened with torture if they would not discover where the army of their brethren was, and what was their plan. The party discovered the plan and the place of their encampment, which was not far off in recesses of the mountain, and received a promise of remuneration if found correct. By this discovery, the imperial army was enabled to surprise the rebels; the latter were dispersed, and their houses burned. Thus were they prevented from *harassing* the Emperor's army, which is their ordinary mode of warfare. To subjugate these people would be impossible: it has often been attempted, but never succeeded. The only lien the Emperor can get of them is, by having at court about his person their sheik, whom he then makes answerable for the obedience of the kabyl.

Moral Justice.

The imperial army being encamped in Temsena, on the confines of Tedla, (see the map,) an Arab chieftain found that a friend [307] of the Emperor came into his *keyma* [192] at night, and took liberties with his wife. The Arab suspected that he was (*shereef*) a prince, and therefore did not dare to kill him, but preferred a complaint to the Emperor. The Emperor was vexed to hear of such a gross breach of hospitality, and asked what time he made his visits? "At one hour after midnight," the Arab replied. Then, said the Emperor, "when he comes, do you let me know by giving the watch-word to this man, and he will then know what to do; and depend thou on my seeing justice done to thee for the aggression." The marauder came; the Arab repaired to the guard of the imperial tent, and gave the word; the guard apprised the emperor, as he was directed, who personally repaired to the tent of the Arab, and, being convinced of the fact, ran the man through with his lance; this was done without a light. The body was brought before the tent, and it was discovered to be an officer of the imperial guard. The Emperor, on seeing that it was not a shereef (a prince) prostrated himself in fervent prayer for a considerable time. The courtiers who were all assembled by this time to witness this extraordinary occurrence, wondered what could induce the Emperor to be so fervent in prayer; which his majesty observing, told them, "that he went alone to the tent, thinking that nobody [308] but a shereef would have dared to commit such a breach of hospitality, in so open a manner; therefore he killed him without having a light, lest, on discovering him to be a prince, personal affection might give way to justice; but that when he discovered that it was not a relation, he returned thanks to God Almighty, that, in his determination to have justice administered, he had not killed his own son!"

Footnote 192: (return) *Keyma* is the name for an Arab's tent; they are made of goats' hair, and are black.

Contest between the Emperor and the Berebbers of Atlas.

March 10, 1797. The Sultan Soliman proceeds with a powerful army against the warlike province of Shawiya, the rebellious Arabs' retreat. The imperial army takes some of the women who are renowned for personal charms. The army can get no food; and, being in danger of starving, returns to Salee. The Arabs promise submission, in hopes of having the women restored; but the Emperor's officers violate them. The Arabs swear vengeance (*alia l'imin* [193]) by their right hand. The emperor attacks them again, is repulsed, and returns to Fas.

Footnote 193: (return) *Alia l'imin*, swearing by the right hand, is a sacred oath; and those who take it will not swerve from its obligation, which is peremptory.

Characteristic Trait of Muhamedans.

One of the Emperor's ministers, when an English fleet was cruising off Salee, and just [309] after some impost had been levied on the merchandise already purchased and warehoused by the Christian merchants, suggested the impolicy at that moment, of harsh measures against Europeans: the Emperor, in a jocose manner, asked what harm he could suffer from the fleets of Europeans? "They could destroy your Imperial Majesty's ports," replied the minister. "Then I would build them again for one-half what it would cost them to destroy them. But if they dared to do that, I could retaliate, by sending out my cruisers to take their trading ships, which would so increase the premiums of insurance (for the (*kaffers*) infidels insure all things on earth, trusting nothing to God [194]), that they would be glad to sue for peace again."

Footnote 194: (return) The Muhamedans abuse the Christians for their mistrust of Providence, exemplified in their insuring ships, merchandise, &c.

Political Deception.

When an embassy is going to the Emperor, the alkaid of the escort endeavours to make the present, which necessarily accompanies every embassy, as bulky and conspicuous as possible, that the Arabs of the kabyls through which they pass, may be dazzled and astounded with the great appearance of the presents, which the alkaid proclaims to consist chiefly of money, or treasure. The Arabs accordingly observed, on Mr. Matra's (the British consul) presents, that [310] the English, who had conquered Bonaparte in Egypt, and were masters of the ocean and seas, yet were tributary to the Sultan. This idea is industriously propagated by the officers of the Emperor's court. "Thinkest thou," they observed, "that these Christians give such large presents with a free-will? Certainly not! They are compelled to do so. The (*Romee*) Europeans are too fond of money to give it away in such loads,--even the English, thou seest, are tributary to the Seed." [195]

Footnote 195: (return) A higher title among the *true Arabs* than Emperor: it implies conjointly, Emperor, Father of the People, Protector, and Brother.

Etiquette of the Court of Marocco.

The European commerce of Mogodor went to pay their respects to the Emperor Seedi Muhamed, on his arrival, from Fas, at Marocco, as is customary. The Emperor's son, Muley El Mamune, was master of the audience, and ordered the commerce to advance into the imperial presence; and standing barefooted, as is the custom before the Emperor, he requested the merchants to take off their shoes, as *he* had done; but they expostulated, and said it was not their custom. The Prince, however, stopped them, and would not allow them to approach the imperial presence without first submitting to this ceremony. Seedi Muhamed, observing the impediment, and knowing the cause, but [311] willing at the same time to initiate the young prince in the custom of foreign countries, called his son to him, and said, "What do muselmen do, when they enter the *Jamaa*?" [196] "Revere the holy ground, by entering barefooted," replied the prince.--"And what do the Christians, when they enter their church?"--"They take off their hats," rejoined the Prince. (*Allah e berk Amer Seedi,* [197]) "God bless your Majesty's life."--"Then, what would you more of these my merchants, than that they pay me, even the same respect that they pay when they pray to *Allah*. Let them approach uncovered, with their shoes on, which they never take off, but to go to bed to rest".

Footnote 196: (return) An Arabic or Korannick word, signifying, the congregation of prayer, or mosque.

Footnote 197: (return) A term invariably used at court, in addressing the Emperor.

The province of Ait Atter, or the Atterites, in Lower Suse, is considered as an independent province, and it pays no tribute. They have a great dislike to *kadis* [198], *talbs*, and attornies, alleging that they only increase disputes between man and man, which is not at all necessary; all disputes are, therefore, decided by the sheik, who is not a logical wrangler, but decides according [312] to the simplest manner. The following decree of their sheik is on record:--

"Four men conjointly bought a mule, which for elucidation, we will call A, B, C, and D: each claimed a leg. D's leg was the off-hind one. In a few days this leg began to swell: it was agreed to cure it by (*el keeh*) burning it with a hot iron, (a common remedy in this country.) This done, the mule was turned out, and went into a field of barley. Some spark was attached to the hoof, and set fire to the corn, which was consumed. The proprietors of the barley applied to the sheik for justice; and A, B, C, and D, the owners of the mule, were summoned to appear. The sheik, finding the leg which caused the barley to be burnt, belonged to D, ordered him to pay the value of the barley. D expostulated, and maintained that he had no right to pay; for, if it had not been for A, B, and C's portions of the mule, the barley would have remained. "How so?" replied the sheik. "Because," quoth D, "the leg which belongs to me cannot touch the ground; but it was brought to the corn-field by the legs of A, B, and C, which were the efficient cause of the ignition of the barley. The sheik reversed his decree, and ordered A, B, and C to pay the damage, and D got off without expense.

Footnote 198: (return) *Kadis*, i.e. judges. *Talbs*, i.e. record writers. *Kadi* is generally spelt by the Europeans of the south *Cadi*, because they have no K in their alphabet: the Arabs have no C; the letter is *Kaf* or K, not C.

[313]

Customs of the Shelluhs of the Southern Atlas, viz.>
of Idaultit (in Lower Suse.)

The mountains of Idaultit are inhabited by a courageous and powerful people, strict to their honour and word, unlike their neighbours of Elala. They make verbal contracts between themselves, and never go to law, or record their contracts or agreements, trusting implicitly to each other's faith and honour. If a man goes to this country to claim a debt due, he cannot receive it while there, but must first leave the country, and trust to the integrity of the Idaultitee, who will surely pay when convenient, but cannot bear compulsion or restraint. They do not acknowledge any sultan, but have a divan of their own, called *Eljma*, who settle all disputes between man and man. These people cultivate the plains, when there is no khalif in Suse; but when there is, they retire to the fastnesses in their mountains, and defy the arm of power; satisfying themselves with the produce of the mountains.

Connubial Customs.

The (*shereef*) Prince Muley Bryhim, son of the present Emperor Soliman, was married to the daughter of the bashaw Abdrahaman ben Nassar, who was powerful and rebellious, and prevented the Emperor for some time from proceeding to the south. This couple was married in 1803. The bashaw died the same year; and in 1805 [314] she was divorced, and sent by the Emperor to Mogodor, with orders to a sheik of Shedma to marry her, it being considered a degradation for a prince to be united to the daughter of a rebellious subject. This happened in January, 1806. The widow of the late Prince Muley Abdrahaman, who rebelled against his father, and who was elder brother to the Emperor Soliman, has been recently sent by the Emperor to Bu Azar, a negro bashaw, and governor of the city of Terodant, in Suse, to marry her. These marriages are promoted by the royal decree, to prevent the females from contaminating the royal blood by illicit connection, if they remain divorced, without a new husband.

Political Duplicity.

A fakeer having interceded in behalf of a state prisoner, his friend, who was confined in the island of Mogodor (the state prison of the empire, except for princes, who are sent to Tafilolt), the Emperor assured him he would release him; and urged the fakeer to proceed to Mogodor, and wait there his Majesty's arrival. The fakeer departed, and soon after his arrival at Mogodor, he learned that the Emperor was not going there; but the alkaid of Mogodor showed him a letter from the Emperor, ordering him to retain the prisoner in safe keeping, and not attend to what the fakeer should say. This system of breaking engagements and promises, is too often denominated policy. "Dost thou [315] think I am a Christian," said an emperor to a prince who was expostulating with him for not fulfilling his engagements,--"Dost thou think I am a Christian, to be a slave to my word?"

Senor P. a Spanish merchant, received a letter from the Emperor, directed to the (*alkaid*) governor of Rabat, ordering him to show Senor P. every attention, and to assist him if he should be desirous of establishing a house at Rabat. Senor P. left the court at Mequinas, well satisfied with his letter; but a few days after his arrival, the alkaid told him he must embark and quit the country in twenty-four hours, by the Emperor's order, which he showed to Senor P. who could read Arabic. He was obliged to embark immediately.

Etiquette of Language at the Court of Marocco.

If the Emperor should enquire about any person that has recently died, it is not the etiquette to mention the word "death,"--a muselmen is supposed never to die;--the answer is *Ufah Ameruh*, "his destiny is closed," or "he has completed his destiny." To which the following answer is invariably given--*Allah ê Erhammoh*, "God be merciful to him." If a Jew's death is announced to any muselman prince, fakeer, or alkaid, the expression is, *Maat hashak asseedi*, "He is dead, Sir." *Ashak* is an Arabic idiom, the exact meaning of which cannot easily be conveyed in English; but it may be assimilated to--"Pardon me for mentioning [316] in your presence a name contemptible or gross (as Jew)." Thus, for further elucidation to the enquirer after the peculiarities of language, *Kie 'tkillem ma el Kaba hashak asseedi,*--"He is talking with a prostitute--your pardon, Sir, for the grossness of the expression."

If a man goes to the alkaid, to make a complaint against any one for doing any indecent act, and in relating the circumstance he omits the word *hashak asseedi*, the persons present will interrupt him thus,--*Kul hashak b'adda*, "Say *hashak* before you proceed." Blood, dung, dirt, pimp, procuress, prostitute, traitor, &c. &c. are words that (in correct company) are invariably followed by the qualifying word *hashak*.

If a Christian is dead, the expression is *Mat el kaffer, or Mat el karan, or Mat bel karan*, "The infidel is dead," "the cuckold, or the son of a cuckold is dead."

Food.

Kuscasoe is, flour moistened with water, and granulated with the hand to the size of partridge-shot. It is then put into a steamer uncovered, under which fowls, or mutton, and vegetables, such as onions, and turnips, are put to boil: when the steam is seen to pass through the *kuscasoe* it is taken off and shook in a bason, to prevent the adhesion of the grains; and then put in the steamer again, and steamed a second time. When it is taken off, some butter, [317] salt, pepper, and saffron, are mixed with it, and it is served up in a large bowl. The top is garnished with the fowl or mutton, and the onions and turnips. When the saffron has made it the colour of straw, it has received the proper quota. This is, when properly cooked, a very palatable and nutritious dish.

Hassua is gruel boiled, and then left over the fire two hours. It is made with barley not ground into flour, but into small particles the size of sparrow-shot. It is a very salubrious food for breakfast, insomuch that they have a proverb which intimates that physicians need never go to those countries wherein the inhabitants break their fast with *hassua*.

El Hasseeda is barley roasted in an earthen pan, then powdered in a mortar, and mixed with cold water, and drank. This is the travelling food of the country--of the Arab, the Moor, the Berebber, the Shelluh, and the Negro; and is universally used by travellers in crossing the Sahara: the Akkabas that proceed from Akka and Tatta to Timbuctoo, Houssa, and Wangara, are always provided with a sufficient quantity of this simple restorative to the hungry stomach.

The Woled Abbusebah, a whole Clan of Arabs,
banished from the Plains of Marocco.

This populous, powerful, and valiant kabyl, during the former part of the reign of the Sultan Seedi Muhamed ben Abdallah, father of the [318] present Emperor Soliman, occupied the plains west of the city of Marocco (being an emigration from the Bedouin tribe of the same name in the Sahara); but their depredatory disposition made travelling through their territory unsafe; wherefore the Emperor, after endeavouring in vain to make an example of them, issued a decree that they should all to a man leave his dominions, and they were driven by his army out of their country to the south, and entered the Sahara. The whole kabyl was thus outlawed, so that they were plundered and killed as they passed through the plains of Fruga, Ait Musie, Haha, and Suse, by the natives of those countries respectively. Not half the number that emigrated, (which was some thousands,) reached the original clan in the Sahara.

The Koran, called also El Kateb el Aziz.

The word Koran conveys the same signification as *Bible*: it means "the reading" or "the book;"--*kora*, "to read; "*el Kateb el Aziz*, i.e. "the dear or beloved book," meaning thereby the *Koran*.

Arabian Music.

The Sultan Seedi Muhamed, after hearing the musical band of the Marquis de Vialli, ambassador from Venice, expressed his gratification at the music of the Italians, and laconically observed that it possessed more harmony than that of any other nation, excepting his own.

[319]

Sigin Messa. (Sigilmessa.)

The country of Sigin Messa, called in the maps Sigilmessa, was the state prison of the kingdom of Suse, when it formed a part of the empire of Muley el Monsore, in the twelfth century of the Christian era. Messa, a port in Suse, was then a large city, and the capital of the kingdom of Suse. The state prisoners were sent to a place of safe keeping, which was east of Tafilelt, and was therefore called Sigin Messa, i.e. the prison of Messa.

Mungo Park at Timbuctoo.

In the month of March, 1806, a letter was received at Mogodor by Seedi L'Abes Buhellal Fasee, from his liberated slave at Timbuctoo. This letter was in Arabic, and the following is an extract literally translated from it by myself:--

"A boat arrived a few days since from the West at Kabra, having two or three Christians in it. One was (*rajel kabeer*) a tall man, who stood erect in the boat, which displayed (*shinjuk bied*) a white flag. The inhabitants of Kabra did not, however, understand the signal to be emblematic of peace, and no one went to the boat, although it remained at anchor before Kabra the whole day, till night. In the morning it was gone."

Troglodytæ.

The Shelluhs of the Atlas, south-east of Santa [320] Cruz, in Suse, during the rainy season, from November till February inclusive, live in caves and excavations in the rocks and earth; laying up provisions sufficient for that period, until the snow begins to melt. The Berebbers of North Atlas have followed the same custom from time immemorial.

Police of West Barbary.

When the present Emperor came to the throne, he gave indefatigable attention to the police. He wished, he said, to make the roads safe for travellers, from the Desert, or Sahara, to the shores of the Mediterranean. He was vigilant in discovering thefts, and rigorous in punishing them. If any one was robbed, he had only to report it to the Emperor, who would forthwith order the douar where the robbery was committed to restore the sum stolen, and to pay a fine to the treasury of the same amount. By adhering strictly to this system, he improved the revenue, and made travelling perfectly safe; so that one may travel now (1805), without danger, with property or money, from one end of the empire to the other. Before this system of policy was renewed, (for it is an old law of the land,) travellers with property were obliged to have a *statta*: thus, if a caravan was going from Terodant or Marocco to Fas, it took a *statta;* that is, two men, natives of the district of Rahamena, who accompanied the caravan in safety [321] to the confines of their territory; they then received a remuneration, and delivered over the caravan to two men of Abda, who conducted it to the border of Duquella: it was then delivered into the hands of two Duquella Arabs; and so it went through the different provinces till it reached Fas, under the protection, through each province, of a *statta*, each of which *statta* receives a remuneration. So that, by the time of arrival at Fas, the merchandise was sometimes subject to a charge of 8 or 10 per cent. for *statta* or convoy through the various provinces.

Before the Emperor Soliman thus established his authority, caravans of gums, almonds, ostrich feathers, gold-dust, &c. &c. from Suse, were sometimes twenty days going from Santa Cruz to Mogodor, a distance of less than one hundred miles, the *statta* being changed and paid at the entrance of every kabyl, of which there are twelve in the province of Haha alone; the camels being also changed at every change of *statta*, increased the charge on the merchandise to an immoderate amount. It would be a great acquisition to England, if His Majesty were to negociate with the Emperor of Marocco for the port of Santa Cruz; for the province of Suse produces in abundance olive oil, almonds, and gums; worm-seed, annis-seed, cummin-seed, and orchilla; oranges, grapes, pomegranates, figs, melons, &c. This port was farmed, during the reign of Muley Ismael, for an annual stipend. It is the key to Sudan, and a communication [322] might be opened on an extensive scale from hence with Timbuctoo, Housa, Wangara, and other regions of Sudan, so as to supply, in a few years, the whole of the interior of Africa with British and East-India manufactures.

Muley Abdrahaman ben Muhamed.

This prince, who was elder brother of the present Emperor Soliman, had accumulated considerable treasure in executing the office of (*khalif*) viceroy of the provinces of Duquella, Abda, and Shedma. His father, jealous of his son's power, when supported by a command of treasure, had recourse to the usual means of transferring it to the imperial treasury. It is held as law in this country, that little is sufficient for every purpose of life. When property becomes accumulated, it is alleged that more than a sufficiency is derogatory of the principles laid down in the Koran, and ought to revolve to the national treasury, there to be deposited as a fund in reserve against the invasion of the country by the Europeans, an event, which they are quite sure, from an ancient tradition, will happen at no very distant period.

Abdrahaman, however, equally avaricious with his father, objected to deliver up his treasure; which so irritated the Sultan, that he ordered a party of his negro soldiers to go to the Prince's house and seize every thing valuable. These men, in their thirst for plunder, out-ran their discretion, as it appears; for they proceeded to [323] examine the ladies in the Horem, putting their base hands on their persons, under the pretence of discovering if they had concealed their jewels and gold. This outrage roused the Prince's indignation and he lost no time in absenting himself for ever from his father's dominions, for this insult on his dignity.--"If my father," said the Prince, "had taken my treasure, it would have passed from my hands to his; but to permit the ignoble hands of slaves to offer me such an indignity, is more than I can or will suffer." Abdrahaman therefore emigrated to the province of Lower Suse, on the confines of Sahara, where he remained encamped, ready, upon any alarm, at a moment's notice, to penetrate into the Desert. He had always two *heiries* ready saddled at the gate of his (*keyma*) tent; one for carrying his treasure, viz. gold dust and jewels, and the other for himself to ride, on any emergency. Many fakeers were sent from the Sultan to the Prince; with the most solemn assurances of his reconciliation, and with urgent solicitations to him to return; but the Prince never forgave or forgot the insult.

Anecdote of Muley Ismael.

Muley Ismael compared his subjects to a bag full of rats.--"If you let them rest," said the warrior, "they will gnaw a hole in it: keep them moving, and no evil will happen." So his [324] subjects, if kept continually occupied, the government went on well; but if left quiet, seditions would quickly arise. This sultan was always in the tented-field: he would say, that he should not return to his palace until the tents were rotten. He kept his army incessantly occupied in making plantations of olives, or in building: rest and rebellion were with him synonymous terms.

Before the Portuguese transplanted their African colonies to South America, they had penetrated far into West Barbary; they frequently made incursions into the country from Mazagan to Marocco, and eastward of that city. They had a church near Diminet, on the declivity of the Atlas, about thirty-five miles east of Marocco, which is still existing: it is a kind of sanctuary; the Berebbers say it is haunted; they will not approach it. There is said to be an inscription on the building in Roman characters, over the entrance; but I never could ascertain what it is.

Library at Fas.

When the present Emperor came to the throne there was a very extensive and valuable library of Arabic manuscripts at Fas, consisting of many thousand volumes. Some of the more intelligent literary Moors are acquainted with events that happened formerly, during the time of the Roman power, which Europeans do not [325] possess. Abdrahaman ben Nassar, bashaw of Abda, was perfectly acquainted with Livy and Tacitus, and had read those works from the library at Fas. It is more than probable that the works of these authors, as well as those of many other Romans and Greeks, are to be found translated into the Arabic language, in the hands of private individuals in West and in South Barbary. This library was dispersed at the accession of Muley Soliman, and books commenting on the Koran only were retained; the rest were burned or dispersed among the natives.

Deism.

Deism was very prevalent throughout the empire. When the present Emperor Soliman came to the throne, the deists went about in large numbers, exclaiming, *La Allah ila Allah*, "There is no God but God." The Emperor soon silenced these people, by proclaiming that if any should be found uttering this truth, without adding, "Muhamed is his prophet," should ([199]*ekul lassah*) be beat. The sect soon disappeared.

Footnote 199: (return) This punishment is inflicted by two men, one on each side; the culprit is stretched naked on the ground, and beat on the back unmercifully, with sticks two yards long, and as thick as a finger.

[326]

Muhamedan Loyalty.

An alkaid of a district in the province of Abda, when that province submitted to the Emperor, went to His Majesty, taking with him the fruit of his government, viz. 100,000 dollars. He prostrated himself before the Emperor, and announced that he had brought this money to the Muselman treasury, being what he had collected since the death of the Emperor's father. "I have lived splendidly, and have never wanted any thing, or I should have brought Your Majesty much more treasure." "You have been," said the Emperor, "a faithful servant, and you shall be rewarded." He was promoted to a government, and had many opportunities of refunding his loss. A large sum was returned to him for his fidelity.

Cairo.

The city of El Kahira is called by Europeans Cairo. When Kairo was founded, in the 359th year of the Hejra, the planet Mars was in ascension; and it is Mars who conquers the universe: "therefore," said Moaz, (the son of El Mansor) to *his* son, "I have given it the name of El-Kahira." [200]

Footnote 200: (return) El Kahira is the Arabic for the planet Mars, and signifies *victorious*.

Races of Men constituting the Inhabitants of
West and South Barbary, and that Part of
Bled el Jereed, called Tafilelt and Sejin Messa,
east of the Atlas, forming the Territories of the
present Emperor of Marocco.

The Moors, who inhabit the towns on the coast, and the cities of Fas, Mequinas, Marocco, and Terodant; who speak a corrupt Arabic language.

The Berebbers, who appear to be the Aborigines, and who retain precisely the same character that was anciently given of the Mauritanians by Sallust. These people inhabit the mountains of Atlas, north of the city of Marocco, and have a language peculiar to themselves. They are a hardy race of warriors, as artful as they are indefatigable in war; when attacked by the imperial troops, they defend themselves valiantly; and, by stratagem and device, often surprise and defeat the Emperor's best troops, the *abeed Seedy Bukaree*. They call the Negro and Arab troops of the Emperor, (*mâden el grudder*), a mine of deceit, and never trust to their vows and promises, even if they swear by the Koran. They are a restless turbulent race, and have never been conquered. They have adopted the Muhamedan doctrines.

The Shelluhs, or inhabitants of the Atlas, who dwell in houses in the mountains south of Marocco, in the province of Haha, and in part of Suse. These are a weaker race, not so [328] athletic and robust as the Berebbers. Their language has been represented to be similar to that of the Berebbers, but that is evidently a mistake; I have travelled through their country, and through the country of the Berebbers, and have conversed with hundreds, nay, I may say, with thousands of them: I have no hesitation in declaring them to be a different race. Their language, costume, and habits differ; the Shelluhs, however, possess the same art and duplicity with the Berebbers.

The Arabs, who live in *douars* of tents, and inhabit the immense plains west of the Atlas, are the agriculturists of the country. They form the principal population of this terrestrial paradise; they are for the most part emigrations from the Sahara, several centuries ago, and speak the true Arabic language. These are a fine race of men, possessing, in a superlative degree, some of the noblest qualities of the human race. To these may be added

The Jews, who wear a distinguishing costume, and a black cap; they are all engaged in trade, and form one-seventh of the population of the walled habitations. They are held in great contempt, and are treated very rudely by the Arabs, and therefore are seldom met with among the encampments of that people.

A *douar* is a village of tents; these tents are made of goats' and camels' hair; they are made by the females, are of a close texture, extremely warm, and impervious to the rain: thus they [329] are cool in the summer, and warm in the rainy season. In countries exposed to the attacks of neighbouring kabyles, they are arranged in a circular form, covering sometimes several acres of ground, having a large keyma or Arab tent in the centre of the circle, which serves for a *jamma*, or meeting for morning and evening prayers, and at other times for an *emdursa*, or seminary, where the Muhamedan youth are taught to read the Koran, and to write, as they call it, (*Sultan men Elsen*) the sultan of languages, or language of languages. The tent-pegs of the respective tents are indented within each other, so that the cattle cannot go out or in; moreover, a hedge of thorny bushes encircles the whole, secured by staves drove into the ground. The camels, horses, mules, horned cattle, sheep, and goats, are all inclosed in a division of the circular area during the night, and a fire is kept all night, to keep off the lions and wild beasts. The incessant barking of dogs, which are very numerous among the Arabs, prevent the travellers unaccustomed to these habitations from sleeping.

Various Modes of Intoxication.

All nations have some method of getting rid of reason, for the purpose of indulging in the vacuum and temporary independence produced by intoxication. We, of Europe, have recourse to wine to effect this purpose: the opulent indulge in the libations of claret, burgundy, [330] and champagne; the middling classes have recourse to brandy, rum, and gin; but the African effects this purpose at far less expense. A muselman procures ample temporary relief from worldly care for a mere trifle: he buys at the (*attara*), drug shop, for a penny, a small pipe of *el keef or hashisha*; this completely effects his purpose. The leaves of this drug, which is a kind of hemp, are called *el hashisha*; the flower of the plant is called *el keef*, and is much more powerful in its inebriating quality than the *hashisha*, but a pipe of the latter will have as powerful an effect as two or three bottles of wine. It is said, that when the patient is under the influence of pleasant imaginations, the fume of this drug increases the sensation into the most pleasing delirium, engendering the most luxuriant images, and promoting a voluptuous vacuum. But when the person's ill fate tempts him to taste it in a melancholy mood, it protracts the gloomy moments, and gives the woes of life a longer duration: he utters sighs and lamentations, he apprehends nothing but misery and misfortune, till the effect of the drug is exhausted, and he awakes from his dream of woe.

Division of Agricultural Property.

Agricultural property is ascertained by a large stone laid at each corner of a plantation of corn, a direct line is drawn from stone to stone at [331] the season of reaping; it has, perhaps, never been known, that these partitions have been removed for the purpose of encroachment; a mutual confidence, and a point of honour renders this mode of discriminating the respective property of individuals adequate to every purpose of hedge or ditch.

Mines.

The mountains that separate the province of Suse from that of Draha, abound in iron, copper, and lead. Ketiwa, a district on the declivity of Atlas, east of Terodant, contains also mines of lead and brimstone; and saltpetre also, of a superior quality, abounds in the neighbourhood of Terodant. In the same mountains, about fifty or sixty miles south-west of Terodant, there are mines of iron of a very malleable quality, equal to that of Biscay in Spain, from which the people of Tagrasert manufacture gun-barrels, equal to those made in Europe. At Elala in Suse, in the same ridge of mountains, are several rich mines of copper, some of which are impregnated with gold: they have also a rich silver mine, the metal of which latter is cast in round lumps, weighing two or three ounces each piece. I have bought of this silver at Santa Cruz, and have paid Spanish dollars for it, weight for weight; it is very pure. Mines of antimony and lead ore are also found in Suse, impregnated with gold, [332] some specimens of which I sent to England to be analyzed; but being informed that it yielded gold sufficient only to pay the expenses of purifying, I gave no farther attention to it, although I have had reason to think, since then, that an importation of the ore would amply pay the importer.

Nyctalopia, Hemeralopia, or Night-blindness,
called by the Arabs Butelleese; and its Remedy.

During my residence at Santa Cruz, I had a cousin with me who was afflicted with this disorder. When the sun sat his blindness came on, and continued till the rising sun. This youth was so afflicted, during a month, with this disorder, that he could scarcely see his way with a candle in his hand, so that it was quite painful to see him groping about. An Arab of the Woled Abbusebah Kabyl, who retain much of the science and art of their ancestors, and whose prosperity I had promoted at Santa Cruz, by facilitating his commercial adventures, communicated to me a simple remedy for this disorder; I put no faith in it, for it was so simple that I was disposed to think it an illusion. He called on me, however, repeatedly, and finding I had not applied it, he brought it one morning himself, and urged me to try it, I did so; and that same evening the eyes of the youth were almost well, and his sight was completely restored the following night. This [333] ophthalmic affection, in an Arabic translation of Hippocrates, is called *Butelleese;* another translation of ancient date calls it *Shebkeret:* the name, however, by which it is known at the present day in Africa, is *Butelleese:* the Latins called it *Lusciosus*, which word denotes precisely the disease, viz. one who sees imperfectly in the morning and evening twilight, but whose vision is clear at broad day-light. *Lusciosus ad lucernam non videt. Vesperi non videre quos lusciosos appellant.* Plaut. Mil. Gl. ii. 3.

This ophthalmia has been by some denominated *hen-blindness*, from the circumstance of hens' eyes being thus affected, when they are unable to see to pick up small grains in the dusk of the evening. I have frequently seen fowls thus affected soon after going to sea, from the coast of Africa, after which they decline and grow sick. A quantity of small gravel should be spread in their coops at sea, which prevents this disorder, and will sometimes cure it. At the commencement of this complaint, the circumstance that first engages the patient's attention is the dimness of his eye-sight at twilight: the nocturnal dimness of vision was such, in the instance before-mentioned, that the youth could scarcely see, even with a candle in his hand, which he described, as seen by him, as if it were misty, or as glimmering in a thick fog. There was no external disfiguration visible in the eyes, but they appeared as usual.

[334]

What the cause of this disorder was I am unable to say; but I have often suspected that it was contracted from the shining of the sun on the white terras of the house where my cousin used to go of a morning to shoot *tibeebs*, a bird somewhat resembling the European sparrow. This youth was rather of a weak or delicate constitution. I did not repeat the above remedy, as the boy's eyes continued well, without any defect in the vision at any time of the day or night, till seven-and-twenty days had elapsed, when the disorder returned. I procured the remedy again, and he took it; it had the same effect as before; he took it again, and then continued well for a month. It again returned a third time, and was cured by one single administration, after which it entirely disappeared, and never returned. Some time after this, I was informed that the British fleet in the Mediterranean was affected with this disorder; that one-tenth, or more, of the crews of our ships had laboured under it; and, on my return to England, I was urged to represent to His Majesty's ministers, that I had an infallible remedy for the disorder. I was referred to Doctor Harness, of the Transport Board. I waited on the Doctor, and afterwards corresponded with him. He appeared very desirous of knowing the remedy; but he was not at liberty to grant me any remuneration for it. I, however, offered to discover it, on being reimbursed the sum which the remedy cost me, on experimental [335] proof being produced of its infallibility; which proposition was rejected by the Transport Board in August, 1812, who informed me at the same time, that the Lords Commissioners of the Admiralty did not judge proper to grant the sum required by me for the discovery of the remedy for Nyctalopia, which, I should add, was between 500*l*. and 600*l*. The remedy, therefore, remains a secret to this day.

A celebrated electrician and galvanist having conversed with me lately respecting this remedy for Nyctalopia, suggested to me the probability, that the same remedy might be effectual also in *gutta serena*, as both those disorders are known to proceed from a defect in the optic nerve. This opinion he corroborated, by quoting, in confirmation of it, the opinion of a well-known author. The electrician perceiving my incredulity, or more properly, my ignorance of the wonderful connection that exists between the intestines and the head, was prompted, as I verily believe, by a philanthropic disposition; and actually proved to me, experimentally, the influence which the eyes have on the intestines, and *vice versa*. A patient with a *gutta serena*, who had been, as he informed me, twelve months under the hands of a celebrated oculist, was recommended by the latter, as a last resource, to try galvanism. He had received no benefit whatever whilst under the direction of the oculist above alluded to, but his intestines were intolerably deranged by the effects of the mercury which he had taken. [336] This gentleman galvanised his eyes, and the man, who is a gunsmith, told me, that when he first went to have the operation performed, he could not see the red border round the hearth-rug in the front parlour, but when he returned into that room, after having been galvanised, he assured me he saw it plainly. He moreover declared that his bowels had been, and then were, in a very deranged state, from the effects of the mercury which he had taken, but that he felt incredible relief after having been galvanised, and that, two or three days afterwards, they were quite restored to health and strength. Being thus satisfied with the influence that so wonderfully exists between the intestines and the eyes, I am now making arrangements with the same gentleman, to administer the remedy for the benefit, *as we hope*, of patients afflicted with *gutta serena*. But I now declare to the public a third time, that the remedy is simple, safe, and effectual, and that I am ready and desirous of administering it to any one who may choose to apply for it, who is afflicted with the disorder, with my positive assurances, that it will effect a cure in eight-and-forty hours at the utmost, but probably in twenty-four.

Vaccination.

Intelligence received from West Barbary was instrumental in promoting the adoption of [337] vaccination. In the latter years of the last century, the small-pox pervaded West and South Barbary. Mr. Matra, the British consul-general to the Empire of Marocco, wrote to me at that period officially, to procure him every information possible, and to inform him if I could discover if cattle in this country were subject to the small-pox. I made every inquiry without delay, and I reported to His Excellency, (who was ambassador as well as consul), that I had ascertained that the horses, mules, asses, and oxen were subject in this country to the small-pox, of which there could be no doubt, as the name given to the disorder in the beasts of the field, was the same as that which designated the small-pox in the human species, viz. Jedrie. In consequence of this information, confirmed afterwards by other enquiries, His Excellency wrote to England on the subject, and, I believe, sent some vaccine pus home; soon after which Dr. Jenner began his experiments on vaccine inoculation, which have since been adopted throughout Europe, and in great part of Asia and America. Although I was thus instrumental in the propagation of vaccine inoculation, yet I never asked for or received any remuneration; but I feel a satisfaction in having been thus instrumental of good to mankind, in this new and eligible system of inoculation, by means of which human life has been preserved; for, according to Sir Gilbert Blane's late statement, 23,134 lives [338] have been saved during the last 15 years by vaccination.

Game.

All kinds of game are plentiful in South and in West Barbary; viz. *el gror*, a bird somewhat similar to the English partridge, but unknown in Europe. I shot some of these birds for Doctor Brussonet, the naturalist, who was intendant of the national garden of botany at Montpelier, which that gentleman prepared in the oven, and sent to the National Institute at Paris. He informed me this bird was a non-descript. Hares, antelopes, woodcocks, snipes, plovers, bustards. There is an abundance of partridges, red ducks as large as geese, ducks, wigeon, and teal; curlews, in immense quantities, are found in the flat parts of the country on the coast; immense quantities of doves, wild pigeons, wood-pigeons, and large sand-larks. Every person is at liberty to shoot; but the princes and the great, consider field-sports beneath their dignity, except hawking, and hunting the wild boar, the lion, and the tiger. The Muhamedans do not prefer game to other food. When they have shot a bird, they immediately cut its throat, that the blood may flow freely; otherwise it is not lawful to eat it. Game is never seen in the public markets. When they shoot for Europeans, they dispense with the ceremony of cutting the throat of the game. They reproach the Christians for eating such food, which they call (*m'jeefa*) "strangled."

[339]

Agriculture.--Mitferes.

The agriculturists, in all the Arab provinces throughout this empire, have subterraneous caverns or apartments, generally in the form of a cone, for the preservation of their corn during a scarcity or famine. During my residence in this country, I have investigated the method, and have learned the art of constructing these depositories of grain. They season them before the corn is deposited. They should not be constructed in a clay soil. In these *mitferes*, throughout the Arab provinces of Duquella, Temsena, Shawiya, &c. they preserve the corn sound during thirty years. I have been present at the opening of them after the corn had been deposited twenty-one years. It was perfectly sound. When these depositories are opened, each family takes a portion of the grain, so as to distribute the whole immediately; otherwise, in a few months, if not consumed, it acquires a peculiar bad flavour, which is called the *mitfere twang*. To prevent this, an Arab, on opening one of these depositaries, lends corn to all his neighbours, and in his turn he receives it back again, when they respectively open theirs. It is unnecessary to expatiate on the expediency of constructing *mitferes* in a country oftentimes visited by locusts, the plague, drought, or inundation. There would be a manifest policy in establishing similar granaries in our colony in South Africa, where I understand they are visited by [340] locusts, and where the soil is similar to that of West and South Barbary. All the valuable gums that Barbary now supplies Europe with, and also many articles of commerce not yet known at the Cape, might be procured from Barbary, and if transplanted to that colony, would undoubtedly thrive, from the similarity of climate and soil.

Laws of Hospitality.

The territory of the Emperor of Marocco, west of the mountains of Atlas, and from the shores of the Mediterranean to the confines of the Shelluh province of Haha, is one continual corn-field, inhabited by Arabs living in douars or encampments: much of the ground, however, lies fallow. These encampments are fixed generally at a considerable distance from the track of travellers, so that a person unacquainted with this circumstance, would be disposed to imagine the country thinly inhabited. The tents in safe countries, where there is no fear of wild beasts, are pitched in a straight line; but where lions or other ferocious animals are found, the tents are disposed in a circular form; and thorny bushes are placed round the douar, to prevent the visits of these unwelcome guests. The Arabs are the agriculturists of the country, and are for the most part emigrations from the original stock in Sahara. These people have preserved from time immemorial the practice of open and unrestrained hospitality. Their prophet [341] confirmed these propensities; and hospitality has been ever since, the predominant virtue of the Arab. Accordingly, Muhamedans are entitled, through their various journeys, to be entertained three days wherever they sojourn. A traveller, therefore, when he chooses to rest from the fatigue of his journey, goes to one of these douars and exclaims (*Deef Allah*) "the guests of God." The sheik then comes forth from his tent to receive him or them: (*Kheyma Deâf*) the travellers' or guests' tent is appropriated to the stranger; food is brought to him, agreeably to his rank in life, but always simple, good, and wholesome. Here he may remain, if he chooses, for three days, without being considered an intruder, and free of all expense whatsoever. If he wishes to exceed the three days allowed by the Muhamedan law, he must prove his poverty; which being done, he may be entertained for a further period of time: but this latter is quite optional; no man is compelled to entertain and provide food for strangers and travellers, without remuneration, above three days.

This hospitality extends not generally to all mankind, but to Muhamedans only. A Christian or a Jew would be expected to pay a trifle for his entertainment; although, in travelling through the province of Suse, the Arabs have absolutely refused to take any remuneration from me; but, that is not generally the case, nor ought such conduct to be expected: in the instances [342] before-mentioned, these people considered themselves so much benefited by the opening of the port of Santa Cruz, that they thought they could not do enough for me. I was, therefore, every where received in that province with the most cordial marks of disinterested hospitality.

The laws of hospitality are sacred and inviolable. This I will elucidate, by relating a circumstance that happened while I was at Marocco. The Emperor was dissatisfied with the conduct of four sheiks of Suse: they had not discharged the duties of their public vocation, but had abused their office; the Emperor had issued orders to arrest them, but by some means they got intelligence of the orders; they therefore immediately ordered their horses, and decamped in the evening from Marocco: they knew they should not be safe any where from the Emperor's grasp, but under the protection of the Khalif Muhamed ben Delemy, whom, however, they had in some manner injured; nevertheless, knowing the noble character of the man, they were resolved to try their fate; accordingly, they made haste to reach the gates of his castle in Shtuka, before the Emperor might discover their departure. They arrived, and exclaiming *Deef Allah*, they were admitted. Delemy told them, that although they had not behaved friendly to him, he would protect them. His gates, he said, were always open to the children of adversity, and they might depend on [343] his protection. The Emperor soon discovered, by diligent enquiry, what route they had taken, and His Imperial Majesty urged Delemy to deliver them up; but the latter expostulated, and observing that he should not deserve the name of an Arabian sheik, if he degraded himself by giving up those who had claimed his protection, in his own country: and he actually granted them protection several months; till, at length, finding they could not escape the hand of power, by any plan but that of going into the Sahara, Delemy agreed to see them safe out of the Emperor's dominions, and accompanied them to Akka, and beyond that place, till they reached the Sahara, where, being perfectly safe, he took his leave of them, and they exchanged *Salems*.

Punishment for Murder.

If a man commits murder, the friends of the murdered claim redress of the alkaid, if in a town,--of the bashaw of the province, if in the country. If the murderer is discovered, he is taken into custody, to suffer death, unless the relations of the murdered man choose to compromise with the relations of the murderer: in which case, a sum of money is paid to the former, and the matter is thus settled.

Insolvency Laws.

An insolvent cannot be detained in prison after his insolvency is ascertained. He gives up his property to his creditors; but if he should [344] afterwards become a man of substance, his creditors can claim the amount of their debts, deducting what they have already received.

Dances.

The dances of the Arabs are peculiar to themselves. The youths dance without females, and the females without youths. On all marriages and rejoicings, music and dancing continue till the dawn of day. Among the encampments of Arabs, in the summer season, the whole country, at night, is in a blaze of light. The kettle-drum, the triangle, the shepherd's pipe, and the *erbeb* an instrument resembling the fiddle, with two strings, form the band of music.

The youths form a double row of six or eight in each, and carry themselves erect, with their arms hanging down close to their side; moving obliquely to the right, then to the left, without taking their feet from the ground, but moving their heels, then their toes on the ground, advancing or gliding slowly along; keeping exact time with the music: they then vault in the air, perform somersets and various feats of agility. They sing also with great taste and judgment, and some of them have excellent voices, being selected for the purpose of affording entertainment to the spectators. The ladies dance also in a similar manner, but without the vaulting and somersets. They have a very elegant shawl-dance, which some of them dance with great taste, and with much graceful movement.

[345]

Circumcision.

The circumcision of male children is the general practice of Islaemism; it is also used among some of the [201] *Khaffers* or *Cafers* of North, Central, and South Africa. Circumcision is not a practice ascribed to a principle of cleanliness, or any other cause, but ancient usage. The period of performing this operation among the Arabs is at the age of eight years.

Footnote 201: (return) *Khaffer* (singular number) is an Arabic term, applied to all who are not Muhamedans; all Pagans, Jews, and Christians, are called *Khaffer*, *K'fer* (plural) *Kaffir billa*, an atheist: hence Caffraria, the name of the country near the Cape of Good Hope.

Invoice from Timbuctoo to Santa Cruz.

Transport of ([202] *Alk Sudan*) gum of Sudan, bought at Timbuctoo, on account of Messrs. James Jackson and Co. by their agent, L'Hage Muhamed O----n, and dispatched to Akka by the spring (*akkaba*) accumulated caravan, in February, 1794.

M. Doll

Footnote 202: (return) This gum is the produce of an enormous tree of Sudan, which flourishes near Timbuctoo, Housa, Wangara, and Bernoh (or Bernou) it is transported by the caravans to Alexandria in Egypt, to Tripoli, Tunis, and Algiers. From the African ports in the Mediterranean it is shipped to Smyrna and Constantinople, and from thence to England, under the denomination of Turkey gum; some goes to Mogodor and Tetuan, and thence to London.

[346]

```
200 camel loads of gum-sudan, each weighing
```

250 lb. net, bought at Timbuctoo, at four Mexico dollars per load,	800
Charges.--Cow-skins to pack it in, sticks to stow it on the camels, &c.	25
200 camels hired to Akka, at 18 Mexico dollars each,	3600
Stata, *i.e.* convoy through the Sahara, from Timbuctoo to Arawan, at 20 cents per camel,	40
Do. from Arawan to East Tagrassa, at 20 cents per camel,	40
Do. from East Tagrassa to Akka, at 40 cents per camel,	40
20 per cent., or one-fifth, on the first cost, to be allowed to the purchaser on safe arrival at Akka,	160
	————
	4705
	————

[347] The adventure is subject to this charge, provided it arrive safe at Akka, not otherwise, as also to encourage the agent at Timbuctoo, to exert himself in procuring trusty guides and competent statas, which he would not do, without having a certain interest in the safe delivery.

N.B. No stata is necessary from Akka to Santa Cruz, but the hire is 3 dollars per camel.

Translation of a Letter from Timbuctoo, which accompanied the foregoing Consignment.

Praise be to God alone; for there is nothing durable but the kingdom of heaven.

To the Christian merchant, Jackson, at Agadeer. Peace be to those who follow the right way.

This being premised, know that I have sent you by this akkabah, two hundred camel load of gum-sudan, agreeable to the account herewith transmitted. The stata will be paid by my friend, L'Hage

Aly, sheik of Akka, whom I request you will reimburse according to the account which I have sent to you by him; and if he goes to Agadeer, be kind, friendly, and hospitable to him on my account, for he stands high in my esteem; and peace be with you.

Written at Timbuctoo, 10th of the month Muharram, year of the Hejra 1208, (corresponding with 15th Feb. A.C. 1794). By your friend,

L'HAGE MUHAMED O----n.
God be merciful to him.

Invoice from Timbuctoo to Fas.

Transport of gold, gum, and cottons, from Timbuctoo to Fas, consigned to L'Hage Seyd and L'Hage Abdrahaman Elfellely, Timbuctoo merchants at Fas, by (*akkaba el Kheriffy*) the autumnal caravan. Dispatched 29th Duelhaja el Hurem, year 1204, corresponding with 10th October, A.C. 1790.

500 skins (*Tibber Wangâree*) gold dust of Wangara, each skin containing 4 ounces, bought on their account, in barter for 800 Flemish plattilias.

100 (*Sibikat deheb Wangaree*). Wangara gold in bars, weighing 20 ounces each, bought in exchange for 400 pieces (*Shkalat*) Irish cloth, averaging 44 cubits each piece (7 cubits are equal to 4 English yards). [348]

10 bed-covers, 9 cubits long, 4 wide, chequered pattern, blue and white cotton, with scarlet silk between the chequers, manufactured at Timbuctoo, bought in barter for 100 lb. sugar, 30 loaves.

50 camel-load gum-sudan, weighing net 120 quintals.

Charges.--Hire of 50 camels to Akka, at 18 dollars each.

Stata to ditto, 1 dollar per load, to be paid by Sheik Aly ben A----r.

Copy of the Letter accompanying the foregoing
Remittance.

Praise be to God alone; for there is neither beginning nor strength, without God, the eternal God.

To my friends, L'Hage Zeyd and L'Hage Abdrahaman Elfellely. Peace be with ye, and the mercy of the High God; and after that, know, that I have sent to our agents at Akka, by the autumnal caravan, 50 camel loads of gum-sudan, being 100 skins; in each skin of gum I have packed 5 skins of gold dust, and 1 bar of gold. L'Hage Tahar ben Jelule will deliver to our agent at Akka, for you, 10 very handsome cotton covers for beds, of Sudan manufacture. May all this arrive safe, with the blessing of God. I will inform you by the spring caravan what merchandize to send here next autumn. I refer you to a long letter, which I have sent to you by L'Hage Tahar. Peace be with you, and the blessing of God be upon you. [349]

Written at Timbuctoo, the 29th Duelhaja El Huram, year 1204.

L'HAGE HAMED ELWANGARIE
. [203]God protect him.

Footnote 203: (return) The Muhamedans, in signing their name, always invoke the protection, mercy, or providence of God upon themselves.

Food of the Desert.

The people, whose interest induces them to cross the desert, (for there are no travellers from curiosity in this country,) obviate the objection to salt provisions, which increases the propensity to drink water, by taking with them melted butter, called *smin*; this is prepared without salt. They also cut beef into long pieces, about six inches long, and one inch square, without fat; these are called *el kuddeed*, which are hung on a line, exposed to the air till dry; they then cut them into pieces, two inches long; these are put into (*buckul*) an earthen pot; they then pour the *smin* into the *buckul* till it is covered. This meat and butter, besides being palatable, is comprised in a small compass, and feeds many. When this butter has been thus prepared and kept twelve or fifteen years, it is called *budrâ*, and is supposed to contain penetrating active medicinal qualities. I have seen some thirty years old.

Antithesis, a favourite Figure with the Arabs.

Mahmoud, sultan of Ghezna in the beginning of the eleventh century, though the son of a [350] slave, was very powerful. He sent to the khalif Alkader, requesting a title suited to his exalted dignity. The latter hesitated; but fearing the power of the sultan, sent him at the expiration of a year the ambiguous title, *Uly*, i.e. a prince, a friend, a slave. Mahmoud penetrated the khalif's meaning, and sent him immediately 100,000 pieces of gold, with a wish to know whether a letter had not been omitted. Alkader received the treasure, and took the hint, instantly dispatching letters patent in full form, creating him *Uäly* which signifies, without equivocation, a sovereign independent prince.

Arabian Modes of Writing.

The Arabs have various modes of writing, the principal of which is that used by the Koreish, the most learned of all the Western tribes, and is denominated the *Niskhi*, or upright character: if this is understood, the others may be easily comprehended. This is the character in which the Koran was originally written. In the seventh century, the Arabs adopted the invention of Moramer ben Morra, a native of Babylonian Irak, which was afterwards improved by the Kufik. The Kufik and the Niskhi are synonymous. Richardson, in his Arabic Grammar, p. 4. say, "The Mauritannick character, which is used by the Moors of Marocco and Barbary, descendants of the Arabians, differs [351] in many respects *considerably* from the other modes of writing." But this is incorrect; for the Mauritannick alphabet, excepting in the order of the letters, is precisely the same with the Oriental, as now written and spoken, with the exception only of the letters *Fa* and *Kaf*, and the formation even of these characters are alike. The punctuation only, differs in the West, that is, west of the Egyptian Nile. The Western punctuation of *Fa*, is one point below the letter, and the punctuation of the letter *Kaf* is one point above. In the East, the former letter has one point above, the latter has two. This is the only difference between the Eastern and the Western alphabets. Richardson, (see his Grammar, page 5,) also says, that "the purest Arabic is spoken at Grand Cairo," but this is not correct: the language of Grand Cairo and of Tunis, Tripoli, Algiers, and Marocco are much alike, but none of them are the pure Koraisch or Korannick Arabic, which is only spoken at Mekka, and among some of the tribes of Bedouins in the West. The language of the Woled Abbusebah, of the Howara, and of the Mograffra is the pure Arabic. Finally, in a note in Richardson's Grammar, page 18, it is said, "Some of our European writers, and amongst others Voltaire, substitute *Koran* for *Alcoran*, but perhaps improperly, as D'Herbelot and other learned Orientalists, write uniformly *l'Alcoran, il Alcorano*, the Alcoran." We have been too apt to copy the orthography of Oriental names from the French, whose pronunciation of the Roman or European characters [352] differs from ours. There cannot be a doubt that D'Herbelot is incorrect. The word *Koran* (for there is no *c* in the Arabic language) is derived from the verb *Kora*, to read; *koran*, reading: *Al* is the article; but, in this instance, D'Herbelot uses this article twice, which is certainly erroneous, for *l'* is the French article in the word in question, and *al* is the Arabic article; whereas *one* article only should precede a noun. *L'Alcoran* and the *Alcoran* are therefore equally incorrect; for the word in French should be *Le Coran*; in English, *the Koran*; therefore Voltaire was correct. I have thought it expedient to make these observations, because standing in Richardson's Grammar on the authority of *learned orientalists*, they are calculated to mislead the Arabic student.

Decay of Science and the Arts among the Arabs.

The literary fire of the Arabs and Persians has been extinguished upwards of 300 years; but before that period, the encouragement to learning in the East was unprecedented, and has never been equalled by any European nation either before or since that period. Kadder Khan, king of Turquestan, was the greatest support to science. When he appeared abroad, he was preceded by 700 horsemen, with silver battle-axes, and was followed by an equal number bearing maces of gold. He supported with magnificent appointment a literary academy in his palace, consisting of 100 men of [353] the highest reputation. Amak, called Abu Näib El Bokari, who was the chief poet, exclusive of a great pension and a vast number of slaves, had, in attendance wherever he went, thirty horses of state richly caparisoned, and a retinue in proportion. The king before-mentioned used to preside at their exercises of genius, on which occasions, by the side of his throne were always placed four large basons filled with gold and silver, which he distributed liberally to those who excelled.

Lebid suspended over the gate at Mecca a sublime poem; Muhamed placed near it the opening of the second chapter of the Koran, which was conceived to be something divine, and it gained the prize of the *Ocadh* assembly.

The remains of this custom of suspending over gates Arabic poems, is perceived at this day among the western Moors. The gates or entrances to Mogodor, Fas, Mequinas, Marocco, &c. have writing over them, which is a kind of Arabic short-hand, that none but the learned understand; these writings, however, are not moveable, being engraven on a square table on the stone itself.

Extraordinary Abstinence experienced in the Sahara.

The Arabs or inhabitants of the Sahara, can support the most extraordinary abstinence. Occasions occur, wherein they will travel several [354] days without food. After suffering a privation of a day or two, they tie their (*hazam*) belt round their loins, every morning tighter than the preceding day, thereby preventing, in some measure, that action of the bowels which promotes appetite. A Saharawan will thus go five or six days without food of any kind, in which case, when he reaches a habitation, or a (*wah*) cultivated spot in the Desert, he will drink about half-a-pint of camel's milk; this remains on the stomach but a short time: he then takes another draught, which, with some, remains and gives nourishment, but with others *it* is also rejected by the stomach; *a third draught is then taken, which restores the exhausted traveller!* I have been assured, that instances have been known in Sahara, wherein a man has been without food of any kind for seven days, and has afterwards been restored by the foregoing regimen!

[355]

LANGUAGES OF AFRICA.

Various Dialects of the Arabic Language --Difference between the Berebber and Shelluh Languages.--Specimen of the Mandinga.--Comparison of the Shelluh Language with that of the Canary Islands, and Similitude of Customs.

Yareb, the son of Kohtan [204], is said to have been the first who spoke Arabic, and the Muhamedans contend that it is the most eloquent language spoken in any part of the globe, and that it is the one which will be used at the day of judgment. To write a long dissertation on this copious and energetic language, would be only to repeat what many learned men have said before; a few observations, however, may not be superfluous to the generality of readers. The Arabic language is spoken by a greater proportion of the inhabitants of the known world than any other: a person having a practical knowledge of it, may travel from the shores of the Mediterranean Sea to the Cape of Good Hope, and notwithstanding that in such a journey he must pass through many kingdoms and empires of blacks, speaking distinct languages, yet he would find men in all those [356] countries versed in Muhamedan learning, and therefore acquainted with the Arabic; again, he might cross the widest part of the African continent from west to east, and would every where meet with persons acquainted with it, more particularly if he should follow the course of the great river called the Neel El Abeed, on the banks of which, from Jinnie and Timbuctoo, to the confines of lower Egypt, are innumerable cities and towns of Arabs and

Moors, all speaking the Arabic. Again, were a traveller to proceed from Marocco to the farthest shore of Asia, opposite the islands of Japan, he would find the Arabic generally spoken or understood wherever he came. In Turkey, in Syria, in Arabia, in Persia, and in India, it is understood by all men of education; and any one possessing a knowledge of the Korannick Arabic, might, in a very short time, make himself master of all its various dialects.

Footnote 204: (return) This Kohtan is the Joktan, son of Eber, brother to Phaleg, mentioned in Genesis. Chapter x, verse 25.

The letters of this language [205] are formed in four distinct ways, according to their situation at the beginning, middle, or end of words, as well as when standing alone; the greatest difficulty, however, to be overcome, is the acquiring a just pronunciation, (without which no living language can be essentially useful;) and to attain which, the learner should be able to express the difference of power and sound between what may be denominated the synonymous [357] letters, such as ط and ث with ت and ع with ا and ص with س and ض and ظ with د and ة with ح and ق with ى and خ and غ with ر.

Footnote 205: (return) The Oriental punctuation is here adopted.

Besides these, there are other letters, whose power is extremely difficult to be acquired by an European, because no language in Europe possesses sounds similar to the Arabic letters خ غ ع, nor has any language, except, perhaps, the English, a letter with the power of the Arabian ث. Those who travel into Asia or Africa scarcely ever become sufficiently masters of the Arabic to speak it fluently, which radical defect proceeds altogether from their not learning, while studying it, the peculiar distinction of the synonymous letters. *No European, perhaps, ever knew more of the theory of this language than the late Sir William Jones, but still he could not converse with an Arabian;* a circumstance of which he was not conscious until he went to India. This great man, however, had he been told that his knowledge of this popular eastern language was so far deficient, that he was ignorant of the separate powers of its synonymous letters, and consequently inadequate to converse intelligibly with a native Arab, he would certainly have considered it an aspersion, and have disputed altogether that such was the fact. Considering how much we are indebted to the Arabians for the preservation of many of the works of the ancients, [358] which would otherwise have never, perhaps, been known to us, it is really surprising, that their language should be so little known in Europe. It is certainly very difficult and abstruse, (to learners particularly,) but this difficulty is rendered insurmountable by the European professors knowing it only as a dead language, and *teaching it without due attention to the pronunciation of the before mentioned synonymous letters, a defect which is not likely to be remedied, and which will always subject the speaker to incessant errors.*

To show the Arabic student the difference between the Oriental and Occidental order of the letters of the alphabet, I shall here give them opposite each other.

[359]

    Oriental   Occidental

1 Alif	ا	1 Alif	ا
2 ba	ب	2 ba	ب
3 ta	ت	3 ta	ت
4 thsa	ث	4 tha	ث
5 jim	ج	5 jim	ج
6 hha	ح	6 hha	ح
7 kha	خ	7 kha	خ
8 dal	د	8 dal	د
9 dsal	ذ	9 dth'al	ذ
10 ra	ر	10 ra	ر
11 za	ز	11 zain	ز
12 sin	س	12 ta	ط
13 shin	ش	13 da	ظ
14 sad	ص	14 kef	ک
15 dad	ض	15 lam	ل
16 ta	ط	16 mim	م
17 da	ظ	17 nune	ن
18 ain	ع	18 sad	ص
19 gain	غ	19 dad	ض
20 fa	ف	20 ain	ع
21 kaf	ق	21 g'rain	غ
22 kef	ك	22 fa	ب ف
23 lem	ل	23 kaf	ف
24 mim	م	24 sin	س
25 nun	ن	25 shin	ش
26 waw	و	26 hha	ه
27 he	ه	27 wow	و
28 ya	ي	28 ia	ي
29 lam-alif	لا لا	29 lam-alif	لا لا

Besides this difference of the arrangement of the two alphabets, the Arabic student will observe that there is also a difference in the punctuation of two of the letters: thus--

Oriental		Occidental	
1 fa	ف	1 fa	ب
2 kaf	ق	2 kaf	ف

[360]

Among the Western Arabs, the ancient Arabic figures are used, viz. 0, 1, 2, 3, 4, 5, 6, 7, 8, 9: they often write 100 thus, 1..--200, 2..

To explain the force of the synonymous letters on paper would be impossible; the reader, however, may form some idea of the indispensable necessity of knowing the distinction by the few words here selected, which to one unaccustomed to hear the Arabic language spoken, would appear similar and undistinguishable.

[361]

[362]

ENGLISH	ARABIC Rendered as near to European pronunciation as the English Alphabet will admit.	ARABIC
A horse	Aoud	عُودٌ
Wood	Awad	اعواذٌ
To repeat	Aoud	عَودٌ
Fish	Hout	حَوتٌ
A gun	Mokhalla	أمكَحلَ
A foolish woman	Mokeela	مقيله
A frying pan	Makeela	مَقلَ
A lion	Seban	ألسبعُ
Morning	Seban	ألصبح
Seventh	Seban	
Hatred	Hassed	
Harvest	Hassed	

180

Learning	Alem, or El Alem	ألسبع
A flag	El Alem	احسب
		احصد
Granulated paste	Kuscasoe	عالِم or العالِم
The dish it is made in	Kuscas	الاعلام
		كسكس
Heart	Kul'b	كسكاس
Dog	Kil'b	قلب
		كلب
Mould	Kal'b	قالب
Captain	Rice	الرّايس
		الرّيش
Feathers	Rish	الغيس
Mud	G'ris	الشّم
		السّم
Smell	Shim	
Poison	Sim [206]	
Absent	G'raib	
Butter-milk	Raib	
White	Bead	
A black	El Abd	
Eggs	Baid	
Afar off	Baid	

A pig	Helloof	الغَايِب
An oath	Hellef	الرَّايِب
Feed for horses	Alf	أبيضُ
A thousand	Elf	العَبدُ
		البَيصُ
		ابعَيدُ
		حلوفُ
		احلفُ
		العَلفُ
		الفُ

Footnote 206: (return) The African Jews find it very difficult in speaking, to distinguish between *shim* and *sim*, for they cannot pronounce the *sh*, ش but sound it like *s* س ; the very few who have studied the art of reading the language, have, however, conquered this difficulty.

It is difficult for any one who has not accurately studied the Arabic language, to imagine the many errors which an European commits in speaking it, when self taught, or when taught in Europe. This deficiency originates in the inaccuracy of the application of the guttural and synonymous letters.

The ain ع and the غ grain cannot be accurately [363] pronounced by Europeans, who have not studied the language grammatically when young. The aspirated *h*, and the hard *s*, in the word for *morning* (sebah), are so much like their synonymes, that few Europeans can discern the difference; the one is consequently often mistaken for the other; and I have known a beautiful sentence absolutely perverted through an inaccuracy of this kind. In the words rendered *Hatred* and *Harvest*, the two synonymes of س and ص or *s* hard and *s* soft, are indiscriminately used by

Europeans in their Arabic *conversations*, a circumstance sufficient to do away the force and meaning of many a sentence.

The poetry as well as prose of the Arabians is well known, and has been so often discussed by learned men, that it would be irrelevant here to expatiate on the subject; but as the following description of the noblest passion of the human breast cannot but be interesting to the generality of readers, and, without any exception, to the fair sex, I will transcribe it.

"Love (العشك) beginneth in contemplation, passeth to meditation; hence proceeds desire; then the spark bursts forth into a flame, the head swims, the body wastes, and the soul turns giddy. If we look on the bright side of love, we must acknowledge that it has at least one advantage; it annihilates pride and immoderate self-love; true love, whose aim is the [364] happiness and equality of the beloved object, being incompatible with those feelings.

"Lust is so different from true love (العشك) , and so far from a perfection, that it is always a species of punishment sent by God, because man has abandoned the path of his pure love."

In their epistolary writing, the Arabs have generally a regular and particular style, beginning and ending all their letters with the name of God, symbolically, because God is the beginning and end of all things. The following short specimen will illustrate this:

Translation of a letter written in the Korannick Arabic by Seedy Soliman ben Muhammed ben Ismael, Sultan of Marocco, to his Bashaw of Suse, &c. &c.

"Praise be to the only God! for there is neither power, nor strength, without the great and eternal God."

L.S.

Containing the Emperor's name and
titles, as Soliman ben Muhamed
ben Abdallah, &c, &c.

"Our servant, Alkaid Abdelmelk ben Behie Mulud, God assist, and peace be with thee, and the mercy and grace of God be upon thee!"

"We command thee forthwith to procure and send to our exalted presence every Englishman that has been wrecked on the coast of Wedinoon, and to forward them hither without delay, and diligently to succour and attend to [365] them, and may the eye of God be upon thee!" [207]

Footnote 207: (return) When they write to any other but Muhamedans, they never salute them with the words, "Peace be with thee," but substitute--"Peace be to those who follow the path of the true God," *Salem ala min itaba el Uda.*

"26th of the (lunar), month Saffer, year of the Hejra 1221. (May, 1806.)"

The accuracy of punctuation in the Arabic language is a matter that ought to be strictly attended to.

The foregoing observations will serve to prove the insufficiency of a knowledge of this language, as professed or studied in Great Britain when unaccompanied with a practical knowledge. These observations may apply equally to the Persian language. [208]

Footnote 208: (return) "One of the objects I had in view in coming to Europe, was to instruct young Englishmen in the Persian language. I however met with so little encouragement from persons in authority, that I entirely relinquished the plan. I instructed, however, (as I could not refuse the recommendations that were brought to me,) an amiable young man, Mr. S------n, and thanks be to God, my efforts were crowned with success! and that he, having escaped the instructions of *self-taught* masters, has acquired such a knowledge of the principles of that language, and so correct an idea of its idiom and pronunciation, that I have no doubt, after a few years' residence in India, he will attain to such a degree of excellence, as has not yet been acquired by any other Englishman." Vide Travels of Mirza Abu Taleb Khan, vol. i. p. 200.

If the present ardour for discovery in Africa be persevered in, the learned world may expect, in the course of a few years, to receive histories and other works of Greek and Roman [366] authors, which were translated into the Arabic language, when Arabian literature was in its zenith, and have ever since been confined to some private libraries in the cities of the interior of Africa, and in Arabia.

Having said thus much with regard to the Arabic of the western Arabs, which, with little variation, is spoken throughout all the finest districts of North Africa, I shall proceed to say a few words respecting the other languages spoken north of Sahara: these are the Berebber and its dialects, viz. the Zayan and Girwan, and Ait Amor; the Shelluh of Suse and South Atlas, all which, though latterly supposed by some learned men to be the same, differ in many respects; any one possessing a knowledge of the Berebber language might, with little difficulty, make himself understood by the Zayan of Atlas, the Girwan, or the Ait Amor; but the Shelluh is a different language, and each so different from the Arabic, that there is not the smallest resemblance, as the following specimen will demonstrate:

[367]

BEREBBER.	SHELLUH.	ARABIC.	ENGLISH.
Tumtoot	Tayelt	Ishira	A girl
Ajurode	Ayel	Ishire	A boy

Askan	Tarousa	Hajar	A thing
Aram	Algrom	Jimmel	Camel
Tamtute	Tamraut	Murrah	A woman
Ishiar	Issemg'h	L'Abd	A slave
Aouli	Izimer	Kibsh	A sheep
Taddert	Tikimie	Dar	House
Ikshuden	Asroen	Lawad	Wood
Eekeel	Akfai	Hellib	Milk
Tifihie	Uksume	El Ham	Meat
Buelkiel	Amuran	Helloof	A hog
Abreede	Agares	Trek	A road
Bishee	Fikihie	Ara	Give me
Adude	Asht	Agi	Come
Alkam	Aftooh	Cire	Go
Kaym	Gäuze	Jils	Sit down
Imile	Imeek	Serire	Little

[368]

Specimen of the Difference between the Arabic and Shelluh Languages.

SHELLUH.	ARABIC.	ENGLISH.
Is sin Tamazirkt	Wash katarf Shelluh	Do you understand Shelluh?
Uree sin	Man arf huh	I do not understand it.
Matshrult	Kif enta	How are you?
Is tekeete Marokshe	Wash gite min Marockshe	Are you come from Marocco?
Egan ras	Miliah	Good
Maigan	Ala'sh	Wherefore?
Misimmink	As'mek	What is your name?
Mensh kat dirk	Shall andik	How much have you got?
Tasardunt	Borella	A mule
Romi	Romi	An European
Takannarit	Nasarani	A Christian
Romi	Kaffer	An infidel
Misem Bebans	Ashkune mula	Who is the owner?
Is'tkit Tegriwelt	Washjite min Tegriwelt	Are you come from Cape Ossem?
Auweete Imkelli	Jib Liftor	Bring the dinner
Efoulkie	Meziana	Handsome
Ayeese	El aoud	A horse
Tikelline	El Baid	Eggs
Amuran	Helloof	Hog

Tayuh	Tatta	Camelion
Tasamumiat	Adda	Green lizard
Tenawine	Sfune	Ships.

Marmol says, the Shelluhs and Berebbers write and speak one language, called Killem Abimalick [209]; but the foregoing specimen, the accuracy of which may be depended on, clearly proves this assertion to be erroneous, as well as that of many moderns who have formed their opinion, in all probability, on the above authority. Now, although the Shelluh and Berebber languages are so totally dissimilar, that there is not one word in the foregoing vocabulary which resembles its corresponding word in the other language, yet, from the prejudice which Marmol's authority has [369] established, it will still be difficult, perhaps, to persuade the learned that such an author could be mistaken on such a subject. My account therefore must remain for a future age to determine upon, when the languages of Africa shall be better known than they are at present; for it is not a few travellers occasionally sent out on a limited plan, that can ascertain facts, the attainment of which requires a long residence, and familiar intercourse with the natives. Marmol had also misled the world, in saying that they write a different language; the fact is, that when they write any thing of consequence, it is in the Arabic; but any trifling subject is written in the Berebber words, though in the Arabic character. If they had any peculiar character in the time of Marmol, they have none now; for I have conversed with hundreds of them, as well as with the Shelluhs, and have had them staying at my house for a considerable time together, but never could learn from any, that a character different from the Arabic had ever been in use among them.

Footnote 209: (return) Killem Abimalick signifies the Language of Abimalick; this is evidently an error of Marmol, the Shelluh language is denominated *Amazirk*; the Berebber Language is denominated *Killem Brebber*.

In addition to these languages, there is another spoken at the Oasis of Ammon, or Siwah, called in Arabic (الواح الغاربي) El Wah El Grarbie, which appears to be a mixture of Berebber and Shelluh, as will appear from the list of Siwahan words given by Mr. Horneman [210], [370] in his Journal, page 19, part of which I have here transcribed, to show the similitude between those two languages, whereby it will appear that the language of Siwah and that of the Shelluhs of South Atlas, are one and the same language.

ENGLISH.	SIWAHAN.	SHELLUH.
Sun	Itfuckt	Atfuct
Head	Achfé	Akfie
Camel	Lgum	Arume
Sheep	Jelibb	Jelibb
Cow	Tfunest	Tafunest
Mountain	Iddrarn	Iddra [211]
Have you a horse?	Goreck Ackmar	Is derk Achmar? [212]
Milk	Achi	Akfie
Bread	Tagor	Tagora [213]

Dates	Tena	Tenia (sing.)Tena (plural.)

South of the Desert we find other languages spoken by the blacks; and are told by Arabs, who have frequently performed the journey from Jinnie to Cairo, and the Red Sea, that thirty-three different Negro languages are met [371] with in the course of that route, but that the Arabic is spoken by the intelligent part of the people, and the Muhamedan religion is known and followed by many; their writings are uniformly in Arabic.

Footnote 210: (return) In reading Mr. William Marsden's observations on the language of Siwah, at the end of Horneman's Journal, in page 190, I perceive that the short vocabulary inserted corresponds with a vocabulary of the Shelluh language, which I presented to that gentleman some years past.

Footnote 211: (return) Plural Iddrarn.

Footnote 212: (return) Or, Is derk ayeese?

Footnote 213: (return) This is applied to bread when baked in a pan, or over the embers of charcoal, or other fire; but when baked in an oven it is called Agarom (g guttural.)

It may not be improper in this place, seeing the many errors and mutilated translations which appear from time to time, of Arabic, Turkish and Persian papers, to give a list of the Muhamedan moons or lunar months, used by all those nations, which begin with the first appearance of the new moon, that is, the day following, or sometimes two days after the change, and continue till they see the next new moon; these have been mutilated to such a degree in all our English translations, that I shall give them, in the original Arabic character, and as they ought to be spelt and pronounced in the English character, as a clue whereby to calculate the correspondence between our year and theirs. They divide the year into 12 months, which contain 29 or 30 days, according as they see the new moon; the first day of the month Muharam is termed

راس العام Ras Elame, i.e. the beginning of the year.

As we are more used to the Asiatic mode of punctuation, that will be observed in these words.

[372]

Muharam	مُحَارُم
Asaffer	أَصَافُر

Arabia Elule

Arabea Atthenie	الرَّابيع الوله
Jumad Elule	الرَّابيع الثاني
Jumad Athenie	جوماد الول
Rajeb	جوماد الثَّاني
Shaban	راجب
	شعبان
Ramadan	رامَدان
Shual	شوال
Du'elkada	دّلكعده
Du Elhajah	دّلحاجَه

The first of Muharram, year of the Hejra 1221, answers to the 19th March of the Christian æra, 1806.

Among the various languages spoken south of the Sahara, we have already observed that there are thirty-three different ones between the Western Ocean and the Red Sea, following the shores of the Nile El Abeed, or Niger: among all these nations and empires, a man practically acquainted with the Arabic, may always make himself understood, and indeed, it is the language most requisite to be known for every traveller in these extensive regions.

The Mandinga is spoken from the banks of the Senegal, where that river takes a northerly course from the Jibel Kuthera to the kingdom [373] of Bambarra; the Wangareen tongue is a different one; and the Housonians speak a language differing again from that.

Specimen of the difference between the Arabic and Mandinga language; the words of the latter extracted from the vocabularies of Seedi Muhamed ben Amer Sudani.

[374]

[375]

[376]

[377]

ENGLISH.	MANDINGA.	ARABIC.
One	Kalen	Wahud
Two	Fula	Thanine
Three	Seba	Thalata
Four	Nani	Arba
Five	Lulu	Kumsa
Six	Uruh	Setta
Seven	Urn'klu	Sebba
Eight	Säae	Timinia
Nine	Kanuntée	Taseud
Ten	Dan	Ashra
Eleven	Dan kalen	Ahud ash
Twelve	Dan fula	Atenashe
Thirteen	Dan seba	Teltashe
Nineteen	Dankanartée	Tasatasli
Twenty	Mulu	Ashreen
Thirty	Mulu nintau	Thalateen
Forty	Mulu fula	Arbä'in
Fifty	Mulu fula neentan	Kumseen
Sixty	Mulu sebaa	Setteen
Seventy	Mulu sebaa nintan	Sebä'in.
Eighty	Mulu nani	T'aramana'een
Ninety	Mulu nani neentaan	Tasa'een
One hundred	Kemi	Mia
One thousand	Uli	Elf
This	Neen	Hadda

English		
That	Waleem	Hadduk
Great	Bawa	Kabeer
Little	Nadeen	Sereer
Handsome	Nimawa	Zin
Ugly	Nuta	Uksheen (k guttur.)
White	Kie	Bead
Black	Feen	Khal
Red	Williamma	Hummer
How do you do?	Nimbana mcuntania	Kif-enta
Well	Kantée	Ala-khere
Not well	Moon kanti	Murrede
What do you want	Ala feta matume	Ash-bright
Sit down	Siduma	Jils
Get up	Ounilee	Node
Sour	Akkumula	Hamd
Sweet	Timiata	Helluh
True	Aituliala	Hack
False	Funiala	Kadube
Good	Abatee	Miliah
Bad	Minbatee	Kubiah
A witch	Bua	Sahar
A lion	Jatta	Sebaâ
An elephant	Samma	El fele
A hyæna	Salua	Dubbah
A wild boar	Siwa	El kunjer
A water horse	Mali	Aoud d'Elma
A horse	Suhuwa	Aoud
A camel	Kumaniun	Jimmel
A dog	Wallee	Killeb
Hel el Killeb or the dog-faced race.	Hel Wallee	Hel El Killeb
A gazel	Tankeen	Gazel (g guttural)
A cat	Niankune	El mish
A goat	Baâ	El mâize
A sheep	Kurenale	Kibsh
A bull	Nisakia	Toôr
A serpent	Saâ	Hensh
A camelion	Mineer	Tatta
An ape	Ku'nee	Dzatute
A fowl or chicken	Susee	Djez
A duck	Beruee	El Weese
A fish	Hihu	El hout
Butter	Tulu	Zibda
Milk	Nunn	El hellib
Bread	Mengu	El khubs (k guttur.)

Corn	Nieu	Zra
Wine	Tangee	Kummer (k guttur.)
Honey	Alee	Asel
Sugar	Tobabualee	Sukar
Salt	Kuee	Mil'h
Ambergris	Anber	Anber
Brass	Tass	Tass
Silver	Kudee	Nukra
Gold-dust	Teber	Tiber
Pewter	Tass ki	Kusdeer
A bow	Kula	El kos
An arrow	Binia	Zerag
A knife	Muru	Jenui
A spoon	Kulia	Mogerfa
A bed	El arun	El ferrashe
A lamp	El kundeel	El kundeel
A house	Su	Ed dar
A room	Bune	El beet
A light-hole or window	Jinnee	Reehâha
A door	Daa	Beb
A town	Kinda	Midina
Smoke	Sezee	Tkan (k guttural)
Heat	Kandia	Skanna (k guttural)
Cold	Nini	Berd
Sea	Bedu baha	Bahar
River	Bedu	Wed
A rock	Berri	Jerf
Sand	Kinnikanni	Rummel
The earth	Binku	Dunia
Mountain	Kuanku	Jibbel
Island	Juchüi	Dzeera
Rain	Sanjukalaeen	Shta
God	Allah	Allah
Father	Fa	Ba
Mother	Ba	Ma
Hell	Jahennum	Jehennume
A man	Kia	Rajil
A woman	Musa	Murrah
A sister	Bum musa	Kat (k guttural)
A brother	Bum kia	Ka
The devil	Buhau	Iblis
A white man	Tebabu	Rajil biad
A singer	Jalikea	Runai (r guttural)
A singing woman	Jalimusa	Runaiah (r guttural)
A slave	June	Abeed

A servant	Bettela	Mutalem

Having now given some account of the languages of Africa, we shall proceed to animadvert on the similitude of language and customs between the Shelluhs of Atlas and the original inhabitants of the Canary Islands. The words between inverted commas, are quotations from Glasse's History of the Discovery and Conquest of the Canary Islands.

"The inhabitants of Lancerotta and Fuertaventura are social and cheerful;" like the Shelluhs of Atlas; "they are fond of singing and dancing; their music is vocal, accompanied with a clapping of hands, and beating with their feet;" the Shelluhs resemble them in all these respects; "Their houses are built of stone, without cement; the entrance is narrow, so that but one person can enter at a time."

The houses of the Shelluhs are sometimes [378] built without cement, but always with stone; the doors and entrances are low and small, so that one person only can enter.

"In their temples they offered to their God milk and butter."

Among the Shelluhs milk and butter are given as presents to princes and great men; the milk being an emblem of good will and candour.

"When they were sick (which seldom happened) they cured themselves with the herbs which grew in the country; and when they had acute pains, they scarified the part affected with sharp stones, and burned it with fire, and then anointed it with goat's butter. Earthen vessels of this goat's butter were found interred in the ground, having been put there by the women, who were the makers, and took that method of preparing it for medicine."

The custom of the Shelluhs on such occasions is exactly similar; the butter which they use is old, and is buried under ground many years in (*bukul*) earthen pots, and is called *budra*: it is a general medicine, and is said to possess a remarkably penetrating quality.

"They grind their barley in a hand-mill, made of two stones, being similar to those used in some remote parts of Europe".

In Suse, among the Shelluhs, they grind their corn in the same way, and barley is the principal food.

"Their breeches are short, leaving the knees bare;" so are those worn by the Shelluhs. [379]

"Their common food was barley meal roasted and mixed with goat's milk and butter, and this dish they call Asamotan."

This is the common food of the Shelluhs of Atlas, and they call it by a similar name, Azamitta.

The opinion of the author of the History and Conquest of the Canary Islands, is, that the inhabitants came originally from Mauritania, and this he founds on the resemblance of names of places in Africa and in the islands: "for," says he, "Telde [214], which is the name of the oldest habitation in Canaria, Orotaba, and Tegesta, are all names which we find given to places in Mauritania and in Mount Atlas. It is to be supposed that Canaria, Fuertaventura, and Lancerotta, were peopled by the Alarbes [215], who are the nation most esteemed in Barbary; for the natives of those islands named milk *Aho*, and barley *Temecin*, which are the names that are given to those things in the language of the Alarbes of Barbary." He adds, that--

"Among the books of a library that was in the cathedral of St. Anna in Canaria, there was found one so disfigured, that it wanted both the beginning and the end: it treated of the Romans, and gave an account, that when [380] Africa was a Roman province, the natives of Mauritania rebelled and killed their presidents and governors, upon which the senate, resolving to punish and make a severe example of the rebels, sent a powerful army into Mauritania, which vanquished and reduced them again to obedience. Soon after the ringleaders of the rebellion were put to death, and the tongues of the common people, together with those of their wives and children, were cut out, and then they were all put aboard vessels with some grain and cattle, and transported to the Canary islands." [216]

Footnote 214: (return) Telde or Tildie is a place in the Atlas mountains, three miles east of Agadeer; the castle is in ruins.

Footnote 215: (return) The Alarbes, this is the name that the inhabitants of Lower Suse and Sahara have, *El Arab* or Arabs.

Footnote 216: (return) One Thomas Nicols, who lived seven years in the Canary Islands, and wrote a history of them, says, that the best account he could get of the origin of the natives, was, that they were exiles from Africa, banished thence by the Romans, who cut out their tongues for blaspheming their gods.

The following vocabulary will show the similarity of language between the natives of Canaria and the Shelluhs (inhabitants of the Atlas mountains south of Marocco).

[381]

LANCEROTTA AND FUERTAVENTURA DIALECT.	SHELLUH OR LYBIAN TONGUE.	ENGLISH.
Temasin	Tumzeen	Barley
Tezzezes	Tezezreat	Sticks
Taginaste	Taginast	A palm-tree
Tahuyan	Tahuyat	A blanket, covering, or petticoat.
Ahemon	Amen	Water
Faycag	Faquair	Priest or lawyer

Acoran	M'koorn	God
Almogaren	Talmogaren	Temples
Tamoyanteen	Tigameen	Houses
Tawacen	Tamouren	Hogs
Archormase	Akermuse	Green figs
Azamotan	Azamittan	Barley meal fried in
oil		
Tigot	Tigot	Heaven
Tigotan	Tigotan	The Heavens
Thener	Athraar	A mountain
Adeyhaman	Douwaman	A hollow valley
Ahico	Tahayk	A hayk, or coarse
garment		
Kabeheira	Kabeera	A head man or a
powerful		
Ahoren	----	Barley meal roasted
Ara	----	A goat
Ana	----	A sheep
Tagarer	----	A place of justice

Benehoare, the name of the natives of Palma.
Beni Hoarie, a tribe of Arabs in Suse between Agadeer and Terodant. [217]

Footnote 217: (return) For further particulars, see Glasse's History of the Canary Islands, 4to. page 174.

[382]

TITLES

OF

THE EMPEROR OF MAROCCO,

STYLE OF ADDRESSING HIM,

AND

SPECIMENS OF EPISTOLARY CORRESPONDENCE.

THE TITLES OF THE EMPEROR

ARE

Servant of God.

Commander, Captain, or Leader of the (Mumeneen) *Faithful* [i.e. in Muhamed], *upheld by the Grace of God.*

Prince of Hassenee. Ever supported by God.

Sultan of Fas, of Maroksh [Marocco], *of Suse, and of Draha, and of Tafilelt and Tuat, together with all the kabyles* [tribes] *of the West, and of the Berebbers of Atlas, &c.*

The Sultan calls his soldiers (*ketteffee*) "my shoulders or support, or strength;" his subjects he calls his sons (*woledee*), and himself the father of his people.

N.B. The Hejra, or Muhamedan æra began A.D. 622. The Muhamedan years are lunar, 33 of which are about 32 solar years. [383]

THE STYLE

USED BY MUSELMEN,

IN ADDRESSING THE EMPEROR,

IS AS FOLLOWS:

"Sultan of exalted dignity, whom God preserve. May the Almighty protect that royal purity, and bestow happiness, increase of wealth, and prosperity on the nation of believers [i.e. in Muhamed], whose welfare and power is attributed entirely to the favour and benevolence of the Exalted God."

The Sultan is head of the ecclesiastical, military, and civil law, and is universally considered by his subjects God's Vicegerent, or Lieutenant on Earth. All letters written to his Imperial Majesty, are begun with the praise of God, and with the acknowledgment, (in opposition to idolatry,) that there is neither beginning nor power but what proceeds from God, the eternal God, (*La hule û la kûa ela billa, Allah el adeem.*) [384]

SPECIMENS

OF

MUHAMEDAN EPISTOLARY CORRESPONDENCE.

The following Letters are literal translations from the original Arabic, and, although not of great importance, yet it is some satisfaction to the enquiring mind, to observe the various modes of address, and to note the style of Epistolary Correspondence practised by the Muhamedans, which is so different from that which is used among European and other nations.

LETTER I.

From Muley Ismael, Emperor of Marocco, to Captain Kirke at Tangier; Ambassador from King Charles the Second, dated 7th Du Elkadah, in the 1093d Year of the Hejra, (corresponding to the 27th October, A. D, 1682.)

Praise be to God, the most High alone! and the blessing of God be upon those who are for his prophet.

From the shereef [218], the servant of God, who putteth his trust in God, the commander of the p. 385 faithful, who is courageous in the way of the omniscient God.

Footnote 218: (return) Shereef is a general term in the Arabic for a prince, king, or emperor, signifying royal blood.

L.S.

Ismael Son of a shereef; God illumine
and preserve him.

God assist his commanders, and give victory to his forces and armies, Amen! To the captain of Tangier, Kirke, *peace be to those who follow the right way;* [219] this by way of preface. Your letter came to the lofty place of our residence, and we understand what your discourse contained. As for the asking a cessation of arms by sea; know, that it was not treated of between us till this present time. Neither did we make truce with you concerning any thing but Tangier alone. When you came to our illustrious house, we treated with you about that matter for four years, and if you had sojourned there yourself, no Muselman would ever have gone into that town hostilely against you, but merely as a peaceable merchant.

Footnote 219: (return) This is a sentence which frequently occurs in the Koran, but when used in epistolary correspondence with Christians (for it is never used by Muhamedans between themselves), it bears the appearance of a salutation, but the allusion is to Muhamedans, who *these people think* are the only men who follow the true path or right way; it is, however, a compliment to all who *think themselves* in the right way.

As to a cessation of arms by sea, it was not negociated by us, neither did we discourse about it; but, when you desired it of us, we wrote to your Master in England, saying, If you desire [386] a cessation of arms by sea, and are willing to receive a firm peace from us, send us two understanding men, of the chief of the Divan of England, by whom the peace of all the Christians here may be confirmed; and, when they shall arrive at the lofty place of our residence, and sit before us, whatsoever they shall hear from us, by way of agreement, shall be acceded to! And we have given you security, at sea, for four months, viz. from the time we sent you our letter to Tangier, till the day that there shall come an answer from your Master, and until the arrival of the two ambassadors aforementioned, after the aforesaid manner. As for those men who in thy letter thou didst say were taken at sea: I neither know nor have heard any thing of them. Your discourse about that matter having been with Aly ben Abdallah, and he administered justice (to you) upon the Muselmen who had taken these men prisoners for the sake of him, for whom you made your complaint to us; and he returned the Christians to you, and imprisoned the sailors for capturing them. Now, if there shall happen to be a peace between me and you at sea, as there is for four years by land, through your mediation, and by reason of your coming to us, I will hang them, and blot out their footsteps, and be revenged on them with the most severe revenge.

Our servant Muhamed ben Hadu Aater, who came from your presence, told us that lions are scarce in your country, and that they are in high [387] estimation, with you. When your servant came to us, he found we had two small young lions, wherefore by him we send them to you. And know, that we have received by our servants from your Master, *three* coach-horses, now a coach requires *four* horses to draw it, wherefore you must needs send us another good one of the same kind and size, that they may draw the coach with four horses. Oblige us in this by all means. Farewell: we depend upon it.

Written 7th of the sacred month *Du El Kadah*, in the year of the Hejra, ninety-three and a thousand, (A.D. 1682.)

LETTER II.

From the same Muley Ismael to Sir Cloudesly Shovel, on board the Charles Galley, off Salee, written Aug. 26. A.D. 1684, year of the Hejra 1095.

L.S.

I, servant of God, and Emperor of
Marocco and King of Mauritania,
whom God preserve in all
his undertakings, &c.

I Salute you and the rest of the captains.

As for the captives you have taken, they belong to several places, and are not all my subjects; and what I do is out of charity, as they are Muhamedans, being forced to go to sea for want of maintenance. As for those that are my soldiers, they go to sea to fight and to die in my quarrels; [388] but, those *Moors* that *you* have taken, are inconsiderable and of no account.

Henceforward I shall have ships as big as yours, if not bigger, hoping to take some of your ships and captains, and cruise for you in your English seas, as you do for us in these.

I have written letters to the King of England, in which are kind expressions: And when you had Tangier, all things were given to you as you wanted, and all done out of kindness; and now that you have left Tangier for the Moors, whatever His Majesty of Great Britain wants, either by sea or by land, it shall be granted, so that there be a peace betwixt the two crowns; for which I pass my word and faith.

Now, *I have written several letters to his Majesty of Great Britain, to which I have received as yet no answer*; but, when it (the answer) reaches my hands, I hope there will be a good accommodation between us.

You have taken several of our ships and destroyed others, and you are cruising on our coast, which is not the way to make a good peace, neither the actions of honesty in you.

God be praised that you have quitted Tangier and left it to us, to whom it did belong: from henceforward we shall keep it well supplied with stores, for it is the best port of our dominions.

As for the captives you have taken, you may do as you please with them, heaving them into the sea, or otherwise destroying them. The [389] English merchants that are here resident, shall satisfy all their debts, which being done, none of them shall remain in my country.

LETTER. III.

Captain Shovel's Answer.

May it please Your Majesty,

We, the King of England's captains, return Your Majesty humble thanks for your kind wishes to us. Your Majesty by this may know, that we have received your letter, and by it we understand, that Your Majesty is informed that most of these people that are taken are not your subjects. We perceive by this, as well as in other things, how grossly Your Majesty has been deceived by those people you trust; else, we doubt not, but that, long before this, our Master, whom God preserve, and Your Majesty had accommodated all differences, and we should have had a firm peace.

Of those fifty-three slaves that are here, (excepting two or three,) they are all Moors of their own country, as they themselves can make appear; but, if they are to be disowned because they are poor, the Lord help them!! Your Majesty tells us, that we may throw them overboard, if we please: all this we very well know; but we are Christians, and they bear the form of men, which is reason enough for us not to do so. [390]

As to Tangier, our Master kept it twenty-one years; and the world is sensible, that in spite of all your force, he could, if he had pleased, have continued to keep it to the world's end; for, he levelled your walls, filled up your harbour, and demolished your houses, in the face of your Alkaid and his army; and when he had done, he left your [220] barren country (without the loss of a man) for your own people to starve in: but our departure from thence, long before this, we doubt not, but you have repented of. When you tell us of those mighty ships Your Majesty intends to build and send to our coast, you must excuse us if we think ourselves the better judges; for we know, as to shipping, what you are able to do.

Footnote 220: (return) The gallant and magnanimous captain was better acquainted with the coast than with the country, which is any thing but barren.

If you think fit to redeem those slaves, at 100 dollars a-piece, they are at Your Majesty's service, and the rest shall be sent to you; or, if you think fit to give us so many English in exchange, we shall be well satisfied; but we think you will hardly comply with that, for the poorest slave that ever our Master redeemed out of *your* country, cost him 200 dollars; and some of these five times that sum, for he freely extended his charity to all, and never forgets his people *because they are poor*. [391]

It is great wonder to us, that you should tax us with unjust proceedings in taking your ships in time of truce, when Your Majesty may remember that, during the time your ambassador was in England, your corsairs took about twenty sail of my Master's ships; and this very year, you have fitted out all the force in your kingdom to sea, who have taken several of our ships, and at the same time pretend to a truce for peace! But some of your ships, for their unjust dealings, have had their reward, and the rest, when they shall come to sea, we doubt not but God Almighty will put them into our hands.

If Your Majesty think fit to send proposals to my Master concerning peace, I shall take care for the speedy and safe conveyance of the same. I desire Your Majesty's speedy answer; for I do not intend to stay long before Salee.

Wishing Your Majesty long life and happiness, I subscribe myself, Your Majesty's

Most obedient and humble Servant,

Cloudesly Shovel.

Sept. 1684 A.D.

[392]

LETTER IV.

A literal Translation of Muley Ismael, Emperor of Marocco's Letter to Queen Anne, in the year of our Lord 1710, extracted from the Harl. MSS. 7525.

L.S.

In the name of the most
merciful God.

He that depends upon God goeth straight to the right way. From the servant of God, the Emperor of the believers, who maketh war for the cause of the Lord of both worlds, Ismael ben Assherif Al Hassanee to the Queen of the English, nay of England, and the mistress of the great parliament thereof, happiness to every one that followeth the right way, and believes in God, and is so directed.

This premised, we have heard from more than one of the comers and goers from thy country, that thou hast seized our Armenian servant, a person of great esteem. We sent him to thee, to compose a difference between us and thee, and we wrote to thee concerning him, that thou shouldst use him well. Then, after this, we heard that thou didst set him at liberty: And wherefore didst thou seize him? Hath he exceeded any covenant, or hath he made any covenant with thee and broke it? We should not have sent him to thee, but on account of our knowledge and assurance of his understanding [393] and integrity; and when he resolved upon his journey into your country, we gave him directions to dispatch some of our affairs. Wherefore we wrote unto thee concerning him, and said, If thou hast any necessity or business with us, he will convey it to us from thee. And we said unto thee, Speak with him, and whatsoever thou sayest unto him, he will communicate unto us, without addition or diminution.

As for what our servant Alkaid Ali ben Abdallah did to ----, the Christian, thy servant, by God we know nothing of it, nor gave him any permission as to any thing that passed between them; and, at the instant that we heard that he had taken thy man, we commanded him to set him at liberty forthwith; and since then we have never manifested any favour to Alkaid Ali, nor was our mind ever right towards him afterwards till he died.

Our Christian servant, the merchant, Bayly, told us, that thou hadst a mind to an ostrich, and we gave him two, a male and a female, which shall come to you, if God will. And, lo! a secretary, our servant, (who is much esteemed by us,) when he cometh he shall bring what goods he hath collected with him, if it please God. And we are in expectation of thy messenger the ambassador; and if he comes, he shall see nothing from us but what is fair; and we will deliver to him the Christians, and do what he pleases, if God will. Wherefore be kind to our servant, with respect. [394]

Written the first of the Glorious Ramadan, in the year of the Hejra 1125 (corresponding with A.D. 1710).

LETTER V.

Translation of an Arabic Letter from the Sultan Seedi Muhamed [221] *ben Abdallah, Emperor of Marocco, to the European Consuls resident at Tangier, delivered to each of them, by the Bashaw of the province of El Grarb, on 1st day of June, 1788, corresponding with the year of the Hejra, 1202.*

Footnote 221: (return) Father of the present Sultan Soliman ben Muhamed.

L.S.

Mohamed ben Abdallah, ben
Ismael, Sultan ben, Sultan,
&c.

In the name of God, for there is no power or strength but from God.

To all the Consuls at Tangier.

Peace (be) to those who follow the right path.

By this you will learn that we are in peace and friendship with all the Christian powers until the month of May of the next year, (of the Hejra, 1203,) and such nations as shall then be desirous to continue in peace and friendship with us, are to write a letter to us, when the month of May comes, to inform us if they are in peace and friendship with us, then we shall be the same with them; but, if any Christian nation desire to go to war with us, they will let us know before [395] the month above-mentioned; and we trust God will keep us in his protection against them; and thus I have said all I had to say.

2d day of Shaban, year of the Hejra 1202, (corresponding with 7th May, 1788.)

Letter VI.

Letter from Muley Soliman ben Muhamed, Emperor of Marocco, &c. &c. to His Majesty George III. literally translated from the original Arabic, by James Grey Jackson, at the request of the Right Hon. Spencer Perceval, after lying in the Secretary of State's Office here for several months, and being then sent ineffectually to the Universities for translation, and after various enquiries had been made on behalf of the Emperor, to the Governor of Gibraltar, the Bashaw of El Garb, and the Alkaid of Tangier, to ascertain if any answer had been returned to his Imperial Majesty.

In the name of God! the all-merciful and commiserating God, on whom is our account, and we acknowledge his support; for there is neither beginning nor power but that which proceeds from God, the High Eternal God.

From the servant of God, the commander of the faithful [in Muhamed] upheld and supported by the Grace of God.

Soliman the son of Muhamed, the son of Abdallah, the son of Ismael, Prince of [the house or dynasty of Hassan] [222] who was ever upheld by the [396] power of God, Sultan of Fas and Marocco, and Suse, and Draha, and Tafilelt, and Tuat, together with all the territories of the West.

Footnote 222: (return) The words between brackets are not in the original, but implied.

L.S.

Soliman, son of Mohamed, son
Abdallah, God illumine and support
him!

To our dearly beloved and cherished, exalted by the power of God, the Sultan [223] George the Third, Sultan of the territories of the United Kingdom of Great Britain, Ireland, Duke of Mecklenburg Strelitz, Prince, descended from the dynasty of the Sultans of Rome and Palestine, &c.

Footnote 223: (return) This perhaps is the only letter extant, wherein a Muselman Prince gives the title of Sultan to a Christian king.

This premised, we inform you, that we make diligent inquiry about you, desiring heartily that you may be at all times surrounded by health and prosperity. We wish you to increase in friendship with us, that our alliance may be more strongly cemented than heretofore, even stronger than it was in the days of our ancestors, whom God guard and protect.

Now therefore we make known to you, that your physician, Doctor Buffé, has been in our royal presence, [which is] exalted by the bounty of God, and we have been well pleased with his medical knowledge and diligent attention, and moreover with the relief he has given to us.

We have therefore to entreat of you to give [397] him your royal order to return to Gibraltar, in our neighbourhood, well provided with all good and necessary medicines; that he, residing at Gibraltar, may be ready to attend quickly our royal presence, whenever we may be in need of his [medical] assistance. We trust you will return him without procrastination to our throne, seeing that he has been of essential service to us.

We recommend you to exalt Dr. Buffé, in your favour and esteem on our account, and we will always be your allies and friends. May you ever be well and in prosperity! Peace be with you, 4th of the month Jumad El Lule in the year [of the Hejra] 1221, (corresponding with 5th July, 1806, A.D.)

LETTER VII.

In Muhamedan countries, an insolvent man continues liable to his creditors till the day of his death, unless the debt is discharged; but he can claim by law his liberation from prison, on making oath, and bringing proof of his insolvency: but then if he succeed afterwards and become possessed of property, he is compelled to pay the debts formerly contracted; so that an European should be cautious how he contracts debts with the Moors, lest the misfortunes that commerce is liable to should oblige him to remain all his life in the country. A letter, similar to the following, should be procured by every European, about to quit the country, to [398] prevent the extortion of the alkaid, who might, as has often happened before, throw impediments in the way for the purpose of extorting presents, &c.

Translation of a Firman of Departure, literally translated from the Original Arabic, by James Grey Jackson.

L.S.

Soliman ben Muhamed, ben
Abdallah, ben Ismael Sultan,
&c.

Praise be to God alone.

Our servants El Hage Mohamed o Bryhim, and Seid Mohamed Bel Akkia, peace and the mercy of God be with you! This premised, I command you to suffer the Christian merchant, Jackson, to embark for his own country, if it appears to you that no one pursues him in law [for debt,] as I wrote to you on this subject in my last letter: if no one claims of him any right by law, allow him to go, and do not impede him. [224] God protect you, and peace be with you. 3d day of Saffer, the good year 1220 of the Hejra, (A.C. 1805.)

Footnote 224: (return) This repetition of the principal subject in Arabic correspondence, is a mode of impressing on the mind more forcibly, the subject intended to be impressed, and is commonly practised by the best Arabian, and African writers; it also frequently occurs in the inspired writings. See Psalms lxxv, l. lxxvii, 1. &c.

LETTER VIII.

As a specimen of the lofty style of writing so much in use among the Eastern authors, I shall [399] add the summons which Hulacu the Tartar conqueror of the East, (who took Bagdad, and entirely subverted the government of the Saracens,) sent to Al Mâlek Annâsar, sultan of Aleppo, in the year of the Hejra 657, (of Christ 1259.)

Let Al Mâlek Annâsar know, that we sat down before Bagdad in the 655th year (of the Hejra,) and took it by the sword of the most high God: and we brought the master of it before us, and demanded two things of him; to which he, not answering, brought deserved punishment upon himself. As it is written in your Koran, "*God doth not change the condition of a people, till their own minds are changed.*" He took care of his wealth, and fate brought him to what he is come to. He chose to exchange precious lives for pieces of money made of vile metal; which is plainly the same that God says *They found* [the reward of] *what they had done present with them.* [225] For we have attained by the power of God, what we desired; and by the help of the most high God we shall increase. Nor is there any doubt of our being the army of God upon his earth. He created us, and gave us power over every one upon whom his anger rests. Wherefore, let what is past be to you an example, and what we have mentioned a warning. Fortifications are nothing in our hands, nor doth [400] the joining of battle avail you any thing; nor will your intreaties be heard or regarded. Take warning therefore by others, and surrender entirely to us, before the veil be taken off, and [*the punishment of*] sin light upon you. For we shall have no mercy upon him that complains, nor be moved by him that weeps. We have wasted countries, we have destroyed men, we have made children orphans, and the land desolate. It is your business to run away; ours to pursue; nor can you escape our swords, nor fly from our arrows. Our horses are racers; our arrows strike home; our swords pierce like lightning; our fortifications are like mountains, and our numbers like the sand. Whosoever surrenders comes off safe: whosoever is for war, repents it. If you will obey our command, and come to our terms, your interest and ours shall be the same; but if you be refractory and persist in your error, blame not us, but yourselves. God is against you, ye wicked wretches: look out for something to screen you under your miseries, and find somebody to bear you company in your affliction. We have given you fair warning, and fair warning is fair play. You have eaten things forbidden [226], you have been perfidious in your treaties. You have introduced new heresies, and thought it a gallant thing to commit sodomy. Prepare yourselves therefore for [401] scorn and contempt. Now you will find what you have done; for they that have done amiss, will now find their state changed. You take it for granted, that we are infidels. We take it for granted, that you are *villains*; and *He* by whose hand all things are disposed and determined, hath given us the dominion over you. The greatest man you have is despicable among us; and what *you* call rich, is a beggar. We govern the world from east to west, and whosoever is worth any thing is our prey; and we take every ship by force. Weigh therefore what is fit to be done, and return us a speedy answer, before *infidelity* [227] shall have kindled its fire, and scattered its sparks among you, and destroy you all from off the face of the earth. We have awakened you by sending to you: make haste with an answer, lest punishment come upon you unawares.

Footnote 225: (return): A quotation from the Koran. The Tartar was a deist, and quotes the Koran in derision.

Footnote 226: (return) The Muhamedans, whose religion is a compound of Judaism and Christianity, have borrowed many customs from either, they abstain like the Jews from swine's flesh, &c.

Footnote 227: (return) As the Muhamedans charge every nation that doth not believe Muhamed to have been a prophet with infidelity, so the Tartar (who was a Deist) returns it upon them.

[402]

LETTER IX.

Translation of a Letter from the Emperor Muley Yezzid, to Webster Blount, Esq. Consul General to the Empire of Marocco, from their High Mightinesses the States-General, of the Seven United Provinces. Written soon after the Emperor's Proclamation, and previous to the Negotiation for the opening of the Port of Agadeer, to Dutch Commerce.

"Praise be to God alone; for there is neither beginning nor power without God."

L.S.

Yezzid ben Muhamed, Sultan
ben Sultan, (i.e. Emperor
and Son of an Emperor.)

"To the Consul Blount. Peace be with those who follow the right way, or the way of the true God: and this being premised, know that I have received your letter, and that we are with you, (the Dutch nation,) in peace and amity and good faith, and peace be with you. 22 Ramadan, year of the Hejra 1204, (A.C. 1792.)"

Translated literally by the Author, from the original Arabic in his possession.

LETTER X.

Translation of a Letter from the Emperor Yezzid, to the Governor of Mogodor, Aumer ben Daudy, to give the Port of Agadeer to the Dutch, and to send there the Merchants of that Nation.

"Praise be to God alone; for there is neither beginning nor power without God, the eternal God." [403]

L.S.

Yezzid ben Muhamed, Sultan
ben Sultan.

"Our servant (or agent) Alkaid Aumer ben Daudy, peace be unto you, with the mercy and blessing of God: this premised, I command that all the duties you have collected be sent to me speedily by my brother [228] Muley Soliman, who will (*berik*) discharge you by receipt for every thing you deliver to him, for he is our representative. We are preparing to go to the siege of Ceuta, with the acquiescence of the High God, by whose power we hope to enter it, and take it. And we command you to send the Alkaid M'saud El Hayanie to my port of Agadeer, with all things necessary for his journey, assisting him with every possible succour, and send with him twenty Benianters [229], who must be sailors skilful in the management of boats; and the Christian merchants of the Dutch nation will go to Agadeer, and establish their houses there; for I have given that port to the Dutch to trade there: and send with them Talb Aumer Busedra, and the eye of God be upon you, and peace be with you."

Footnote 228: (return) The duties were at this time collected in kind; viz. one tenth of every thing imported from Europe: and the present Emperor Muly Soliman was deputed to convey them to the camp before Ceuta, to his brother, the Emperor Muley Yezzid, whose army was besieging that fortress.

Footnote 229: (return) *Benianters*, are a kabyle of Shelluhs of Suse, who are employed to work, and row the boats, and land the goods at Mogodor.

[404]

Seventh day of Arrabea Ellule, year (Hejra) 1205. [230]

Translated by the Author, from the original Arabic in his possession.

"Be vigilant with respect to the matter of the establishment of Agadeer, and of M'saud El Hayanie." [231]

Footnote 230: (return) Corresponding with A.C. 1793.

Footnote 231: (return) The Emperors of Marocco, and the Arabian writers in general thus repeat the principal subject of a letter or discourse, to impress it more forcibly on the mind.

LETTER XI.

Epistolary Diction used by the Muhamedans of Africa, in their Correspondence with all their Friends who are not of the Muhamedan faith.

"Praise be to God alone; for there is neither beginning nor strength without God, the eternal God.

"From the servant of the great God, El Hage Abdrahaman El Fellely, to my friend Consul Jackson, peace be to those who follow the right way, or who pursue the right path; and then, O my friend, I have received your letter, and I have taken good notice of its contents, &c. &c."

The letter, after explaining matters of business, concludes thus:--

"Do not leave me without news from you; and peace be with you, and peace from me to our friend L'hage Muhamed Bu Zeyd; and peace from me to Seed Muham'd bel Hassen, and to the Fakeer Seed Abdallah, and praise be to God, I am very well, and prosperous. [405] Written 15th day of Shaban, year of the Hejra 1209, (1797, A.C.)"

The style in which letters are addressed is generally as follows:--

"This shall arrive, God willing, to the hands of Consul Jackson, at Agadeer. May God prosper it."

LETTER XII.

Translation of a Letter from the Sultan, Seedi Muhamed Emperor of Marocco, to the Governor of Mogodor.

"Praise be to God alone,

"I order my servant Alkaid Muhamed ben Amran, to deliver the treasure and the merchandise to the Christian merchants at Mogodor, which is in the possession of the Jews, Haim Miram, and Meemon ben Isaac Corcos, and others of the Jews, friends of the Christian merchants. God assist you, and peace be with you. 23d of the month Jumad Ellule, year of the Hejra 1203.

"By order of the Sultan, empowered by God. Written by Talb El Huderanie."

The courier who receives the letter is ordered by the minister whom to deliver it to. It is then inclosed in a blank leaf or sheet of paper, without any address, and not sealed. It is presumed, that the courier or messenger will not dare to open it, or discover the contents to any one; such a breach of confidence might cost him his head, if discovered. [406]

Doubts having been made in the Daily Papers, concerning the accuracy of the two following Translations of the Shereef Ibrahim's account of Mungo Park's Death; the following Observations, by the Author, are laid before the Public in elucidation of those Translations.

The following is a copy of a letter, supposed to be a description of Mungo Park's death; brought to England from Ashantee in Africa, by Mr. Bowdich; and that gentleman assured me, about six months after his arrival in England, and a few days previous to the publication of his interesting account of a mission to Ashantee, that he had by every means in his power endeavoured, but ineffectually, to get this manuscript *decyphered* and translated into English; that he had sent it to several persons, who had retained it in their hands a considerable time, but had returned it without a decypher, or even a complete translation. When delivered into my hands, I transmitted him a *decypher*, and a translation immediately. The following is my translation, which, in that gentleman's account of Ashantee, is coupled with another translation, *not perspicuous, but unintelligible*; for which see Bowdich's "Account of a Mission to Ashantee," Appendix, No. 2.

The original Arabic document, of which I have given a decypher in the work before mentioned, [407] is, (for the information of gentlemen desirous of referring to the same,) deposited in the British Museum. There are also, in the same work on Ashantee, several papers decyphered by me, of certain routes in Africa. Now I think it expedient here, to declare to the public, that whenever the British Government, the Court of Admiralty, or private individuals, have stood in need of translations, and decyphers from the Arabic, they have invariably found it expedient, ultimately, to apply to me for the same, after having, however, endeavoured ineffectually to procure their information at the Universities, the Post Office, and elsewhere: but as this declaration may appear to many incredible, I will mention three instances in elucidation of this my assertion, which, as they are all on record, will place this fact beyond doubt.

1st. A vessel under Marocco colours, was, during last war, taken by a British cruiser, and sent or brought into Plymouth, or other port, in England. The captain and the ship were detained a considerable time here; the former, at length, whose patience became exhausted, expostulated at his detention, and insisted on being released, if no interpreter in this commercial nation could be found competent to translate his passport. *Mr. Slade, an eminent proctor in Doctors' Commons*, then applied to me, after a detention of, I believe, two months, and I translated the passport. Mr. Slade very liberally told me, that whatever I chose to [408] charge for this service, which he had *sought in vain to accomplish*, should be gratefully paid. I charged five guineas; and it was instantly paid. The passport consisted of two lines and a half. This was in the Court of Admiralty. Mr. Slade, who is an honourable and respectable man, will of course not hesitate to corroborate the accuracy of this statement.

2d. A letter was written by the present Sultan Soliman, emperor of Marocco, &c. to our late revered sovereign, George III., in a more courteous style than is usual for Muhamedan potentates to write to Christian kings; with liberal offers on the part of the Sultan, courting an augmentation of friendly intercourse, &c. This letter (contrary to the usual courtesy of European courts) was neglected some months, no answer being returned to it. It was sent to the Universities for translation, but ineffectually; then to the Post Office; and, at the expiration of some months, it was accidentally transmitted to me, through the hands of the Right Honourable Spencer Perceval, at that time Chancellor of the Exchequer, and I delivered, at the request of that gentleman, a translation of it in English. This letter was ten or fifteen times as long as the passport before mentioned, and I charged thirty pounds for the service. But the Treasury thought ten pounds a sufficient remuneration, which I accepted!!

This service was rendered to the British government, [409] and I have letters and documents in my possession, which corroborate this fact.

3d. Was the translation of an Arabic manuscript, respecting Mungo Park's death; delivered gratuitously to a private individual, viz. Mr. Bowdich, before mentioned; to satisfy the curiosity of my country, whose interest was excited respecting the fate of that enterprising and indefatigable African traveller. Mr. Bowdich, who is an honourable man, will undoubtedly confirm the truth of this statement, to any gentleman who may be desirous of ascertaining the fact.

The Shereef Ibrahim's account of Mungo Park's Death.

(THE AUTHOR'S TRANSLATION.)

"In the name of God, the Merciful and Clement!

"This narrative proceeds from the territory in Husa, called Eeaurie or Yeaurie. We observed an extraordinary event or circumstance, but we neither saw nor heard of the river which is called Kude. And as we were sitting we heard the voice of children; and we saw a vessel, the like to which in size we never saw before. And we saw the king of Eeaurie send cattle and sheep, and a variety of vegetables, in great abundance. And there were two men and one woman, and two slaves; and they tied them in the vessel. There were also in the vessel two [410] white men, of the race called Christians: and the Sultan of Eeaurie called aloud to them, to come out of the vessel, but they would not. They proceeded to the country of Busa, which is greater than that of the Sultan of Eeaurie. And as they were sitting in the vessel, they hung [232], or were stopped by the cape, or head-land of Kude."

Footnote 232: (return) Probably by an impetuous current.

"And the people of the sultan of Busa called to them, and poured their arms into the vessel; and the vessel reached the head-land or cliff, and became attached or fixed to the head of the mountain or projection in the river, and could not pass it. Then the men and women of Busa collected themselves hostilely together, with arms of all descriptions; and the vessel being unable to clear the head-land, the man in the vessel killed his wife, and threw the whole of her property into the river; they then threw themselves into the river through fear. The news of this occurrence was then conveyed to the Sultan Wawee, until it reached, by water, the territory of Kanjee, in the country of the Sultan Wawee. And we buried it in its earth; and one of them we saw not at all in the water. And God knows the truth of this report from the mouth of the Shereef Ibrahim. The end."

OBSERVATION.

After giving the foregoing translation, it behoves [411] me to inform the intelligent reader, that I wrote a letter to Mr. Bowdich, communicating to him my observations on several notes, transmitted to him by Sir William Ouseley, on the manuscript of which the foregoing is a translation, in which I informed him, that in decyphering the Arabic manuscript, I had observed the Oriental or Asiatic punctuation; knowing that Mr. Bulmer had not letters with the occidental punctuation. Several observations I made, respecting the Arabic manuscripts which could not be elucidated here without the Arabic type. I shall, therefore, omit them, and conclude by observing, that in translating this manuscript, two gentlemen (Arabic scholars) had translated *akkadan Fie Asfeena*, "two maids in the ship;" which words I have translated, "were tied or bound in the vessel:" the word *akkadan* being the preterite of the verb *akkad*, to bind. I was not surprised to hear that *one* translator had made such an interpretation; knowing that incredible errors have been frequently committed by professed Professors in the Hebrew language as well as in the Arabic. But when I heard, as I did, that another Arabic scholar had given a similar interpretation, I must confess that I was not a little surprised. However, a circumstance soon after unravelled the mystery; for I discovered that these two gentlemen, at a loss no doubt to ascertain the meaning of *akkadan*, had referred to [412] Richardson's Arabic Dictionary, wherein the word is quoted to signify, in a figurative sense, a virgin. *In a figurative sense!* In translating an ill-written, illiterate, and ungrammatical manuscript, these two translators had had recourse to *rhetorical figures*, and actually substituted a trope for what was a verb, generally used in the West, signifying "to bind!"

As it has been asserted in the following extract, that my translation of the foregoing manuscript differs *only in a trifling degree* from that of Mr. Abraham Salamé, I here insert my answer to that assertion, leaving the intelligent reader to determine, whether they are alike or materially different.

Extract from The Times, 3d May, 1819.

MUNGO PARK.

The death of this enterprising traveller is now placed beyond any doubt. Many accounts of it have been received, and although varying as to the circumstances attending it, yet all agreeing that it has taken place. One statement was given to Mr. Bowdich, while on his mission to the King of the Ashantees, in 1817, by a Moor, who said that he was an eye-witness; and the same gentleman procured an Arabic manuscript declaratory of Mr. Park's death. This manuscript has been deposited with the African Association, formed for the purpose of extending [413] researches in that part of the world. Two translations have been made of this curious document; one by Mr. Salamé, an Egyptian, who accompanied Viscount Exmouth in his attack on Algiers, as interpreter; and the other by Mr. Jackson, formerly consul at one of the Barbary courts. The following is Mr. Salamé's translation, from which, however, *the one by Mr. Jackson only differs in a trifling degree.* The words in italics have been inserted by Mr. Salamé, in order to render the reading more perfect, and are not in the original:--

A literal Translation of a Declaration written in a corrupted Arabic, from the Town of Yaud, in the Interior of Africa.

"'In the name of God, the merciful and the munificent. This declaration is issued from the town called Yaud, in the county of Kossa. We (the writer) do witness the *following* case (statement.) We never saw, nor heard of the sea (river) called Koodd; but we sat to hear (understood) the voice (report) of some persons, *saying,* 'We saw a ship, equal to her we never saw before; and the King of Yaud had sent plenty of every kind of food, with cows and sheep; *there* were two men, one woman, two male slaves, and two maids in the ship; *the* two white men *were* derived from the race (sect) of Nassri (Christ, or Christianity.) The King of [414] Yaud asked them to come out to him (to land); but they refused coming out (landing); and they went to the *King* of the country of Bassa, who is greater than the King of Yaud; and *while* they *were* sitting in the ship, and gaining a position (rounding) over the Cape of Koodd, and *were* in society with the people of the King of Bassa, the ship reached (struck) a head of mountain, which took (destroyed) *her* away, and the men and women of Bassa all together, with every kind of arms (goods); and the ship could find no way to avoid the mountain; and the man who *was* in the ship, killed his wife, and threw all his property into the sea (river), and *then* they threw themselves *also,* from fear. Afterwards they took one *out of the* water till the news reached the town of Kanji, the country of the King of Wawi; and the King of Wawi heard of it; he buried him in his earth (grave), and the other we have not seen; perhaps he is in the bottom of the water. And God knows best.' Authentic from the mouth of Sherif Abraham.--Finis.'

"In addition to the foregoing, another corroboration has been obtained. Lieut. Col. Fitzclarence, when on his voyage down the Mediterranean on board the *Tagus* frigate, Capt. Dundas, with despatches from the Marquis of Hastings, learnt from the governor to the two sons of the Emperor of Marocco, who had been on a pilgrimage to Mecca, and were then returning home, that he (Hadjee Tahib) had [415] been at Timbuctoo in 1807, and had heard of *two white* men, who came from the sea, having been near that place the year before; and that they sold beads, and had no money to purchase grain. This person added, that they went down the *Nile* to the eastward, and that general report stated that they *died of the climate.* There can be little doubt but the *two white* men here alluded to were Mr. Park and his companion, Lieutenant Martyn, who were at Sandsanding in Nov. 1805, and could, in the following year, have been near Timbuctoo. Sandsanding is the place from whence the last despatches were dated by Mr. Park; and Amadi Fatouma, who was his guide afterwards, was sent to learn his fate, and returned with an account of Mr. Park being drowned. The statement of this person was, however, of such a nature as to excite suspicions of its correctness; and hopes were entertained that Mr. Park had not met with such an untimely fate. Fourteen years have now almost elapsed since the date of his last dispatches; and this circumstance is of itself sufficient to demonstrate, that he is to be added to the catalogue of those who have perished in their attempts to explore the interior of Africa.-- *Englishman*."

TO THE EDITOR OF THE BRITISH STATESMAN.

Sir;--Seeing in your Paper of yesterday a translation of the Arabic manuscript respecting [416] Mr. Mungo Park's death, which is deposited with the African Association, and *deciphered and transcribed by me* in Mr. Bowdich's account of a Mission to Ashantee, p. 480, and perceiving that the errors in *that translation* are thus propagated to the public through the medium of the London Papers; which although perhaps of little consequence to the general reader, yet, as they are of importance to the critic, and to the investigator of African affairs, I shall take the liberty of offering a few observations on the subject.

The following passage, in the translation above alluded to, might have passed the public eye without animadversion as the language of a foreigner, (as we have understood Mr. Salamé to be,) but from the intelligent Editor of a London daily paper, might we not have expected more correct phraseology? [233]

Footnote 233: (return) "The phrases thus objected to by our learned Correspondent, were contained in the translations furnished to us in common with other papers, and not the language of the Editor. Indeed, this appears to be admitted by our Correspondent himself, in the apparently very just comments he has thus favoured us with.--Editor."

"The ship reached a head of mountain which took her away, and the men and women of Bassa, altogether with every kind of arms, and the ship could find no way to avoid the mountain."

I have no hesitation in declaring to be incorrect the first two lines of Mr. Abraham Salamé's [417] translation, inserted in your paper of yesterday, which runs thus:--

"*This declaration is issued from the town called Yaud, in the country of Kossa.*"

My translation of this passage, inserted in Mr. Bowdich's account of a Mission to Ashantee, page 478, runs thus:--

"*This narrative proceeds from the territory in Hausa called Ecauree.*"

No one, I presume, will say that there is not a *manifest* difference between these two translations-- between *the town called Yaud, in the country of Kossa*, and the *territory of Hausa, called Ecauree*.

One of these translations must therefore necessarily be incorrect. The Arabic manuscript deciphered and transcribed by me, is inserted in Mr. Bowdich's work, page 480. Those who may feel interested in ascertaining which is the correct and precise translation, are requested to refer to the transcript above-mentioned, or to the original manuscript, in the possession of the African Association. As for myself, I presume I am right; and would submit the decision to the judgment of either Sir Gore Ousley, or to that of Sir William, or to the opinion of any Arabic scholar, to decide this question.

If, Mr. Editor, you had an Arabic type, to save the trouble of referring to the original, I should ask the Arabic scholar if it were possible for any man to translate the following passage in that document:--"Bled Hausa eekalu Ecuree"--"the [418] town called Yaud, in the country of Cossa;" whilst I should maintain that it would admit of no other translation but the following, viz.--"the country of Hausa, called Ecauree."

If you think this elucidation of the translation of the Manuscript of Park's death sufficiently interesting to the public to deserve a place in your intelligent paper, it is very much at your service.

From, Sir,
Your most obedient servant,
James Grey Jackson,

Professor of African Languages, and formerly British Consul and Agent for Holland, Sweden, and Denmark, at Santa Cruz, South Barbary. [234]

Circus, Minories,
May 4. 1819.

Footnote 234: (return) See British Statesman, May 6th, 1819.

[419]

LETTERS RESPECTING AFRICA,

FROM

J.G. JACKSON AND OTHERS.

On the Plague.

To JAMES WILLIS, Esq. late Consul to Senegambia.

London, October 30, 1804.

My dear Sir,

Your letter reached my hands yesterday; but I am afraid I shall not be able to satisfy you in every enquiry which you have made relative to the plague in Barbary in 1799. I have, however, no doubt but the plague which has prevailed in Spain has originated from it. Some of the following observations may probably be of service to you.

It does not appear to be ascertained how the plague originated in Fas in the year 1799. Some persons have ascribed it to infected merchandise received at Fas from the East; whilst others maintain that the locusts which had infested Western Barbary during seven years, destroying the crops, the vegetables, and every green thing, even to the bark of the trees, produced such a scarcity, that the poor could obtain scarcely [420] any thing to eat but the locusts; and living on them for several months, till a most abundant crop enabled them to satisfy the cravings of nature, they ate abundantly of the new corn, which producing a fever, brought on the contagion. At this time the small-pox pervaded the country, and was generally fatal. The small-pox is thought to be the forerunner of this species of contagion, as appears by an ancient Arabic manuscript, which gives a full account of the same disorder having carried off two-thirds of the inhabitants of West Barbary about four hundred years since; but, however the dreadful epidemy originated, the leading features of the disorder were novel, and more dreadful than the common plague of Turkey, or that of Syria or Egypt, as the following observations will demonstrate.

In the month of April, 1799, a plague of the most dreadful kind manifested itself at the city of Old Fas, which soon after communicated itself to the new city. About this time the Emperor Muley Soliman ben Muhamed was preparing a numerous army, and was on the eve of departure to visit his Southern dominions, and to take possession of the province of Abda, which had not acknowledged him as Emperor, but was, as well as the port of Saffy, in a state of rebellion. The Emperor left Fas early in the summer, and proceeded to Sallee, Mazagan, and Saffee; thence to Marocco and Mogodor. Now the plague began to kindle in all the Southern provinces, first carrying off one or two the first day, three or four the second day, six or eight the third day, [421] and increasing progressively till it amounted to a daily mortality of two in a hundred of the whole population; continuing *with unabated violence*, ten, fifteen, twenty days, being of longer duration in old than in new towns; then diminishing in a progressive proportion from one thousand a-day, to nine hundred, to eight hundred and so continuing to decrease till it disappeared.

When it raged at the town of Mogodor, a small village (Deabet) situated two miles South-east of Mogodor remained uninfected, although the communication was open between these two places. On the thirty-fourth day after its first appearance at Mogodor, this village received the infection, where, after committing dreadful havoc among the human species for twenty-one days carried off one hundred persons out of one hundred and thirty-three, the population of the village before the plague visited it. After this, none died; but those who were infected recovered, some losing the use of a leg, or an arm, or an eye.

Many similar circumstances might be mentioned relative to the numerous villages scattered about the extensive province of Haha, all which shared the like, or a worse fate. Travelling through this province after the plague had disappeared, I saw many ruins, which had been flourishing villages before the plague. Making enquiry concerning the population of these dismal remains of the pestilence, I was informed, [422] that one village contained six hundred inhabitants; that only four had escaped. Others, which had contained four and five hundred, had left seven or eight to lament the calamities they had suffered.

Whenever any families retired to the country, to avoid the infection; on returning to town, when apparently all infection had disappeared, they were generally attacked, and died. The destruction of the human species in the province of Upper and LowerSuse was much greater than elsewhere. The capital city of this province (Tarodant) lost, when the infection was at its *acmé*, about eight hundred each day; the city of Marocco lost one thousand each day; the cities of Old and New Fas from twelve to fifteen hundred each day; insomuch, that, in these large towns, the mortality was such, that the living had not time to bury the dead: they were therefore thrown altogether into large holes, which were covered over when full of dead bodies.

Young and healthy robust persons were generally attacked first; then women and children; lastly, thin, sickly, and old people. *After the plague had totally subsided, we saw men, who had been common labourers, enjoying their thousands, and keeping horses, without knowing how to ride them. Provisions became extremely cheap, for the flocks and herds had been left in the fields, and had nobody now to own them. Day-labour increased enormously. Never was equality in the human species more evident than at this time. [423] When corn was to be ground, or bread made, both were done in the houses of the rich, and prepared by themselves; for the very few poor people whom the plague had spared were insufficient for the wants of the affluent, and they were consequently obliged to work for themselves.* The country being now depopulated, vast tribes of Arabs from the Desert poured into Suse and Draha; settling themselves on the river Draha and in Suse, and wherever they found little or no population.

The symptoms of the disorder varied in different patients; in some it manifested itself by a sudden shivering, in others by delirium, succeeded by a violent thirst. Cold water was drank eagerly by the imprudent, and generally proved fatal. Some had one, two, or three, some more biles, generally in the groin, under the arm, or near the breast; some had more. Some had no biles, nor any outward disfiguration; these were invariably carried off in less than twenty-four hours. I recommended Mr. Baldwin's remedy [235], applied according to his directions; and I do not know one instance of its failing, when properly applied, and sufficiently persevered in.

Footnote 235: (return) Of unction of the body with olive oil.

I have no doubt but the epidemy, which has been ravaging Spain lately, is the same disorder with the one above described. We have been told that it was communicated originally to Spain by two infected persons, who went from Tangier [424] to Estapona, and eluded the vigilance of the guards. We have been assured that it was communicated by some persons infected, who landed in Spain from a vessel that had loaded produce at Laraich, in West Barbary. We have also been informed that a Spanish privateer, which had occasion to land its crew for water in some part of West Barbary, caught the infection, and afterwards went to Cadiz and communicated it to the town.

James G. Jackson.

Death of Mungo Park.

May, 1812.

The doubts which may have existed of the fate of this eminent man are now removed, by the certain accounts lately received from Goree, of his having perished, through the hostility of the natives, on one of the branches of the Niger. The particulars have been transmitted to Sir Joseph Banks, by Governor Maxwell, of Goree, who received them from Isaco [236], a Moor, sent inland by the Governor, for the purpose of enquiry. In a letter to Mr. Dickson, of Covent-garden, brother-in-law to Mr. Park, Sir Joseph thus writes:--

"I have read Isaco's translated journal; by which it appears, that the numerous European retinue of Mungq Park quickly and miserably [425] died, leaving, at the last, only himself and a Mr. Martyn. Proceeding on their route, they stopped at a settlement, from which, according to custom, they sent a present to the chief whose territory they were next to pass. This present having been treacherously withheld, the chief considered it, in the travellers, as a designed injury and neglect. *On their approaching, in a canoe, he assembled his people on a narrow channel of rocks [237], and assailed them so violently with arrows, that some of the rowers were killed.* This caused Mr. Park and Mr. Martyn to make an effort by swimming to reach the shore; in which attempt they both were drowned. The canoe shortly afterwards sunk, and only one hired native escaped. Every appurtenance also of the travellers was lost or destroyed, except a sword-belt which had belonged to Mr. Martyn, and which Isaco redeemed, and brought with him to Goree."

Footnote 236: (return) Isaco was a Jew, not a Moor.--J.G.J.

Footnote 237: (return) There is a remarkable confirmation of this quotation from Sir Joseph's letter in Mr. *Jackson's* translation of the Arabic manuscript of Mungo Park's death, for which see Bowdich's Account of a Mission to Ashantee, p. 480.; also Annals of Oriental Literature, No. I.

Death of Mr. Rontgen, in an Attempt to explore the Interior of Africa.

May, 1812.

The young German gentleman of the name of Rontgen, who left England about a twelve-month since for Africa, in order to prosecute [426] discoveries in the interior of that country, has, it is said, been murdered by the Arabs, before he had proceeded any great distance from Mogodor, where he spent some time perfecting himself in the Arabic language. He was a promising young man, and an enthusiast in the cause in which he was lost, and supposed to understand the Arabic language better than any European who ever before entered Africa. At an early age he formed the plan of going to that country, and gave up his connections and a competency in Germany, to prosecute his intentions. His father was a character well known in Europe, who raised himself from obscurity to the greatest celebrity by his talent for mechanics. He was at one time worth a million, but was ruined by the French revolution.

The following Letter from James Willis, Esq. late Consul to Senigambia, is extracted from the Gentleman's Magazine for May, 1812.

COMMERCIAL INTERCOURSE WITH AFRICA.

May 5. 1812.

At a time when our ancient rivals and enemies are exerting all their powers to destroy the British commerce, and have nearly effected their gigantic schemes of cutting off all communication between Great Britain and the various ports, states, and kingdoms of Europe; at such a time when we are in imminent danger of losing the markets of a quarter of the globe, it becomes [427] essentially important to discover other channels for our commerce, and other markets for our manufactures.

In this point of view, the information lately communicated to the public by Mr. James Grey Jackson, in his "Travels in Africa," becomes highly interesting to the statesman as well as to the merchant. From the account which he has given of the city of Timbuctoo, and its commercial relations, there is great reason to conclude, that if we could find means to open and maintain a safe and easy communication with that great emporium, and with the rich, fertile, and populous regions in its vicinity, we might acquire a market for our manufactures, that would in time compensate for the loss of that of Europe.

In the warehouses of Timbuctoo, are accumulated the manufactures of India and of Europe; and from thence the immense population that dwells upon the banks of the Niger is supplied. There is no doubt that we could furnish the articles they want, upon much lower terms than they can obtain them at present; and, in return, we should furnish the best market they could have for their gold, ivory, gums, and other rich products, and raw materials.

Now, it certainly appears to me, and I think it must appear to every man who takes the trouble of investigating the subject, that, provided Government would give proper support to the enterprise, this important communication might easily be established. *For this purpose, nothing more [428] is necessary than to take a fortified station upon the African coast, somewhere about the 29th degree of north latitude, near the confines of the Marocco dominions, to serve as a safe magazine or emporium for merchandize. From this station it would be easy to maintain a direct correspondence with the opulent merchants of Timbuctoo; regular caravans might be established to depart at fixed periods; the protection of the Arabs can at all times be purchased at stipulated prices, which may be considered as premiums of insurance, or as a tax for convoy*, and thus in a little time these caravans might carry out merchandize, to and from Timbuctoo, with as much regularity and safety, and with less expense, than our fleets convey our goods to and from the West Indies.

The expense of such a fortified station as is here proposed, would be very moderate, in comparison with the advantages it would produce; and it would be easy to draw out a plan for it; but I do not think it would be proper to go into a detail here,--*"non est hic locus."*

It has been well observed, that commerce is the key of Africa; and I shall only add, that if the plan I have suggested were carried into execution, these interesting regions of Africa, that have heretofore baffled the attempts of curiosity and enterprise, and remained for so many ages a "sealed book" to the inhabitants of Europe, would soon be explored and laid open. This is an object that cannot be indifferent to a prince, [429] who has so evidently evinced a desire to patronise science, and who is undoubtedly desirous to encourage, to facilitate, and to increase, still further the vast geographical discoveries which have added such lustre to the reign of his august father.

To return to Mr. Jackson's book. This work contains, besides the information that more directly concerns the statesman and the merchant, much interesting matter for the natural and moral philosopher, as well as for the general reader. The author makes no pretension to fine writing; his style is plain, unaffected, and perspicuous, and there is as much new, authentic, and important matter in the book, as in the hands of the French writers of African travels, (Golberry, Vaillant, and Savary, for instance,) would have been spread over three times the space. Upon the whole, it is the most valuable work of the kind that has appeared for many years. I hope the author will reap the reward which his labours have so well deserved.

James Willis.

Of the Venomous Spider.--Charmers of Serpents.--Disease called Nyctalopia, or Night-blindness.--Remedy for Consumption in Africa.--Western Branch of the Nile, and Water Communication between Timbuctoo and Egypt.

Sir,

The venomous spider (*Tendaraman*). This beautiful reptile is somewhat similar to a hornet in size and colour, but of a rounder form; its [430] legs are about an inch long, black, and very strong; it has two bright yellow lines, latitudinally crossing its back; it forms its web octagonally between bushes, the diameter being two or three yards; it places itself in the centre of its web, which is so fine, as to be almost invisible, and attaches to whatever may pass between those bushes. It is said to make always towards the head, before it inflicts its deadly wound. In the cork forests, the sportsman, eager in his pursuit of game, frequently carries away on his garments the *tenderaman*, whose bite is so poisonous, that the patient survives but a few hours.

Charmers of serpents (*Aisawie*).--These *Aisawie* have a considerable sanctuary at Fas. They go to Suse in large bodies about the month of July to collect serpents, which they pretend to render harmless by a certain form of words, incantation, or invocation to *Seedy ben Aisah*, their tutelary saint. They have an annual feast, at which time they dance and shake their heads quickly, during a certain period, till they become giddy, when they run about the towns frantic, attacking any person that may have a black or dark dress on; they bite, scratch, and devour any thing that comes in their way. They will attack an *unjumma*, or portable fire, and tear the lighted charcoal to pieces with their hands and mouths. I have seen them take the serpents, which they carry about, and devour them alive, the blood streaming down their clothes. The incredible [431] accounts of their feats would fill a volume; the following observations may suffice to give the reader an idea of these extraordinary fanatics. The *buska* and the [238]*el effah* are enticed out of their holes by them; they handle them with impunity, though their bite is ascertained to be mortal; they put them into a cane basket, and throw it over their shoulders: these serpents they carry about the country, and exhibit them to the people. I have seen them play with them, and suffer them to twist round their bodies in all directions, without receiving any injury from them. I have often enquired how they managed to do this, but never could get any direct or satisfactory answer; they assure you, however, that faith in their saint, and the powerful influence of the name of the divinity, (*Isim Allah*,) enables them to work these miracles: they maintain themselves in a miserable way, by donations from the spectators before whom they exhibit. This art of fascinating serpents was known by the ancient Africans, as appears from the *Marii* and *Psilii*, who were Africans, and showed proofs of it at Rome.

Footnote 238: (return) For a description of these deadly serpents, see Jackson's Account of Marocco, &c. chapter on Zoology.

Bu Telleese (Nyctalopia).--This ophthalmic disease is little known in the northern provinces; but in Suse and Sahara it prevails. A defect of vision comes on at dusk, but without pain; the patient is deprived of sight, so that he cannot see [432] distinctly, even with the assistance of candles. During my residence at Agadeer, a cousin of mine was dreadfully afflicted with this troublesome disease, losing his sight at evening, and continuing in that state till the rising sun. A Deleim Arab, a famous physician, communicated to me a sovereign remedy, which being extremely simple, I had not sufficient faith in his prescription to give it a trial, till reflecting that the simplicity of the remedy was such as to preclude the possibility of its being injurious, it was applied inwardly; and twelve hours afterwards, to my astonishment, the boy's eyes were perfectly well, and continued so during twenty-one days, when I again had recourse to the same remedy, and it effected a cure, on one administration, during thirty days, when it again attacked him; the remedy was again applied with the same beneficial effect as before.

Offer to discover the African Remedy for Nyctalopia, or Night Blindness.

(TO THE EDITOR OF THE LITERARY PANORAMA.)

Sir,

Having read your animadversions on the additional matter introduced in my second edition of an "Account of Marocco, Timbuctoo," &c. (see Literary Panorama for April last, p. 713.) wherein you conceive that I am reprehensible [433] for not having discovered publicly the remedy alluded to as an infallible cure to the *Butellise* or *Nyctalopia*, I should observe that I was not apprised, (till I read those animadversions,) that this was a disorder incident to the inhabitants in Europe, or that it affected our seamen on the Mediterranean station. But, if that be the case, and it should be found expedient and beneficial to the interests of Great Britain, that this remedy should be divulged for the alleviation of our meritorious seamen in His Majesty's service, I am willing to make the discovery to any respectable medical man who may be appointed by Government as physician or surgeon on the Mediterranean station.

James G. Jackson.

May 18. 1812.

TO THE EDITOR OF THE LITERARY PANORAMA.

Circus, Minories, June 21. 1815.

Sir,

I request you will contradict in your next publication the assertion of my *decease*, which is calculated to injure considerably my interests abroad as a merchant. (Vide your Review of Parke's Travels, page 377.) In answer to this unfounded information, which has been propagated in your review of last month, I have to acquaint you that I am not only in the land of the living, but in excellent health, and waiting to hear the testimony of some stranger or European [434] traveller (since the Africans are not to be relied on), who shall establish the fact of *the junction of the Nile of Sudan with that of Egypt; or at least, the approximation of these two mighty streams*. And notwithstanding *the* insidious reflections and censures passed on the native Africans, from whom

I gathered much of the information communicated to the public in my account of Marocco, it must be allowed by all liberal-minded men, that a native is more likely to give an accurate account of his country than a foreigner; and a residence of sixteen years in a country may be allowed to give a man of common observation experience enough to select judiciously such intelligence as might be relied on; and I have no hesitation in declaring it to be my unalterable opinion, that *so soon as a traveller shall have returned from the interior of Africa, many of my assertions respecting those regions will be confirmed*, and that information founded on the testimony of unprejudiced and disinterested Africans, will be found not so contemptible as some learned persons have imagined.

James G. Jackson.

[435]

Critical Observations on Abstracts from the Travels of Ali Bey, and Robert Adams, in the Quarterly Journal of Literature, Science, and the Arts, edited at the Royal Institution of Great Britain, Vol. I. No. II. page 264.

London, Dec. 19. 1817.

In the discussion on Aly Bey's Travels, in the Journal of Science and the Arts, above mentioned, p. 270. are the following words:--

"Aly Bey has added, in a separate chapter, all the information he received, respecting a mediterranean sea, from a merchant of Marocco, of the name of Sidi Matte Buhlal, who had resided many years at Timbuctoo, and in other countries of Sudan or Nigritia, the most material of which was, that Tombut is a large town, very trading, and inhabited by Moors and Negroes, and was at the same distance from the Nile Abid, (or Nile of the Negroes, or Niger,) as Fez is from Wed Sebu, that is to say, *about three hundred English miles*."

As this passage is quoted from Aly Bey, by the first literary society of Great Britain, and is, therefore, calculated to create a doubt of the accuracy of what I have said, respecting the distance of the Nile El Abeed from Timbuctoo, in the enlarged editions of my account of Marocco, &c. page 297. I consider it a duty which I owe to my country and to myself, not to let [436] this sentence pass through the press without submitting to the public my observations on the subject.

Sidi Matte Buhlal is a native of Fas: the name is properly Sidi El Mattie Bû Hellal. This gentleman is one out of twenty authorities from whom I derived the information recorded in my account of Marocco, respecting Timbuctoo and the interior of Africa; his whole family, which is respectable and numerous, are among the first Timbuctoo merchants that have their establishments at Fas. I should, however, add, that among the many authorities from whom I derived my information relative to Timbuctoo, there were two muselmen in particular,-- merchants of respectability and intelligence, who came from Timbuctoo to Santa Cruz, soon after *I opened that port to Dutch commerce, in the capacity of agent of Holland, by order of the then Emperor of Marocco, Muley Yezzid*, brother and predecessor of the present Emperor Soliman. These two gentlemen had resided at Timbuctoo, and in other parts of Sudan, fifteen years, trading during the whole of that period with Darbeyta, on the coast of the Red Sea, with Jinnie, Housa, Wangara, Cashna, and other countries of the interior, from whom, and from others, equally intelligent and credible, I procured my information respecting the *mediterranean sea in the interior of Africa, called El Bahar Assudan, i.e. the Sea of Sudan*, situated fifteen days' journey east of Timbuctoo. These two [437] muselmen merchants had amassed considerable fortunes at Timbuctoo, and were on their journey to Fas, their native place; but in consequence of a civil war at that time raging throughout West Barbary, particularly in the province of Haha, through which it was indispensable that they should pass, on their way to Fas, they sojourned with me two months; after which they departed for Fas with a caravan.

These intelligent Moors gave me much information respecting Timbuctoo, and the interior countries where they had resided; they sold me many articles of Sudanic manufacture, among which were three pieces of fine cotton cloth, manufactured at Timbuctoo, and some ornaments of pure gold *in or molu*, of exquisite workmanship, of the manufacture of Jinnie; one of these pieces of Timbuctoo manufacture, of cotton interwoven with silk, of a square blue-and-white pattern, dyed with *indigo of Timbuctoo*, I had the honour to present to the British Museum, in April, 1796 [239], where it is now deposited.

Footnote 239: (return) This piece of cloth, about two yards wide and five long, I had the honour of offering to Sir Joseph Banks, who declined receiving it; but at the same time suggested that it was a manufacture deserving public notice, and would be considered an acceptable present by the British Museum.

I have been led into this digression from certain insinuations that have been [240] insidiously propagated, reflecting on the accuracy of my statements respecting the interior of Africa; [438] and I must add, that I always have felt, and still feel confident, that in proportion as we shall become more acquainted with the interior of this unexplored continent, my account will be so much the more authenticated: my confidence in this opinion, (however dogmatical it may appear,) is founded on the original and intelligent sources of my information; on a long residence and general acquaintance with all the principal inhabitants of West Barbary, whose connections lay in Sudan, and at Timbuctoo; in a competent knowledge and practical acquaintance with the languages of North Africa, and a consequent ability to discriminate the accuracy of the sources of my intelligence.

Footnote 240: (return) See my letter to the editor of the Monthly Magazine, for March, 1817; page 125.

This being premised, I now proceed to offer to the public my animadversions on the above quotation from the Journal of Science and the Arts.

I have actually crossed the Wed Sebu, or the River Sebu, alluded to in the above quotation, which passes through the Berebber Kabyl of Zimure Shelleh; I have crossed the same river several times at the city of Mequinez, and also at Meheduma, where it enters the Atlantic Ocean, in lat. 34° 15' north, and from this experimental knowledge of the course of that river, I can affirm, with confidence, that it is not inaccurately laid down in my map of West Barbary [241], and that it is not three hundred English miles from Fas, but only six English miles from [439] that city. I can also assert, from incontestable testimony, that Tombut, or Timbuctoo, is [242] not three hundred miles from the Nile El Abeed, but only about twelve English miles from that stream, the latter being south of the town.

Footnote 241: (return) For which see page 55.

Footnote 242: (return) Vide Jackson's enlarged Account of Marocco, &c. p. 297.

Respecting the following passage in the above quoted Journal of Science and the Arts, p. 272, "This river contains the fierce animals called *Tzemsah*, which devour men," I shall only observe, that *Tzemsah* is the word in Arabic which denominates the *crocodile*. Farther on, in the same page, we have the words,--"We must suppose that the Joliba makes at this spot a strange winding, which gives to the inhabitants of Marocco the opinion they express." This supposed winding is actually asserted to exist, and is denominated by the Arabs [243] *El Kose Nile*, i.e. the arch or curve of the Nile, and is situated between the cities of Timbuctoo and Jinnie.

Footnote 243: (return) Idem, note, p. 305.

I should here adduce some further testimony respecting the course of the Nile El Abeed; but as the quotation from Aly Bey in the above Journal of Sciences and the Arts, page 271. asserts it to be towards the east, and again, in page 272. declares it to be towards the west, such incoherence, I presume, requires no confutation. I consider that it originates from Moorish inaccuracy. [440]

The *La Mar Zarak* of Adams, if any such river exists, may be a corruption of *Sagea el Humra*, i.e. the Red Stream, a river in the southern confines of Sahara, nearly in the same longitude with Timbuctoo. This river the late Emperor of Marocco, Muley Yezzid, announced as the southern boundary of his dominions; but from the accounts which I have had of it, it was not of that magnitude which Adams ascribes to the Mar Zarak, nor was it precisely in the neighbourhood of Timbuctoo, when I was a resident in South Barbary: rivers, however, *which pass through sandy or desert districts*, often change their courses in the space of twenty-four hours, by the drifting of the moving sands impelled by the wind; instances of which I have myself often witnessed.

If this river proceeded from the Desert, it might have had the name of *El Bahar Sahara*, i.e. the River of Sahara; the word *La Mar* is a lingua franca, or corrupt Spanish word, signifying the sea, and might have been used to this poor sailor by a native to make it the more intelligible to him.

Many Spanish words having crept into the Arabic vocabulary, and are occasionally used by those Africans who have had intercourse with Europeans.

The next passage for animadversion is as follows:-- [441]

"The state in which he represented Timbuctoo, and its being the residence of a Negro sovereign, instead of a muselman."

The state in which he has represented Timbuctoo, is, I think, extremely inaccurate; and being a slave, it is more than probable, that he was placed in a Fondaque [244], or Caravansera, belonging to the King, which he *mistook* for his palace; but that his narrative should be deemed inaccurate, because he has described the town of Timbuctoo to be under the sovereignty of a Negro prince, is to me incomprehensible.

Footnote 244: (return) Vide Jackson's enlarged Account of Marocoo, &c. p. 298.

The various sources of information that I have investigated, uniformly declare that sovereign to be a Negro, and that his name in the year 1800, was Woolo. This account, it appears, is confirmed by Adams, who says, [245] Woolo was King of Timbuctoo in 1810, and that he was then old and grey-headed. Some years after the above period, Riley's Narrative, epitomised in Leyden's Discoveries and Travels in Africa, vol. i., *speaking of the King of Timbuctoo, says, this sovereign is a very large, old, grey-headed black man*, called *Shegar*, which means Sultan. This, however, I must observe is a misinterpretation of the word *Shegar*, which is an African-Arabic word, and signifies *red or carrotty*, and is a word applicable to his physiognomy; but certainly not to his rank:--*Abd Shegar*, a [442] carrotty or red Negro. If these two testimonies, since 1800, be correct, then the *anachronism* of which I am accused in the New Supplement to the Encyclopedia Britannica, (title Africa,) is misapplied.

Footnote 245: (return) Since publishing this letter, Mr. Bowdich, in his Account of Ashantee, pages 194, 195, says, Woolo was King of Timbuctoo in 1807, or ten years before Mr. Bowdich was at Ashantee.

Many of this king's civil officers, however, in 1800, were muselmen; but the military were altogether Negroes.

However fervent the zeal of Muhamedanism may be at Timbuctoo, it is not, I imagine, sufficient to convert the Negroes, who have not the best opinion of the Muhamedan tenets. The Negroes, however, are disposed to abjure idolatry for any other form of religion that they can be persuaded to think preferable, or that holds out a better prospect; a convincing proof of which has been seen by the readiness of the Africans of Congo and Angola, to renounce their idolatry for the Christian faith, by the conversion of thousands to that faith by the indefatigable zeal of the catholic missionaries, when the Portuguese first discovered those countries, and which, if the Sovereign of Portugal had persevered with that laudable zeal with which he began to promote the conversion of the Africans, the inhabitants of those extensive and populous countries might, at this day, have been altogether members of the Christian church!! [443]

On the Junction of the Nile of Egypt with the Nile of Timbuctoo, or of Sudan.

TO THE EDITOR OF THE MONTHLY MAGAZINE. [246]

Footnote 246: (return) Inserted in March, 1817.

London, Jan. 25. 1817.

Sir,

Having read some annotations, in the Journal of a Mission to the Interior of Africa, by Mungo Park, in 1805, which are calculated to persuade some persons, that my Account of the Interior of Africa is not altogether authentic, I feel myself called upon to offer some cursory observations to the public, in refutation of those aspersions. (Vide Appendix, No. IV. to Mungo Park's Second Journey, in 1805, pages 114. and 115.)

Although I assert, on the concurrent testimony of the best informed and most intelligent natives of Sudan, that there exists a [247]water communication between Timbuctoo and Cairo, I do not maintain that the [248]Nile of Sudan falls into the [249]Nile of Egypt, but that it hath a communication with it, or with some river that [444] connects itself with the Nile of Egypt, which opinion is confirmed by Mr. Hornemann, on African authority.

Footnote 247: (return) Vide Jackson's Marocco, second or third edition, page 310.

Footnote 248: (return) (*Nile el Kabeer*) the Great Nile, (*Bahar el Abeed*, or *Nile el Abeed*) the Nile of Slaves or Negroes, (*Nile Sudan*) the Nile of Sudan or Nigritia, are the various names applied to the river that passes by Timbuctoo, and through the interior of Sudan, from west to east.

Footnote 249: (return) *Nile Masser* is the name applied to the Nile of Egypt.

It is very probable that this junction is formed by a stream that flows westward towards Wangara through the country called [250] Bahar Kulla, and Lake Dwi, from the source of the Nile of Egypt, or from that part of the Jibbel Kumri, or Lunar Mountains, which form the southern boundary of Donga.

If this be so, the junction of the Nile el Abeed, of Timbuctoo, and the Bahar el Aheäd of Donga [251], (or more properly the Bahar el Abeed,) is established, and the water communication between

Timbuctoo and Cairo is proved; admitting, however, that the Negroes reported by me to have performed the [252] voyage by water, took their boat or canoe ashore, to ascend the cataracts, in the country between Wangara and Donga.

Footnote 250: (return) *Bahar Kulla* is an Arabic term, signifying the sea altogether, implying an alluvial country, (probably forming a part of the mediterranean sea of central Africa). See Major Rennel's Map in the Proceedings of the African Association, vol. i. 8vo. page 209. lat. N. 10°, long. 18°.

Footnote 251: (return) Vide Major Kennel's Map in the Proceedings of the African Association, 8vo. edition, vol. i. page 209.

Footnote 252: (return) Vide Jackson's Marocco, second or third edition, page 312.

Mr. Park's annotator, in the spirit of controversy with which he appears to be endued, may say, the fact of this stream running to the west towards Wangara, cannot be admitted, because [445] Mr. Browne saw a ridge of mountains extending in that direction; but Mr. Browne did not ascertain that this was an uninterrupted ridge; the river might therefore pass through some chasm similar to that which I have seen in crossing the Atlas Mountains, or through some intermediate plain.

The annotator further says [253], "It is needless to comment upon such hearsay statements, received from an African traveller." This assertion being calculated to impress on the public mind, that I founded my hypothesis respecting the junction of the Niles of Africa on the simple and single statement of one individual African traveller; I feel it incumbent on me thus publicly to declare, that *the junction alluded to is founded on the universal and concurrent testimony of all the most intelligent and well informed native African travellers* (for the most part natives of Sudan), not one of whom differed in this opinion, but unanimously declared it to be an uncontroverted fact, that the waters of the Nile of Egypt joined the waters of the Nile el Abeed, which passes near Timbuctoo to the east; and that there exists, without a doubt, a water communication between Cairo in Egypt, and Timbuctoo in Sudan. Now, if, as M. de Bailly observes, "*la vérité se fait connaître par le concours des témoignages*," it must be admitted, [446] by men of liberal sentiments, that it is somewhat more than a hearsay statement; and what better foundation can there possibly be for the truth of any geological fact, than the concurrent testimony of the best-informed natives of the country described?

Footnote 253: (return) Vide Appendix, No. IV. to Park's Second Journey page 115.

With respect to precision being unfavourable to authenticity [254], I consider this a new dogma; and if I were disposed to confute it, (but it carries with it its own confutation,) I should point out many hearsay evidences, precisely recorded in my Account of Marocco, which have been confirmed already by Ali Bey (El Abassy) and many others; but "*non est hic locus.*"

J.G. Jackson.

Footnote 254: (return) Vide Appendix, No. II. to Park's Second Journey page 103.

Strictures respecting the Interior of Africa, and Confirmation of Jackson's Account of Sudan, annexed to his Account of the Empire of Marocco, &c.

London, 16th Jan, 1818.

It is a satisfaction to perceive (after a lapse of eight or nine years since the publication of my account of Marocco and the interior of Africa), that in proportion as we are becoming better acquainted with the interior of that continent, my account becomes more authenticated, notwithstanding the attempts that have been so insidiously made to invalidate it. [447]

The various hypotheses, for the most part founded in theory, that have within the last seven years, been adopted respecting the course of the *Nile el Abeed* (Niger), are beginning now to fall to the ground, and the learned and judicious editor of the Supplement to the New Encyclopedia Britannica, founding his opinions, as it should seem, upon the facts that have been corroborated respecting the interior of Africa, has actually adopted my opinion; [255] viz.

That there is an union of waters between the Nile of Egypt, and that of Sudan [256]; where the common receptacle is, I have not ventured to declare, but it is probable that it may be in the Bahar Kulla [257], in Wangara, or in the [258]Sea of Sudan; the opinion that the junction is formed in the Sea of Sudan is supported by the Shereef Imhammed, who saw the Nile at Cashna, and declared that it was so rapid there from east to west, that vessels could not stem it.

Footnote 255: (return) See my letter to the Editor of the Monthly Magazine, vol. xliii. March, 1817, page 125.

Footnote 256: (return) It is incorrect to say, that the word *Nile* is applied, in Africa, to any great river: the name, I can with confidence declare, is never applied to any river in North Africa, except the Nile of Egypt, and that of Sudan; whoever has propagated this opinion has mistaken the matter altogether. See Proceedings of the African Association, vol. i. page 540.

Footnote 257: (return) See Major Rennell's Map of North Africa, lat. north 6°, long, west 18°, &c.

Footnote 258: (return) See Jackson's enlarged Account of Marocco, Timbuctoo, &c. page 310.

Again: Parke's intelligence, in his second [448] journey, demonstrates an union of waters in the (Baseafeena [259]) Sea of Sudan; for he says, the current was said to be sometimes one way, and sometimes another; which I will take the liberty to interpret thus:--

That the current from the Eastern Nile, was westward into the Sea of Sudan, and the current of the Western Nile was eastward into the same sea of Sudan: thus the current would be sometimes one way, and sometimes another, making the Sea of Sudan the common receptacle for the Eastern as well as for the Western Nile.

Ptolemy's Sea of Nigritia is undoubtedly the same with my Sea of Sudan; *Lybia Palus* [260] being the Latin denomination, as *Bahar Sudan* is the Arabic for the interior lake called the Sea of Sudan; but whether this sea of Sudan will ultimately prove to be situated [261] as I have described it, fifteen journies [262] east of Timbuctoo, or 450 English miles, or as Ptolemy has described it, or in the intermediate distance between the two extremes, must be left for future travellers to ascertain.

Footnote 259:(return) Another name for the Sea of Sudan, as will hereafter appear.

Footnote 260:(return) See Ptolemy's Map of North Africa.

Footnote 261:(return) See Jackson's enlarged Account of Marocco, page 310.

Footnote 262:(return) Fifteen journies horse travelling, which are the journies here alluded to, at thirty miles a-day, is 450 British miles.

The enterprising and indefatigable, the patient and persevering genius of Burkhardt, deriving incalculable advantages from a long residence in the eastern regions of Africa, may probably decree

[449] him to be the person to clear up this long-contested geographical point, unless the fascination of Arabian manners, or some Utopia in the interior regions of that continent, should wean him from the desire to re-visit his native country.

This intelligence of Park may be considered some corroboration of what I have maintained respecting the union of waters between the Eastern and Western Niles. [263]

The following testimonies are some confirmation of my report respecting decked vessels, &c. in the interior of Africa. [264]

Dr. Stetzen, a German physician residing at Alexandria [265], says, that he has received intelligence from a pilgrim, on his way to Mecca, a native of *Ber Noh,* or *Bernou* [266], that the river within a mile of the city is as large as the Egyptian Nile, and overflows its banks; *it is navigated by vessels of considerable dimensions, carrying sails and oars.*

Footnote 263: (return) See Monthly Magazine, March, 1817, page 125.

Footnote 264: (return) See Jackson's enlarged Account of Marocco, &c. page 309.

Footnote 265: (return) For full particulars, see New Supp. to Ency. Brit. article "Africa."

Footnote 266: (return) This Bernou, or according to the Arabic orthography, *Ber Noh*, is asserted by the Arabs to be the birth-place of the Patriarch Noah.

Mr. Barnes states, that the Niger discharges itself into a large lake; that he has heard from the Black traders that there are white inhabitants upon the borders of this lake; and has been [450] told, by people who have seen them, that they dress in the style of Barbary Moors, and wear turbans, but do not speak Arabic. See Report of Committee of Council. [267]

Footnote 267: (return) See Jackson's enlarged Account of Marocco, &c. p, 309.

Park, in his second journey, was informed, that "one month's travel south of Baedo, through the kingdom of Grotto, will bring the traveller to the country of the Christians, who have their houses on the banks of the *Ba Seafeena* [268], which they describe as incomparably larger than the lake Dehebby (Dibbie)."--This is another corroboration of the accuracy of my account of the interior of Africa; but before I dismiss this subject, I should observe, that from the general ignorance of the African Arabic, an important circumstance respecting this *Ba Seafeena*, is not yet (it appears) discovered. It is this:--the words *Ba Seafeena*, or, according to the correct Arabic orthography, *Bahar Sefeena*, literally translated into English, signifies the Sea of Ships, and is evidently only another name for the Sea of Sudan, declaring it to be a sea wherein ships are found!

Footnote 268: (return) See New Supp. to Ency. Brit. article "Africa."

Here then are two topographical facts first asserted by me, among the moderns, to exist in the heart of Africa, and since confirmed by Ali Bey, Park, and Dr. Sietzen, or, as the enlightened editor of the Supplement to the New Encyclopedia Britt. observes,

"We have thus three independent testimonies [269] [451] from opposite quarters, meeting exactly in the same point; nor does there, as far as we know, exist any evidence *at all respectable* to the contrary."

Footnote 269: (return) The testimonies here alluded to are Hornman, Park, and Jackson.

It now remains for me to declare (that as opinions have been industriously propagated tending to discredit my account of Marocco, and the interior of Africa,) that nothing has been set down therein, until I had previously investigated the qualifications of the narrators, their means of knowledge, and whether the respective vocations of the several narrators made it their interest to disguise or misrepresent the truth of their communications; and, after ascertaining these important points, I have generally had recourse to other testimonies, and have seldom recorded any thing until confirmed by three or four *concurrent* evidences: on this *pyramidical basis* is founded the intelligence in my account of Marocco, and of the interior of Africa, annexed to that account.

This assertion is to be understood in respect to intelligence that I could not ascertain by ocular demonstration.

Finally, my description of the black heartheaded serpent, called Bouska [270], has been doubted; but a late traveller [271] has confirmed the accuracy [452] of my account; even of this extraordinary animal.--In Riley's Narrative of his Shipwreck on the [453] Coast of Sahara is given an account of an exhibition by two *Isawie* [272], who do not appear to [454] have been adepts in the art of fascinating these serpents; for I have frequently seen them manage [455] and charm the *Bouska* much more adroitly than those who exhibited at Rabat before Riley, although its bite is more deadly, and its strength considerably greater, than that of the *El Effah!*

Footnote 270: (return) See Jackson's enlarged Account of Marocco, &c. p. 109.

Footnote 271: (return)

"I paid two dollars for a station, and I looked into the room without interruption. It was about twenty feet long, and fifteen broad, paved with tiles and plastered within. The windows had also been secured by an additional grating made of wire, in such a manner as to render it impossible for the serpents to escape from the room: it had but one door, and that had a hole cut through it six or eight inches square: this hole was also secured by a grating. In the room stood two men, who appeared to be Arabs, with long bushy hair and beards; and I was told they were a particular race of men, that could charm serpents.

"A wooden box, about four feet long and two wide, was placed near the door, with a string fastened to a slide at one end of it; this string went through a hole in the door. The two serpent-eaters were dressed in haiks only, and those very small ones. After they had gone through their religious ceremonies most devoutly, they appeared to take an eternal farewell of each other: this done, one of them retired from the room, and shut the door tight after him. The Arab within seemed to be in dreadful distress. I could observe his heart throb, and his bosom heave most violently: and he cried out very loudly, "*Allah houakiber*," three times; which is, as I understood it, *God have mercy on me.* [273]

"The Arab was at the farthest end of the room: at that instant the cage was opened, and a serpent crept out slowly; he was: about four feet long, and eight inches in circumference; his colours were the most beautiful in nature, being bright, and variegated with a deep yellow, a purple, a cream colour, black and brown, spotted, &c. As soon as he saw the Arab in the room, his eyes, which were small and green, kindled as with fire; he erected himself in a second, his head two feet high; and darting on the defenseless Arab, seized him between the folds of his haik, just above his right hipbone, hissing most horribly; the Arab gave a horrid shriek, when another serpent came out of the cage. This last was black, very shining, and appeared to be seven or eight feet long, but not more than two inches in diameter: as soon as he had cleared the cage, he cast his *red fiery eyes* on his intended victim, thrust out his forked tongue, *threw himself into a coil, erected his head, which was in the centre of the coil*, three feet from the floor, and flattening out the skin above his head and eyes, in the form, and nearly of the size of a human heart, and springing like lightning on the Arab, struck its fangs into his neck near the jugular vein, while his tail and body flew round his neck and arms in two or three folds. The Arab set up the most hideous and piteous yelling, foamed and frothed at the mouth, grasping the folds of the serpent, which were round his arms with his right hand, and seemed to be in the greatest agony, striving to tear the reptile from around his neck, while with his left he seized hold of it near its head, but could not break its hold: by this time the other had turned itself around his legs, and kept biting all around the other parts of his body, making apparently deep incisions: the blood, issuing from every wound (both in his neck and body,) streamed all over his haik and skin. My blood was chilled in my veins with horror at this sight, and it was with difficulty my legs would support my frame.

"Notwithstanding the Arab's greatest exertions to tear away the serpents with his hands, they turned themselves still tighter, stopped his breath, and he fell to the floor, where he continued for a moment, as if in the most inconceivable agony, rolling over, and covering every part of his body with his own blood and froth, until he ceased to move, and appeared to have expired. In his last struggle, he had wounded the black serpent with his teeth, as it was striving, as it were, to force its head into his mouth, which wound Footnote: seemed to increase its rage. At this instant I heard the shrill sound of a whistle, and looking towards the door saw the other Arab applying a call to his mouth: the serpents listened to the music, their fury seemed to forsake them by degrees, they disengaged themselves leisurely from the apparently lifeless carcase, and creeping towards the cage, they soon entered it, and were immediately fastened in.

"The door of the apartment was now opened, and he without ran to assist his companion: he had a phial of blackish liquor in one hand, and an iron chissel in the other: finding the teeth of his companion set, he thrust in the chissel, forced them open, and then poured a little of the liquor into his mouth; and holding the lips together, applied his mouth to the dead man's nose, and filled his lungs with air: he next anointed his numerous wounds with a little of the same liquid, and yet no sign of life, appeared. I thought he was dead in earnest; his neck and veins were exceedingly swollen; when his comrade taking up the lifeless trunk in his arms, brought it out into the open air, and continued the operation of blowing for several minutes before a sign of life appeared; at length he gasped, and after a time recovered so far as to be able to speak. The swellings in his neck, body, and legs gradually subsided, as they continued washing the wounds with clear cold water and a sponge, and applying the black liquor occasionally; a clean haik was wrapped about him, but his strength seemed so far exhausted that he could not support himself standing, so his comrade laid him on the ground by a wall, where he sunk into a sleep. This exhibition lasted for about a quarter of an hour from the time the serpents were let loose until they were called off, and it was more than an hour from that time before he could speak. I thought I could discover that the poisonous fangs had been pulled out of these formidable serpents' jaws, and mentioned that circumstance to the showman, who said, that they had indeed been extracted; and when I wished to know how swellings on his neck and other parts could be assumed, he assured me, that though their deadly fangs were out, yet that the poisonous quality of their breath and spittle would cause the death of those they attack; that after a bite from either of these serpents, no man could exist longer than fifteen minutes: and that there was no remedy for any but those *who were endowed by the Almighty with power to charm, and to manage them*; and that he and his associates were of that favoured number! The Moors and Arabs call the thick and beautiful serpent *El Effah*, and the long black and heartheaded one *El Bouskah*.

"I afterwards saw engravings of these two serpents in *Jackson's Marocco*; which are very correct resemblances. They are said to be very numerous on and about the south foot of the Atlas mountains and border of the Desert, where these were caught when young, and where they often attack both men and beasts."--Vide *Riley's Shipwreck and Captivity in the Great Desert*, p. 550.

Footnote 272: (return) Disciples of Seedy ben Isa, whose sanctuary is at Fas, and who possess the art of fascinating serpents.

Footnote 273: (return) N.B. This is a misinterpretation of the Arabic words here used, which, literally translated, signify, *God alone, is great!*--J.G.J.

Animadversions on the Orthography of African Names.

(TO THE EDITOR OF THE MONTHLY MAGAZINE, INSERTED MAY, 1818.)

Bennet's-hill, Feb. 1818.

Sir,

I should be much surprised to find that Jackson's account of what he has heard is doubted, if I did not remember that Bruce's account of [456] what he had seen was disbelieved. Nothing human can appear to me more deserving of implicit credit than the intelligence the former of these writers gives respecting Timbuctoo. He has not seen it, it is true. I have not seen Lisbon; but, if I had, and were to sit down to write an account of it, some things would be necessary to be described, with regard to which I should feel a degree of uncertainty; and, having given an account of Lisbon, if I were to visit it again, I should find others on which I had been mistaken. But let me arrange in my own mind the information I want respecting Lisbon; let me make enquiries of twenty intelligent persons who have resided there; let me carefully compare their different accounts, and who shall doubt the accuracy of the result?

Mr. Jackson has had an opportunity of acquiring information respecting Timbuctoo that no other European ever had, by having the direction of commerce in a city frequented by Timbuctan merchants; a city, the port of which is called, in Arabic, *Bab Sudan*, the Gate of Sudan. Mr. Jackson was qualified to make use of this advantage to an extent that no other European ever was, by a practical, and even critical knowledge of the general language of the country,--the African Arabic. To these Mr. Jackson added an ardent spirit of research, an industry which neglected no opportunity, a caution to compare, a judgment to discriminate, and a firmness to decide. Who, that weighs [457] these things, can doubt the accuracy of his intelligence respecting Sudan? I even regard his orthography as the standard of correctness, and am surprised that any person should continue to write Timbuctoo instead of Timbuctoo, or Fez instead of Fas.

I am inclined to believe that Adams has been at Timbuctoo, though I do not consider it as proved; but, supposing that he has, and that I wished to become acquainted with that city, would I apply for information to an illiterate slave, who was confined within narrow precincts? Or would I rely upon the united testimony of twenty persons of education, who had each a wider field of observation?

I have read "Jackson's Account of Marocco" twice through, at different periods, with great attention; and I do most heartily join in the confidence expressed by the enlightened and judicious author, that, in proportion as the interior of Africa shall be more known, the truth of his account of it will be made evident.

Catherine Hutton.

Hints for the Civilisation of Barbary, and Diffusion of Commerce.

March 16, 1818.

Algiers, and the territory belonging to it, is governed by despotic Turks, the refuse of the Ottoman troops; who maintain their power over the Moors and Arabs of the plains (who are the [458] cultivators of the country), and over the Berebbers (who are the aborigines of the country), or inhabitants of the mountains of Atlas, which terminate this sovereignty on the south, and divide Algiers from Bled-al-Jereed. The first principle of this barbarous and sanguinary government, according io an African adage, is to "*Maintain the arm of power, by making streams of blood flow, without intermission, around the throne!*" This country,--the government of which reflects disgrace on Christendom, which has been, during many ages the scourge of Christian mariners, and of all who navigate the Mediterranean Sea,--has often been conquered. The Romans reduced Numidia and Mauritania into Roman provinces. This beautiful garden of the world was afterwards conquered by the Vandals; then by the Greeks, during the reign of Justinian, under Belisarius; and, finally, three times by the Arabs, viz. in the 647th year of Christ, by Abdallah and Zobeer; in the year 667, by Ak'bah for the Kalif Moawiah; and in the year 692, by Hassan, the governor of Egypt, for the Kalif Abd Elmelik. Not one of the armies of these warriors ever exceeded 50,000 men.

After these general conquests, the partial conquests of the Portuguese and Spaniards, about the end of the fifteenth and beginning of the sixteenth century, were effected by a mere handful of men; and, in 1509, the latter rendered the kingdom of Algiers tributary to them: but, afterwards, they lost it by the ferocity of their [459] chiefs, and by the fanaticism of their soldiers and priests; and, finally, by their perfidy and intolerance, they made themselves enemies to the various (*Kabyles*) tribes of Mauritania, and thereby lost their conquest.

The repeated insults, offered by these ruffians to civilised Europe, cannot be efficiently punished by a bombardment; a measure which punishes many innocent subjects for the insults offered by their government. No one acquainted with the character of the natives of Barbary will maintain, that the destruction of a few thousands of the peaceable inhabitants, or the burning of many houses, is a national calamity in the eyes of a Muselman chief; who would himself commit the same ravage and destruction that was so gallantly effected by the British fleet, under Lord Exmouth, for half the money it cost to accomplish it.

When Lord St. Vincent was off Cadiz with the British fleet, and could not obtain the object which he sought of the Emperor of Marocco; his Lordship, after refusing to comply with the Emperor's request, communicated to his Lordship by the Emperor's envoy, or agent, Rais Ben Embark, told the Rais to inform his Emperor, that, if he did not change his conduct very soon, he would begin a war with him, and such a war as he had neither seen nor read of before. When the Rais reported this to the Emperor Soliman, he enquired what kind of war an admiral could wage against him; some one of the divan observed, that he would destroy the ports on the [460] coast; adding, that it would cost a certain large sum of money to effect that destruction. Upon which the Emperor exclaimed, that, for half that amount, he would himself destroy all these ports.--This affair happened in September, 1798.

There is a prophecy in Barbary, that, from time immemorial, has been generally credited by the inhabitants. It has been transmitted to them by some fakeer, that the land of the Muselmen will be wrested from them by the Christians; and there is an impression, that the period when this event will take place is not far distant. They also believe that this event will happen on a Friday (the Muselman Sabbath), whilst they are occupied at their devotions at the *Dohor*, service of prayer. Accordingly, at this period,--viz. from twelve till half-past one o'clock,--the gates of all the town's on the coast are shut and bolted every Friday. This attack, forsooth, is to happen whilst they are occupied at prayer, because they are so infatuated with an opinion of their own valour, that they will not believe that Christians would presume to attack them openly, when armed and prepared for the combat. It should seem that these people begin now seriously to anticipate the near approach of this predestined conquest, and have accordingly entered into a kind of holy alliance, offensive and defensive: to which, it is said, the Emperor of Marocco, and the Deys of Tunis and Tripoli, have acceded; and that this holy alliance is crowned by the Ottoman Emperor. [461]

It is more than probable, that the Dey of Algiers, goaded by the blow inflicted by Lord Exmouth,--which has increased his hatred to Christians, and has inflamed his desire of revenge,--will not fail to seek every opportunity (according to the known principles of Muhamedanism), of retaliating and insulting the Europeans, whenever a favourable opportunity may offer, even at the risk of another bombardment. This opinion has been confirmed by his late conduct; and by the activity that has been manifested in the fortifications, in increasing their military force, in building and equipping new vessels, to infest the Mediterranean with their abominable piracies; all which proceedings demonstrate the hostile intentions of the Dey beyond all doubt.

Plan for the Conquest of Algiers.

The inhabitants of the plains are bigoted to the Muhamedan tenets; but they would readily exchange the iron rod that rules them for a more mild and beneficial form of government. A well-disciplined European army of 50,000 men, would assuredly effect their complete conquest without much difficulty: such an army, directed by a Wellington, would perform wonders, and astound the Africans. After the conquest, an energetic, decisive, but beneficent form of government, would be necessary, to retain the country, and to conquer and annihilate [462] the repugnancy which these people entertain to our religious tenets. A system of rule formed on the principles of the English constitution,--directed by good policy, benevolence, and religious toleration,--would not fail to reconcile these hostile tribes, and attach them to rational government. The Berebbers would readily assimilate to such a government; and, although by nature a treacherous race, they would rejoice to see the country in possession of a government which, they would perceive, strove to promote the welfare and prosperity of the mountaineers, as well as the inhabitants of the plains; and their own interest would thus gradually subdue the antipathy resulting from religious prejudices.

A general knowledge of the African Arabic would be essentially necessary; and I think a school might be established in England, on the Madras system, for initiating youths (going out to Africa) in the rudiments of that language. This would be attended with most important advantages; and might be accomplished in a very short time. The conquest of Algiers being thus effected, that of the neighbouring states would follow, without difficulty, by a disciplined army of European troops; keeping the principle ever in view, of conciliating the natives, without swerving from an energetic and decisive mode of government.

The advantages that would necessarily result from a successful attack upon Africa, would be-- [463]

1. An incalculable demand for spices, and East India manufactures of silk and cotton.

2. A similar demand for coffees, and for sugars, manufactured and unmanufactured; as well as for other articles of West India produce.

3. An incalculable demand for all our various articles of manufacture.

On the other hand, we should obtain from this fine country,--

1. An immense supply of the finest wheat, and other grain, that the world produces.

2. We should be able to open a direct communication with the interior regions of Africa,--which have baffled the enterprise of ancient and modern Europe: the fertile and populous districts which lie contiguous to the Nile of Sudan, throughout the whole of the interior of Africa, would become, in a few years, as closely connected to us, by a mutual exchange of benefits, as our own colonies; and such a stimulus would be imparted to British enterprise and industry, as would secure to us such stores of gold as would equal the riches of Solomon, and immortalize the prince who should cherish this great commerce to its maturity.

Vasco De Gama.

[464]

(TO THE EDITOR OF THE EUROPEAN MAGAZINE.)

Liverpool, Dec. 17. 1818.

Sir,

In "*The Portfolio*," a Monthly Miscellany for May, 1817, published at Philadelphia, there is rather an interesting review of Ali Bey's travels. The writer says, "Ali Bey has rectified various errors in the common maps of Marocco. The river Luccos, for instance, flows to the South, and not to the North of Alcasser; and the city of Fas, according to Ali Bey, is situated in 34° 6' north latitude, and not as laid down in the Maps of Arrowsmith, Rennell, Delille, Golberri, &c."--If, however, he had given himself the trouble to consult the map of West Barbary, in Jackson's Account of Marocco, &c. &c. (which is by far the most accurate extant, and whose geographical orthography has been adopted in all the best modern English maps,) he would have seen that Fas is in 34° north latitude; that the river Elkos, or Luccos, is described in that map, (which was published several years before Ali Bey's travels,) as running south of Alcasser.

In describing the funeral cry at Marocco, the editor, or reviewer, impresses his reader with an idea that this funeral cry is that of the Moors, whereas it is no such thing: it is the practice of the Jews only in West Barbary to cry "Ah! Ah!" and lacerate their faces with their finger [465] nails; after which they wash, drink brandy, and enjoy themselves.

The large sea in the interior of Africa, described by Ali Bey to be without any communication with the Ocean, had been described (*years before Ali Bey's travels were published*) by Jackson, in his Account of Marocco, &c. &c. third edition, p. 309, and called first by him *Bahar Sudan*, and represented as a sea having decked vessels on it. Mr. Park, in his Second Journey, calls this sea the Bahar Seafina, without, however, informing the public, or knowing, that the Bahar Sefeena is an Arabic expression implying a sea of ships, or a sea where ships are found; and the situation he places it in coincides exactly with Jackson's prior description. There are thus three concurrent testimonies of the situation of the Bahar Sudan, or Sea of Sudan, *first noticed by Jackson*, and since confirmed by Ali Bey and Park. [274]

Footnote 274: (return) There is an able discussion of this subject in the New Supplement to the Encyclopedia Britannica, article "Africa," p. 104, and 105.

El Hage Hamed El Wangary.

On the Negroes.

(TO THE EDITOR OF THE EUROPEAN MAGAZINE.)

Eton, 5th Dec. 1818.

Sir,

Many maintain that the Negroes are a docile and tractable race, and more easily to be governed than Europeans; others maintain, that [466] they are liars, thieves, vindictive, and a demoralised race. That they are vindictive, no one who is acquainted with their character will deny; but are not most barbarous and uncivilised nations the same? What are the Muhamedans and Pagans? The latter, who form nearly two-thirds of the population of the earth, are generally of the same character, and the vindictive character of the former is notorious.

Propagate among the Negroes the benign principles of the Christian doctrine, and they will gradually (as those principles are inculcated) become good subjects, and useful members of society. It is that religion which will bring forth their latent and social virtues--a religion, the moral principles of which are the admiration even of its enemies, the Muhamedans themselves: a religion which exalts the human character above the brutes, and brings forth its beauties as the brilliancy of the diamond is brought forth by the hand of the polisher.

Destroy their witchcraft and idolatry, and on their ruins inculcate the divine doctrines of Christ, and we shall soon see that they will possess sentiments that exalt the human character, and that nothing has contributed more to their mental degradation than the cruel treatment of their masters in the European colonies of the West.

Vasco De Gama.

[467]

Cursory Observations on Lieutenant-Colonel Fitzclarence's Journal of a Route across India, through Egypt, to England.

Eton, 7th May, 1819.

It is remarkable, that in proportion as our mass of information respecting the interior of Africa increases, the truth of Mr. James Grey Jackson's account of that country, in the appendix to his account of Marocco, &c. receives additional confirmation. Some literary sceptics have been so far prejudiced against this author's report as to doubt its veracity altogether; but let us see how far the interesting report of Lieut.-Colonel Fitzclarence, in his journal of a route across India, through Egypt, to England, lately published, corroborates Mr. Jackson's description of Timbuctoo, published so long since as 1809.

It is to be lamented, that Jackson's African orthography is not altogether adopted: with the superior and practical knowledge which he evidently possesses of the African Arabic language, it cannot, I presume, be doubted by the learned and impartial, that his orthography is correct; and, judging from what has already transpired, I do not hesitate to predict, that his African orthography, from an evidence of its accuracy, will, in a few years, be adopted throughout; although the learned world have been ten years in correcting *Tombuctoo* into *Timbuctoo*; the latter being Mr. Jackson's orthography [468] in his account of Marocco, Timbuctoo, &c. published in 1809.

The late account of Mr. Bowdich's mission to Ashantee has been the first to corroborate this author in this respect; and Lieut.-Colonel Fitzclarence has confirmed it with this additional observation, in his Journal of a Route, &c. page 493: "Upon enquiring about *Timbuctoo* the Hage laughed at our pronunciation, the name of the city being *Timbuctoo*." The next improvement in African geographical orthography, will probably be the conversion of Fez into *Fas* (for there is absolutely no more reason for calling it Fez than there has been for calling Timbuctoo, Timbuctoo), this word being spelled in Arabic with the letters *Fa, Alif*, and *Sin*, which cannot be converted into any other orthography but *Fas*; the same argument would hold with various other words spelled correctly by this author, an accurate elucidation of which might encroach too much upon your valuable pages. I shall therefore briefly state, that in page 480 of Colonel Fitzclarence's Journal, the name of the Moorish gentleman to whose care the sons of the Emperor of Marocco, Muley Soliman, were confided, is stated to be El Hadge Talib ben Jelow: this is incorrect orthography, there is no such name in the Arabic language as *Jelow*, it is a barbarism; ben Jelow signifies ben Jelule, and the proper name is *El Hage Taleb ben Jelule*.

Page 494. Behur Soldan is evidently another [469] barbarism or corruption of the Arabic words *Bahar Sudan: vide* Jackson's Account of Marocco, Timbuctoo, &c. page 309, published by Cadell and Davies.

It has been observed by an intelligent French writer, that "*Le pluspart des hommes mesurant leur foi par leur connoissance acquise croyent fort peu de choses*." In confirmation of this opinion, many intelligent men, at the time of the publication of Jackson's Account of Marocco, Timbuctoo, &c. doubted the existence of the *Heirie*, as described by him; but in proportion as our knowledge of Africa improves, we see that the truth of these wonders is confirmed: and Colonel Fitzclarence mentions one that travelled four days in one; but we should not be surprised to hear, before this century shall terminate, that an Englishman had travelled from Fas to Timbuctoo on a Heirie, accompanied by an accredited agent of the Emperor of Marocco, in ten or fifteen days!

It appears by this ingenious traveller's Journal of a Route, &c. page 493, that all religions are tolerated at Timbuctoo. This is a confirmation of what is reported by Jackson, in the Appendix annexed to his Account of Marocco, &c. page 300.

The fish in the river of Timbuctoo, the Neel El Abeed or Neel of Sudan, is described by Colonel Fitzclarence as resembling salmon: this is a corroboration of Jackson, who says, the [470] *shebbel* abound in the Neel of Sudan, and the shebbel is the African salmon. See appendix to Jackson's Account of Marocco, &c. page 306.

In page 494, Colonel Fitzclarence says, the Nile at Kabra is a quarter of a mile wide; Jackson says it is as wide as the Thames at London. See Appendix to Jackson's Marocco, &c. page 305.

In page 496 of the Colonel's narrative, an account is given of the rate of travelling through the Desert; which, allowing for an arbitrary difference, in the resting days, corroborates Jackson's Account, page 286.

In page 497, El hage Taleb ben Jelule's report to the Colonel, of an account of two white men, (undoubtedly Mungo Park and another,) who were at Timbuctoo in 1806, is a remarkable confirmation of the account brought by Mr. Jackson from Mogodor in January, 1807, and reported by him to the Marquis of Hastings, to Sir Joseph Banks, and to Sir Charles Morgan, which is inserted in the Morning Post and other papers, about the middle of August, 1814.

I am, Sir, Your most obedient servant,
VASCO DE GAMA

[471]

On the Arabic Language, as now spoken in Turkey in Europe, in Asia, and in Africa.

London, May 10, 1819.

In this enlightened age, when our intercourse is increasing with nations remote from our own, and possessing different religions, languages, laws, and customs; when the ambassadors of the Muhamedan potentates of Europe, Asia, and Africa, are resident in our metropolis, all understanding *the Arabic language*; when, with a knowledge of this language, a person may travel and hold colloquial intercourse with the inhabitants of Turkey, with the greater part of Asia, and with Africa; and, lastly, when we consider the valuable and immense stores of Arabian literature, of the best periods which still remain unexplored, is it not remarkable under all the exciting circumstances above enumerated, that in this powerful and opulent country, there should not be found, with all our boasted learning and eagerness of research, three or four Englishmen capable of writing and conversing intelligibly in that beautiful and useful language? The extent of this disgraceful ignorance would be scarcely credible, were there not proofs beyond doubt, that our principal seats of learning are as deficient in this knowledge as the public in general [275], and that [472] letters or public documents written in that language, have been in vain sent to them for translation. What I have long considered as chiefly tending to diminish the desire of acquiring this language, is an opinion dogmatically asserted, and diligently propagated, that the Arabic of the East and West are so different from each other, as almost to form distinct languages, and to be unintelligible to the inhabitants of either of those regions respectively; but, having always doubted the truth of this assertion, I have endeavoured, from time to time, *during the last ten years*, to ascertain whether the Arabic language spoken in Asia be the same with that which is spoken in Africa, (westward to the shores of the Atlantic ocean,) but without success, and even without the smallest satisfactory elucidation, until the arrival in London [473] last winter, of the most *Reverend Doctor Giarve, Bishop of Jerusalem*, who has given such incontestible proofs of his proficiency in the Arabic language, that his opinion on this important point cannot but be decisive; accordingly, on presenting to the reverend Doctor some letters from the Emperor of Marocco to me, desiring that he would oblige me with his opinion, whether the Arabic in those letters was the same with that spoken in Syria, the Rev. Doctor replied in the following perspicuous manner, which, I think, decides the question: *"I can assure you, that the language and the idiom of the Arabic in these letters from the Emperor of Marocco to you, is precisely the same with that which is spoken in the East."*

Footnote 275: (return) See page 408. respecting a letter sent to our late revered Sovereign, by the Emperor of Marocco. In consequence of the inattention to that letter, the Emperor determined never to write again to a Christian king in the Arabic language; and, with regard to Great Britain, I believe he has faithfully ever since kept his word! Some time before this letter was written, I being then in Marocco, the Emperor's minister asked me if the Emperor his master were to write an Arabic letter to the *Sultan George Sultan El Ingleez*, (these were his expressions,) whether there were persons capable of translating it into English: I replied, that there were men at the Universities capable of translating every learned language in the known world; and accordingly the letter above alluded to was written in Arabic, and addressed to His Majesty. This letter was written by the Emperor himself, which I am competent to declare, having letters from him in my possession, and being acquainted with his hand-writing and style.

It is, therefore, thus ascertained, that the Arabic language spoken in the kingdom of Tafilelt, of Fas, of Marocco, and in Suse or South Barbary, is precisely the same language with that which is now spoken in Syria, and Palestine in Asia; countries distant from each other nearly 3000 miles, and from information since obtained, there appears to be no doubt that the Arabic language spoken by the Arabs in Arabia, by the Moors and Arabs in India and Madagascar, by the Moorish nations on the African shores of the Mediterranean, are one and the same language with that spoken in Marocco, subject only to certain provincial peculiarities, which by no means form impediments to the general understanding of the language, [474] no more, or not so much so, as the provincial peculiarities of one county of England differ from another!!

Unwilling to encroach too much on your valuable pages, I will leave, for the subject of my next letter, the inconceivable misconstructions and errors into which the ignorance of this language has led European travellers in Africa, of which I shall state some examples in a recent publication respecting Africa.

I am, Sir,
Your most obedient Servant,
James G. Jackson.

Cursory Observations on the Geography of Africa, inserted in an Account of a Mission to Ashantee, by T. Edward Bowdich, Esq. showing the Errors that have been committed by European Travellers on that Continent, from their Ignorance of the Arabic Language, the learned and the general travelling Language of that interesting part of the World.

June 17, 1819.

The Niger, after leaving the lake Dibber, was invariably described as dividing in two large streams.--*Vide* "Bowdich's Account of a Mission to Ashantee," p. 187.

The Lake Dibber is called in the proceedings of the African Association Dibbie, but the proper appellation is *El Bahar Tibber,* or *El Bahar Dohebbie.* The Bahar Tibber signifies the sea of gold dust; the *Bahar Dehebbie* signifies the sea [475] or water abounding in gold. Jinnee, which is on or near the shore of this lake, (I call it a lake because it is fresh water,) abounds in gold, and is renowned throughout Africa for the ingenuity of its artificers in that metal, insomuch that they acknowledge the superiority of Europeans in all arts except that of gold work. There are some specimens of Jinnee gold trinkets, very correctly delineated in the recent interesting work of "Lieutenant-Colonel Fitzclarence's Journal of a Route across India, through Egypt to England," p. 496.

Page 187, "Yahoodie, a place of great trade."

This place is reported to be inhabited by one of the lost tribes of Israel, possibly an emigration from the tribe of Judah. Yahooda, in African Arabic, signifies Judah. Yahoodee signifies Jew. It is not impossible, that many of the lost tribes of Israel may be found dispersed in the interior regions of Africa, when we shall become better acquainted with that Continent; it is certain, that some of the nations that possessed the country eastward of Palestine when the Israelites were a favoured nation, have emigrated to Africa.

An emigration of the Amorites [276] are now in possession of the declivity of the Atlas Mountains, westward of the sanctuary [277] of Muley Driss, and in the neighbourhood of the ruins of Pharaoh; they live in encampments, consisting of [476] two, three, or four tents each: they resemble the Arabs of the Desert in their predatory excursions. I speak from practical knowledge, having twice travelled through their country, and visited their encampments.

Footnote 276: (return) They are called *Ite-amor*, Amorite.

Footnote 277: (return) *Vide* Jackson's Account of Marocco, chap. viii. enlarged edition.

Page 189. "Mr. Beaufoy's Moor says, that below Ghinea is the sea into which the river of Timbuctoo discharges itself."

This might have been understood to signify the Sea of Sudan, if the Moor had not said below Ghinea, (by which is meant Genowa, or as we call it Guinea,) which implies, that the *Neel El Abeed* (Niger) discharges itself in the sea that washes the coast of Guinea; this, therefore, corroborates Seedi Hamed's, or rather Richard's hypothesis.

Page 190. "This branch of the Niger passing Timbuctoo, is not crossed until the third day going from Timbuctoo to Houssa."

This quotation from "Dapper's Description of Africa," is corroborated by L'Hage Abdsalam, Shabeeni, whose narrative says, "Shabeeni, after staying three years at Timbuctoo, departed for Houssa, and crossing the small river close to the walls, reached the Neel in three days, travelling through a fine, populous, and cultivated country."

The confusion of rivers, made mere equivocal by every new hypothesis, receives here additional ambiguity. If there were (as Mr. Bowdich affirms) three distinct rivers near Timbuctoo; viz. the Joliba, the Gambarro, and the Niger, (*i.e.* [477] the *Neel El Abeed*) how comes it that they have not been noticed by Leo Africanus, who resided at Timbuctoo; by Edrissi, who is the most correct of the Arabian geographers; or whence is it, that these rivers have not been noticed by the many Moorish travelling merchants who have resided at Timbuctoo, and whom I have repeatedly questioned respecting this matter [278], or whence is it that Alkaid L'Hassen Ramy, a renowned chief of the Emperor of Marocco's army, with whom I was well acquainted, and who was a native of Houssa, knew of no such variously inclined streams. This being premised, I am certainly not disposed to relinquish the opinion I brought with me from Africa in the year 1807, viz. that the *Neel El Abeed* is the only mighty river that runs through Africa from west to east; but I admit that its adjuncts, as well as itself, have different names; thus, in the manuscript of Mr. Park's death, a copy of which is inserted in "Mr. Bowdich's Account of Ashantee," it is called Kude; many hundred miles eastward it is called Kulla, from the country through which it passes; but Kude and Kulla are different [478] names, and ought not to be confounded one with the other; neither ought Quolla (*i. e.*, the Negro pronunciation of Kulla) to be confounded with Kude, the former being the Negro term for the same river, in the same manner as Niger is the Roman name for the *Neel Elabeed*, which is the Arabic name for the same river. There is a stream which proceeds from the Sahara, the water of which is *brackish*; this stream hardly can be called a river, except in the rainy season. It passes in a south-westerly direction near Timbuctoo, but does not join the *Neel Elabeed*. I could mention several intelligent and credible authorities, the report of respectable merchants, who have resided, and, who have had establishments at Timbuctoo, in confirmation of this fact; but as the authorities which I should adduce would be unknown, even by name, to men of science in Europe, I would refer the reader to the interesting narrative of an intelligent Moorish merchant, who resided three years at Timbuctoo, and who was known to the committee of the African Association; this travelling merchant's name is L'Hage Abdsalam Shabeeny, and his narrative, a manuscript of which (with critical and explanatory notes by myself) I have in my possession, has the following observation: [279]--"Close to the town of Timbuctoo, on the south, is a small rivulet in which the inhabitants wash their clothes, and [479] which is about two feet deep; it runs into the great forest on the east, and does not communicate with the Nile, but is lost in the sands west of the town: its water is brackish; that of the Nile is good and pleasant."

Footnote 278: (return) The Arabs who conduct the *cafelahs* or caravans across the Sahara, are often seen at Agadeer or Santa Cruz, and sometimes even at Mogodor; and if there was a river penetrating to the north through the Sahara, would it not have been noticed by them? Is it possible that such a prominent feature of African geography, as a river of sweet water passing through a desert, could fail of being noticed by these people, who are, in their passage through the Desert, continually in search of water?

Footnote 279: (return) See page 8.

Page 199. Mr. Murray recently observes, "Joliba seems readily convertible into Joli-ba, the latter syllable being merely an adjunct, signifying river; this I was also given to understand."

This is an etymological error. The Joliba is not a compound word, if it were it would be Bahar Joli, not Bajoli, or Joliba; thus do learned men, through a rage for criticism, and for want of a due knowledge of African languages, render confused, by fancied etymologies, that which is sufficiently clear and perspicuous.

Page 191. "The river of Darkulla mentioned by Mr. Brown."

This is evidently an error: there is probably no such place or country as Darkulla. There is, however, an alluvial country denominated *Bahar Kulla*, (for which see the map of Africa in the Supplement of the Encyclopaedia Britannica, p. 88. lat. N. 8°, long. E. 20°). I apprehend this Darkulla, when the nations of Europe shall be better acquainted with Africa and its languages, will be discovered to be a corruption of *Bahar Kulla*, or an unintelligible and ungrammatical term: *Dëaar Kulla* is grammatical, and implies a country covered with houses! *Dar Kulla* is an ungrammatical and an incorrect term, which being [480] literally translated into English, signifies *many house*. This being premised, we may reasonably suppose, that *Bahar Kulla* is the proper term which, as I have always understood, forms the junction of the Nile of the west with the Nile of the east, and hence forming a continuity [280] of waters from Timbuctoo to Cairo.

Footnote 280: (return) See my letter in the Monthly Magazine for March, 1817, page 128.

191. In this geographical dissertation the word Niger is still used, which is a name altogether unknown in Africa, and calculated to contuse the geographical enquirer. As this word is unintelligible to the natives of Africa, whether they be Arabs, Moors, Berebbers, Shelluhs, or Negroes, ought it not to be expunged from the maps?

P. 192. In the note in this page, "Jackson's Report of the source of the *Neel el Abeed*, and the Source of the Senegal," is confirmed by the Jinnee Moor.--See Jackson's Appendix to his Account of Marocco, enlarged edition, p. 311.

"It is said, that thirty days from Timbuctoo they eat their prisoners!" Does not this allude to Banbugr [281], and has not this word been corrupted by Europeans into Bambarra. See Mr. [481] Bowdich's MS. No. 3, p. 486; Banbugr, who eat the flesh of men. Jackson's translation.

Footnote 281: (return) The Gr in Banbugr, is the Arabic letter, grain. Richardson, in his Arabic Grammar, renders this letter gh; which demonstrates, that his knowledge of the Arabic was only scholastic, not practical. It has no resemblance or affinity to gh, and would be unintelligible if so pronounced to an Arab.

Page 193. The government of Jinnee appears to be Moorish; because *Malai Smaera*, which should be written *Mulai Smaera*, signifies in the Arabic language, the *Prince Smaera*: the term does not belong to Negroes, but exclusively to Muhamedans. *Malai Bacharoo* is a Negro corruption of the word; it should be *Mulai*, or *Muley Bukaree*; i.e. the *Abeed Mulai Bukaree*, or *Abeed Seedi Bukaree*. They are well known among the Negroes of Sudan; the Negroes of this race form the present body-guard of the Emperor of Maroceo's troops, consisting of 5000 horse. They are dexterous in the management of the horse, are well-disciplined troops, and are the only military in the Emperor's army that can cope with the Berebbers of the Atlas.

Note, p. 194. Dapper's description of Africa is here quoted in confirmation of the decay of Timbuctoo; and Jackson is accused of extravagance. The latter I shall pass over, it being an assertion unsupported by any substantial testimony; but immediately afterwards is the following passage.

"The three last kings before Billa (*i.e. Billabahada*) were Osamana, (*i.e.* Osaman; Osamana being the feminine gender,) Dawoloo, and Abass. Mr. Jackson says there was a King Woolo reigning in 1800; and a Moor who had come from Timbuctoo to Comassee ten years ago (viz. about 1807, or ten years before Mr. Bowdich [482] visited Ashantee), did not know King Woolo was dead, as he was reigning at the time he left Timbuctoo."

With regard to Dapper's assertion, it should be remembered, that if Timbuctoo was decaying in his time, that is about the period that Muley Ismael ascended the throne of Marocco, viz. in 1672; it revived very soon after, that is before the close of the 17th century. This powerful and warlike prince had the address to establish and to maintain a very strong garrison at Timbuctoo; and accordingly, during his long reign of fifty-five years, viz. from 1672 to 1727, Timbuctoo carried on a constant, extensive, and lucrative trade with Marocco, Tafilelt, and Fas, in gold dust, gum-sudan, ostrich-feathers, ivory, and slaves, &c. *Akkabahs* [282], and *cafilahs*, or caravans, were going continually from Timbuctoo to Tafilelt, Marocco, Fas, and Terodant. Travelling across the Desert was then as safe as it is now in the plains of Marocco, or on the roads in England; the only months during which the caravans did not travel were July and August, because the *Shûme*, or hot wind of the Desert, prevails during these two months. It is reported, that Muley Ismael was so rich in gold, that the bolts of the gates of his palaces, and his kitchen utensils, were of pure gold. Timbuctoo continued to carry on a most lucrative trade with [483] Marocco, &c.; during the Feign of the Emperor Muley Abd Allah, son and successor of Ismael, and also during the reign of Seedy [283] Muhamed ben Abd Allah, who died about the year 1795, a sovereign universally regretted, and hence aptly denominated the father of his people: since the decease of Seedy [284] Muhamed ben Abd Allah, the father of the reigning emperor, Muley Soliman, the trade of Sudan has rapidly decreased, because the policy of the present emperor is, to discourage commerce, but to encourage the agriculture and the manufactures of his own country, so as to make them sufficient for itself, and independent of foreign supplies!

Footnote 282: (return) An Akkabah is an accumulation of many *cafilahs* or caravans.

Footnote 283: (return) It should be observed, that an emperor having the name of the Arabian prophet, is called Seedy; but having any other name, he is called Muley; the former signifies master, the latter, prince.

Footnote 284: (return) If therefore the trade with Timbuctoo declined in Leo's time, *i.e.* A.D. 1570, it unquestionably revived in Ismael's reign, and also continued with but little diminution during the reign of his son Abd Allah, and his grandson Muhamed.

Da Woolo is a reverential term, and is synonymous with Woolo, signifying King Woolo.

Park says, Mansong was king of Timbuctoo [484] in 1796, and in 1805, implying that he reigned from 1796 to 1805. The Moor before mentioned, who came from Timbuctoo to Comassie in 1807, told Mr. Bowdich, that Woolo was then reigning at Timbuctoo. Isaaco says, Woolo was predecessor to Mansong; consequently, according to this Jew, Woolo was king before the year 1796; therefore, if Mr. Park's testimony be correct, Woolo must have been predecessor and successor to Mansong; otherwise, Mr. Park was incorrect in saying that Mansong was king of Timbuctoo in 1796, and in 1805. Adams says, Woolo was king of Timbuctoo in 1810, and was old and grey-headed. Riley's narrative also confirms his age and grey hairs. With regard to my testimony, viz. that Woolo was king [285] of Timbuctoo in 1800, I had it from two merchants of veracity, who returned from Timbuctoo in 1800, after residing there 14 years: they are both alive now, and reside at Fas; their names I would mention, were I not apprehensive that it might lead to a reprimand from the emperor, and create jealousy for having communicated intelligence respecting the interior of the country. I should not have entered into this detail *in confirmation of my assertion that Woolo was king of Timbuctoo in* 1800, if the editor of the Supplement to the Encyclopedia Britannica (article Africa), had not asserted, that I have committed an anachronism in asserting, that he was king in that year; thereby insinuating that Park was right, and that I was wrong.

Footnote 285: (return) See my Letter on the Interior of Africa, in the Anti-Jacobin Review for January, 1818, p. 453.

[485]

Page 195. The Editor of Adams's Narrative is, I apprehend, incorrect in asserting, that the name Fatima affords no proof that the queen, or the wife of Woolo, was a Muhamedan. Fatima

is incontestably an Arabian proper name; and it would be considered presumption in a Negress unconverted to Muselmism, to assume the name of Fatima. She must, therefore, have been necessarily a Mooress, or a converted Negress; the name has nothing to do with a numeral, as Mr. Bowdich suggests, and above all not with the *numeral five*, for that is a number ominous of evil in Africa, and as such, would never have been bestowed as a name on a beloved wife.

Page 196. Note of W. Hutchison, "The four greatest monarchs known on the banks of the Quolla, are Baharnoo, Santambool, Malisimiel, and Malla, or Mallowa."

Baharnoo should be written *Ber Noh*; i.e. the country of Noah the patriarch; it is called in the maps Bernoo, and the whole passage is calculated greatly to confuse African geography. The information is unquestionably derived from Negro authority, and that not of the most authentic kind. Santambool is the Negro corruption of *Strambool*, which is the Arabic name for Constantinople: *Malisimiel* is the Negro corruption of Muley Ismael. [286] The first signifies the empire of Constantinople; the second signifies the empire of Muley Ismael, who was emperor of Marocco in the early part of the 18th century, and whose authority was acknowledged at Timbuctoo, where he maintained a [486] strong garrison, and held the adjacent country in subjection, where his name is held in reverence to this day. This being premised, it follows of course, that one of these four great monarchies here alluded to, viz. that of Santambool is certainly not on the Quolla, unless the Quolla be considered the same river with the Egyptian Nile, and that Egypt be considered a part of the empire of Santambool; then, and then only, can it be said, that the empire of Santambool is situated on the Quolla.

Footnote 286: (return) See Jackson's Marocco, chap. xiii. p. 295, and note, p. 296.

Page 198. Two large lakes were described close to the northward of Houssa; one called Balahar Sudan, and the other Girrigi Maragasee; the first of these names is a Negro corruption, or an European corruption of the term *Bahar Sudan* [287]; the other is a Negro name of another, if not of the same lake or sea. The situation of the *Bahar Sudan* is described by me in the 13th chapter, in my account of Marocco, to be fifteen journeys east of Timbuctoo, and the *Neel El Abeed* passes through it. I had this information from no less than seven Moorish merchants of intelligence and veracity; the same is confirmed by Ali Bey [288], the Shereef Imhammed, Park, and Dr. Seitzen; all these authorities must therefore fall to the ground if Mr. Bowdich's report is to overturn these testimonies, [487] which has placed it three degrees of latitude north of the *Neel El Abeed*, or [289]*Neel Assudan*, and in the Sahara [290], *unconnected with any river*! I doubt if any, but a very ignorant Pagan Negro (for the Muhamedan Negroes are more intelligent), would have given the Sea of Sudan this novel situation.

Footnote 287: (return) See Jackson's Marocco, chap. xiii.

Footnote 288: (return) For an elucidation of these opinions, see my Letter on the Interior of Africa, in the European Magazine, Feb. 1818, page 113.

Footnote 289: (return) Neel Sudan and Neel Assudan are synonymous, the *as* being the article.

Footnote 290: (return) See Mr. Bowdich's Map, in his Account of a Mission to Ashantee.

Page 200. The Quolla appears to be the Negro pronunciation of the Arabic name *Kulla*; i.e. the *Bahar Kulla*, to which the *Neel Assudan* is said to flow. *Bahar Kulla* is an Arabic word signifying the sea altogether, or an alluvial country. The *Neel Assudan* here joins the waters of a river that proceed westward from the Abysinian Nile, and hence is formed the water communication between Cairo [291] and Timbuctoo.

Footnote 291: (return) See Jackson's Account of Marocco, enlarged edition, p. 313. See also his Letter to the Editor of the Monthly Magazine for March, 1817. p. 125.

Page 201. Quolla Raba, or Kulla Raba, signifies the Kulla forest, as the Negroes express it; the Arabs call it *Raba Kulla*, i.e. the forest of *Kulla*, If any further proof of the accuracy of this interpretation be necessary, it maybe added, that the position agrees exactly with Major Rennell's kingdom of *Kulla*, for which see the Major's map in proceedings of the African Association, vol. i. page 209, lat. N. 9°, long. W. 10°. [488]

Page 203. The lake Fittri is a lake, the waters of which are said to be filtered through the earth, as the name implies. The Nile is here said to run under ground. The Arabs and Moors have a tradition, that the waters of Noah's flood rested here, and were absorbed and filtered through the earth, leaving only this large lake. I never understood this sea to be identified with the *Bahar Heimed* [292]; i.e. the Hot or Warm Sea. The Hot Sea and the Filtered Sea are distinct waters; the former lies about mid-way, in a right line between Lake Fittri and Lake Dwi. (See Laurie and Whittle's Map of Africa, published in 1813.) This is another inaccuracy of Mr. Hutchison; who appears, indeed, to have collected information from natives, without considering what title they had to credibility. Another error is added to the note in page 203 and 204, viz. what he calls sweet beans are unquestionably dates, which have not the least affinity in taste, shape, growth, or quality, to beans. The Arabic name correctly converted into European letters, is *timmer*, not *tummer*. The Arabic words designating sweet beans, is *Elfool El Hellue*. The passage signed William Hutchison here alluded to, is this: "The Arabs eat black rice, corn, and *sweet beans called tummer*."

Footnote 292: (return) *Heimed* is an Arabic term, signifying that degree of heat which milk has when coming from the cow or goat.

Note, page 204. I do not know whence the Quarterly Review has derived its information [489] respecting the derivation of the word Misr (a corruption of Massar); the word Massar is compounded of the two Arabic words Ma and Sar; i.e. Mother of Walls. Possibly some Arabic professor versed in bibliographic lore, to favor a darling hypothesis, has transmuted Massar into Misr, to strengthen the plausibility of the etymology of Misr from Misraem!!

Note, page *205. Bahar bela ma* is an Arabic expression, importing it to be a country once covered with water, but now no longer so. In the note in this page, I recognise the word Sooess to designate the Isthmus of Suez. The Bahar Malee, and the Sebaha Bahoori, are Negro corruptions of the Arabic words *Bahar El Maleh*, and *Seba Baharet*: the former does not apply particularly to the Mediterranean, but *is a term applicable to any sea or ocean that is salt* (as all seas and oceans assuredly are); the latter term signifies literally, the Seven Seas or Waters: neither is this a term applicable to the Mediterranean, but to any sea supplied by seven rivers, as the Red Sea: these, therefore, are evidently other inaccuracies of Mr. Hutchison. I apprehend Mr. Hutchison's Arabic tutor at Ashantee was not an erudite scholar. The term, and the only term in Africa, applicable to the Mediterranean Sea, is the *Bahar Segrer* (literally the Small Sea); and *El Bahar El Kabeer* (is the Atlantic Ocean, or literally the Great Sea); the latter is sometimes figuratively called the *Bahar Addolum*, i.e. the Unknown Sea, or the Sea of Darkness. [490]

Note, p. 206. Is it possible that the author doubts that Wangara is east of Timbuctoo? It should seem that he did, as he quotes Mr. Hutchison as authority for making it to contain Kong, a mountainous district many journeys south of the *Neel Assudan*. Mr. Park's testimony is also called in support of this opinion, but they are both erroneous. Wangara is as well known in Africa to be east of Timbuqtoo, as in England York is known to be North of of London.

Oongooroo is a barbarous Negro corruption of Wangara; therefore, this note, if suffered to pass through the press unnoticed, would be calculated to confuse, not to elucidate, African geography; neither can it be called, according to Mr. Horneman's orthography, Ungura: the name is *Wangara* which cannot be converted accurately into any word *but* Wangara. Ungura Oongooroo, &c. are corruptions of the proper name, originating in an imperfect, and but an oral knowledge of the African Arabic.

Page 210. I apprehend the reason why Wassenah was not known at Ashantee by the traders, is because it was out of their trading track. I have no doubt of the existence of Wassenah or Massenah (for when the names of African towns and countries are recorded, we should not be particular about a letter or two, when we find so many orthographical variations are made by different authors); neither is there any reason (that I know of) to doubt the description of [491] Wassenah given in Riley's Narrative; but it is not extraordinary, that this place should be unknown at Ashantee, if there were no commerce or communication between these countries respectively; it is certain, that the Africans neither know, seek, or care, for places or countries with which they have no trade or communication.

It appears well deserving of observation (for the purpose of rendering Arabic names intelligible to future African travellers), that Mr. Bowdich has demonstrated that, what is called in our maps, 1. Bambarra, 2. Gimbala, 3. Sego, 4. Berghoo, 5. Begarmee, being written in the Arabic language, with the guttural letter *grain*, would be quite unintelligible, if pronounced to an African *as they are written* by our letters, the nearest approximation to the Arabic words would be as follows, taking *Gr* for the nearest similitude that our alphabet affords to the guttural letter [Arabic غ] *grain*.

Correct Pronunciation. African Orthography. Called in the Maps.

1. Banbug'r	بَنبغ	Bambara.
2. Grimbala	غـمبَل	Gimbala.
3. Shagr'u	شاغّ	Sego.
4. Bergr'u	برغوأ	Berghoo.
5. Bagrarmee	باغرِم	Begarmee.

[492]

The African traveller should be precise in his attention to the sound of these words, otherwise he will be quite unintelligible to the Africans, and to the Muhamedans.

Richardson, in his Arabic Grammar, is certainly incorrect, when he says, the letter غ *grain* should be pronounced *gh*. No one acquainted *practically* with the Arabic language, could possibly be of this opinion; *gh* having no more resemblance to the sound of the letter غ *grain*, than *g* has to *h*: and every traveller going to Africa with this erroneous opinion, will, undoubtedly, be unintelligible to the Africans.

Finally, the Arabic document, if it may be permitted to call it Arabic, facing page 128 of this interesting work of Mr. Bowdich, is a most miserable composition of *Lingua franca*, or corrupt Spanish, of unintelligible jargon, consisting of many words quite unintelligible to the Africans, whether Negroes or Moors, or others. The language of this document, although it has some Arabic words in it, is worse, if possible, than the scrawl in which it is written; neither is it a correct translation of the English which precedes it. But purporting to be a letter issued from the *accredited servants of the King of the English*, it is certainly a disgrace to the country from whence it issues, and a rare specimen of our knowledge of the Arabic language.

James Grey Jackson.

[493]

Commercial Intercourse with the Interior of Africa.

TO THE EDITOR OF THE JOURNAL OF TRADE, &c.

Eton, June 30, 1818.

Sir,

The last expedition from Sierra Leone, in addition to many others sent out for the purpose of *exploring the interior of Africa*, having failed, and the enterprising and persevering Mr. Burckhardt, having frustrated the well grounded hopes of the African Association, by his having paid the debt of nature, it is not improbable that His Majesty's government *will now direct their attention with energy to the only plan that can possibly make that interesting and extraordinary country a jewel in the British crown.*

This important discovery, which would immortalise the prince, who should cherish it to its maturity, *can be effected only through the medium of commerce.* But it should be attempted not only with energy and decision, but with *dispatch*, before the enterprising and commercial spirit of a foreign power (seeing how abortive our efforts have been), shall snatch from us the glorious opportunity now offered of *laying open the interior regions of Africa* to the commercial enterprise of Great Britain.

I am, Sir,
Your most obedient servant,
Vasco de Gama.

[494]

The following curious Memoir was composed by Edmund Hogan, in the reign of Queen Elizabeth, and lately found amongst the papers of one of his descendants.

(A TRUE COPY.)

"The Embassage of Mr. Edmund Hogan, one of the Sworne Esquires of her Ma't's Person, from her Highnesse to Muley Abdelmelech, Emperour of Morocco, and King of Fes and Sus, in the Yeare 1577. Written by himselfe.

"I Edmund Hogan, being appointed Embassadour from the Queens Ma'tie to the above-named Emperour and King Muley Abdelmelech, departed with my company and servants from London the 22d April, 1577, being imbarked in the good ship called the Gallion, of London, and arrived in Azafi, a port of Barbary, the 21st of May next following. Immediately I sent Leonell Egerton ashoare with my letters directed to John Williams and John Bampton, who dispatched a courier to Morocco to know the Kings pleasure for my repaire to the court, which letters came to theire hands on the Thursday night. They with all speed gave the King understanding of it, who being glad thereof, speeded the next day certaine captaines, with souldiera and tents, with other provision, to Azafi; so that upon Whitsunday at night, the said captaines, with John Bampton, Robert [495] Washborne, and Robert Lion, and the Kings officers, came late to Azafi. In the meane time I remained aboard, and caused some of the goods to be discharged, for lightning of the ship; and I wrote in my letter that I would not lande 'till I knew the Kings pleasure. The 26th day, being Saturday, the Mark-speed arrived in the roade about two of the clock in the afternoone. The 27th day, being Whitsunday, came aboard the Gallion, John Bampton, and others, giving me to understand how much the King rejoyced of my safe arrivall, coming from the Queens Ma'tie; and how that for my safe conduct to the court he had sent four captaines, and an hundred souldiers well appointed, with a horse furnished, which he used himself to ride on, with all other furniture accordingly; they wished me also to come on land in the best order I could, as well for my self as my men, which I did, having to the number of ten men, whereof three were trumpeters. The ships being four, appointed themselves in the best order they could, for the best shew, and shott off all theire ordinance to the value of twenty marks in powder. At my coming, ashoare, I found all the souldiers well appointed on horseback, the captaines and the Govern'r of the towne standing as neer the water side as they could, with a jennet of the Kings, and rec'd me from the boate, declaring how glad his Ma'tie was of my safe arrivall, coming from the Queens Ma'tie my Mistresse, and that he had sent them [496] to attend upon me, it being his pleasure that I should tarrie there on shoare five or six dayes for my refreshing; so being mounted upon the jennet, they conducted me through the towne into a faire fielde upon the sea side, where there was a tent provided for me, and all the ground spread with Turkie carpets, and the castle discharged a peale of ordinance, and all things necessarie were brought into my tent, where I both tooke my table and lodging, and had other convenient tents for my servants. The souldiers inviron'd the tents, and watched about us day and night as long as I lay there, altho' I sought my speedier dispatch. On the Wednesday towards night, I tooke my horse, and travelled ten miles to the first place of water that wee could finde, and there pitched our tents 'till the next morning, and so traveled till ten of the clock, and then pitched our tents 'till four, and so traveled as long as day light would suffer, about twenty-six miles that day. The next day being Fryday, I traveled in like order but eight and twenty miles at the most; and by a [293]river, being about six miles within sight of the Citty of Morocco, wee pitched bur tents. Imediately after came all our English Merchants, and the French, on horseback, to meete me; and before night there came an Alcayde from the King with fiftie men, and divers mules laden with victuall and banket for my supper, declaring [497] unto me how glad the King shewed himselfe to hear of the Queens Ma'tie, and that his pleasure was I should be received into his countrey as never any Christian the like; and desired to know what time the next day I would come into his Citie, because he would that all the Christians, as also his Nobilitie, should meete me; and willed John Bampton to be with him early in the morning, which he did. About seven of the clock, being accompanied with the French and English Merchants, and a great number of souldiers, I passed towards the Citie, and by that time I had traveled two miles, there met me all the Christians of the Spaniards and Portugals to receive me, which I know was more by the Kings commandment then of any good wills of themselves; for some of them, although they speake me faire, hung downe theire heads like dogs, and especially the Portugals; and I countenanced them accordingly. So I passed on, 'till I came within two English miles of the Citie; and then John Bampton returned, shewing me that the King was so glad of my coming, that he could not devise to doe too much, to shew the good will that he did owe to the Queens Ma'tie and her Realme; His counsellors met me without the gates; and at the entrie of the gates, his footmen and guard were placed on both sides of my horse, and so brought me to the King's palace. The King sate in his chaire, with his Counsell about him, as well the Moores as the Alkaids; and, according [498] to his order given unto me before, I there declared my message in Spanish, and made deliverie of the Queens Ma't's letters, and all that I spake at that present in Spanish, he caused one of his Alkaids to declare the same to the Moores present in the Arabic tongue; which done, he answered me againe in Spanish, yeelding to the Queens Ma'tie great thankes, and offering himselfe and his countrey to be at her Graces comandment; and he comanded certaine of his counsellors to conduct me to my lodging, not being farr from the Court. The house was faire, after the fashion of that countrey, being dayly well furnished with all kinde of victuall at the Kings charge. The same night he sent for me to the court, and I had conference with him about the space of two houres; where I throughly declared the charge co'mitted unto me from her Ma'tie, finding him conformable, willing to pleasure, and not to urge her Ma'tie with any demands, more then conveniently she might willingly consent unto, hee knowing that out of his countrey the Realme of England might be better served with lackes, then he in comparison from us. Further, he gave me to understand, that the King of Spain had sent unto him for a licence that an Embassadour of his might come into his countrey, and had made great meanes, that if the Queens Ma'tie of England sent any unto him, that he would not give him any credit or entertainment; albeit (said he) I know what the King of Spaine, [499] and what the Queene of England and her realme is; for I neither like of him, nor of his religion, being so governed by the Inquisition, that he can doe nothing of himselfe. Therefore, when he cometh upon the licence which I have granted, he shall well see how little account I will make of him and Spaine, and how greatly I will extoll you for the Queenes Ma'tie of England; he shall not come to my presence as you have done, and shall dayly, for I minde to accept of you as my companion, and one of my house, whereas he shall attend twentie dayes after he hath done his message. After the end of this speech, I delivered Sir Thomas Gresham's letters; when as he tooke me by the hand, and led me downe a long court to a palace, where there ranne a faire fountaine of water, and there sitting himselfe in a chaire, he comanded me to sitt downe in another, and there called for such simple musicians as he had. Then I presented him with a greate base lute, which he most thankfully accepted, and then he was desirous to hear of the musicians; and I tolde him, that there was great care had to provide them, and that I did not doubt but upon my returne they should come with the first ship. He is willing to give them good entertainment, with provision of victuall, and to let them live according to theire law and conscience, wherein he urgeth none to the contrary. I finde him to be one that liveth greatly in the fear of God, being well exercised in the [500] Scriptures, as well in the Old Testament, as also in the New, and he beareth a greater affection to our nation then to others, because of our religion, which forbiddeth worship of idols; and the Moores called him the Christian King. The same night, being the first of June, I continued with him till twelve of the clock, and he seemed to have so good likeing of me, that he tooke from his girdle a short dagger, being sett with 200 stones rubies and Turkies, and did bestowe it upon me; and so I, being conducted, returned to my lodging for that time. The next day, because he knew it to be Sunday, and our Sabboth day, he did let me rest; but on the Monday in the afternoone he sent for me, and I had conference with him againe, and musick. Likewise on the Tuesday, by three of the clock, he sent for me into his garden, finding him layed upon a silk bed, complaining of a sore leg; yet, after long conference, he walked into another orchard, whereas having a fair banketing house, and a great water, and a new gallie in it, he went aboard the gallie, and tooke me with him, and passed the space of two or three houres, shewing the great experience he had in gallies, wherein (as he said) he had exercised himselfe eighteene yeares in his youth. After supper he shewed me his horses, and other co'modities that he had about his house; and since that night I have not seene him, for that he hath kept in with his sore legg; but he hath sent to me dayly. The 18th of June, at [501] six of the clock at night, I had againe audience of the King, and I continued with him, till midnight, having debated, as well for the Queenes co'mission, as for the well-dealing with her merchants for their traffick here in these parts, saying, he would do much more for the Queenes Ma'tie and the Realme; offering that all English ships with her subjects may with good securitie enter into his ports and dominions, as well in trade of merchandize, as for victuall and water, as also in time of warr with any of her enemies, to bring in prizes, and to make sales as occasion should serve, or else to depart againe with them at theire pleasure. Likewise for all English ships that shall passe along his Coast of Barbary, and threw the Streights into the Levant seas, and so to the Turks dominions, and the King of Algiers, as his owne; and that he would write to the Turke, and to the King of Algiers, his letters for the well using of our ships and goods. Also, that hereafter no Englishman that by any meanes may be taken captives, shall be sold within any of his dominions; whereupon I declared that the Queenes Ma'tie, accepting of these his offers, was pleased to confirme the intercourse and trade of our Merchants within this his countrey, as also to pleasure him with such commodities as he should have need of, to furnish the necessities and wants of his country in trade of merchandize, so as he required nothing contrary to her honour and law, and the breach of league with the Christian Princes [502] her neighbours. The same night I presented the King with the case of combes, and desired his Ma'tie to have speciall regard that the ships might be Iaden back againe, for that I found little store of salt-peter in readinesse in John Bampton's hands; he answered me, that I should have all the assistance therein that he could, but that in [294] Sus he thought to have some store in his house there, as also that the Mountainers had made much in a readinesse; I requested that he would sende downe, which he promised to doe. The eighteenth day I was with him againe, and so continued there till night; and he shewed me his house, with pastime in ducking with water spaniels, and baiting bulls with his English doggs. At this time I moved him againe for the sending downe to Sus, which he granted to doe; and the 24th day there departed Alcayde Mammie, with Lionell Egerton, and Rowland Guy, to Sus; and carried with them, for our accounts and his company, the Kings letters to his brother Muly Hammet, and Alcayde Shavan, and the Viceroy. The 23d day the King sent me out of Morocco to his garden called Shersbonare, with his guard and Alcayde Mamoute; and the 24th at night I came to the Court to see a Morris-dance, and a play of his Alkaids; he promised me audience the next day, being Tuesday, but he putt it off [503] 'till Thursday; and the Thursday at night I was sent for to the King after supper, and then he sent Alcayde Rodwan and Alcayde

Gowry to conferr with me; but, after a little talk, I desired to be brought to the King for my dispatch. And being brought to him,. I preferred two bills of John Bampton's, which he had made for provision of salt-peter, also two bills for the quiet traffique of our English Merchants, and bills for sugars to be made by the Jewes, as well for the debts past, as hereafter, and for good order in the Ingenios. Also I moved him againe for the salt-peter, and other dispatches, which he referred to be agreed upon by the two Alcaydes. But the Fryday, being the 20th, the Alcaydes could not intend it, and upon Saturday Alcayde Rodwan fell sick; so on Sunday wee made meanes to the King, and that afternoone I was sent for to conferre upon the bargaine with the Alcaydes and others; but did not agree. Upon Tuesday I wrote a letter to the King for my dispatch; and the same afternoone I was called againe to the Court, and referred all things to the King, accepting his offer of salt-peter. That night againe the King had me into his gallie, and the spaniels did hunt the duck. The Thursday I was appointed to weigh the 300 quintals grosse of salt-peter,, and that afternoone the Tabybe came unto me to my lodging, shewing me that the King was offended with John Bampton for divers causes. The Sunday night late, being the 7th July, I got the King [504] to forgive all to John Bampton, and the King promised me to speake againe with me upon Monday. Upon Tuesday I wrote to him againe for my dispatch, and then he sent Fray Lewes to me, and said, that he had order to write. Upon Wednesday I wrote againe; and he sent me word that I should come and be dispatched, so that I should depart upon Fryday without faile, being the 12th July. So the Fryday after, according to the Kings order and appointment, I went to the Court; and whereas motion and petition was made for the confirmac'on of the demands which I had preferred, they were all granted, and likewise which were on the behalfe of our English Merchants requested, were with great favour and readinesse yeilded unto. And whereas the Jewes there resident, were to our men in certaine round sum'es indebted, the Emperor's pleasure and co'mandment was, that they should without further excuse or delay pay and discharge the same. And thus at length I was dismissed with great honour and speciall countenance, such as hath not ordinarily bene shewed to other Embassadors of the Christians. And touching the private affairs intreated upon betwixt her Ma'tie and the Emperour, I had letters from him to satisfie her Highnesse therein. So to conclude, having received the like honourable conduct from his Court, as I had for my part at my first landing, I imbarked myself with my foresaid company; and arriving not long after [505] in England, I repaired to her Ma'ties Court, and ended my embassage to her Highnesses good liking, with relation of my service performed."

Footnote 293: (return) The Tensift.

Footnote 294: (return) Great quantities of superior saltpetre are produced at Terodant in Suse.

Letter from the Author to Macvey Napier, Esq. F.R.S.L. and E.

Sir, London, 17th January, 1818.

Having read, with considerable satisfaction, your very able and judicious dissertation respecting Africa, in the new Supplement to the Encyclopedia Britannica, I will take the liberty to offer some animadversions that have occurred to me in the perusal of that very interesting article.

Bahr Kûlla I conceive to be an immerged country, of considerable extent, similar to Wangara; for the name, which is Arabic, implies as much. The correct orthography, translated literally into English is *Bahr Kûlha*, which signifies the sea, wholly or altogether, implying, therefore, an alluvial country.

Respecting goat-skins dyed red or yellow, these are not brought by caravans from central Africa to Marocco, but are manufactured at Marocco, Fas, Mequinas, and Terodant the metropolis of Suse, from which manufactories they are conveyed to the interior regions for sale. Goat-skins, with the hair, in the raw state only, are exported from Mogodor to England. [506]

When Moore asserted that there was no such river as the Niger, he evidently meant that the *natives of Africa* knew it not by that name; which is undoubtedly correct; for the word being an European word, it would not be known in Africa: but its translation into Arabic is *Bahar El Abeed*, i. e. the river of Negroes. Edrissi called it Niger, from the same motive, viz. because it was so named by *Europeans*, and by them only.

I conceive that the hypothesis which has been credited by some, viz. that there is no receptacle for the two Niles, between Cashna and Timbuctoo, must now necessarily fall to the ground; since the sea of Sudan, first declared by me to be between Cashna and Timbuctoo, and since confirmed by Ali Bey, and by Park, in his second journey, can (as I apprehend) no longer be doubted: and it is not improbable that this is the common receptacle of the Nile of the West and the Nile of the East. This hypothesis is strengthened by the testimony of the Shereef Imhammed, who has said, that he himself saw the Nile, at Cashna, flowing so rapidly westward, that vessels could not stem the current. If this be true, the [295]*Ba Sea Feena* of Park, which is only another name for the *Sea of Sudan*, must lie west of Cashna, and, probably, about the same point that it is stated by me to [507] be situated, viz. fifteen journeys of horse-travelling, or from 400 to 450 British miles east of Timbuctoo.

Footnote 295: (return) The Arabic orthography is *Bahar S'feena* which being literally translated into English, signifies the Sea of Ships.

The word *Djinawa* is the African word that denominates Guinea, but I cannot imagine that it was ever intended to signify Gana. (See Supplement to Encyclopædia Britannica, p. 104.)

You say there are, in Africa, two rivers to which the name of *Niger* has been given: this is evidently an error, but possibly of the press only. There are, however, two rivers in Africa to which the name of *Neel* has been given.

The Proceedings of the African Association, vol. i. p. 540, declare that the Nile is a name applied in Africa to any great river; but as this assertion is calculated to produce confusion in the geographical elucidation of the interior of that continent, and as it certainly is not the fact, I must here beg leave to contradict it, and declare that there are absolutely but two rivers in Africa, that bear the name Neel or Nile, viz. the Neel El Kabeer, Neele Sudan, or Neel El Abeed, i.e. the great Nile, the Nile of Sudan or the Nile of the Negroes; and Neele Masser, i.e. the Nile of Egypt. [296]

Footnote 296: (return) *Nile* is a French term, and loses its proper pronunciation and is unintelligible when pronounced by an Englishman to an African; but if written *Neel*, and pronounced by an Englishman, it is intelligible.

If my knowledge of the African Arabic can be of any service in giving you the signification or correct orthography of African [508] words, in the event of your favouring the public with a future edition of your New Supplement to the Encyclopædia Britannica, any information that I can communicate to you will be very much at your service; and you may in this and in any other respect that regards Africa freely command my services.

Observations on an Historical Account of Discoveries and Travels in Africa, by the late John Leyden, M.D., by Hugh Murray, Esq. F.R.S.E.

TO HUGH MURRAY ESQ. F.R.S.E.

London, Feb. 1818.

Sir,

You have certainly rendered to your country a service, in the publication of "The Travels and Discoveries in Africa, of the late John Leyden," the perusal of which has been to me a fund of instruction and entertainment; it is a most valuable work, and such a one as was wanted by the literary world, inasmuch as the judicious collection of the matter forms a most valuable epitome of African knowledge, collecting what was before distributed into many folios.

I anticipate that the information in this work, communicated to the public, will soon be circulated, and you will be called upon to supply a second edition. In the mean time, I take the liberty of submitting to your perusal a few cursory observations which I have made during the perusal of it, on the accuracy of which you may [509] assuredly rely. These apply for the most part to Arabian words, which have been by the moderns, as well as the ancients variously corrupted and mutilated. Desirous (for the information of those who really seek after African knowledge) that this book will pass through many editions. I am, &c.

James Grey Jackson.

Cursory Observations.

"The *Ludaia*, are not inhabitants of *Ludama*, they are a very numerous and warlike tribe of Arabs, inhabiting the Sahara, of which there are two or three emigrations or encampments in different and distant parts of Sahara; the Emperor of Marocco has some thousands of them in his army, and they are esteemed (next to the negroes, called Abeed Seedy Bukaree) his best troops. See the Map of the tracts from Fas and Arguin to Timbuctoo, facing page 1. Lat. N. 24°. long. W. 3°.

"This serpent is the *Bûska*, described in Jackson's enlarged Account of Marocco, &c. p. 109. Providence has afforded to man an opportunity of evading the attack of this deadly animal; for when it coils itself up, and by the strength of its tail darts forward fifteen or twenty yards at once, the person attacked, by watching vigilantly its motions, evades the attack, by moving only a short distance from the right line, in which it is prepared to dart forwards; neither can the [510] *Bûska* govern itself in the extent of its movement, but necessarily goes as far as its strength will permit, and then coils itself up again in a circular form, again erects its head, and darts a second time to its object. I have conversed with Arabs, who have been attacked by this monster, and they have assured me, that, by vigilantly watching its motion, and the direction of its head, when preparing to dart forward, they may escape its attack. [297]

"It is not correct to assert that *Nasari is a general term*, applied to infidels in Muhamed; it is applied to Christians only. *Kaffer is the general term* applied to all who have not faith in the Arabian Prophet. [298]

"That which you call the Talk Tree, is the tree which produces the Barbary gum; the name is *talh*. [299]"

Footnote 297: (return) Vide Leyden's Africa. p. 306.

Footnote 298: (return) Ibid, p. 429.

Footnote 299: (return) Ibid. 204.

"The *Keydenah*.--This is the Sudanic name for the tree which produces the Argan nut, or olive, the *kernel* of which resembles a bitter almond, and from *it*, not from the shell, they extract the oil, so celebrated for frying fish, and for burning; a pint of which will afford light as long as two pints of olive oil.

"The She plant, or properly Sheh is not wild thyme, nor does it resemble it, it is the wormseed plant, the seed of which is an article of exportation, from the ports of Marocco, The [511] sheh resembles the absynthum. The wild thyme is called *zatar*, also an article of exportation from the ports of the Marocco empire. [300]

"The *Alsharra* signifies the Book of Laws of Muhamed. [301]

"*Gebel Ramlie* should be written *Jibbel Rummelie*, i.e. the Sandy Mountain. [302]

"The Elwah [303]Elgarbie is inhabited by the Maggrebee Arabs. My late friend, Muley Abd Salam, elder brother to Muley Soliman, the reigning Emperor of Marocco, had a very large estate in this Wah, called Santariah. In the 1793d year of the Christian era, he sent his friend and servant Alkaid Muhammed ben Abd Saddack, late governor of Mogodor, to effect the sale of this estate. He was absent on this embassy two years and three months. [304]

"*Sheb* is the Arabic for alum, the correct orthography is *Shib*. [305]

"*Marybucks* should be *Marabet*, i.e. Priests, or Holy Muhamedans. [306]

"The primitive plough is used in all the African countries inhabited by the Arabs, or their descendants; the negroes, however, use the hoe." [307]

Footnote 300: (return) Vide Leyden's Africa, p. 312.

Footnote 301: (return) Ibid, p. 334.

Footnote 302: (return) Ibid, p. 398.

Footnote 303: (return) Let the African traveller be careful to pronounce these g's guttural خ

Footnote 304: (return) Ibid, p. 399.

Footnote 305: (return) Ibid. ibid.

Footnote 306: (return) Ibid. p. 225.

Footnote 307: (return) Ibid. p. 227.

[512]

"The Mouselmines is a French corruption of the term Muselman, i.e. Mohamedans.

"Mongearts, i.e. Moguert, the g guttural.

"Ouadelim, i.e. Wooled Deleim, or the sons of Deemy.

"Labdessebah, i.e. Woled Abbusebah, 'the sons of Abbusebah.' [308]

"Wed de Non, i.e. Wedinoon.

"The herb, with a decoction of which they dye their nails and hands, is called by the Arabs *El Henna*: it imparts a coolness and softness to the hands, and diminishes the excessive perspiration incident to warm climates. [309]

"Hooled ben Soliman ought to be Woled ben Soliman, 'the sons of the sons of Soliman;' and Benioled, should be Ben El Waled, 'the sons of Elwaled.' [310]

"The small beautiful species of deer, is the *El Horreh:* it is an inhabitant of the confines of the Saharah; it is said never to lie down. It produces the anti-poison called bezoar stone, (called in the Arabic *Bide El Horrek*, i.e. the testicle of the Horreh.) This is an article of commerce at Santa Cruz, and Wedinoon. The back and sides of the skins of these animals are of a red brown, and of a vivid white underneath." [311]

Footnote 308: (return) Vide Leyden's Africa, p. 262.

Footnote 309: (return) Ibid. p. 291.

Footnote 310: (return) Ibid. p. 299.

Footnote 311: (return) Ibid. p. 303.

[513]

TO JAMES GREY JACKSON, ESQ.

Edinburgh, May 3. 1818.

Sir,

I have lately been favoured with two communications from you:--the one a letter to Mr. Napier, editor of the Encyclopædia Britannica, on the subject of the article *Africa*, of which I was the author, and which Mr. Napier, therefore, put into my hands; the other, a letter direct to myself, on the subject of my edition of "Leyden's Discoveries in Africa." I fully intended to have answered them before now, but the pressure of other business, with the wish to bestow upon them the leisurely consideration which they merited, has hitherto prevented me. I feel much gratified by the favourable opinion which you express of what I have done on this subject, and much obliged to you for your communications, and offers of further information. I experienced very much the disadvantage arising from a want of knowledge of the languages of North Africa, with which you appear to have a *very extensive acquaintance. Indeed, several of the etymologies which you have given, are very interesting.* I was particularly pleased to receive that of the term *Ba Sea Feena*, though I cannot conceal that it tends to strengthen the doubts which I have entertained of its applying to the sea on the Gold Coast. The distance, the direction southwards, the Christians, the motion one way and another, and even the ships, are all circumstances which [514] would agree. There are arguments, however, against it; and it is certain that Park did not so understand it. Do you think there is any chance that the Bahr Soudan could be the Gulf of Guinea?

If you are acquainted with any circumstances which could tend to confirm or refute the narrative of Sidi Hamet, as given by Riley, or throw light upon Riley's general credibility; or if you have ever heard any report of such a city as *Wassanah*, I should feel particularly obliged to you for communicating such information: and whenever I find myself at a loss, I shall gladly avail myself of the liberality with which you show yourself disposed to impart the knowledge of which you have become possessed.

I shall communicate this letter to Mr. Napier; and it is but fair to mention, that, from the circumstances already stated, I am solely responsible for the too long delay which has taken place in answering your letter to him, as well as that to myself.

Hugh Murray.

On the Niger and the Nile.

London, 7th April, 1820.

In the 25th number of the Quarterly Review, (article Park's Travels,) the hypothesis there laid down as almost indisputable, is the non-continuity of the two Niles of Africa, or (according [515] to the European phraseology of the day) of the Niger and the Nile.

This hypothesis founded on the opinion of Major Rennel, carries with it no evidence whatever, but the speculative theory of that learned geographer. The identity or connection of the two Niles, and the consequent water communication between [312] Cairo and Timbuctoo receives (supposing the Quarterly Review to be correct), as our intelligence respecting Africa increases, additional confirmation: and even the Quarterly Reviewer, who denominated the opinion recorded by me, the gossipping stories of Negroes, (*vide* Quarterly Review, No. 25, p. 140.) now favours this opinion!

The Quarterly Reviewer appreciates Burckhardt's information on this subject, and depreciates mine, *although both are derived from the same sources of* [313] *intelligence, and confirm one another*: the reviewer says, Mr. Burckhardt has revived a question of older date; viz. "that the Niger of Sudan and the Nile of Egypt are one and the same river: this general testimony to a physical fact can be shaken only by direct proof to the contrary."

Footnote 312: (return) *Vide* Jackson's enlarged Account of Marocco, p. 310.

Footnote 313: (return) *i.e.* Intelligence from natives of Africa.

This is all very well: I do not object to the Quarterly Reviewer giving up an opinion which he finds no longer tenable; but when I see in the same review (No. 44, p. 481.) the following words,--"we give no credit whatever to the [516] report received by Mr. Jackson, of a person (several Negroes [314], it should be) having performed a voyage by water from Timbuctoo to Cairo," I cannot but observe with astonishment, that the Reviewer believes Burckhardt's report, that they are the same river, when, at the same time he does not believe mine.

Footnote 314: (return) *Vide* Jackson's enlarged Account of Marocco, p. 312.

Is there not an inconsistency here, somewhat incompatible with the impartiality which *ought* to regulate the works of criticism? I will not for a moment suppose it to have proceeded from a spirit of animosity, which I feel myself unconscious of deserving. But the reviewer further says, the objection to the identity of the Niger and the Nile, is grounded on the incongruity of their periodical inundations, or on the rise and fall of the former river not corresponding with that of the latter. I do not comprehend whence the Quarterly Reviewer has derived this information; I have always understood the direct contrary, which I have declared in the enlarged editions of my account of Marocco, page 304, which has been confirmed by a most intelligent African traveller, Ali Bey, (for which see his travels, page 220.)

I may be allowed to observe, that although the Quarterly Reviewer has changed his opinion on this matter, I have invariably maintained mine, founded as it is on the concurrent testimony of the best informed and most intelligent native African travellers, and I still assert, on [517] the same foundation, *the identity of the two Niles, and their continuity of waters*.

I have further to remark what will most probably ere long prove correct; viz. that the *Bahar Abiad* [315], that is to say, the river that passes through the country of Negroes, between Senaar and Donga, is an erroneous appellation, originating in the general ignorance among European travellers of the African Arabic, and that the proper name of this river is Bahar Abeed, which is another term for the river called the Nile-el-Abeed, which passes south of Timbuctoo towards the east (called by Europeans the Niger).

It therefore appears to me, and I really think it must appear to every unbiassed investigator of African geography, that every iota of African discovery, made successively, by Hornemann [316], Burckhardt, and others, tends to confirm *my water communication between Timbuctoo and Cairo*, and the theorists and speculators in African geography, who have heaped hypothesis upon hypothesis, error upon error, who have raised splendid fabrics upon pillars of ice, will ere long close their book, and be compelled, by the force of truth and experience, to admit the fact stated about twelve years ago by me in my account of Marocco, &c. viz. *that the Nile of* [518] *Sudan and the Nile of Egypt are identified by a continuity of waters, and that a water communication is provided by these two great rivers from Timbuctoo to Cairo*; and moreover, that the general African opinion, *that the Neel-el-Abeed* (Niger) *discharges itself into the* (Bahar el Mâleh) *Salt Sea, signifies neither more nor less than that it discharges itself at the Delta in Egypt, into the Mediterranean Sea*!

James Grey Jackson.

Footnote 315: (return) Bahar Abiad signifies White River; Bahar Abeed signifies River of Negroes.

Footnote 316: (return) *Vide* my letter in Monthly Magazine on this subject for March, 1817, p. 124.

[519]

APPENDIX;

BEING HISTORICAL FRAGMENTS IN ELUCIDATION OF THE FOREGOING PAGES.

First Expedition on Record to Timbuctoo.--Timbuctoo and Guago captured by Muley Homed, (son of Muley Abdelmelk, commonly called Muley Melk [317], or Muley Moluck,) in the 16th Century, (about the Year 1580.)

Footnote 317: (return) See the Spectator, No. 349.

Muley Abdelmelk, commonly called Muley Moluck, in 1577, A.C. fought the celebrated battle with Don Sebastian, King of Portugal, near Alkassar, which is at a short distance from L'Araich, wherein Don Sebastian was killed; and Abdelmelk being, before the battle, extremely ill, his son Muley Hamed went to his litter, to communicate to the Emperor his father, that the Moors had gained the victory, when he found his father dead and cold. Muley Hamed concealed this event till the battle was over; and was then proclaimed Emperor, and reigned twenty-six years: he cultivated the arts and sciences, mathematics and astronomy, which last was of essential service to him in crossing the Sahara to Timbuctoo and Guago; during which perilous journey the compass is so indispensable, that there is no certainty of travelling without it. He lost some thousands in this expedition; [520]but if gold could recompense the waste of human life, he was rewarded for his journey of abstinence and privation across the Sahara, for he brought from Guago seventy-five quintals, and from Timbuctoo sixty quintals, of gold-dust, making together one hundred and thirty-five quintals, or 16,065 lb. English avoir-du-poids weight of gold.

A Library of Arabic Manuscripts taken by the Spaniards,--Contests among Christians reprimanded.

Muley Sidan, son of Muley Hamed, disputed the throne of Marocco, A.C. 1611, with three brothers, one of whom was supported by the Spaniards, whose succour was purchased by his delivering into their hands the port of L'Araich, soon after which they gained a naval victory over the forces of Sidan, which was very disastrous to the Africans; for the Spaniards, besides other plunder, got possession of 3000 Arabic books, on theology, philosophy, and medicine. Sidan, however, notwithstanding this disaster, maintained his right to the crown. He was of a liberal and charitable mind. He protected and granted to the Christians various privileges; but *he ordered that Christians of all sects, and denominations should live in peace one with another*.

One day, some (*Userah*) Christian slaves of Provence, in France, who were Catholics, had a controversial dispute with others from Rochelle, who were Calvinists. This dispute ended in a violent contest, accompanied with blows on either side; this scene excited the curiosity of the Muselmen, who were surprised to see Christians thus fight among themselves on points of their own law! The report of this battle was carried to Sidan, who ordered all these slaves to be brought before him. He condemned some to a bastinado, which was inflicted in his [521]presence. He then addressed them thus:--"I command you all, on pain of death, not to dispute in future on the various dogmas of your law: every one has the presumption to think *himself* right; and as I allow every individual in my dominions to follow the religion that he chooses for himself; *slaves ought to have among themselves the same toleration*".

Muley El Arsheed, (a second Expedition to Timbuctoo and Sudan.)

This Sultan preceded the renowned Muley Ismael, on the throne of Marocco: he united to great ability the most ferocious disposition, and was continually inebriated.--He crossed the Sahara to Timbuctoo, with a numerous army, about the year of Christ 1670; proceeding to *Suse*, he laid siege to the Sanctuary of *Seedi Aly ben Aidar*, near *Ilirgh*: Seedi Aly, making his escape in disguise, fled to Sudan, whither he was followed by Muley El Arsheed, who, on his arrival on the confines of Sudan, between Timbuctoo and Jinnie, was met by a numerous host of Negroes, commanded by a black sultan: the Emperor demanded Aly ben Aidar; but the sultan of Bambarra replied, that, as he had claimed his protection, it would be an infringement on the laws of hospitality to deliver him up, adding, that he desired to know if the views of El Arsheed were hostile or not; to which the latter replied, after endeavouring in vain to procure the person of Aly, that he was not come hostilely, but was about to return, which he forthwith did: and the Bambareen sultan, having received from Aly two beautiful renegade virgins, was so much flattered with the present, that he promised him any thing that he should ask; whereupon, he requested permission to go to Timbuctoo, and to settle there with his numerous followers; which being granted, he proceeded [522]thither, and having established a Moorish garrison, resided there several, months, and afterwards returned to Barbary, bringing with him many thousand Bambareen negroes: but, on his reaching Suse, he heard of the death of Muley El Arsheed, and having then no farther occasion for these negroes, he dismissed them. They went to various parts of the country, serving the inhabitants in order to procure daily subsistence; but the arch-politician Muley Ismael, who had then recently been proclaimed as his successor, ordered them to be collected together, and incorporated in his negro army, which was, however, before this, very numerous, consisting for the most part of blacks, brought away from Sudan by Muley El Arsheed the preceding year. The Sultan Ismael also seized this opportunity of establishing his authority at Timbuctoo, and he met with little or no opposition in putting that place under contribution. Having sent fresh troops to occupy the Moorish garrison there, the inhabitants were glad to make a contribution, in exchange for the protection and power which it afforded them; for previous to this, they had been subject to continual depredations, from the Arabs of the adjacent country, to whom they had been compelled to pay tribute, as a security for their caravans, which were constantly passing the country of these Arabs, who are of the race of Brabeesh. In the year 1727,

A.C. when Ismael died, it is reported that he possessed an immense quantity of gold, of the purity of which, his gold coins, to be seen at this day at Timbuctoo, bear testimony; it is also said, that the massive bolts of his palaces were of pure gold, as well as the utensils of his kitchens. After his decease, however, the tribute was discontinued, and the Moorish garrison at Timbuctoo, intermarrying with the natives, and dispersing themselves in the neighbouring country, has given to Timbuctoo that tincture of Muselman manners, which they are known to possess; their [523]descendants forming, at this period, a considerable portion of the population of Timbuctoo.

Third Expedition to Timbuctoo and Sudan.

Muley Ismael died of an abscess in 1727, and was succeeded by his youngest son Muley Hamed Dehebby, a most avaricious prince, whose treasure, collected in his government during the life of his father, amounted to ten millions; to which was now added his father's treasury, amounting to fifty millions, besides jewels and diamonds to a much larger amount.

Dehebby [318], sanguinary and cruel when sober, was mild, affable, and humane when intoxicated: unlike Muselmen, he believed not in predestination, but had always several surgeons and doctors in his suite, and consulted them with the most unlimited confidence when ill. He decorated the palace of Marocco: in one of the apartments of the seraglio, of which he had had painted, in a superior style, the twelve signs of the zodiac; for which his ignorant and bigoted subjects accused him of having conspired against the Deity, in imitating, by gross and ill-formed images, the works of the Almighty. This prince was an intolerable drunkard; so that the Marabets and chiefs of the empire called Abdelmelk to the throne, whom they enabled to take possession of Mequinas. This prince, anticipating the revenge of Dehebby, proposed to deprive him of his eye-sight; but the Marabets and chiefs opposed this resolution and replied to him in the following words:--"It is not for his crimes that we have deposed thy brother, but for his continual intoxication, which prevented him from watching over the government and his officers: he has therefore only been [524]guilty of weakness, which is not a punishable crime." Abdelmelk dared not push his point, but was contented to send his brother to the (*Bled Shereef*), country of princes, i.e. Tafilelt. Before Dehebby was dethroned, he marched with a numerous army across Sahara, to Timbuctoo, of which he took possession, and brought home immense quantities of gold.

Footnote 318: (return) His proper name was Muley Hamed ben Ismael, the name Dehebby is figurative of his riches in gold.

1730.--Muley Hamed Dehebby dying, should have been succeeded by his son Muley Bouffer; but money and intrigue gave power to Abdallah, a son of Muley Ismael, who was proclaimed in spite of the efforts of his nephew, whom he attacked at Terodant, the capital of Suse. Bouffer was taken, together with a Marabet, his confidential friend and counsellor. Abdallah ordered them both to be brought before him.--"Thou art young," said he to his nephew; "thou hadst imprudently undertaken more than thou couldst accomplish; and in consideration of thy youth and inexperience, I pardon thee, but I will be revenged of thy counsellor." Then turning himself to the Marabet, "Thou, art a rebel," said he. "Didst thou imagine that thy sacred character, which thou hast abused against thy (*Seed*) Lord or King would prevent him from punishing thee? Let us see if thy sanctity will turn the edge of my sword."--In uttering these words, he struck off the saint's head.

INDEX.

A.

Commerce, the key of Africa,428.

Communication with Africa to be effected by the medium of commerce, 493.

Connubial customs, 313.

Copper mines, 331.

Corn, abundant at Dar el Beida and at Fedalla, 110. Abundance of, in West Barbary,208, 340.

Couriers, confidence reposed in them, 405.

Coffee of Timbuctoo, 279.

Consuls of the European powers, their residence, 130.

Congo, Africans of, how converted to the Christian faith, 442_.

Continental markets of Europe, contemplation how they will be supplied with colonial produce, 229.

Cuscusoe, or more properly Kuskasoe, an excellent food, mode of preparing it, 97.

Customs, Muhamedan, 230..

Cuba, slave-trade and produce of, increased, 270.

Customs of the shelluhs of Idaultit, and laws of, remarkable,313.

Customs, ceremonies at funerals, 465.

D.

Dances of the Arabs described, music of, 140, 344.

Dates abundant at Tafilelt, 80.

Dar el Beida, a corn country, 110.

Dead, bodies of the, never interred in towns or in the mosques, 272. Ceremony of interment, 273.

Deism, 325.

Deef Allah, what, 341.

Decay of science and the arts among the Arabs, 352.

Delel, i.e. auctioneer of slaves at Marocco, 95.

Deleim, woled Arabs, 138.

Decked vessels in the interior of Africa, 449.

Delemy, sheik of the Deleim Arabs,138. Invites the author and his companion, Signor Andrea de Christo, to pass the night at a douar of the Woled Abbusebah Arabs, 139. Garden of, described, 147. Renown of, 148. A main pillar to the throne of Marocco, 148. Receives an exhortation from the prince Abdsalam to give battle to the usurper Buhellessa, 288. Dextrous in the management of a horse, 289.

Desert, rate of travelling through, 470.

Dews of the night, how they secure themselves against, when sleeping, 154.

Deef Allah, custom of uttering, 233.

Dimenet, in the Atlas, attacked by the emperor,305.

Difference between the oriental and occidental Arabic alphabets, 351.

Djinawa, definition of the name, 507.

Distances from port to port, along the coast, calculated, 132.

Discovery of Africa, plan for, 200.

Disgrace of inhospitality,240.

Doctors, itinerant, their apparatus, 242.

Douars, or villages of tents, described, 328.

Draha, province of, 2. Hire of camels from Tafilelt to, 2. Dates, the names of the different species, 3. Plantations of, 3. Inhabitants of nearly black, 2. Character of them, 2, 7.
Drahim, what, 3.
Driss Zerone Muley, renowned sanctuary of, 118. Author's hospitable reception there, and admission to the adytum, 119.
Duplicity of the Africans exemplified, 293, 314.

E.

East India trade, our, how likely to be affected by French colonisation, in Senegal, 229.
Ebekoaits, or Ait Ebeko, a tribe of Berebbers, 124.
Effah el, exhibition of that venomous serpent, 453.
Elephants, 8.
Elegant females, 142.
Emperor admits an ambassador without prostration, and why, 282.
-------- Yezzid is wounded, and dies, 285. His body exhumated, 286. Compared to his majesty George the Fourth, 287.
Emperor, anecdote of one, 307. His contest with the Berebbers, 308. Letter from him to his bashaw of Suse respecting English seamen wrecked on the western coast of Africa, 364. Titles of H.I.M., 382.. Style of addressing him, 382.
Emperor's letters, 384, 387, 392, 394, 395, 398, 402, 403, 405.
---- plan of reconciling catholics with protestants, 520.
---- table, simplicity of the furniture of, 96.
---- audience of business of the, 98. Audience of leave in the garden of the Nile, 98.
Embassy, British, to Marocco, result of, 128.
Encroachments of the French anticipated on our colonial arkets, 230.
Encyclopedia Britannica, misapplication of an anachronism, 442. The editor of has adopted the author's opinion respecting the course of the Niger, 447.
Epistolary correspondence, 382.
Epistolary diction used by Muhamedans, 404.
Equity, case of, 312.
Esshume, See *Shume*.
Euphorbium plant, 74.
European merchants at Mogador in danger of being decollated by order of the emperor, on a charge of high-treason, 284.

F.

Fas, bankrupts, how treated at, 16. Is the metropolis of the north, 87. Talb Cadus, 87.
----, gold thread manufactured at, of a superior quality, 126. Manufactures, various of, 126.
----, houses of the merchants of, described, and gardens at, 275. Library at, 324.
Fakeers, or muselmen-saints excite hostility between Christians and Muhamedans, 267..
Fedalla, corn country, 110.
Fig-trees, very large, 82.
Food, 316. Food of the desert, 349.

I.(J.)

Invocation for the author's welfare made by the Fakeers of the sanctuary of Muley Dris Zerone, 119.

---------- for the welfare of the British embassy.

Journey, in disguise, at a critical period, 135.

Journies, viz. from Mogodor to Rabat; to Mequinas; to the sanctuary of Muley Dris Zerone; and to the ruins of Pharaoh; through the country of Amorites to L'Araich and Tangier, 105.

Irrigation, wheel for, 13.

Iron mines, 331.

Isa Seedy ben, fascinators of serpents, 455.

Isawie (fascinators of serpents) their performance, 453.

Justice, moral, 306.

K.

Kaaba, Muhamed's mausoleum, so called, 273.

Kadder Khan, king of Turkostan, a great support to science, 352.

Kaffer, the application of this term, 510.

------, (or Caffre) its signification, 267, 345.

Kassar Kabeer el, a beautiful country, 124.

Kereb, what, 5.

Key of Africa is commerce, 428.

Keyma, its definition, 307.

Khalif Delemys, noble conduct to the prince Abdsalsm, 288.

Kibla, i. e. the tomb of Muhamed, 9.

Kiffen, signification of, 273.

King George IV. compared to the late emperor of Marocco, Muley Yezzid, 287. A patron to science and the arts, 429.

Kitiwa ait, or Kituvites, a tribe of Berebbers, 124.

Koba, or coba, 88.

Koran, called the beloved book. Etymology of the word, 318. Incorrectly called the Alcoran, l'Alcoran, or il Alcorano, 351. Written in good language, 353.

L.

L'âad of the Arabs described, 289.

Language, etiquette of, at the court of Marocco, 315.

Languages of Africa, 355.

L'Araich, forest of. Ferry of, 125.

Laws of insolvency, 343.

Lead mines, 331. Lead-ore mines, 331.

Leather superior manufactory of, at Mequinas and Marocco, 217. Articles used in the manufacture of leather, 218.

Leghorn, its indirect commerce with Timbuctoo, 255.

Leper's town or village near Marocco, 90. Mendicant lepers, 91.

Library at Fas, 324.

Lions, country abounding in. Mode of destroying them. Preservation against, 115.

Liquorice root, abundant in Suse, 74_.

Locusts, their incredible devastation described, 221. Mode of collecting them, 222. Used as food; method of preparing them; much esteemed as food, 222. Remarkable instance of these insects having devoured every blade of grass south of the river Elkos, but not north of that river, 223.

Love, Arabian definition of, 363.

Loyalty of the sheiks of Suse, 288. Of Muhamedans, 326.

Ludaia are not Ludama, 507.

Lybia palus and sea of Sudan synonymous, 448.

M.

Majesty, His, George IV. patron of science and the arts, 429. Compared to the late emperor Yezzid, 287.

Mandinga language compared with the Arabic, 373.

Manufactures of Fas; superior manufacture of gold-thread there, 214.

Marabets, what, 511.

Marabet, punishment of one, 524.

Market called Soke Elkhummes, 94.

Marocco, emperor's march to, 73. Country abundant in corn of a superior quality, 78. Reception at salutations of the Moors, 78. Gate called Beb el Lushoir; its situation, 78. Garden of the Nile, an imperial garden, 79. Tafilelt rose flourishes at Marocco; its powerful perfume; otto of roses, 79. Roses; various flowers abundant; Persian wheel in general use throughout the country, 82. Divisions of the empire of, 86. The summer residence of the emperor, 86. The metropolis of the south, 87. Town or village of lepers at, 90. Policy of concealing the appearance of wealth at, 95. Furniture of houses at, 95. Customs at, 95. All trades carried on at, 98.

--------, etiquete of the court of, 310. Emperor dispenses with, 311.

Marseilles, its commerce indirectly with Timbuctoo, 254.

Massacre of the Jews at Algiers, 283.

Matamores, what, 14, 195.

Matra, J.M., his excellency the British ambassador, treated by the emperor like a prince, 128.

--------, his intelligence respecting vaccine pus, 237.

Mauritannick writing, what, 351.

Mazagan, 109. Country of, and inhabitants described, 109.

Mekka caravan, i. 4.

Mendicant lepers, their exclamation, 91.

Mensoria el, 110.

Mequinas, city of the court-town; travelling, mode of; 88. Imperial palace at, 117. Beauty of the ladies of, 118.

--------, superior leather and shoes made at, 98.

Merchandize, consignment of, from Timbuctoo to Fas, 348.

----------, the various, the produce of Sudan, 256.

Messa, visit to the port of, 145. Gold and silver mines of, 146.

Minister's house at Marocco, a noble one, 90.

-------- suggestions recommended to their attention, 230.

N.

Nasari, the application of the term, 510.

Nassar, Abdrahaman Ben, the bashaw of Abda, interview with, 136..

Nations, the respective costumes of, enjoined, 296..

Negro languages, thirty-three different ones spoken, 370.

Negroes, opinion respecting, 466. Mental degradation of, imputable, in some measure, to the cruel treatment of them in the West India islands, 466.

Neel, a name applied to two rivers in Africa only, 507.

Nile, at Kabra, its width, 471.

----, the correct orthography in English is Neel, 79.

Niger, contemplated result of the discovery of its course and termination, 99. Opinion concerning its course, 103. Nile el Kabeer, Nile Assudan, synonymous with Niger, 201.

----, or Nile of Sudan, discharges itself in a lake, 449.

------ and the Nile, 515. Theory respecting, 515. The author's opinion of this river never varied, 516.

------ or Neel el Abeed, discharges itself into the Mediterranean sea at the Delta, in Egypt, 518.

Nile, this word is improperly spelled, 507.

Niles, anticipation of the confirmation of their junction, 434.

Nile Abid, or Neel el Abeed, error respecting its situation, 435.

Niles, junction of, where supposed to take place, 444. Not doubted in Africa, but supported by the general testimony of the natives, 445.

Nile, the word applied only to two rivers in Africa, 447.

Nishki, manner of writing, 350. Synonymous with the Kufie.

Nyctalopia, or night-blindness, 332.

----------, description of, and remedy, 432. Offer to discover the remedy, 432.

----------, an ophthalmia, that affects our seamen in the Mediterranean, 433. Offer to discover the remedy for to government, 433.

O.

Oasis, western, 280.

Oil of olives, 67. Oil organic, 91.

Olive plantations of Ras el Wed, 77.

Ophthalmia, disorders at Marocco prevail among the Jews, 92.

Opinions of the Africans respecting Jews, Christians, and themselves, 315.

Oranges of Rabat, superior in quality, and low in price, 114.

Oranges, 75. Orange-trees, very large, 82.

Ostrich's feathers, 67.

Ostriches presented by the Emperor Muley Ismael to Queen Anne, 393.

P.

Palace, imperial, at Tafileet, magnificent, 80.

Palaces described, 274. Architecture of, 274.

Partridges, mode of hunting among the Arabs, 107.

Park, Mungo, at Timbuctoo, 319.

Pyramidical basis on which is founded the intelligence in Jackson's Account of Marocco, &c., 451.

Q.

Quarterly journal, of literature, science, and the arts, error of, 435, 438.
Queen Elizabeth, embassy to the emperor of Marocco, 494.

R.

Rabat, arrival at, 110. Town described. Aqueduct. Mausoleum of the Sultan Muhamed at, described. Battery of, bomb-proof. Bastions. Roman spring at. Old Roman town of Sheila at, described. Old Roman coins, 111. Mosques, tower of Hassan, similar to one at Timbuctoo, &c. described, 112.
Rabat and Salee, abundant countries, 113.
Religions, of all kinds, tolerated at Timbuctoo.
Repast, or dinner, sent by the prince Muley Teib, 192.
Retaliation for murder, an incumbent duty on tha individuals of a family, 295.
Revenge of the Shelluhs, described, 152.
-------- of the Shelluhs for murder rigidly pursued, 291.
Richardson, incorrect in calling the Arabic guttural letter, *grain*, ghain, 492.
Richardson's Arabic grammar, some errors in, 351.
Riches of the Arabs, in what it consists, 247.
Rivers, in sandy districts, change their courses, 440.
Robbery, singular mode of, 116.
Rontgen, African traveller, death of, 425.

S.

Santa Cruz, the port of, delivered to the Dutch, 403.
--------, See *Agadeer*.
-------, or Agadeer, the key to Sudan, 268.
-------, invoice from Timbuctoo to, 345.
------- opened to Dutch commerce by the author, 436.
Sanctuary of Muley Dris Zerone, 80.
Saffy, its road for shipping described, 108. Situation and description of, 108.
Sahara, north part described, no water, 4. South part described, 7. Water carried in goat-skins, 5. Sheiks of, independent.
--------, Arabs of, prefer sleeping in the open air, 155.
Salee, dungeon of, for Christian captives, 114.
------ and Rabat, the adjacent country productive, 113.
Salutations, peculiar character of their, 235.
Saneet Urtemma, a dangerous country, 110.
Sand baths, 279.

Suse, province of, inaccessible to an invading army from the north, 76.
Synonymous words in sound, 362..

T.

Tabia walls, what, 2. Mode of building them.
Tafilelt, 1. A rendezvous for caravans; kassars of; hire of camels from Fas to; a country of princes, 2. Market at, 2. Palace, imperial, magnificent at, 80. Dates abundant at, 80. Magnificent plantations and extensive forests of, 81. Faith and honour of the natives proverbial; robberies unknown there, 81.
Talleyrand, his favourite African scheme, 229.
Talh-tree defined, 510.
Tangier garrison, salute to the British ambassador on his entry there, 127.
Tas, what it is, 231.
Tatta, a depôt for camels, 248.
Tendaraman, venomous spider described, 429
Tensift, river of, 108.
Tildie, repast, Arab, at; Portuguese tower at, 63. Cookery of the Arabs at, 64.
Timbuctoo, situation of, and charge of travelling to, 7. City of; river close to it, 8. Population of; extent of; caravanseras of; slaves at, 10. Houses; government, 11. Revenue of, 12. Moors pay no duty at, but negroes do, 14. Subject to Housa, 14. Army of; subsidies; administration of justice at; punishments, 15. Good police of, 16. Insolvent debtors at; slaves entitled to freedom at; property, succession to and distribution of; rational treatment of slaves at; wills not written, 18. Laws of inheritance; marriage; rape; adultery, 19. Trade and articles sold at, 20. Manufactures, 23. Measures, 23. Husbandry, 24_. Sowing season; provisions, 25. Animals; birds, 26. Fish; prices of various articles, 27. Costume, 28. Diversions, 31. Time, measurement of; Religion, 32. Diseases, 33. Manners and customs, 34. Neighbouring nations, 35.
--------, opportunity of opening a trade with, why declined, 145.
--------, how likely to be made tributary to Great Britain, 249. Circuitous commerce of, explained, 256. Direct and eligible route to, through Sahara from the shores of the Atlantic Ocean, 257.
--------, value of merchandize at, 260. Immense profit actually made in, 261. Immense quantities of gold to be procured from Sudan, 261. Goods entering the city at the gate of the desert pay no duty, 263. Timbuctoo coffee, 179. Invoice from, 345, 347. Letter from, 346, 348.
Timbuctoo, Mungo Park at, 319.
----------, warehouses of, contain the manufactures, of India and Europe, 427. Communication with, plan for opening, 428.
----------, intelligence respecting, whence derived, 436.
----------, cotton manufacture, made in the city of, interwoven with silk, of a chequered pattern, deposited in the British Museum, 437. Situation of, in respect to the Neel el abeed, 439. Under the sovereignty of a negro prince, 441. Fish at, resembling salmon, 469.
-------- first expedition to and conquest of, 519.
-------- second expedition to, 521.
-------- third expedition to, 523.
Titles of emperor, 382.
Togreda, ceremony of, how performed, 231.

Tomie, or Sebah Biure, port of; the author visits it by the prince's request, 138. Arab dance and festivity in the neighbourhood of, 141. Music of, 140.

Trade with Sudan, 277.

Travellers, solitary or scientific, little expectations from, 258.

Travelling in Barbary, 293.

Treaties with Muhamedan princes, 283.

Troglodyte, 319.

U.

Uffran, a depôt for camels, 248. *Uly* and Ualy, material difference between these two terms, 350. *Unity* among Christians a necessary prelude to the conversion of Africa. The several sects of Christians should unite, instead of being divided, as an expedient measure necessary to precede the conversion of Africa, 129. *Union* of waters between Timbuctoo and Cairo, 447.

V.

Vaccination, intelligence transmitted from West Barbary instrumental in the propagation of, 337. 23,134 lives saved by vaccination, 338.

Vasco de Gama's observations on intercourse with Africa, 258.

Vincent, Lord St. his message to the Emperor of Marocco, 459.

Vines, the grapes of which are of an extraordinary size, 74.

W.

Water communication between Timbuctoo and Cairo, 443. This opinion is confirmed by Mr. Hornmann, 444.

------ communication between Cairo and Timbuctoo, the opinion respecting, receives additional confirmation, 517.

------ melons at Salee and Rabat peculiarly sweet, 114.

------ carried through the Sahara in goat's skins.

Wah el, what, 6.

Wahs of Sahara, how supplied with fish, 257. Western oasis, 280.

Wangara, jewel from, 103.

Wassenah, or Massenah, conjecture why not known at Ashantee, 491.

Wed el fees, river of, 82.

Whedinoon, a depôt for camels. *Wheat*, superior at Marocco, 95.

------, a superior kind or quality, 125.

Wild myrtle grows in the Sahara, 6.

Wine Company recommended, 212.

Woled Aisah, encampment of Arabs. Produce of that country, 109.

Wool, exportation of, granted by the emperor.

Woladia el, an eligible place for a naval depôt, 108.

Woolja, not Woolga, 109.

THE END.